UNEP

Depleted Uranium in Bosnia and Herzegovina

Revised Edition: May 2003

Post-Conflict Environmental Assessment

This report by the United Nations Environment Programme was made possible by the generous contributions of the Governments of Italy and Switzerland

Depleted Uranium in Bosnia and Herzegovina

TABLE OF CONTENTS

Foreword

In 2001, the United Nations Environment Programme (UNEP) published the findings from the first-ever assessment on the environmental impact of the use of depleted uranium (DU) originating from a real conflict situation. This work was conducted in Kosovo in 2000 and followed-up one year later in Serbia and Montenegro. Since then, UNEP has become a reference in the scientific community regarding the impacts of DU when used in a conflict situation. When, in the summer of 2002, the Council of Ministers of Bosnia and Herzegovina (BiH) requested UNEP to conduct a similar assessment in BiH related to the use of DU ordnance in 1994-95, UNEP was naturally ready to initiate action.

In this new study, we learn that more than seven years after the end of the conflict it is still possible to detect DU in soil and sensitive bio-indicators at sites where DU had been used. A large number of contamination points (holes were DU penetrators hit the ground), as well as loose contamination, including DU penetrators, fragments and jackets/casings were found. UNEP could confirm local DU contamination around impact points, although the levels were low and no significant level of radioactivity could be measured.

Importantly, for the first time during an assessment in the Balkans, it was possible to detect DU contamination in drinking water. The contamination, however, was very low and remained below the World Health Organization's (WHO) reference value. Finally, DU was also detected in several of the air samples where it had been unexpected to find any DU particles in the air so long after the end of the conflict. Again, detected levels remained below international safety limits. However, for precautionary purposes, confirmation of DU contamination inside some buildings leads UNEP to recommend to the local authorities decontamination and clean-up measures .

The mission also analysed the handling and storage conditions of radioactive sources within BiH. The representative from the International Atomic Energy Agency (IAEA) provided valuable analysis on these issues.

During this challenging work, our cooperation with BiH authorities has been excellent. The government shared their scientific and health expertise with UNEP, as well as their important civil protection and mine clearance experience. NATO/SFOR co-operated with UNEP throughout the study, and UNMIBH, as our local UN partner, helped make this work possible in many ways.

All of the scientific members on this mission were experienced from earlier UNEP assessments. I want to congratulate these scientists not only for a work well done, but also for producing new and valuable information on the behaviour of DU. Close cooperation with our colleagues from the IAEA and the WHO was a success. Health related information was presented and reviewed by the WHO during meetings with hospitals and government health officials. The WHO assessment, as the competent United Nations agency on health issues, is included in this report.

This work could never been conducted in such an efficient manner without the professional work by the national institutes of Greece, Italy, Russia, Sweden, Switzerland, the United Kingdom and the United States, ensuring the highest quality discussion and results. Above all, my gratitude goes to the governments of Italy and Switzerland that provided UNEP with experts, laboratory assistance and generous financial support.

Following this third DU assessment in the Balkans, the collective information from these reports can now be used to minimize any health and environmental risks from depleted uranium. These studies confirm that the behaviour of DU is a complex issue, and that DU can be found in soil, vegetation, water and air in certain conditions many years after the conflict.

For this reason, UNEP strongly encourages further studies in the areas where risks could be higher than in the Balkans.

Klaus Töpfer
United Nations Under-Secretary-General
Executive Director of the United Nations Environment Programme

CROATIA

Cazin

Bihac

Prijedor

Sanski Most

Banja Luka

Prnjavor

Gradacac

Bijeljina

Belgrade

Save

Vrbas

Bosna

Save

Drina

Tesanj

Maglaj

Tuzla

SERBIA

BOSNIA AND HERZEGOVINA

Jajce

Turbe

Travnik

Vitez

Zenica

Vlasenica

Srebrenica

Kiseljak

Sarajevo

Zepa

Pale

Jablanica

Konjic

Gorazde

Visegrad

Drina

Neretva

Mostar

Stolac

Novi Pazar

Neum

Vojvodina

Tisa

Danube

Ibar

Tara

ELEVATION :

2 000 m
1 500 m
1 000 m
500 m
200 m
0

■ Investigated
Sites

0   50   100 km

Trebinje

MONTENEGRO

Podgorica

ALBANIA

Philippe Rekacewicz, UNEP GRID Arendal, 1997.

Introduction

The question on environmental and health impacts originating from the use of depleted uranium (DU) ammunition has, after several conflicts, become a much debated issue. Since there has been very little scientific fieldwork with proper measurements as well as laboratory work outside of the military community, until recently it has been difficult to come to any significant conclusions.

In the autumn of 2000, UNEP carried out the first-ever international assessment on the environmental behaviour of DU following its use in a real conflict situation. In March 2001, UNEP published the report, entitled *Depleted Uranium in Kosovo - Post-Conflict Environmental Assessment.*

To reduce the uncertainties about DU's environmental impacts, a second phase was carried out in Serbia and Montenegro with a field mission in October 2001. This study investigated six sites, as well as - for the first time - one targeted military vehicle, which was studied in detail. UNEP subsequently published the report, entitled *Depleted Uranium in Serbia and Montenegro - Post-Conflict Environmental Assessment in the Federal Republic of Yugoslavia* in March 2002.

In Serbia and Montenegro, authorities had already conducted some decontamination and clean-up operations, which were in line with the findings of the UNEP field studies. Both the Kosovo and the Serbia and Montenegro reports were well received by local stakeholders, as well as by the international scientific community. These reports helped alleviate some of the public concerns with respect to DU by scientifically demonstrating the low contamination levels and providing recommendations to reduce future risks at affected sites.

The request by the Bosnia and Herzegovina (BiH) authorities to conduct similar studies over seven years after the use of DU was a new challenge for the scientists in UNEP's team. 15 international experts comprised the UNEP mission to BiH, which took place on 12 - 24 October 2002.

UNEP had selected 15 sites to be visited during the mission. One of the sites was unfortunately inaccessible due to the heavy presence of mines. For the remaining 14 sites, the presence of mines and other unexploded ordnance (UXO) was a factor that occasionally restricted the work to a degree. Five of these fifteen sites were areas where NATO had reported using DU munitions. The remaining 10 sites were areas where the local population or authorities were concerned that DU might have been used.

The possible health risks and questions for safe storage of radioactive waste were integrated into the tasks of this mission. Therefore, experts from the relevant UN agencies - the WHO and the IAEA - participated on this mission. The valuable contributions and recommendations made by these experts are included in this report.

Soil sampling at the Kalinovik Ammunition Destruction Site with the remains of an old Turkish fort in the background

A total of 132 samples were collected: 4 penetrators, 46 surface soil, 3 soil profiles of 60 cm, 5 smear, 2 scratch, 19 water, 24 air, and 29 vegetation samples. Both the Swiss Spiez Laboratory and the Italian APAT Laboratory conducted sample analyses. Of the 14 sites investigated, three clearly showed DU contamination, confirming the earlier use of DU ordnance. These sites correspond to the information on DU targets provided by NATO.

Four new and significant findings are contained within this report. First, detailed laboratory analyses of surface soil samples revealed low levels of localized ground contamination. At most, local ground contamination could be detected around contamination points at distances below 200 meters, but usually much closer. None of the sites showed widespread contamination, meaning a contamination over large surfaces in the range of a couple of hundred meters. Ground surface DU contamination detectable by portable beta and gamma radiation detectors was typically limited to areas within 1 - 2 meters of penetrators and localized points of contamination caused by a penetrator impact.

Second, penetrators buried near the ground surface and recovered by UNEP had decreased in mass by approximately 25% over 7 years. Based on this finding, correlated with those penetrators studied in UNEP's earlier studies, a DU penetrator can be fully oxidized to corrosion products (e.g. uranium oxides and carbonates) in 25 to 35 years after impact. Following that

Depleted Uranium in Bosnia and Herzegovina

1

Penetrators and fragments fully corrode 25 - 35 years after impact

time period, no more penetrators – metallic DU – will be found buried in the Balkans soil. In contrast, penetrators lying on the ground surface showed significantly lower corrosion rates.

Third, for the first time, DU contamination of drinking water could be found at one site. DU could be clearly identified in one drinking water sample. A second drinking water sample from a well also showed traces of DU, but was detectable only through the use of mass spectrometric measurements. Contamination of the well water may be due to the fact that the well is positioned in what would have been the line of attack by planes. The concentrations are very low and the corresponding radiation doses are insignificant for any health risk. This is also true considering the toxicity of uranium as a heavy metal. However, because the mechanism that governs the contamination of water in a given environment is not known in detail, it is recommended that water sampling and measurements should continue for several years, and that an alternative water source should be used if DU is found in the drinking water.

Finally, the presence of DU in air was found at two sites, including air and certain surface contamination inside two buildings at two different sites. Resuspension of DU particles due to wind and/or human activities from sources such as contamination points, corroded penetrators or fragments laying on the surface are the most likely cause. The concentrations were very low and resulting radiation doses are minor and insignificant. However, as some of these buildings are currently under use by the civil population or by military, UNEP considers exposure to such a source unnecessary. Therefore, precautionary decontamination and clean-up steps for these buildings are recommended.

In addition to these key findings, some important remarks must also be added. Throughout the mission, the UNEP team observed that workers and civilians, as well as military and mine clearance personnel with access to sites where DU presence was confirmed, were unaware of or misunderstood the risks and issues surrounding DU ammunition. Awareness raising activities should be considered, including information about DU in general, associated risks, handling and storage and contact information for relevant authorities. A flyer or leaflet, like the ones used to advocate mine safety, could be produced and distributed.

The importance of having correct locations and coordinates for DU-affected sites and of obtaining access to these sites for the purpose of conducting surveys and measurements is essential. The longer the elapsed time since the date of the attack, the more difficult it is to implement countermeasures, including decontamination, if necessary. As 6 coordinates of confirmed attack sites are still missing according to the NATO web page, these coordinates should be disclosed without delay.

Another important issue related to information on what had happened to the radioactive material that had previously been collected and stored in BiH. During the assessment study, UNEP wanted to confirm the whereabouts of a box containing DU penetrators collected earlier from Hadzici. The information received from NATO confirms that NATO/SFOR military authorities have properly stored it outside of BiH.

On-line and random survey techniques were used over hard surfaces in Ustikolina

UNEP also visited certain ammunition destruction sites to confirm that DU had not been included among detonated ammunition, as well as to analyse another environmental aspect; the contamination by heavy metals as a result of such destruction activities. Selected water and soil samples were analysed for their heavy metals content. High surface soil contamination of heavy metals was measured at three sites. Such contamination could represent a future health risk. Results indicate that past ammunition production, as well as current ammunition destruction activities, have produced heavy metal contamination of the soil. Ammunition destruction sites should therefore not be situated in areas where secondary contamination could occur; for example, contamination of the groundwater and any animals grazing nearby.

Overall, the findings of this study are consistent with the findings of UNEP's earlier DU studies. The levels of DU contamination are not a cause for alarm, but some uncertainty remains with respect to future potential groundwater contamination from penetrator corrosion products. Both general and site-specific recommendations are included in this report for follow-up and implementation.

This study is UNEP's third contribution to the scientific debate on the environmental risks and the behaviour of DU. UNEP is committed to working with other UN organisations to extend DU studies to other post-conflict regions where the long-term effects of DU contamination should be studied. As part of this commitment, UNEP was invited in Spring 2002 by the IAEA to participate in a DU mission to Kuwait.

An air sampler operating near Foca bridge (Srbinje)

I would like to extend my genuine thanks and appreciation to all the national and international experts who worked so hard to contribute to the success of this study. All scientists made excellent contributions. I would like to extend my gratitude to three in particular. Jan Olof Snihs, from the Swedish Radiation Protection Authority (SSI), has been the Scientific Leader of all three UNEP DU studies in the Balkans. His role in keeping the scientific quality of these reports at a high level has been exceptional. Gustav Åkerblom, also from SSI, has been the Technical Leader of each mission. Based on his experience, appropriate methods for finding and measuring DU ammunition have been developed by UNEP. Finally, Mario Burger, from Spiez Laboratory in Switzerland, has been a key scientist in all three missions in the Balkans and, for the Bosnia and Herzegovina assessment, acted as UNEP's Project Coordinator. Without their respective dedicated and professional work, the UNEP assessments on depleted uranium would not have been possible.

Based on its work in the Balkans, UNEP strongly encourages further assessments to be undertaken in other regions and climate zones where DU has been used in earlier conflicts in order to reduce any uncertainties about its potential environmental impacts in the longer term.

Conflicts and wars are never good news. I believe that the findings of this study will contribute both to conflict-prevention and to the protection of human health and environment debate during times of conflicts.

Pekka Haavisto
Chairman, UNEP Depleted Uranium Assessment Team
Geneva, 10 March 2003

Post-Conflict Environmental Assessment

Background

2.1 UNEP'S ROLE IN POST-CONFLICT ENVIRONMENTAL ASSESSMENT

UNEP's Post-Conflict Assessment Unit first emerged in May 1999 as a joint UNEP/UNCHS (Habitat) 'Balkans Task Force' with the aim of producing an overall assessment of the consequences of the Kosovo conflict on the environment and human settlements. Its particular focus was on the Federal Republic of Yugoslavia (Kosovo, Montenegro and Serbia).

As part of this work, an international expert group - the 'Depleted Uranium Desk Assessment Group' - was appointed to "assess the potential health and environmental impact of depleted uranium (DU) used in the Kosovo conflict". However, the use of DU in Kosovo had not been officially confirmed at that time and no information was available on the locations of sites possibly targeted by DU munitions.

Thus, the work was carried out, *inter alia*, by:

- collecting background information on the potential effects of DU on human health and/or the environment, the quantity and quality of depleted uranium used in the conflict, and the locations of affected sites;
- assessing the medium- and long-term potential health and environmental impacts of DU used in the Kosovo conflict by means of a scenario-based desk study;
- undertaking a fact-finding mission to Kosovo to make preparations for a possible future sampling campaign; and
- analysing information in order to both quantify problems 'on the ground' in potentially affected areas and to provide qualitative answers concerning the possible risks to human health and the environment.

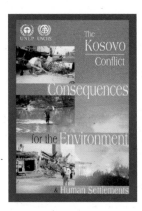

The fact-finding mission did not encounter elevated levels of radiation, either in and around the wreckage of destroyed military vehicles, or on/alongside roads. Based on these preliminary measurements, UNEP concluded that there was no evidence or indication of the presence of DU at the locations visited. However, it was stressed that any further investigations could only be meaningful if and when confirmation was received that DU ammunition had been used and, if so, where.

Such confirmation arrived in July 2000. Following approaches from the United Nations Secretary-General, NATO made available a detailed list of sites where DU had been used. Operating under the newly formed 'Balkans Unit', UNEP then moved quickly to assemble a team of international experts to prepare a scientific mission to Kosovo from 5-19 November 2000. In March 2001, UNEP published the findings in the report *'Depleted Uranium in Kosovo'* (see section 2.2 for a summary of these findings).

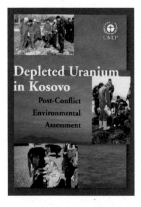

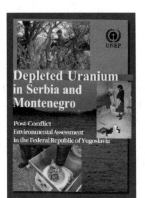

With the continued help of NATO and local authorities, a similar mission to Serbia and Montenegro (FRY) took place from 27 October to 5 November 2001. Building on the Kosovo report, this mission also took air samples in addition to water, soil and lichen samples. The report, *'Depleted Uranium in Serbia and Montenegro'*, was published in March 2002 (see section 2.2).

The success of these missions created a need for UNEP to expand its scope beyond the Balkans. In late 2001, the 'Balkans Unit' became the Post-Conflict Assessment Unit (PCAU) in order to "extend the work to other areas of the world where the natural and human environment has been damaged as a consequence of conflict".

In mid-2002, UNEP received an official invitation, this time from Bosnia and Herzegovina (BiH), to make a third DU assessment focusing on the use of depleted uranium during air attacks against armoured vehicles, tanks and artillery positions in 1994 and 1995. The benefits of this project would also extend beyond the boundaries of BiH, as important new information would be discovered on the environmental behaviour of DU more than seven years after its use in combat. In order to assess the feasibility and safety of such an assessment so long after the end of the conflict, a fact-finding mission was undertaken from 5-14 September 2002. Following the success of this undertaking, the third DU assessment mission took place from 12-24 October 2002.

2.2 SUMMARY OF FINDINGS FROM THE KOSOVO AND SERBIA/MONTENEGRO MISSIONS

In Kosovo, the mission did not find any widespread contamination of the soil or ground surface, though some localized points of contamination were identified at some of the sites where the use of DU had been reported. The major part of ground contamination was found in the upper 10-20 cm directly below a penetrator. No DU contamination of water or domesticated cow milk was found during the mission and subsequent laboratory testing, and there was no evidence to suggest any immediate health problems. However, it was concluded that there could be future risk of DU contamination of groundwater. Analyses of bio-indicators (i.e. lichen, bark, moss and grass) at four sites indicated that DU had been used at these sites, but did not uncover any conclusions about the aerosolisation of DU or airborne contamination.

In the subsequent Serbia and Montenegro mission, all the sites investigated had previously been visited, cleaned, fenced-off and assessed by the FRY authorities. This had not been the case in Kosovo. UNEP could not find any significant contamination of the ground surface or the soil except at localized points of concentrated contamination. Nine penetrators and 13 contamination points were identified. The penetrators were removed and the contamination points marked for later decontamination by the FRY authorities. However, laboratory analyses of soil samples enabled contamination to be detected several metres from contamination points. DU contamination was found in some soil samples within the fenced areas (i.e. the target areas). With the exception of Cape Arza, none of the soil samples collected outside the fenced areas showed any DU contamination. Thus, there was no indication that DU had spread outside the fenced areas or over a large distance. Importantly, however, the contamination levels inside the fenced areas were of such a low level that they were considered insignificant from the human health point of view.

In terms of groundwater contamination arising either from DU at contamination points or from more widespread ground contamination, the possible consequences in Serbia and Montenegro were insignificant. The general conclusion for the five sites investigated in Serbia was that there were no penetrators remaining on the surface in the areas that were searched by UNEP. However, at some sites there were indications that penetrators (and contamination points) were present outside the searched areas and might be present outside the areas fenced-off by the FRY authorities in Serbia. There were good reasons for believing that most of the DU rounds fired against targets at the investigated sites did not fragment, but instead entered the ground more or less intact. In this case, the buried penetrators constitute a source of uranium that might, in the future, influence the concentration of uranium in drinking water. During the mission and subsequent laboratory testing, there was no detectable DU in any of the water samples.

Post-Conflict Environmental Assessment

Two of the sites showed a clear indication of DU in the air sampled. However, digging for penetrators was undertaken at the same time as the operation of the filters used for air sampling, making it difficult to find an unequivocal explanation for this finding.

As was found in the 2000 Kosovo mission, lichen appeared to be a reliable indicator of airborne DU contamination. Of the lichen samples taken in Serbia and Montenegro, only those obtained from four sites showed any significant indication of DU.

2.3   DEPLETED URANIUM

What is depleted uranium?

Depleted uranium is a by-product from the process used to enrich natural uranium ore for use as fuel in nuclear reactors and nuclear weapons. It is distinguished from natural uranium by differing concentrations of certain uranium isotopes. Natural uranium has a uranium-235 (abbreviated as U-235 or ^{235}U) content of 0.7 per cent, whereas the content of U-235 in DU is reduced to about one-third of its original content (0.2-0.3 per cent). The U-235 content in DU used in DU ammunition in the Balkans was found to be 0.2 per cent (UNEP 2001; UNEP 2002).

Like naturally occurring uranium, DU is an unstable, radioactive heavy metal that emits ionizing radiation of three types: alpha, beta and gamma. Because of its radioactivity, the amount of uranium in a given sample decreases continuously but the so-called 'half-life' (the period required for the amount of uranium to be reduced by 50 per cent) is very long, 4.5 billion years in the case of the isotope uranium-238 (U-238 or ^{238}U). Therefore, the level of radioactivity does not change significantly over human lifetimes. The unit of measurement for radioactivity is becquerel (Bq), 1 Bq being the disintegration of one atom per second.

A heavily corroded penetrator is collected from the soil at Han Pijesak

When uranium decays, another nuclide or isotope is created, which in turn is also radioactive, leading to a long chain of radionuclides (uranium daughter products) being produced (see Appendix O *'Data on Uranium'*). DU is roughly 40 per cent less radioactive than natural uranium and, consequently, less radiotoxic. This is because during the industrial process by which uranium ore is converted to uranium metal, uranium is chemically separated from all its daughter products beyond U-234, i.e. radium, radon and others.

In the enrichment process used for the production of nuclear fuel, the uranium concentration of the isotope U-235 is enriched from 0.7 per cent in natural uranium to roughly 4 per cent in the uranium destined for fuel in nuclear reactors.

The by-product is uranium with a lower concentration of U-235, i.e. depleted uranium (DU). The U-235 concentration in the DU produced is usually 0.2-0.3 per cent. In enrichment plants, U-235, which is slightly lighter in mass than U-238, is used to separate the two isotopes, allowing the enrichment process of U-235.

Since U-234 is an even lighter isotope, its concentration is correspondingly higher in fuel uranium and lower in DU when compared with natural uranium. The fact that DU has

Depleted Uranium in Bosnia and Herzegovina

lower concentrations of U-235 and U-234 than natural uranium also explains why DU is less radioactive than natural uranium. Data on the specific activity of DU are given in Table 2.1.

Table 2.1 Depleted Uranium, DU (^{235}U 0.2%, ^{238}U 99.8%)

Isotope	Chemical composition [1]	Specific activity [Bq/mg DU]
U-238	99.7990%	12.38
U-235	0.2000%	0.16
U-234	0.0010%	2.29
Th-234	Traces (Decay Product)	12.27
Pa-234 m	Traces (Decay Product)	12.27
Th-231	Traces (Decay Product)	0.16
DU ammunition	Sum	39.42

[1] Browne et al., 1986

Uranium occurs naturally in all rock, soil, water and biota. The typical concentration of activity - expressed as specific activity (activity per mass unit) - of U-238 in the Earth's crust is 5 to 125 becquerels per kilogram (Bq/kg), equivalent to 0.5-10 mg/kg (1 mg/kg = 1 ppm = 1 gram/ tonne). Typical values for U-235 are around 0.2 to 5 Bq/kg. The specific activity of U-238 in uranium ore of good quality (0.5 to 30 per cent uranium) is $0.6 \cdot 10^5$ to $3.6 \cdot 10^6$ Bq/kg. The specific activity of pure uranium metal in radioactive equilibrium with its immediate decay products is $50.23 \cdot 10^6$ Bq/kg (50.23 Bq/ mg ^{nat}U). Details on the specific activity of uranium in soils, rocks, water and air are given in Appendix O (Tables O.18 and O.19).

The overwhelming part of the radiation emitted from the nuclides in the U-238 series is emitted from the isotopes that follow after U-234. Compared with the sum of the energy of alpha radiation emitted per transformation from all isotopes in the U-238 series, the isotopes that follow after U-234 emit about 89 per cent of the alpha energy, roughly 58 per cent of the beta radiation energy and about 98.6 per cent of the gamma radiation energy (Appendix O, Table O.4).

Beta radiation is measured from a penetrator fragment found in the concrete at Hadzici

If reprocessed uranium from a nuclear reactor is used (fully or partially) as feed material in the enrichment process of uranium, or if this was the case during earlier runs of the technical facilities of the enrichment plant, the DU may contain tiny traces of fission products, uranium isotopes and transuranic elements that are specific to reprocessed reactor fuel. In DU penetrator material found during earlier UNEP missions to the Balkans region (UNEP, 2001; UNEP, 2002), traces of U-236 and Pu-239/240 could be identified. U-236 was analysed around 0.003 per cent (mass per cent), and Pu-239/240 contamination of the DU was around 20 Bq/kg (10^{-2} micrograms per kilogram), which is equivalent to the very low content of one plutonium atom per 100 billion uranium atoms. This indicates that the DU found in the

Balkans came into contact with reprocessed uranium at some point during its fabrication process. The concentration of contaminating nuclides is indeed so low that their contribution to the total radiation dose of DU is insignificant and can be neglected in assessing risk to humans or the environment.

Uranium occurs naturally in the +2, +3, +4, +5, and +6 valence states, but it is most commonly found in the hexavalent form at the Earth's surface. In nature, hexavalent uranium is commonly associated with oxygen as the uranyl ion, UO_2^{2+}. The different uranium isotopes are chemically identical and thus exert the same chemical and toxicological effects.

Metallic DU reacts chemically in the same manner as metallic uranium, which is considered to be a reactive material. The general chemical character of uranium is that of a strong reducing agent, particularly in aqueous systems. In air at room temperature, solid uranium metal oxidizes slowly and first assumes a golden-yellow colour. As oxidation proceeds, the colour darkens and at the end of three to four weeks, the metal appears black (Blasch *et al.*, 1970).

Metallic DU, particularly as a powder, is a pyrophore, which means that it spontaneously ignites in air at temperatures of 600-700°C. When DU burns, the high temperatures oxidize the uranium metal to a series of complex oxides, predominantly triuranium octaoxide (U_3O_8), but also uranium dioxide (UO_2) and uranium trioxide (UO_3) (RAND, 1999).

Upon oxidation, uranium metal first forms UO_2. A typical oxidation rate for massive uranium metal would be penetrations of 0.005 mm/day (0.19 mg/cm^2 per day) at 175°C. Significant oxidation of UO_2 does not occur except at temperatures above 275°C (Bennellick, 1966). Uranium oxides are sparingly soluble in water but in a moist environment will gradually form hydrated oxides. Under such conditions, the addition of 0.75 per cent titanium to DU metal used in penetrators appears to slow the oxidation rate by approximately a factor of 16 (Erikson, 1990).

Microbial action can speed the corrosion rate of uranium. The corrosion rate is controlled by several variables, including the oxygen content, presence of water, size of metal particles, presence of protective coatings and the salinity of any water present. The principal factor controlling corrosion is the size of the particles and hence, surface area. Thus, small particles of uranium metal, produced by abrasion and fragmentation, corrode rapidly, whereas large masses of uranium metal usually corrode very slowly. In the long term, all uranium metal will oxidize to U^{4+} and U^{6+} (US AEPI, 1994). Studies carried out on penetrators collected by the UNEP DU mission to Kosovo in 2000 showed that impact on the ground causes numerous fine cracks in penetrators (UNEP, 2001). This favours increased rates of corrosion and dissolution. Rapid corrosion was further confirmed by studies made on penetrators collected during the 2001 UNEP mission to Serbia and Montenegro (UNEP, 2002).

DU can expose people to radiation both from the outside (external radiation) and from the inside (internal radiation) if DU enters the body by inhalation or ingestion. The harmful effect of such radiation is mainly an increased risk of cancer, with the magnitude of risk depending on the part of the body exposed (particularly exposure of the lungs through the inhalation of insoluble compounds) and on the radiation dose.

Like naturally occurring uranium and other heavy metals, DU is also chemically toxic. The toxic effect depends on the amount ingested by the body and the chemical composition of the uranium. Depleted uranium's toxicity is normally the dominant risk factor to consider in the case of ingestion.

For complete, specific data on uranium and depleted uranium see Appendix O. The military uses of DU are summarized in Appendix N.

Depleted Uranium in Bosnia and Herzegovina

2.4 ASSESSING THE RISKS

The concept of risk, its meaning and application are discussed in detail in Appendix A *'Risk Assessment'*. The following is a summary, intended to equip readers with the necessary background for interpreting the *Overall Findings, Conclusions* and *Recommendations* presented respectively in Chapters 4, 5 and 6 of this report.

Line surveys with field instruments were undertaken at all sites during the mission

'Risk' can either refer to the probability, sometimes possibility of occurrence of a given event, or to the consequences of an event if it occurs. A third possibility is a combination of both probability and consequence. Regardless of how the term is used, it is clear that scientific quantification of a given risk has to be expressed clearly and concisely so that appropriate judgements and responses can be made.

The effects of being exposed to DU are both radiological (i.e. due to radiation) and chemical (i.e. as a result of biochemical effects in the human body). Corresponding health consequences may, depending upon the dose or intake, include cancer and malfunction of body organs, particularly the kidneys.

In order to avoid consequences developing from day-to-day procedures in which radioactive and toxic materials are used, a range of applicable standards have been established, including limits for exposure to radiation and toxic materials. However, although such limits and standards exist, these do not imply that if these values are surpassed that there will automatically be severe or adverse consequences, such as serious illness. Wide safety margins are built in before any unconditional or high probability of serious illness could occur. Nonetheless, from a safety point of view, such a situation would be unacceptable.

A potential way to judge the consequences of events or circumstances where DU exposure may have occurred is to compare findings, measurements or assessments with natural levels, and with given 'safety' limits or standards (see Appendix O). In this report, the consequences are those that might be caused by intake of DU through ingestion or inhalation and/or through external radiation exposure to DU.

The consequences of radiation may be expressed directly in terms of the radiation dose, which is measured in millisieverts (mSv) or microsieverts (μSv). Comparisons can be made with natural levels and with established limits and action levels. Consequences of radiation, in this report, are considered insignificant for doses less than 1 mSv per year (or per

Post-Conflict Environmental Assessment

infrequent event), and significant for doses higher than 1 mSv. Because there is an assumption of a linear non-threshold relationship for biologically detrimental effects of ionizing radiation, there is also a decreasing probability of occurrence with decreasing radiation doses. Therefore, an insignificant radiation dose means, in reality, a low and insignificant probability of getting a serious illness from that dose as compared with the overall probability of contracting that same illness from all other potential sources.

With respect to chemical toxicity, consequences are treated as insignificant in this report for concentrations or total intakes below applicable health standards or guidelines, and significant for those above.

In the site-specific findings in Chapter 7, judgements of risk are made on the basis of measured DU ground contamination and measurements of possible DU contamination of drinking water and air. The relationship between measurements and risks are discussed in Appendix A *'Risk Assessment'*. There is also a summary of risk assessment in relation to a given situation (known as the *Reference Case* and taken from the 1999 UNEP *DU Desk Assessment Report*). This assumes ground-surface contamination of 10 g DU per square metre, hereafter referred to as the Reference Level.

The presence of minefields prevented full access to the site in Ustikolina

Some levels of exposure lead to significant risks (consequences, radiation doses, intakes, as compared with chemical toxicity standards), others to insignificant risks. If ground contamination is less than 0.1 to 1 g/m^2, the consequences are normally insignificant. In the current report, the risks considered and assessed - in terms of significance or insignificance of consequences for the environment and human health - are the following:

- If there is widespread measurable contamination of the ground surface by DU, there is a risk that some DU will become airborne through wind action and subsequently be inhaled by people. There is also a possibility of contamination of food (fruit, vegetables, meat, etc.) and drinking water.

Depleted Uranium in Bosnia and Herzegovina

- If there are localized points of concentrated contamination (referred to in this report as 'contamination points'), there is a risk of contamination of hands and/or of direct ingestion of contaminated soil. There is also a possible risk of airborne contamination and contamination of drinking water.

- Solid pieces of DU lying on the ground surface - either fragments of or complete penetrators - can be picked up by persons completely unaware that they are handling uranium. Consequently, there is a risk of being exposed to external beta radiation and to internal radiation (i.e. from inside the body) if corroded DU dust or DU fragments enter the body.

- A large percentage of DU rounds that hit soft targets, or missed the intended target completely, will have penetrated into the ground and become corroded over time (to a widely varying degree, depending on site-specific environmental conditions). As a result, there is a risk of future contamination of groundwater and nearby wells used to supply drinking water. There is also a risk that DU fragments will be brought up to the surface through reconstruction activities.

As more than seven years had elapsed since the attacks with DU munitions in BiH (1994-1995), the conditions influencing the environmental consequences have changed and, thereby, the risks to people. For instance, the risks of airborne contamination from resuspension of DU dust on the ground surface should decrease over time due to the expected dispersion into the ground by dissolution in water, as well as an increasing cover of grass, leaves, etc. On the other hand - and for the same reasons - the probability of water contamination increases over time as DU from surface dust and corroded penetrators enters the water table.

Furthermore, over the aforementioned seven-year period, people may have been exposed to any of the risks described in Appendix A. The possible health consequences of such exposures need to be taken into account by the relevant competent bodies within BiH.

Waters were collected from various sources

The risks of contamination from touching a penetrator on the ground increase, given the possibility of hands or clothes becoming contaminated by corroded DU and the risk of subsequent internal contamination through ingestion. However, this increased risk may be offset by the decreased probability of finding a penetrator that is hidden by vegetation. In conclusion, and as discussed in further detail in Appendix A, the overall risks from DU decrease with time.

UNEP Mission

3.1 MISSION OBJECTIVES

Since UNEP's first depleted uranium (DU) mission to Kosovo in November 2000, a great deal of experience has been gathered concerning the behaviour of DU in the natural environment. A variety of international studies covering such behaviour, as well as medical aspects and risks, have been published in key documents on DU: National Research Center for Environment and Health (GSF) Germany, January 2001; World Health Organisation (WHO) Geneva, April 2001; The Royal Society UK, May 2001 and 2002; Italian Ministry of Defence Italy, May 2001; Scientific and Technological Options Assessment Series (STOA) 100 EN 05-2001, May 2001; Swedish Defence Research Agency (FOI) Sweden, August 2001.

What made this mission distinctive from the two previous missions was that a significantly longer period of time - seven years - had elapsed between the end of the conflict in Bosnia and Herzegovina (BiH) and the DU assessment. During this time, it could be expected that environmental contamination from DU had probably altered in both quantity and quality owing to natural processes.

The objectives of the present mission can be summarized as follows:

The most important objective was to examine the possible risks from any remaining DU contamination of ground, water, air and biota, as well as from solid pieces of DU (i.e. intact or fragmented penetrators) still in the environment, and on that basis recommend any justified countermeasures. The measurements of biota focused, as in the earlier UNEP DU studies, on bio-indicators such as lichens, bark, mushrooms and mosses in order to study their use as 'fingerprints' of earlier DU dispersion in air.

A second objective involved comparing the measurement results with those published by various experts/expert groups (see above), as well as in UNEP's previous assessment reports, and thereby improve UNEP's earlier conclusions with these data. Of particular interest was the long-term behaviour of DU in the natural environment and the conclusions that might be drawn on the corresponding long-term risks of DU. These conclusions would also be applicable to other places with similar environmental properties and where DU has likewise been used.

Thirdly, UNEP wanted to gain an overview on the storage of radioactive waste and sources, as well as radioactive waste management within the country in general. This task was undertaken by the IAEA representative of the UNEP team and is reported in Appendix M *'Storage of radioactive waste and depleted uranium residues in Bosnia and Herzegovina'*.

An important final objective was to obtain an indication of the current level of any existing health databases, both in general and specifically with respect to any population which was expected or rumoured to have been exposed to DU at the time of conflict (i.e. DU dust during an attack). This assignment was undertaken by the medical sub-team comprised of health experts from the WHO and the US Army Center for Health Promotion and Preventive Medicine and is reported in Appendix L *'WHO Assessment of the information on cancer in Bosnia and Herzegovina'*.

Key questions facing the UNEP mission were:

1. What are the present levels of DU contamination in the area, over seven years after the firing of DU ammunition?
2. What are the corresponding radiological and chemical risks, both now and in the future?
3. Is there any need for remedial measures or restrictions?
4. If so, which measures are reasonable and realistic?

The UNEP team received a briefing at each site prior to starting their investigations

The operational objectives and scope of the mission were aimed to answer these questions while bearing in mind: i) the conclusions and recommendations of the October 1999 UNEP *DU Desk Assessment*; ii) the results and recommendations of the two previous UNEP DU missions; iii) the possible constraints on the mission; and iv) the need to conduct the mission in a scientifically sound manner in order to achieve results of high quality. These conditions and prerequisites are developed further in Appendix B *'Prerequisites and Limitations'*.

Specifically, the operational objectives and scope of the mission were:

- to confirm the presence or absence of DU at selected/confirmed locations;
- to determine the distribution of solid pieces of DU (penetrators, fragments, jackets) in the environment and other localized (concentrated) points of contamination (called 'contamination points' or 'hotspots') at the investigated sites;
- to determine how widespread any potential contamination of soil, water, biota etc. is at the investigated sites;
- to determine the possible presence of DU dust in air caused by re-suspension of DU from the ground;
- to determine the corrosion status of penetrators;
- to determine the depth distribution of DU corrosion products beyond a penetrator by studying soil cores;
- to determine the precise isotopic composition of penetrators/fragments;
- to assess the corresponding risks from DU;
- to judge the necessity of establishing precautionary measures;
- to gain experience with regard to the possibilities and limitations that need to be taken into account when planning and executing DU missions in the future;
- to draw conclusions and recommend possible follow-up activities; and
- to inform concerned parties.

Of additional interest, UNEP also sought to determine possible (non-radioactive) heavy metal (e.g. lead) concentrations in selected water and soil samples.

A total of 11 sites known to be attacked in 1994-1995 by A-10 planes using 30 mm DU ammunition was published by NATO (see Appendix P). Five of these sites were available with the exact coordinates and were subject to UNEP's field investigation, whereas the exact positions of the other sites remain undisclosed. The other sites chosen for investigation during the field mission were done on the basis of the NATO document C-M(2001)43, in combination with local information and rumours about sites, as well as a UNEP fact-finding Pre-Mission (see section 3.3 below).

Since 1999, significant efforts have been undertaken in the Balkans region by international expert teams with NATO support in order to localize and measure contamination from DU on the ground. The outcome of NATO's efforts is published on their website (www.nato.int/du/docu/d010523b.pdf; Tables in Annex 2 to NATO UNCLASSIFIED document C-M(2001)43). Those teams covered a range of sites that stood under SFOR troop jurisdiction. Dose rate measurements were conducted and, in some cases, different environmental samples such as soil and water were taken. These were analysed in detail mainly by gamma spectrometric measurements and other chemical parameters. The teams essentially detected no risk from DU at the sites. Some of the previously examined sites were also subject to the UNEP assessment presented here.

NATO had previously been involved in limited clean-up activity at an unspecified time to remove loose DU contamination (i.e. penetrators and jackets) from the ground surface at one of the sites visited during the UNEP mission - the former Hadzici Tank Repair Facility. The penetrators and jackets were removed and placed within a box, which was photographed by the press and published worldwide prior to being removed from the area (see www.nato.int/sfor/indexinf/105/s105p03a/t0101243a.htm).

3.2 COMPOSITION OF THE TEAM

The UNEP DU mission to Bosnia and Herzegovina was undertaken by an 18-member team, most of whom were involved in the two earlier UNEP DU assessments. Experts came from UNEP, the International Atomic Energy Agency (IAEA), the Swedish Radiation Protection Authority (SSI), the United States Army Center for Health Promotion and Preventive Medicine (USACHPPM), the Nuclear Safety Institute of the Russian Academy of Sciences, the Greek Atomic Energy Commission, WHO, the University of Bristol (UK), and two national laboratories: the Swiss Spiez Laboratory and the Italian Environmental Protection Agency and Technical Services (APAT). The WHO health expert did not visit any of the sites, but was involved with meeting government health officials and local hospital representatives. Due to the heavy mine and unexploded ordnance situation, a security expert, formerly of the Finnish Institute of International Affairs, advised the team throughout the mission.

The UNEP team ready to embark on a day in the field

The remaining team members comprised UNEP's PCAU Chairman, the DU Assessment Project Coordinator, the Report Writer and a Project Assistant.

The composition of the team was mainly determined by the need for diverse technical experience and competence in order to ensure a suitably qualified, scientific and wide-ranging examination of the DU issue. It was also necessary to have members with appropriate positions of seniority for conducting negotiations with the military and administrative authorities during the mission.

For that purpose the team included the following functions and expertise:

- Team leader / project coordinator
- Scientific leader
- Technical leader
- Safety and security expert
- Experts in the fields of:
  - Health and environmental effects of depleted uranium
  - Radiation protection
  - Equipment use and maintenance
  - Surveying and field measurements
  - Sampling (air, biota, water and soil)
  - Laboratory work
  - Military advice
  - Mapping
  - Logistics
  - Reporting
  - Public relations.

In practice, one person was often able to cover several tasks and areas of expertise so that two or more experts dealt with a number of subjects.

Beta radiation measurements during the pre-mission helped identify contamination spots

3.3 SELECTION OF SITES

A fact-finding pre-mission, held on 5-14 September 2002, looked at 18 sites based on information provided by local authorities, NATO, and research. This included information published on the NATO website indicating positions targeted by DU munitions, together with dates of firing and the numbers of rounds used. The final choice of which sites - targeted or rumoured - were to be investigated was made solely and independently by UNEP. Eleven sites from the pre-mission were retained for investigation during the full DU assessment. They were selected on the basis of preliminary indications of DU munitions use and information provided by local authorities, as well as rumoured bombing sites. Shortly before the October mission, NATO provided UNEP with two additional site coordinates for confirmed DU attacks. These sites were added for investigation and assessment, for a total of five NATO confirmed sites to be investigated.

With additional information acquired from local authorities throughout the course of the October mission, two further sites were included for investigation. These sites involved ammunition destruction and could have been contaminated by DU if the ammunition had been inadvertently destroyed in such areas. UNEP also asked the authorities whether any vehicles hit by DU could be investigated, but none could be located. Within each study area, a more detailed selection of specific sites suitable for investigation was made *in situ*, based mainly on instructions from military experts and UNEP's security advisor concerning i) the presence of mines and unexploded ordnance, and ii) estimates of the probable direction of attack.

The criteria for selecting sites were as follows:

- The approximate number of DU rounds fired was known.
- Indications of a DU attack were identified during the pre-mission.
- Information and rumoured information were supplied by local authorities.
- The sites taken together were representative of a range of environmental conditions and properties.
- The locations taken together were representative of the region's varied ethnic composition.
- The areas to be examined were considered safe from mines and unexploded ordnance.
- The areas were close to residential areas and needed to be investigated for humanitarian reasons.

3.4 FIELDWORK, SAMPLING AND LABORATORY ANALYSIS

The mission used five complementary technical methods in conducting its investigations:

- Field measurements of beta radiation (total beta);
- Field measurements of gamma radiation (total gamma);
- Field sampling of soil, water and vegetation (bio-indicators), with subsequent laboratory analysis;
- Field air sampling by special air filter samplers, with subsequent laboratory analysis; and
- Field analysis of higher radioactive background levels (gamma spectrometric measurements, e.g. from lightning rods, cesium-137 fallout from the 1986 Chernobyl accident, natural radiation).

The surveys of radiation in the environment were made using beta and gamma instruments held close to the ground, usually employing the 'line-up' survey technique. This technique involved team members walking several abreast at fixed distances from each other, and sometimes along parallel transect lines (see Appendix C for a full description). As a complement to these formal searches, individual survey measurements were made. Although carried out in a more random way than the line-up surveys, likely search areas were selected by observing the assumed direction of attack and looking for signs of ammunition impacts. These individual surveys were often very effective. The results of field measurements of radioactivity are given as 'counts per second' (cps) or microsieverts per hour - abbreviated as µSv/h.

Depleted Uranium in Bosnia and Herzegovina

Each measurement taken was governed by uncertainties that had to be estimated. Besides the usual statistical uncertainties, there are possible systematic errors in the field measurements caused by absorption of the radiation, and in laboratory work by varying analytical techniques used.

Analyses of soil, soil cores, water, biological and air samples were carried out at both the Spiez and APAT laboratories.

Starting a 'line-up survey' at Pjelugovici

Field instruments effectively detected increased gamma radiation

Following the Kosovo and Serbia and Montenegro missions, a quality control exercise for selected IAEA certified reference materials was conducted. Both Spiez and APAT laboratories passed that quality control test. The reference materials IAEA-326 (soil), IAEA-336 (lichen), IAEA-140TM (sea weed) and IAEA-381 (sea water) were analysed, with the results reported in Appendix C *'Methodology and Quality Control'*. The analysis of penetrators was performed solely at Spiez Laboratory.

The results of laboratory samples (of soil and biota) are given either in terms of weight, i.e. milligrams of uranium isotope (U-238 etc.) per kilogram of sample (abbreviated as 'mg U/kg sample'), with DU expressed as a percentage of total uranium concentration, or in terms of activity in becquerels per kilogram, Bq/kg.

For water samples, results are given as micrograms per litre (μg/L). or microbecquerels per kilogram (μBq/kg) and for air in μBq/m^3.

Specific components of the measurement and sampling campaign included:

- field measurements using beta instruments (sometimes in combination with gamma instruments to identify strong hidden contamination or hidden penetrators) held close to the ground to search for possible widespread DU contamination and contamination points;
- field measurements using a gamma instrument held close to the ground to find DU penetrators and jackets/casings lying on or close to the surface;
- field measurements using a gamma spectrometric instrument placed close to objects of interest;
- sampling of soil from around and beneath penetrators and contamination points, in order to study the migration of DU in soil;
- sampling of soil from the wider environment to search for possible widespread DU contamination (complement to the field measurements);

- sampling of water from both streams and reservoirs (tap water) to search for possible DU contamination of water supplies;
- sampling of biota (e.g. lichen, bark, mushrooms and moss) in order to check for the possible presence of DU as evidence of earlier or ongoing contamination;
- sampling of air at several locations within most sites.

The number of samples taken at each site, the number of penetrators and jackets found, and the approximate number of DU rounds fired against the respective site are given in Table 3.1.

Retrieving a penetrator imbedded in cobblestone at Hadzici

The results of all the laboratory analyses are given in detail in Appendices D, E, F, G and H. The geographical (UTM) coordinates of each sampling position can be found in Chapter 7, together with corresponding maps. The analytical methods used are fully described in Appendix C.

3.5 IAEA: STORAGE OF RADIOACTIVE WASTE AND DEPLETED URANIUM RESIDUES IN BOSNIA AND HERZEGOVINA

One of the tasks assigned to the UNEP team for this mission was to conduct an investigation of the regulatory and technical infrastructure the country has in place concerning the storage of radioactive waste and, in particular, DU residues. As part of this task, the IAEA representative, accompanied by a UNEP team member, carried out a series of meetings with national authorities and visited the interim low-level radioactive waste storage facility of the Federation of Bosnia and Herzegovina (FBiH). Appendix M describes the outcome of this investigation.

3.6 WHO ASSESSMENT OF THE INFORMATION ON CANCER IN BOSNIA AND HERZEGOVINA

The WHO developed an assessment on the information on cancer due to DU exposure, as well as cancer rates in general, in BiH. A health consultant to UNEP, coming from the US Army Center for Health Promotion and Preventive Medicine (USACHPPM), accompanied the WHO in the visits and meetings. Visits were made to the cities of Sarajevo (in both the FBiH and Republika Srpska (RS)), and Banja Luka. See Appendix L for the report.

Table 3.1 Summary of samples collected and on-site findings in Bosnia and Herzegovina*

Site name	Sample type (collected)						Penetrators found on the surface	Contamination points found	Rounds
	Air	Water	Botanical	Soil	Smear	Fragments/ penetrators			
Hadzici Tank Repair	9	4	7	12	-	1	Yes	240	1 500
Lukavica	4	1	5	4	-	-	No	No	Unknown
Hadzici Barracks	2	2	1	3	-	-	No	No	Unknown
Hadzici Ammunition Storage	-	-	2	2	-	-	Yes	6	1 500
76mm Selp-prop AT Gun (Rosca)	Unable to access						-	-	860
Pjelugovici (T55)	-	-	2	2	-	-	No	2 (caused by cesium-137)	120
Han Pijesak Barracks	6	2	4	6 (+3 soil cores)	4 (+2 scratch)	3	Yes	48 (+1 caused by cesium-137)	2 400
Han Pijesak Ammunition Storage	-	-	-	-	-	-	No	No	Unknown
Pale Koran Barracks	-	1	-	2	-	-	No	6 (caused by cesium-137)	Unknown
Vogosca Ammunition Production	2	2	4	5	1	-	No	No	Unknown
Ustikolina Barracks	-	2	1	3	-	-	No	No	Unknown
Foca (Srbinje) Bridge	1	1	1	2	-	-	No	No	Unknown
Kalinovik Water Reservoir	-	1	-	1	-	-	No	No	Unknown
Kalinovik Ammunition Destruction Site	-	1	1	2	-	-	No	No	-
Bjelasnica Plateau Ammunition Destruction Site	-	2	1	2	-	-	No	No	-
Total	24	19	29	46 (+3)	5 (+2)	4			

* Additional smear samples were taken by the Russian expert as part of a special study on surface contamination. Results are discussed in Appendix J.

Storage boxes for samples collected during the mission

Post-Conflict Environmental Assessment

Overall Findings

4

4.1 OVERVIEW

The following sites were investigated during the mission to Bosnia and Herzegovina (BiH): the former Hadzici Tank Repair Facility, Lukavica, Hadzici Army Barracks, the former Hadzici Ammunition Storage Depot, a hill at Pjelugovici (site of a T55 tank), the Han Pijesak Artillery Storage and Barracks, the Han Pijesak Storage Area, Pale's Koran Barracks, Vogosca's former Ammunition Production Facility, a barracks site in Ustikolina, a bridge in the town of Foca (Srbinje), a water reservoir site in Kalinovik, the Kalinovik Ammunition Destruction Site, and the Bjelasnica Plateau Ammunition Destruction Site. The sites were chosen for investigation based on information which was provided stating that depleted uranium had probably been used or that certain areas could have a potential risk of DU contamination due to other activities.

DU was found at three of these sites; the former Tank Repair Facility and former Ammunition Storage Depot in Hadzici, and Han Pijesak Artillery Storage and Barracks. Clear and unambiguous findings of penetrators or contamination points on the ground and soil was found at each of these sites, as well as water contamination at one site, air contamination at two sites, and in botanical samples taken at three sites. No DU was found at any of the other sites, which may be due to some or all of the following reasons:

- There is no presence of DU in the area (the most likely scenario).

- DU contamination has been covered by soil, grass and other growth in the time that has passed since the military conflict and is therefore no longer detectable by direct field measurements. However, subsequent laboratory analyses of soil and botanical samples would have revealed such hidden activity.

- DU penetrators have penetrated so deeply into the ground that they are undetectable by both direct field measurements and laboratory analyses.

- One hundred per cent of the area was not searched due to the risk of mines. Where only a minor part of the total area was inaccessible, conclusions could be made by extrapolation; however, no clear conclusions could be drawn where a major part of the area was inaccessible.

- Samples were somehow taken only in uncontaminated parts of an area. However, by taking samples from several locations within a site, the risk of missing something is significantly reduced.

- The area was searched prior to the mission and DU penetrators removed and contamination cleaned up.

As sophisticated equipment was used both in the field and laboratory, it was concluded that there was no DU contamination at investigated sites when nothing was detected.

The overall findings for the 14 sites investigated are summarized below. No findings for the Rosca site (*76 mm AT Self-Prop Gun*) are included as investigations were not possible due to the heavy presence of mines. The corresponding *Conclusions* and *Recommendations* are presented in Chapters 5 and 6, respectively. The assessments of risk mentioned below are discussed in more detail in Appendix A.

4.2 FINDINGS

(a) Localized contamination of surface soil

If a large number of penetrators hit hard surfaces and partly aerosolise on impact, there is a risk of inhaling airborne DU dust if people are nearby during an attack. As the aerosols disperse and fall out, resulting contamination of the ground surface may be localized or widespread, depending on the properties of the aerosols and the prevailing meteorological conditions.

No DU was present in the soil samples collected from Foca (Srbinje)

The same conditions occur during destruction by blasting of ammunition containing DU, although under controlled conditions the risk of inhalation and contamination of the surrounding area can be minimized. Importantly, no indications of DU were measured at such sites (*Kalinovik* and *Bjelasnica Plateau* Ammunition Destruction sites), neither in water or soils samples, nor during radiometric surveys.

Using portable beta and gamma radiation detectors, UNEP could not find any detectable and significant widespread contamination of the ground surface, soil, or biota-environment except at localized points of concentrated contamination, referred to as 'contamination points' (see (b) below). These were close to penetrators lying on the ground, penetrator impact sites or penetrator holes. The level of DU detected decreased rapidly with distance from contamination points and was no longer detectable by field measurements beyond a distance of 1 m.

However, through laboratory analyses of soil samples, ground contamination could in some cases be detected around contamination points at distances less than 200 m from the nearest identified contamination point, defined in this report as localized ground contamination. Of the 14 sites investigated, only three had DU in soil that was detectable using sampling and laboratory analyses. Importantly, as not all soil samples at these three sites showed contamination, this indicates more localized - as opposed to widespread - contamination of the sites. Undetectable DU contamination of the soil means that possible DU contamination was so small that it could not be differentiated from natural uranium present in the soil. All the soil samples were taken by and analysed at Spiez Laboratory in Switzerland.

Assessment of risk

Contamination of the ground surface and upper layer (0-5 cm) of the ground was very low. Therefore, the corresponding radiological and chemical risks are insignificant.

(b) Contamination points

Localized points of ground contamination occurred at the site of penetrator impact or close to a penetrator that had remained on the surface and been subject to corrosion. DU concentration can be very high at these points, but the contamination was quite localized (normally within a radius of 0.1 m) with widely variable concentrations: 0.01-100 g DU/kg of soil.

One of many corroded penetrator fragments collected from the Hadzici Tank Repair Facility

Remarkably, close to 300 contamination points were found during the mission, most of these at the *Tank Repair* site in Hadzici. These findings are intriguing from three points of view:

i)   A great deal of precipitation has fallen over the intervening eight-year period and yet this has dissolved and removed perhaps only a minor part of the DU;

ii) Contamination has not been dispersed by wind;

iii) Although certain contaminated areas have been used by various vehicles, the apparent mechanical agitation has not helped the contamination to disappear.

These observations of slow dispersion in soil and resistance to mechanical agitation lead to the conclusion that ground and soil contamination may be permanent in nature.

It is possible that more contamination points exist away from the searched areas. Due to the risk of mines and unexploded ordnance, surveys of some sites were quite limited.

Assessment of risk

One risk is related to the possibility of some contaminated soil becoming airborne, through wind action or movement by people or animals, and being inhaled. Another risk is related to the possibility that DU from the contamination points eventually contaminates groundwater through drainage. However, in both these cases, the amount of DU at the contamination points was too low to cause any radiological and chemical problems either now or in the future. The corresponding risks are insignificant.

The only risk of any significance would be from the possibility that someone came into direct physical contact with the contamination points and thereby contaminated their hands or directly ingested contaminated sand/soil. However, even if several grams of soil are ingested, the resulting exposure is insignificant with regard to the radiation from ingested uranium (less than 10 µSv). On the other hand, such exposure might be significant from the standpoint of heavy metal toxicity.

Depleted Uranium in Bosnia and Herzegovina

OVERALL FINDINGS

(c) Dispersion in ground

There are scientifically valid reasons to believe that the chemical and physical properties of DU make it more liable to dispersion in soil than is the case for natural uranium. The issue of DU dispersion into the ground is of particular relevance in judging the risk of future groundwater contamination and, ultimately, drinking water supplies (see Appendix E for further details).

Soil profiles collected from Han Pijesak revealed limited dispersion of DU into the ground

The depth of contaminated soil caused by dispersion of DU below contamination points or a penetrator was carefully studied. The major part of soil contamination was found in the upper 0-10 cm and the concentration then fell by 1-2 orders of magnitude for each 10 cm further below. These results were similar to the ones from the UNEP DU mission to Kosovo in 2000, however, the depth of detectable dispersion had increased from 10 to 40 cm during the five additional years of dispersion as compared to the Kosovo findings. Importantly, the major part of measured activity (~98 per cent) remained in the upper 10 cm. This vertical distribution results from dissolution and dispersion of DU from the initial superficial contamination (or from the penetrator lying on the surface). When comparing results with Kosovo, it should be noted that soil conditions at the investigated sites might be different from these in Kosovo.

(d) Penetrators

As outlined in Chapter 2.3, and discussed in more detail in Appendix H '*Analysis of DU Penetrators, Fragments and Jackets*', the fate of a DU penetrator after firing is governed by a wide range of variable factors (e.g. type of target, resistance of surface substrate, etc). Consequently, there are several possible explanations of why penetrators were found at some sites but not at others.

Altogether at the three sites where DU was discovered, some ten penetrators, two jackets and several dozen fragments were found. The presence of a further 100 penetrators hidden in the ground were indicated by measurements. In most cases, the penetrators were located either on the ground surface, or superficially covered by leaves and grass. Those that were covered by less than 10 cm of soil were heavily corroded and, given a similar continued rate of

An intact penetrator still in its jacket

Post-Conflict Environmental Assessment

corrosion, would disappear as solid objects from the environment within 25-35 years after impact into the ground. The penetrators that were lying on the ground surface were only mildly corroded. What occurs in the case of penetrators hidden deep in the ground has not yet been studied by UNEP and is an important unanswered scientific question.

Most penetrators that were found on the surface or just below were picked up, but some of them were left *in situ*, as mentioned in Chapter 7 '*Site-specific findings*'. These sites therefore have to be searched and possible penetrators and contaminated soil dealt with.

NUC-2002-028-403

A penetrator cleaned from soil and DU corrosion products shows structural damage

As described above, the soil underneath and around penetrators on the ground surface was contaminated by DU. This finding is closely related to the corrosion of penetrators, which also illustrates one possible pathway for internal exposure. If a person not wearing protective gloves touches a corroded penetrator, hands may become contaminated, leading to a risk of DU ingestion.

Due to the lack of widespread contamination, there are good reasons to believe that most of the DU rounds that were fired at the sites investigated did not fragment, but instead entered the ground more or less intact. In this way, they are a source of uranium that might influence the uranium concentration in drinking water in the future. Exceptionally, the amount of additional uranium in the affected areas might be 10-100 times naturally occurring levels. However, the additional amount would normally only represent a doubling of natural uranium levels.

Penetrators were also analysed with regard to their plutonium content (Pu-239/240), uranium-236 (U-236) and neptunium (Np-237) (see Appendix H). The isotopic composition and radiochemical analysis confirmed the overall picture for penetrators and fragments that emerged from the UNEP DU missions to Kosovo, and Serbia and Montenegro. The depletion level in all samples measured was constant (i.e. $0.200\pm0.001\%$ U-235 by weight). In addition, the level of U-236 in penetrators was confirmed to be 0.0028 per cent by weight.

Depleted Uranium in Bosnia and Herzegovina

The radiochemical analyses also confirmed the very low presence of plutonium and neptunium in the penetrators. For plutonium, activity concentrations were 0.0050-0.0878 Bq/g penetrator, which corresponds to 2.2E-12 to 38.2E-12 g Pu/g penetrator. For neptunium, the concentration was very low at less than 0.004 to 0.0162 Bq/g.

The presence of these radioactive elements in the DU indicates that at least some of the depleted uranium came from reprocessed material from spent nuclear fuel or from contamination of equipment during the reprocessing of spent nuclear fuel. The amount of plutonium, neptunium and U-236 found did not have any significant impact on the overall radioactivity of penetrators or corresponding health risk.

Assessment of risk

People may pick up penetrators lying on the ground. Several grams of corroded uranium could easily be removed from the penetrators through mechanical contact. This would constitute a potential risk of being internally contaminated through ingestion. Even if only a small part of the available DU were to pass into the body, the resulting radiation dose, although relatively high, would still be less than 1 mSv. In terms of health standards relating to chemical toxicity, the possible intake is not small with respect to annual tolerable intakes.

Another risk of exposure from a heavily corroded penetrator is by inhalation. Care has to be taken in handling a penetrator to avoid corroded DU becoming airborne. With conservative assumptions, inhalation might lead to significant doses (more than 1 mSv).

A third risk of exposure is by external beta radiation to the skin where a penetrator is placed close to the body, such as in a pocket. Continuous exposure of the skin for several weeks can lead to local radiation doses (in excess of radiation safety guidelines), even though skin burns from radiation may not occur. The resulting gamma radiation exposure will be insignificant and, at most, of the same order of magnitude as natural radiation.

Penetrators on the surface, and particularly those in the ground, may dissolve in time and slowly contaminate groundwater and drinking water (see Appendix E). As discussed in point (g) below, drinking water has natural uranium content. Normal natural uranium concentration and annual intake by water in the areas visited is low, 10^{-5}-10^{-3} mg U/L water and 0.01-1 mg uranium/year respectively, leading to radiation doses of less than 1 μSv/year.

The increase of uranium from hidden penetrators at the sites could - very locally - be 10-100 times the natural uranium content in the first metre below the surface. If that resulted in a corresponding increase of uranium concentration in water, the radiation dose would still be less than 1 mSv per year, but the uranium concentration could exceed WHO health standards for drinking water. However, many uncertainties exist and therefore some future analysis of uranium in drinking water close to the affected sites will be needed.

Penetrators currently hidden in the ground may be dug up during future construction work. Should this occur, there would be corresponding risks of external exposure from beta radiation and the risk of internal exposure by contamination of hands and by inhalation, as described above.

There are no risks of any significantly increased uptake of DU in plants either now or in the future as a consequence of penetrators remaining in the environment (compare with point (b) above).

The measured concentration of plutonium in DU was 87.8 Bq/kg DU at the most. This has to be compared with the activity of U-238 in DU, which is 12 400 000 Bq/kg DU, i.e. about 150 000 times higher. The radiation dose per Bq of Pu is much higher than per Bq of DU, particularly with regard to doses caused by inhalation. By combining the relative activity and the dose factor, it is concluded that the Pu contained in the studied penetrators is about 1 000 times less hazardous than the DU itself.

Analysis of uranium-236 in the penetrators showed a concentration of 0.0028 per cent of the total uranium. The content of U-236 in the penetrators is so small that the radiotoxicity is unchanged when compared to DU without U-236.

(e) Jackets/Casings

A jacket is the part of the projectile that holds the penetrator. It stops upon impact against a hard surface, while the penetrator enters the target. Only two jackets were found, this small number being another indication that most of the penetrators missed hard targets and penetrated the ground with the jacket attached.

Assessment of risk

The potential risks from jackets are much lower than those from penetrators because they are made of aluminium and are only slightly contaminated with DU.

(f) Military vehicles hit by DU

Although many vehicles were probably hit by DU during the conflict, none could be investigated by UNEP. It was reported that the vehicles had been removed from the sites, but no information could be provided on where they may now be stored, or how they were disposed of.

Tanks and APCs are the usual targets when using depleted uranium munitions

Assessment of risk

If any DU-hit vehicles are identified, even if the risk of contamination may be small, some precautions should be taken to avoid any unnecessary risk before entering a vehicle. Some decontamination of the interior of the vehicle might be needed before being considered safe. A qualified expert, taking due regard for appropriate safety regulations, should carry out the decontamination work.

Tap water from a local source near the Bjelasnica plateau

(g) Contamination of water

Nineteen water samples from 11 investigated sites were taken for laboratory analyses. All the water measurements are summarized in Appendix E. The uranium concentration was found to vary from 0.02-2.7 µg/L water (i.e. within the normal range of uranium concentration in drinking water).

Depleted Uranium in Bosnia and Herzegovina

Unlike the two previous assessments, DU contamination of groundwater was found at one of the sites (*Hadzici Tank Repair Facility*). The concentration was low and insignificant from a radiological and chemical-toxicological point of view, but was indicative of possible future water contamination over time. This finding justifies the need for continued checking of possible DU contamination of drinking water in the future.

Assessment of risk

On the basis of these findings, there are no significant risks from DU in water at present.

Modern air samplers were run for several hours at most sites

(h) Contamination of air

Air samples were taken at six sites. With the exception of the Foca (Srbinje) bridge site, sampling was done at two or more locations within the fenced areas, and was chosen based on wind direction or either inside or in proximity to any contaminated buildings. The concentration of uranium in air varied from $0.011\ 10^{-6}$ mg/m^3 (0.14 µBq/m^3) to $3.6\ 10^{-6}$ mg/m^3 (43 µBq/m^3) (see Appendix G, Table G.6). All but two of the samples showed concentrations within the normal range of uranium in air. All results from air samples are summarized in Appendix G.

Two sites showed clear indications of DU in the air. Of the two samples with higher than 'normal' uranium concentration, one was collected at the former *Hadzici Tank Repair Facility* and the other at the *Han Pijesak Artillery Storage and Barracks*. These samples contained over 90 per cent DU, which was caused by wind resuspension of DU dust on the ground.

Where significant dust and particles are present in the air from nearby ground surfaces, and DU dust is present on these local surfaces, it is likely that DU will be found in air under certain wind conditions or human activities that raise the dust into the air. In these circumstances, air samplers provide a good measure of potential inhalation risk and DU should be detectable.

DU in air can also depend on resuspension caused by human activities such as moving around, digging, driving vehicles, etc. Only one air sample was taken during ongoing human activities at both sites, which could have impacted the results.

Assessment of risk

The natural concentration of uranium in air normally causes very low doses from the uranium isotopes alone, in the order of 0.1-1 µSv/year. This was also the case at all sites measured, including the two sites with measurable DU concentration in air.

(i) Contamination of botanical material

Samples of botanical material such as moss, bark and lichen were taken at 11 sites in order to search for possible DU uptake and to identify any previous or ongoing airborne contamination. As illustrated in UNEP's previous DU assessments, moss, bark and lichen are sensitive indicators of past airborne contamination for DU dust or particles generated at the time of attack or by later resuspension.

Post-Conflict Environmental Assessment

The presence of DU in lichen, bark and moss samples indicates the earlier presence of DU in air in three of the 11 sites (the former *Hadzici Tank Repair Facility* and *Ammunition Storage Depot*, and *Han Pijesak Artillery Storage and Barracks*). This indicates that at least some of the penetrators at these sites hit hard targets and surfaces, partly aerosolised into dust, and dispersed into the air.

(j) Box of loose DU ordnance

One of UNEP's tasks was to investigate the history and location of the box containing DU penetrators, fragments and jackets/casings originally located at the former *Hadzici Tank Repair Facility* (see Chapter 7.1). Despite numerous enquiries, additional information concerning the location of the box was unavailable both from SFOR and local workers and authorities. Based on information later provided by NATO, it was confirmed that the box containing DU collected material was transferred in Spring 2001 to US national facilities outside Bosnia and Herzegovina for disposal.

Lichen samples from trees and other surfaces helped reveal the earlier presence of DU at certain sites

Jackets and penetrators recovered by SFOR at Hadzici (source: NATO)

(k) International Atomic Energy Agency (IAEA)

The low-level radioactive waste repository of the Federation of Bosnia and Herzegovina (FBiH) provides an adequate facility for the safe storage of radioactive waste, including depleted uranium residues. Work on the construction of a treatment and conditioning facility for the radioactive waste has started. The treatment facility will improve the capability of the Centre for Radiation Protection to deal with radioactive waste. Unfortunately no repository for low-level radioactive waste is operational in Republika Srpska, although progress has been made towards identifying a possible location where the repository could be built.

There were a significant number of radioactive sources, such as industrial sources, lightning rods and smoke detectors, in use on the territory of BiH before the war. Many of these sources have become obsolete or were lost or damaged during the war and have yet to be recovered. The risks from potential exposure to them are significantly higher than those from exposure to DU residues. Consideration should be given to the storage and eventual disposal of these sources and in particular to those lost or damaged during the war.

(l) World Health Organisation (WHO)

Information on cancers, cancer rates and trends is incomplete in both the FBiH and the Republika Srpska. Claims of increases in many types of cancers were made by physicians based on clinical observations but were not substantiated by information on cancer rates, which relate the number of cases to the population these cases come from. Therefore, no

Depleted Uranium in Bosnia and Herzegovina

4

A crater created by
ammunition blasting at
the Bjelasnica Plateau

conclusions can be made on whether there is any change in cancer frequency. However, this situation is improving. In particular, the cancer registries aimed at establishing complete ascertainment of cancers and to avoid double counting have been set up in parts of the FBiH and in the Republika Srpska.

(m) Heavy Metal contamination
During the mission, heavy metal contamination of topsoil was found at both a former Ammunition production site (*Vogosca*), and two Ammunition destruction sites. Contamination through such activities at those types of sites is a known occurrence elsewhere in the world. However, for certain heavy metals (such as lead, copper, nickel, etc) the intervention levels for soil contamination were already reached. This is reason for some concern.

Opšti nalazi

4.1 PREGLED

Tokom misije u Bosni i Hercegovini, istražene su sledeće lokacije: nekadašnji objekat za popravku tenkova u Hadžićima, Lukavica, kasarna u Hadžićima, nekadašnje skladište municije u Hadžićima, brdo kod Pjelugovića (mesto tenka T55), kasarna u Han Pijesku, skladište u Han Pijesku, kasarna Koran na Palama, nekadašnji objekat za proizvodnju municije u Vogošći, lokacija kasarne u Ustikolini, most u gradu Foča, lokacija rezervoara vode u Kalinoviku, lokacija za uništenje municije u Kalinoviku, lokacija za uništenje municije na platou na Bjelašnici. Ove lokacije izabrane su za istraživanje na osnovu dobijenih informacija o tome da je tu verovatno korišćen osiromašeni uranijum ili da možda postoji opasnost od kontaminacije osiromašenim uranijumom zbog drugih aktivnosti.

Osiromašeni uranijum pronadjen je na tri gore navedene lokacije: na lokaciji nekadašnjeg objekta za popravku tenkova i nekadašnjeg skladišta municije u Hadžićima, kasarne i skladišta artiljerijskog naoružanja u Han Pijesku. Na tim lokacijama pronadjeni su jasni i nedvosmisleni nalazi radioaktivnih zrna ili tačaka kontaminacije na tlu i u zemlji; na jednoj od ovih lokacija utvrdjena je i kontaminacija vode, na dve kontaminacija vazduha, a na tri kontaminacija u uzorcima flore. Osiromašeni uranijum nije pronadjen na ostalim lokacijama, što može proisticati iz pojedinih ili svih dole navedenih razloga:

- Nema prisustva osiromašenog uranijuma u toj oblasti (najverovatniji scenario)

- Tlo kontaminirano osiromašenim uranijumom je od vremena vojnog sukoba prekrila zemlja, trava i drugo rastinje i zato se više ne može otkriti neposrednim merenjem na terenu. Medjutim, takva skrivena aktivnost bi u tom slučaju bila otkrivena u uzorcima zemljišta i biljaka koje su kasnije podvrgnute laboratorijskoj analizi.

- Radioaktivna zrna sa osiromašenim uranijumom su toliko duboko prodrla u zemlju da ih je nemoguće detektovati bilo neposrednim terenskim merenjem, bilo laboratorijskim analizama.

- Zbog opasnosti od mina, nije pretraženo 100% svake lokacije. Ako samo mali deo sveukupnog prostora nije dostupan, zaključci se mogu izvoditi ekstrapolacijom. Ukoliko je obrnuto slučaj, ne mogu se izvesti nikakvi jasni zaključci.

- Uzorci su uzimani samo u nekontaminiranim delovima neke lokacije. Medjutim, uzimanjem uzoraka sa nekoliko mesta na jednoj lokaciji, značajno smanjuje rizik da je nešto propušteno.

- Lokacija je pregledana pre misije i zrna sa osiromašenim uranijumom i kontaminacija su uklonjena.

Medjutim, s obzirom da je korišćena sofisticirana oprema kako na terenu, tako i u laboratorijama, zaključeno je da na istraženim lokacijama na kojima nije detektovana kontaminacija osiromašenim uranijumom takve kontaminacije nema.

Sledi kratak pregled opštih nalaza sa četrnaest istraženih lokacija. Nalaza za petnaestu lokaciju (samohodni top76 mm AT) nema jer nije bilo moguće istražiti tu lokaciju zbog prisustva velikog broja mina. Odgovarajući Zaključci i Preporuke izloženi su u Poglavljima 5 i 6. Dole navedene procene rizika detaljnije su obrazložene u Aneksu A.

4.2 NALAZI

(a) Lokalizovana kontaminacija površinskog sloja zemljišta

Ukoliko veliki broj radioaktivnih zrna udari u tvrde površine i delimično se rasprši u čestice u vidu aerosola u trenutku udara, postoji opasnost da ljudi koji se nalaze blizu mesta udara tokom napada udahnu prašinu osiromašenog uranijuma koju prenosi vazduh. Pošto se aerosoli raspršuju i padaju, rezultirajuća kontaminacija površinskog tla može biti lokalizovana ili rasprostranjena, u zavisnosti od osobina aerosola i preovladjujućih meteoroloških uslova.

Isti uslovi postoje prilikom aktivnosti uništavanja municije koja sadrži osiromašeni uranijum, iako se opasnost od udisanja i kontaminacije okoline može svesti na najmanju moguću meru pod kontrolisanim uslovima. Važno je da na takvim lokacijama (lokacije na kojima je uništavana municija u Kalinoviku i na platou na Bjelašnici) nisu utvrdjeni nikakvi pokazatelji osiromašenog uranijuma, kako u analiziranim uzorcima vode ili zemlje, tako ni tokom radiometrijskih merenja.

Korišćenjem portabl detektora beta i gama zračenja, ekipa UNEP nije detektovala bilo kakvu i značajnu rasprostranjenu kontaminaciju površine tla, zemlje ili flore, osim na lokalizovanim mestima koncentrisane kontaminacije koje se nazivaju "tačkama kontaminacije" (videti niže, pod (b)). Te tačke su bile blizu radioaktivnih zrna koja su se nalazile na tlu, blizu mesta udara zrna ili rupa koje su napravila zrna. Nivo detektovanog osiromašenog uranijuma brzo je opadao sa razdaljinom od tačaka kontaminacije i nije se više mogao detektovati terenskim merenjem na razdaljini većoj od jednog metra.

Medjutim, laboratorijske analize i uzorci tla su u nekim slučajevima otkrili tragove kontaminacije zemljišta na razdaljini manjoj od 200 metara od najbliže identifikovane tačke kontaminacije. U ovom izveštaju se to definiše kao lokalizovana kontaminacija zemljišta. Od 14 istraženih lokacija, samo na 3 je detektovano prisustvo osiromašenog uranijuma u zemljištu i to putem uzorkovanja i laboratorijskih analiza. Važan pokazatelj da je kontaminacija na te tri lokacije lokalizovana, a ne rasprostranjena, proizilazi iz toga što nisu svi uzorci tla na te tri lokacije pokazali kontaminaciju. Odsustvo detektovanja zagadjenja tla osiromašenim uranijumom znači da je moguća kontaminacija osiromašenim uranijumom tako mala da se nije mogla utvrditi razlika izmedju osiromašenog i prirodnog uranijuma koji je prisutan u zemljištu. Sve uzorke zemljišta su uzele i analizirale Spiez laboratorije u Švajcarskoj.

Procena rizika

Kontaminacija površine tla i gornjeg sloja (0-5 cm) zemlje je veoma niska. Dakle, odgovarajući radiološki i hemijski rizik je beznačajan.

(b) Tačke kontaminacije

Lokalizovane tačke kontaminacije površine tla pojavljuju se na mestima udara radioaktivnog zrna ili blizu zrna koji je ostao na površini i bio izložen koroziji. Koncentracija osiromašenog uranijuma može biti veoma visoka na tim tačkama, ali je kontaminacija prilično lokalizovana (obično u radijusu od 0,1 m) a koncentracija veoma varira, od 0,01 do 100 gr osiromašenog uranijuma po kilogramu zemlje.

Zanimljivo, tokom misije je pronadjeno skoro 300 tačaka kontaminacije, većina na lokaciji objekta za popravku tenkova u Hadžićima. Ovi nalazi su interesantni sa tri stanovišta:

i) Mnogo padavina je palo tokom razdoblja od osam godina ali su one izgleda rastvorile i odnele samo mali deo osiromašenog uranijuma.

ii) Kontaminacija nije raspršena putem vetra.

iii) Iako su različita vozila prelazila preko odredjenih kontaminiranih delova, očigledno mehaničko delovanje nije doprinelo nestanku kontaminacije.

Ova zapažanja sporog prodora u zemlji i otpora mehaničkom delovanju navode na zaključak da je kontaminacija površine tla i zemlje možda po svojoj prirodi postojana.

Moguće je da postoji još tačaka kontaminacije izvan istraženih lokacija. Zbog opasnosti od mina i neeksplodirane municije, istraživanje nekih lokacija bilo je prilično ograničeno.

Procena rizika

Jedan od rizika vezan je za mogućnost da se zagadjena zemlja vazduhom prenosi vetrom, kretanjem ljudi ili životinja ili da se u vidu prašine udiše. Druga opasnost vezana je za mogućnost da osiromašeni uranijum na tačkama kontaminacije pre ili kasnije otekne i kontaminira podzemne vode. Medjutim, u oba ova slučaja, količina osiromašenog uranijuma na tačkama kontaminacije je isuviše mala da bi prouzrokovala bilo kakve radiološke ili hemijske probleme u sadašnjosti ili budućnosti. Odgovarajući rizici su beznačajni.

Jedina opasnost od značaja proistekla bi od mogućnosti da neko dodje u neposredan fizički kontakt sa tačkama kontaminacije i tako kontaminira ruke ili direktno proguta kontaminirani pesak/zemlju. Medjutim, čak i ako se proguta nekoliko grama zemlje, rezultirajuća izloženost je neznatna u smislu ozračenja progutanim uranijumom (manje od 10 µSv). S druge strane, takva izloženost može biti značajna sa stanovišta toksičnosti teških metala.

(c) Disperzija u zemlji

Postoje naučno valjani razlozi za verovanje da je zbog svojih hemijskih i fizičkih osobina osiromašeni uranijum podložniji disperziji u zemljištu nego prirodni uranijum. Pitanje disperzije osiromašenog uranijuma u tlu je od posebne važnosti pri proceni rizika buduće kontaminacije podzemnih voda i, konačno, zaliha vode za piće (videti Aneks E za detalje).

Pažljivo je proučavana dubina zagadjenja zemljišta izazvanog disperzijom osiromašenog uranijuma ispod tačaka kontaminacije ili radioaktivnih zrna. Najveći deo kontaminacije tla pronadjen je u gornjih 0-10 cm, a koncentracija je zatim opadala po 1-2 reda veličine svakih 10 cm. Ovi rezultati su slični onima do kojih je došla misija UNEP koja je proučavala prisustvo osiromašenog uranijuma na Kosovu 2000.g; medjutim, dubina disperzije, koju je moguće registrovati, povećana je sa 10 cm na 40 cm tokom 5 dodatnih godina ove disperzije u poredjenju sa nalazima sa Kosova. Važno je što je veliki deo izmerene aktivnosti (~98%) ostao u gornjih 10 cm. Ova vertikalna distribucija rezultat je rastvaranja i disperzije osiromašenog uranijuma od početne površinske kontaminacije (ili od radioaktivnog zrna koje leži na površini). Pri poredjenju rezultata sa onima sa Kosova, treba napomenuti da je moguće da se uslovi zemljišta na istraženim lokacijama razlikuju od onih na Kosovu.

(d) Radioaktivna zrna

Kao što je izloženo u Poglavlju 2.3 a detaljnije razmatrano u Aneksu H "Analiza radioaktivnih zrna sa osiromašenim uranijumom, fragmenata i košuljice zrna", sudbina zrna sa osiromašenim uranijumom posle ispaljivanja zavisi od velikog broja promenjivih faktora (napr: vrste mete, otpora materijala u koji udara itd). Zato postoji nekoliko mogućih objašnjenja zašto su na nekim lokacijama pronadjena radioaktivna zrna, a na nekima ne.

Sveukupno je pronadjeno oko 10 radioaktivnih zrna, dve košuljice, i nekoliko desetina fragmenata na tri lokacije gde je detektovan osiromašeni uranijum. Merenja su pokazala da je još 100 zrna prisutno skriveno u zemlji. U većini slučajeva, zrna su se nalazila ili na površini tla ili su bila neznatno prekrivena lišćem i travom. Radioaktivna zrna koja su bila pokrivena sa manje od 10 cm zemlje bila su veoma korodirana i, pod uslovom da se sličan tempo korozije nastavi, možda će nestati iz životne sredine kao čvrsti predmeti za nekih 25-35 godina od prodora u zemlju. Radioaktivna zrna koja su ležala na površini zemlje bilo su samo blago korodirana. UNEP još nije proučavao šta se dešava u slučaju radioaktivnih zrna skrivenih duboko u zemlji i ovo je jedno važno naučno pitanje na koje nije odgovoreno.

Većina radioaktivnih zrna koja su pronadjena na površini tla ili odmah ispod površinskog sloja zemljišta su uklonjena, ali neka su ostala u prvobitnom položaju, kao što je rečeno u Poglavlju 7 "Nalazi na pojedinačnim lokacijama". Zato ove lokacije treba istražiti i rešiti problem eventualnih radioaktivnih zrna i kontaminiranog zemljišta.

Kao što je gore opisano, tlo ispod i oko radioaktivnih zrna je na površinskom sloju bilo kontaminirano osiromašenim uranijumom. Ovaj nalaz je blisko povezan sa korozijom radioaktivnih zrna, što takodje ilustruje jedan od mogućih načina unutrašnje izloženosti. Ukoliko osoba, koja ne nosi zaštitne rukavice, dotakne korodirano radioaktivno zrno, može doći do kontaminacije ruku, što dovodi do rizika gutanja osiromašenog uranijuma.

S obzirom da kontaminacija nije rasprostranjena, postoje valjani razlozi za verovanje da se veliki deo zrna sa osiromašenim uranijumom koja su ispaljena na istražene lokacije nisu raskomadala, već su se više-manje neoštećena zabila u zemlju. Na taj način, ona predstavljaju izvor uranijuma koji ubuduće može uticati na koncentraciju uranijuma u vodi za piće. Izuzetno, količina dodatnog uranijuma u pogodjenim lokacijama može biti i 10-100 puta viša od prirodnog fona. Medjutim, ta dodatna količina obično predstavlja samo udvostručavanje nivoa aktivnosti prirodnog uranijuma.

Takodje su analizirana radioaktivna zrna u odnosu na sastav plutonijuma (Pu 239/240), uranijuma-236 (U-236) i neptunijuma (Np-237) (Videti Aneks H). Analiza sastava izotopa i radiohemijska analiza potvrdili su opštu sliku o radioaktivnim zrnima i fragmentima koja je dobijena tokom misija UNEP procene osiromašenog uranijuma na Kosovu i Srbiji i Crnoj Gori. Nivo osiromašenja u svim izmerenim uzorcima bio je konstantan (tj 0,200 ± 0,001% U-235 po težini). Takodje, potvrdjeno je da nivo U-236 u radioaktivnim zrnima 0,0028% po težini.

Radiohemijske analize su takodje potvrdile veoma nisko prisustvo plutonijuma i neptunijuma u radioaktivnim zrnima. Za plutonijum, koncentracije aktivnosti bile su od 0,0050 do 0,0878 Bq/g po radioaktivnom zrnu, što odgovara od 2,2E-12 do 38,2E-12 g Pu/g radioaktivnog zrna. Koncentracija u slučaju neptunijuma bila je veoma niska, manje od 0,004 do 0,0162 Bq po gramu.

Prisustvo ovih radioaktivnih elemenata u osiromašenom uranijumu ukazuje na to da je bar nešto osiromašenog uranijuma poteklo od prerade materijala od iskorišćenog nuklearnog goriva ili kontaminacije opreme tokom prerade iskorišćenog nuklearnog goriva. Količina pronadjenog plutonijuma, neptunijuma, i U-236 nije imala nikakav značajan uticaj na sveukupnu radioaktivnost radioaktivnih zrna, niti predstavljala odgovarajuću opasnost po zdravlje.

Procena rizika

Dešava se da ljudi podignu radioaktivna zrna sa površine tla. Mehaničkim kontaktom je lako sa radioaktivnog zrna skinuti nekoliko grama korodiranog uranijuma. Ovo bi moglo predstavljati potencijalni rizik od unutrašnje kontaminacije gutanjem. Ukoliko bi čak i mali deo dostupnog osiromašenog uranijuma ušao u telo, rezultirajuća doza radijacije, iako relativno visoka, i dalje bi bila ispod 1 mSv. U smislu zdravstvenih standarda vezanih za hemijsku toksičnost, potencijalni unos nije mali u odnosu na godišnji unos koji se toleriše.

Udisanje aerosola osiromašenog uranijuma takodje prestavlja rizik od izloženosti veoma korodiranom radioaktivnom zrnu. Ljudi moraju pažljivo da rukuju sa takvim radioaktivnim zrnom kako bi izbegli prenos korodiranog osiromašenog uranijuma vazduhom. Pesimistična pretpostavka je da se takvo udisanje može odraziti značajnim dozama ozračivanja (više od 1 mSv).

Treću opasnost od izloženosti prestavlja spoljno ozračavanje kože beta radijacijom do koje može doći ukoliko neka osoba stavi radioaktivno zrno blizu tela, naprimer, u džep. Kontinurana izloženost kože tokom nekoliko nedelja može dovesti do lokalnih doza zračenja (koje premašuju doze navedene u preporukama vezanim za radiološku sigurnost) iako radijacija ne mora izazvati opekotine na koži. Rezultirajuća izloženost gama zračenju biće beznačajna i, u najgorem slučaju, istog reda veličine kao i prirodno zračenje.

Radioaktivna zrna na površini tla, a pogotovo ona u zemlji, mogu se vremenom rastvoriti i polako kontaminirati podzemne vode i vodu za piće (videti Aneks E). Kao što se napominje niže u tački (g), voda za piće sadrži prirodni uranijum. Normalna koncentracija prirodnog uranijuma i godišnji unos vodom u posećenim lokacijama su niski, $10^{-5} – 10^{-3}$ mg uranijuma po litru vode ili 0,01-1 mg uranijuma godišnje, što se ogleda u dozama zračenja koje ne prelaze 1 µSv godišnje.

Povećanje uranijuma iz skrivenih radioaktivnih zrna na lokacijama bi moglo biti - veoma lokalno - 10 do 100 puta veće od sadržaja prirodnog uranijuma na prvom metru dubine ispod površine tla. Ukoliko bi to rezultiralo odgovarajućim povećanjem koncentracije uranijuma u vodi, doza radijacije bi i dalje bila manja od 1 mSv godišnje, ali bi koncentracija uranijuma bila veća od zdravstvenih standarda koje je Svetska zdravstvena organizacija

Depleted Uranium in Bosnia and Herzegovina

propisala za vodu za piće. Medjutim, tu i dalje postoje mnoge nesigurnosti i zato bi trebalo u budućnosti izvršiti analizu uranijuma u vodi za piće blizu pogodjenih lokacija.

Moguće je da tokom gradjevinskih radova u budućnosti budu iskopana radioaktivna zrna koja su trenutno skrivena u zemlji. Ukoliko se ovo dogodi, postojali bi odgovarajući rizici od spoljne izloženosti beta zračenju i opasnost od unutrašnje izloženosti kontaminacijom ruku i udisanjem, kao što je gore opisano.

Ne postoji opasnost da će sada ili ubuduće apsorpcija osiromašenog uranijuma od strane biljaka biti značajno povećana zbog toga što se radioaktivna zrna i dalje nalaze u životnoj sredini (porediti sa gornjom tačkom (b)).

Izmerena koncentracija plutonijuma u osiromašenom uranijumu nije premašivala 87,8 Bq po kilogramu osiromašenog uranijuma. To se mora porediti sa aktivnošću U-238 u osiromašenom uranijumu, koja iznosi 12.400.000 Bq po kilogramu osiromašenog uranijuma, tj. viša je od plutonijumove oko 150.000 puta. Doza radijacije plutonijuma po jedinici zračenja Bekerelu mnogo je viša od doze zračenja osiromašenog uranijuma po Bekerelu, pogotovu kada su u pitanju doze izazvane udisanjem. Kombinovanjem relativne aktivnosti i faktora doze, zaključuje se da je plutonijum pronadjen u proučavanim radioaktivnim zrnima oko 1.000 puta manje štetan nego sam osiromašeni uranijum.

Analiza Uranijuma 236 u radioaktivnim zrnima pokazala je koncentraciju od 0,0028% ukupnog uranijuma. Sadržaj U-236 u radioaktivnim zrnima je toliko mali da je radiotoksičnost nepromenjena u poredjenju sa osiromašenim uranijumom bez U-236.

(e) Košuljice/čaure

Košuljica je deo projektila u kojem se nalazi radioaktivno zrno. Ona se zaustavlja pri udaru o tvrdu površinu dok radioaktivno zrno ulazi u metu. Pronadjene su samo dve košuljice. Mali broj pronadjenih košuljica predstavlja dodatni pokazatelj da većina radioaktivnih zrna nije pogodila tvrde mete i da je prodrla u zemlju zajedno sa košuljicom.

Procena rizika

Potencijalni rizici od košuljica mnogo su niži od rizika od radioaktivnih zrna zato što se košuljice proizvode od aluminijuma i samo su neznatno kontaminirane osiromašenim uranijumom.

(f) Vojna vozila pogodjena osiromašenim uranijumom

Iako je verovatno veliki broj vozila pogodjen osiromašenim uranijumom tokom sukoba, tim UNEP nije mogao da istraži nijedno vozilo. Rečeno je da su vozila uklonjena sa lokacija, ali niko nije mogao da pruži informacije o tome gde se sada ta vozila čuvaju ili šta se sa njima dogòdilo.

Procena rizika

Ukoliko se identifikuje ijedno vozilo pogodjeno osiromašenim uranijumom, čak i ako je rizik kontaminacije mali, treba preduzeti neke mere predostrožnosti pre ulaska u vozilo kako bi se izbegao nepotreban rizik. Možda će biti potrebno izvršiti neku dekontaminaciju unutrašnjosti vozila pre no što se ono može smatrati bezbednim. Dekontaminaciju treba da vrši kvalifikovani stručnjak, koji će uzimati u obzir odgovarajuća pravila sigurnosti.

(g) Kontaminacija vode

Uzeto je 19 uzoraka vode sa 11 istraženih lokacija radi laboratorijske analize. Sva merenja vode ukratko su izložena u Aneksu E. Koncentracija uranijuma je varirala od 0,02 do 2,7 μg po litru vode (tj. u okviru normalnog opsega koncentracije uranijuma u vodi za piće).

Za razliku od prethodne dve misije, na jednoj lokaciji (u objektu za popravku tenkova u Hadžićima) utvrdjena je kontaminacija podzemnih voda osiromašenim uranijumom. Koncentracija je bila niska i beznačajna s radiološkog i hemijsko-toksikološkog stanovišta, ali indikativna s obzirom na kontaminaciju vode do koje vremenom može doći. Ovaj nalaz opravdava kontinuiranu proveru moguće kontaminacije vode za piće osiromašenim uranijumom u budućnosti.

Procena rizika

Na osnovu sadašnjih nalaza, sada ne postoji značajna opasnost od osiromašenog uranijuma u vodi.

(h) Kontaminacija vazduha

Uzorci vazduha uzeti su na šest lokacija. S izuzetkom lokacije mosta u Foči, uzorci zu uzimani na dve ili više tačaka unutar ogradjenih lokacija, a te tačke su odabrane na osnovu pravca vetra, ili unutar ili blizu kontaminiranih zgrada. Koncentracija uranijuma u vazduhu varirala je od $0,011 \cdot 10^{-6}$ mg/m^3 (0,14 μBq po m^3) do $3,6 \cdot 10^{-6}$ mg/m^3 (43 μBq po m^3) (videti Aneks G, Tabelu G.6). S izuzetkom dva uzorka, svi ostali uzorci pokazali su koncentraciju u normalnom opsegu uranijuma u vazduhu. Svi rezultati analize uzoraka vazduha prikazani su ukratko u Aneksu G.

Dve lokacije su pokazale jasne indikacije prisustva osiromašenog uranijuma u vazduhu. Jedan od uzoraka sa višom od "normalne" koncentracije uranijuma uzet je kod nekadašnjeg

Depleted Uranium in Bosnia and Herzegovina

objekta za popravku tenkova u Hadžićima, a drugi je uzet kod kasarne u Han Pijesku. Ovi uzorci su sadržali preko 90% osiromašenog uranijuma, a uzrok tome je što je vetar sa zemlje ponovo podigao prašinu sa osiromašenim uranijumom.

Ukoliko se u vazduhu nalazi značajna količina prašine i čestica sa obližnjih površina tla (napr: lokacije) a prašina osiromašenog uranijuma je prisutna na ovim lokalnim površinama, verovatno je da će u vazduhu biti pronadjen osiromašeni uranijum pod dejstvom odredjenih vetrova ili ljudskih aktivnosti koji podižu prašinu u vazduh. U tom smislu instrumenti predstavljaju dobro sredstvo za merenje potencijalnog rizika od udisanja aerosola osiromašenog uranijuma i njima bi bilo moguće detektovati osiromašeni uranijum.

Prisustvo osiromašenog uranijuma u vazduhu takodje zavisi od njegovog ponovnog podizanja u vazduh izazvanog ljudskim aktivnostima, kao što je kretanje, kopanje, vožnja vozila itd. Na obe lokacije je uzet samo po jedan uzorak vazduha tokom ljudskih aktivnosti koje su mogle da utiču na rezultate.

Procena rizika

Prirodna koncentracija uranijuma u vazduha obično izaziva veoma niske doze. Samo od izotopa uranijuma ona je reda veličine 0,1-1 µSv godišnje. Ovo je slučaj i kod svih izmerenih lokacija, uključujući i dve lokacije sa merljivom koncentracijom osiromašenog uranijuma u vazduhu.

(i) Kontaminacija materijala flore

Uzorci materijala flore, kao što je mahovina, kora drveta i lišajevi, uzeti su sa 11 lokacija kako bi se istražila mogućnost apsorpcije osiromašenog uranijuma i identifikovala ranija ili sadašnja kontaminacija putem vazduha. Kao što je ilustrovano u prethodnim procenama osiromašenog uranijuma od strane UNEP-a, mahovina, kora drveta i lišajevi predstavljaju osetljive indikatore ranije kontaminacije prašinom ili česticama osiromašenog uranijuma putem vazduha, a koje su nastale tokom napada ili kasnijim ponovnim podizanjem te prašine ili čestica u vazduh.

Prisustvo osiromašenog uranijuma u uzorcima lišajeva, kore drveta i mahovine ukazalo je na ranije prisustvo osiromašenog uranijuma u vazduhu na 3 od 11 lokacija (objekat za popravku tenkova i stovarište municije u Hadžićima i kasarna u Han Pijesku). To ukazuje da su bar neka radioaktivna zrna na tim lokacijama udarili tvrde mete i površine, delom se raspršili i pretvorili u prašinu i razneli se u vazduhu.

(i) Kutija sakupljene municije osiromašenim uranijumom

Jedan od zadataka UNEP je bio da istraži istorijat i lokaciju kutije sa zrnima sa osiromašenim uranijumom, fragmentima, košuljicama i čaurama koja se prvobitno nalazila u objektu za popravku tenkova u Hadžićima (videti 7.1). Bez obzira na mnogobrojna raspitivanja, dodatne informacije u vezi sa mestom gde se kutija nalazi nisu mogli da pruže ni SFOR, ni lokalni radnici, ni vlasti. Na osnovu informacija koje je kasnije pružio NATO, potvrdjeno je da je kutija sa sakupljenim materijalom sa osiromašenim uranijumom u proleće 2001.g. prebačena u nacionalni objekat SAD izvan Bosne i Hercegovine radi odlaganja.

(j) Medjunarodna agencija za atomsku energiju (IAEA)

Odlagalište radioaktivnog otpada niskog nivoa Federacije predstavlja adekvatan objekat za bezbedno skladištenje radioaktivnog otpada na teritoriji Federacije, uključujući ostatke osiromašenog uranijuma. Rad na izgradnji objekta za obradu i skladištenje radioaktivnog otpada je otpočeo. Taj objekat će poboljšati sposobnost Centra za zaštitu od zračenja da odlaže i čuva radioaktivni otpad. Nažalost, u Republici Srpskoj nijedno odlagalište radioaktivnog otpada niskog nivoa ne radi, mada je učinjen napredak u pronalaženju moguće lokacije na kojoj bi se takvo odlagalište izgradilo.

Pre rata je na teritoriji BiH korišćen značajan broj radioaktivnih izvora, kao što su industrijski izvori, gromobrani i javljači požara. Mnogi od tih izvora su zastareli, izgubljeni ili oštećeni tokom rata i tek treba da budu pronadjeni. Rizici od potencijalne izloženosti ovim izvorima su značajno veći od rizika od izloženosti ostacima osiromašenog uranijuma. Treba dati prioritet skladištenju i kasnijem odlaganju ovih izvora a pogotovo pronalaženju i bezbednom skladištenju ili odlaganju izvora koji su izgubljeni ili oštećeni tokom rata.

(k) Svetska zdravstvena organizacija (WHO)

Informacije o raku, stopama oboljevanja od raka i trendovima nepotpuni su i u Federaciji i u Republici Srpskoj. Tvrdnje o većoj učestalosti mnogih vrsta raka izneli su lekari na osnovu kliničkih zapažanja, ali njihove tvrdnje nisu potkrepljene informacijama o stopama oboljevanja od raka, koje dovode u vezu broj slučajeva i stanovništva gde se ti slučajevi pojavljuju. Dakle, nikakvi zaključci se ne mogu izvesti o tome da li postoji promena u učestalosti raka. Medjutim, situacija se poboljšava. Konkretno, u delovima Federacije Bosne i Hercegovine i Republike Srpske uvedene su evidencije oboljevanja od raka koje imaju za cilj utvrdjivanje svih slučajeva oboljenja od raka i izbegavanje dvostrukog evidentiranja.

(l) Kontaminacija teškim metalima

Tokom misije je pronadjena kontaminacija teškim metalima površine tla kako na lokaciji nekadašnjeg objekta za proizvodnju municije, tako i na dve lokacije na kojoj se uništava municija. Poznato je da se i u drugim delovima sveta na takvim lokacijama pojavljuje zagadjenje prouzrokovano pomenutim aktivnostima. Medjutim, već su dostignuti nivoi zagadjenja tla nekim teškim metalima (kao što su olovo, bakar, nikl) koji zahtevaju intervenciju. Ovo je donekle zabrinjavajuće.

5 Conclusions

5.1 INTRODUCTORY NOTES

(a) The conclusions and observations in this section refer to the 15 sites that were visited and investigated during the UNEP mission to Bosnia and Herzegovina (BiH) from 12-24 October 2002.

(b) A 'significant' radiological risk is defined in this report to be where the expected radiation dose would be more than 1 mSv per year. A 'significant' toxicological risk means that the expected concentration or intake would exceed WHO health standards (WHO 1998A, 1998B). 'Insignificant' radiological risks are those where the corresponding dose is less than 1 mSv. 'Insignificant' toxicological risks correspond to intakes below WHO health standards (see Appendix A).

(c) Although corresponding radiological and toxicological risks in most cases are insignificant, UNEP calls for precautionary clean-up steps at certain sites as it is deemed unnecessary for any local populations to be exposed when simple, inexpensive measures can be taken to either remove or ameliorate the DU contamination.

(d) In comparison with the two previous UNEP missions, many different conditions applied to the work conducted in BiH. Yet, the results from each mission remain broadly compatible. One essential difference was that seven years had elapsed since the military conflict. This had led to further corrosion of DU penetrators lying in the ground, more growth covering impact points, and to increased possibilities of DU contamination in water.

5.2 CONCLUSIONS

Based on the findings discussed in Chapter 4 (and on a site-specific basis in Chapter 7), the overall conclusions of the UNEP mission are as follows:

1) **Investigated sites:**
   a) The UNEP team visited 15 sites of which one of the NATO-confirmed sites was inaccessible due to the presence of mines (*76 mm AT Self-Prop Gun*). Three of the 14 sites investigated clearly showed DU contamination, confirming the earlier use of DU ordnance (i.e. in Hadzici both the former *Tank Repair Facility* and *Ammunition Storage Depot*, and *Han Pijesak Artillery Storage and Barracks*). These sites corresponded to confirmed NATO coordinates. Importantly, there are six NATO coordinates in the vicinity of Sarajevo which are still missing. These sites could therefore not be investigated.

   b) No DU contamination was found on the other 11 sites investigated. Based on the information collected in the field and subsequent laboratory work, it is highly unlikely that DU would have been used at these sites. Even if there had been a full clean-up of the sites following the attacks, analytical methods would have detected traces of DU in the soil, water and/or biota samples.

2) **Localized ground contamination:**
   None of the sites showed signs of widespread contamination of the ground surface as nothing was detected by portable beta and gamma radiation detectors. At most, localized ground contamination was detected around contamination points at distances below

200 m, but often much closer, as confirmed by the much more sensitive laboratory analyses of soil samples. This also indicates that most DU rounds probably never fragmented but penetrated into the ground. When penetrators enter ground that is more or less soft, significantly less DU dust results. The corresponding radiological and toxicological risks from such low-level contamination are insignificant. These observations are consistent with the findings from UNEP's two previous assessments.

3) **Contamination points:**
   a) Over seven years had elapsed since the military conflict and UNEP's assessment mission. In 2000-2001, other international expert teams had searched many of the sites investigated by UNEP for penetrators and contamination points. Despite this, many penetrators and contamination points were still found and identified by UNEP. Ground surface DU contamination that is detectable by portable beta and gamma radiation detectors was typically limited to areas within 1-2 m of penetrators and localized points of contamination caused by penetrator impacts. Almost 300 contamination points were identified during the mission, but most of them were only slightly contaminated. Each was marked for the authorities to address.

   b) Based on results of air filter measurements, contamination points may be formed by resuspension of DU particles in the air. However, no significant risk is expected to arise from these points through inhalation by local populations or possible contamination of water or plants.

   c) The only risk of any potential significance would be through touching a contamination point, thereby contaminating the body (with a risk of subsequent transfer to the mouth), or directly ingesting contaminated soil. However, with reasonable assumptions on intake of soil, the corresponding radiological risk would be insignificant, while from a toxicological point of view the possible intake might be somewhat higher than applicable health standards or guidelines.

4) **Penetrators and fragments:**
   a) During the mission three penetrators were collected for detailed analysis. There were also indications from field measurements of a large number hidden in the ground (contamination points). At the former *Hadzici Tank Repair Facility*, an unknown number of penetrators had been collected by both locals and SFOR troops. Given that several thousand DU rounds were reportedly fired against the target sites investigated, the number found is still low. It is concluded that there could be four possible explanations:

   - the majority of the penetrators are buried deep in the ground;
   - they are spread over larger, inaccessible areas within mine fields;
   - they have been removed during random site clean-up or during mine clearing activities;
   - they have been removed in circumstances beyond the control of the authorities (for instance by local people)

   The most probable and most widely applicable explanation is the first one, but the other three scenarios might also have occurred.

   b) **Penetrator corrosion:** Corrosion occurs relatively quickly when the penetrator remains in the ground and is surrounded by soil. A penetrator can be completely corroded to emitting corrosion products (e.g. uranium oxides and carbonates) in the 25-35 years following impact. These corrosion products may in turn dissolve and disperse in water. However, the rate of corrosion depends on the composition of the soil. If the penetrator is lying on the ground surface the corrosion rate is significantly lower.

c) **Penetrator contact:** The corroded uranium is loosely attached and easily removable. Consequently, if such a penetrator is picked up, it could easily contaminate anyone handling it. Even if the probable resulting intake into the body is small, the radiological and toxicological risks should not be ignored. If a penetrator is placed near the body, such as in a pocket, there will be external beta radiation to the skin. After some weeks of continuous exposure, this could lead to localized radiation doses above safety standards. Even so, it is unlikely that there would be any adverse health effects from such exposure.

d) **Accidental penetrator recovery:** Buried penetrators and jackets may be accidentally brought to the surface in the future through digging as part of soil removal or construction works. The corresponding risks would then be the same as for penetrators and jackets currently lying on the surface.

e) **Penetrator composition:** The transuranic elements plutonium-239/240 and neptunium-237, as well as the uranium isotope U-236, were found to be present in the depleted uranium of those penetrators analysed. However, the concentrations were very low, in the published range of the open military literature, and did not have any significant impact on their overall radioactivity or health risk. The composition is consistent with penetrators found in earlier assessments.

5) **Soil contamination:**
The contamination of subsurface soil above and below penetrators was studied. The penetrators lay in undisturbed, grass covered ground at a depth of 3-8 cm below the soil surface. Soil contamination around the penetrator was 45 g of DU per kg of soil. Within 10 cm below the penetrator the DU concentration decreased by two orders of magnitude, and within the next 30 cm by a further three orders of magnitude. From these observations it is concluded that the mobility of corroded DU in the present soil composition is low due to the fact that it is retarded by sorption and coprecipitation with minerals. Groundwater contamination is unlikely due to the low mobility of DU corrosion products.

6) **Water contamination:**
a) DU could be clearly identified in one of the drinking water samples. A second drinking water sample from a well showed traces of DU contamination, which were detectable only through the use of mass spectrometric measurements. The concentrations are very low and the corresponding radiation doses are insignificant for any health risk. This is also the case with respect to toxicity of uranium as a heavy metal. However, because the mechanism that governs the contamination of water in a given environment is not known in detail, it is concluded that water sampling and measurements should continue for several years.

b) As concluded above, it is probable that the majority of penetrators are hidden in the ground. They may constitute a risk of future groundwater and drinking water contamination where they lie close to water sources, as is the case for those samples indicating contamination (i.e. the wells were most likely lying in the line of attack). Although DU mobility is low, if a penetrator is located in the immediate vicinity of a water source, contamination may occur. Heavy firing of DU in an area could increase the potential source of uranium contamination of groundwater by a factor of 10 to 100, compared to the case of a single penetrator. While the radiation doses will be low, the resulting uranium concentration may exceed WHO health standards or guidelines for drinking water.

7) **Bio-indicator contamination:**

The presence of DU was found in lichen samples at the three sites mentioned above. This is an indication that some penetrators hit targets and hard surfaces, partly split into dust and dispersed into the air. This also illustrates that analysis of lichen samples is a useful method in monitoring the quality of the environment.

8) **Vegetable samples:**

Two vegetable samples (cabbage) were taken in the vicinity of the former *Hadzici Tank Repair Facility*. Results from these two samples are insufficient to allow for any scientific conclusion. There are no reasons to expect any DU in food due to the low dispersion rate in the ground and low uptake factor in food.

9) **Air contamination:**

a) DU contamination of air was found at two sites where DU use had been confirmed. This can be due to resuspension of DU particles by wind or human activities from contamination points, corroded penetrators or fragments lying on the surface. The concentrations were very low and resulting radiation doses were minor and insignificant. At distances over 100 m from contaminated areas, no DU could be detected in the air. This may be due to limits on instrumentation detection.

b) DU contamination of air and some surfaces was found inside two buildings at the two sites mentioned above. This can be due to resuspension of DU particles by wind or human activities from contamination points, corroded penetrators or fragments laying on the surface inside, as well as any DU dust contained within the building since the time of attack. Although the low levels measured result in doses which are minor and insignificant, UNEP considers exposure to such a source unnecessary. Therefore, precautionary clean-up steps for areas of contamination are recommended.

10) **Awareness raising:**

Throughout the mission, UNEP observed that workers and civilians with access to these sites, as well as military and mine clearing personnel, were unaware of or misunderstood the risks and issues with respect to DU ammunition in general.

11) **Methodology:**

The techniques, equipment and methodologies used worked very well during the mission and the experience from earlier missions contributed to the successful evaluations.

12) **Radiation protection and radiation safety:**

a) The radiation safety infrastructure in BiH has only recently been established. In the Federation of Bosnia and Herzegovina (FBiH), the new Law on Radiation Protection and Radiation Safety establishing the basis for the new regulatory system was approved by Parliament in 1999. In the Republika Srpska (RS), legislation complying with the IAEA's international standards for protection against ionizing radiation was adopted in 2001. The efforts made in establishing an institutional radiation protection framework in BiH since the end of the conflict are commendable, considering the limited resources available and the encouraging results achieved, although more work is necessary to improve radiation protection.

b) In addition to two independent legal frameworks for radiation protection, two separate regulatory authorities and radiation protection organizations have been created in the FBiH and RS. This results in a duplication of services and activities which is particularly inappropriate in view of the shortage of resources available. The lack of cooperation between the two radiation protection organizations negatively affects the establishment and implementation of an efficient radiation safety regime in BiH.

c) The low-level radioactive waste repository of the FBiH provides an adequate facility for the safe storage of radioactive waste in the territory, including depleted uranium residues. Work on the construction of a treatment and conditioning facility for the radioactive waste has started, although no significant progress has been made in the last year. The treatment facility will improve the capability for the Centre for Radiation Protection to deal with radioactive waste. Unfortunately, no repository for low-level radioactive waste is operational in Republika Srpska, although progress has been made towards identifying a possible location where the repository could be built.

d) There were a significant number of radioactive sources, such as industrial sources, lightning rods and smoke detectors, in use throughout BiH before the war. Records for these are no longer available. Many of these sources have become obsolete or were lost or damaged during the war and have yet to be recovered. The risks from potential exposure to them are significantly higher than those from exposure to DU residues. Consideration should be given to the storage and eventual disposal of these sources and in particular to those which were lost or damaged during the war.

e) While normal environmental monitoring is not a high priority for BiH, where there are no significant sources of radioactive discharges from facilities, it is of concern that no activities are carried out to ensure the protection of members of the public in areas accessible to them and where radiation and/or risks from contamination may exist. This concerns particularly those areas where damaged or abandoned and uncontrolled sources may exist as a result of the disruption caused by the war.

13) Health concerns:

Due to the lack of a proper cancer registry and reporting system, claims of an increase in the rates of adverse health effects stemming from DU cannot be substantiated. It is encouraging that the BiH authorities are in the process of implementing a registry and reporting system to detect and report cancers within the country. This should allow the verification of concerns about changes in the frequency of cancers. The scientific data on uranium and DU health effects developed over the last half century, and the extremely low exposure identified in this UNEP mission, indicates that it is highly unlikely that DU could be associated with any of these reported health effects.

14) DU box:

One of UNEP's tasks was to investigate the history and location of the box containing DU penetrators, fragments and jackets/casings originally located at the former *Hadzici Tank Repair Facility* (see Chapter 7.1). Based on a NATO fax dated 3 December 2002, the box containing DU material was transferred in spring 2001 to US national facilities outside Bosnia and Herzegovina for disposal.

15) Heavy metals:

At three of the sites investigated, high surface contamination of heavy metals was measured (*Vogosca's Ammunition Production Facility*, and ammunition destruction sites at *Kalinovik* and the *Bjelasnica Plateau*). Such contamination could represent a potential future health risk. As the intervention values for certain elements in soil have already been reached, further investigation is required to properly assess the situation.

Post-Conflict Environmental Assessment

Zaključci

5.1 UVODNE NAPOMENE

(a) Zaključci i zapažanja u ovom odeljku odnose se na 15 lokacija koje su posećene i istražene tokom misije UNEP u Bosni i Hercegovini (BiH) 12-24. oktobra 2002.g.

(b) "Značajan" *radiološki* rizik je u ovom izveštaju definisan u slučajevima kada je očekivana doza zračenja viša od 1 mSv godišnje. "Značajan" *toksikološki* rizik znači da očekivana koncentracija ili unos premašuje zdravstvene standarde WHO (WHO, 1998A, 1998B). "Beznačajni" *radiološki* rizici su oni gde je odgovarajuća doza manja od 1 mSv. "Beznačajni" *toksikološki* rizici odgovaraju unosu nižem od zdravstvenih standarda WHO (videti Aneks A).

(c) Iako su u većini slučajeva odgovarajući radiološki i toksikološki rizici beznačajni, UNEP poziva na mere predostrožnosti čišćenja odredjenih lokacija jer smatra nepotrebnim da lokalno stanovništvo igde bude izloženo takvim rizicima ako se mogu preduzeti jednostavne i jeftine mere kako bi se uklonila ili sanirala kontaminacija osiromašenim uranijumom.

(d) U poredjenju sa prethodne dve misije UNEP, tokom ove misije u BiH na rad misije su uticali mnogi različiti uslovi. Medjutim, rezultati svih misija su u suštini medjusobno saglasni. Jedina suštinska razlika je u tome što je prošlo sedam godina od vojnog sukoba. Rezultat toga je dalja korozija radioaktivnih zrna s osiromašenim uranijumom koja leže u zemljištu, veće mogućnosti kontaminacije vode osiromašenim uranijumom i više rastinja koje je u medjuvremenu prekrilo tačke udara.

5.2 ZAKLJUČCI

Na osnovu nalaza iznetih u Poglavlju 4 (i iznetih po lokacijama u Poglavlju 7), slede opšti zaključci misije UNEP:

1) *Istražene lokacije:*

a) Tim UNEP je posetio 15 lokacija od kojih jedna lokacija, za koju je NATO potvrdio da je gadjao osiromašenim uranijumom, nije bila dostupna zbog prisustva mina (samohodni top 76 mm AT). Na tri od istraženih 14 lokacija jasno je izmerena kontaminacija osiromašenim uranijumom, čime je potvrdjena ranija upotreba municije sa osiromašenim uranijumom (npr. u nekadašnjem objektu za popravku tenkova i skladištu municije u Hadžićima, kao i u kasarni u Han Pijesku). Ove lokacije su se poklopile sa potvrdjenim koordinatama NATO. Važno je to da i dalje nedostaju koordinate NATO za šest lokacija u blizini Sarajeva. Zato nije bilo moguće istražiti i te lokacije.

b) Na ostalih istraženih 11 lokacija nije pronadjena bilo kakva kontaminacija osiromašenim uranijumom. Na osnovu informacija sakupljenih na terenu i kasnijeg laboratorijskog rada, postoji veoma mala verovatnoća da je osiromašeni uranijum korišćen na tim lokacijama. Čak i da su te lokacije bile potpuno očišćene posle napada, tragovi osiromašenog uranijuma bili bi detektovani analitičkim metodama u uzorcima zemljišta, vode i/ili flore.

2) *Lokalizovana kontaminacija zemljišta:*
Ni na jednoj lokaciji nije bilo znakova rasprostranjene kontaminacije površinskog sloja

zemljišta pošto portabl detektori beta i gama zračenja nisu ništa detektovali. Najviše što je detektovano je zagadjenje lokalizovanog zemljišta oko tačaka kontaminacije na razdaljini manjoj od 200 m, ali često mnogo bliže, kao što su potvrdile mnogo osetljivije laboratorijske analize uzoraka tla. Ovo takodje ukazuje na to da se verovatno većina zrna sa osiromašenim uranijumom nikada nije rasparčala, već da se zabila u zemlju. Kada radioaktivno zrno prodre u zemlju koja je manje više mekana, pojavi se znatno manje prašine osiromašenog uranijuma. Odgovarajući radiološki i toksikološki rizici od takve kontaminacije niskog nivoa su beznačajni. Ova zapažanja su u skladu sa nalazima prethodne dve misije UNEP-a.

3) Tačke kontaminacije:

a) Više od 7 godina prošlo je od vojnog sukoba i posete misije UNEP. Tokom 2000. i 2001.g. drugi medjunarodni stručni timovi su istraživali mnoge lokacije koje su istražili i stručnjaci UNEP u potrazi za radioaktivnim zrnima i tačkama kontaminacije. Medjutim, moguće je da još mnogo radioaktivnih zrna i tačaka kontaminacije bude pronadjeno i identifikovano. Zagadjenje osiromašenim uranijumom površine tla koje se može detektovati portabl detektorima beta i gama zračenja tipično je ograničeno na radijus od 1-2 metra od radioaktivnih zrna i lokalizovanih tačaka kontaminacije prouzrokovanih udarima radioaktivnih zrna. Tokom misije je identifikovano skoro 300 tačaka kontaminacije ali većina je bila samo neznatno kontaminirana. Sve tačke su obeležene kako bi vlasti mogle da ih saniraju.

b) Na osnovu rezultata merenja filtera za vazduh, tačke kontaminacije bi mogle predstavljati jedan od izvora ponovnog podizanja čestica osiromašenog uranijuma u vazduh. U vezi sa ovim tačkama kontaminacije, ne očekuje se postojanje značajne opasnosti da će lokalno stanovništvo udisati takav vazduh ili od moguće kontaminacije vode ili biljaka.

c) Jedini rizik od mogućeg značaja bio bi kada bi neko dotakao tačku kontaminacije, čime bi kontaminirao svoje telo (i rizikovao kasniji prenos do ustiju) ili neposredno progutao zagadjenu zemlju. Medjutim, uzimajući u obzir razumne pretpostavke o unosu zemlje, odgovarajući radiološki rizik bio bi beznačajan, dok bi sa toksikološkog stanovišta moguć unos bio nešto viši od postojećih granica navedenih u zdravstvenim standardima ili preporukama.

4) Radioaktivna zrna i fragmenti:

a) Tri radioaktivna zrna su sakupljena tokom misije radi detaljne analize. Takodje su terenska merenja ukazala na to da je veliki broj radioaktivnih zrna skriveno u zemlji (tačke kontaminacije). Na lokaciji nekadašnjeg objekta za popravku tenkova u Hadžićima, lokalno stanovništvo i vojnici SFOR su sakupili nepoznat broj radioaktivnih zrna. S obzirom da je navodno više hiljada metaka sa osiromašenim uranijumom ispaljeno na istražene lokacije koje su bile mete, broj pronadjenih radioaktivnih zrna je i dalje mali. Zaključuje se da postoje četiri moguća objašnjenja:

- Većina radioaktivnih zrna se nalazi duboko ukopana u zemlji;
- Radioaktivna zrna su rasuta po velikoj, nedostupnoj teritoriji, u minskim poljima;
- Uklonjena su tokom nasumičnog čišćenja lokacija ili tokom aktivnosti uklanjanja mina;
- Uklonjena su u okolnostima izvan kontrole vlasti (npr. od strane lokalnog stanovništva).

Najverovatnije i najpodesnije objašnjenje je prvo, a takodje je moguće da su se i ostala tri scenarija odigrala.

b) *Korozija radioaktivnih zrna:* Korozija se odvija relativno brzo kada radioaktivno zrno ostane u tlu, okruženo zemljom. Radioaktivno zrno može potpuno da korodira u proizvode korozije (npr. uranijumske okside i karbonate) u roku od 25-35 godina po udaru. Ovi proizvodi korozije, pak, mogu da se rastvore i raznesu u vodi. Medjutim, brzina korozije zavisi od sastava zemljišta. Ukoliko radioaktivno zrno leži na površini tla, brzina korozije je znatno sporija.

c) *Dodirivanje radioaktivnog zrna:* Korodirani uranijum nije čvrsto vezan i lako se odvaja. Dakle, osoba koja podigne takvo radioaktivno zrno bi lako mogla da bude kontaminirana. Čak i ako je verovatni unos u telo koji sledi mali, ne treba zanemariti radiološke i toksikološke rizike. Ako se radioaktivno zrno stavi blizu tela, npr. u džep, uslediće spoljašnje ozračavanje kože beta zracima. Nekoliko nedelja kontinuirane izloženosti može dovesti do lokalizovanog ozračavanja dozama zračenja koje premašuju sigurnosne standarde. Čak i u tim slučajevima, nije verovatno da bi takva izloženost rezultovala bilo kakvim štetnim posledicama po zdravlje.

d) *Slučajno pronalaženje radioaktivnih zrna:* Ukopana radioaktivna zrna i njihove košuljice mogu biti slučajno izneti na površinu kopanjem s ciljem uklanjanja zemlje ili pri gradjevinskim radovima. Odgovarajući rizici bi tada bili isti kao u slučaju radioaktivnog zrna i košuljice koji trenutno leže na površini tla.

e) *Sastav radioaktivnog zrna:* U analiziranim radioaktivnim zrnima pronadjeno je prisustvo transuranijumskih elemenata, plutonijuma 239/240 i neptunijuma-237, kao i izotopa uranijuma U-236 u osiromašenom uranijumu. Medjutim, koncentracija tih elemenata bila je veoma niska, u okviru granica navedenih u vojnoj literaturi dostupnoj javnosti, i nije imala ikakav značajan uticaj na njihovu opštu radioaktivnost ili bila opasna po zdravlje. Sastav je u skladu sa radioaktivnim zrnima pronadjenim tokom prethodnih misija.

5) *Kontaminacija zemljišta:*

Ispitivana je kontaminacija potpovršinskog zemljišta iznad i ispod radioaktivnih zrna. Radioaktivna zrna su ležala u nedirnutoj zemlji prekrivenoj travom, na dubini od 3-8 cm ispod površine tla. Kontaminacija zemljišta oko radioaktivnog zrna iznosila je 45 g osiromašenog uranijuma po kilogramu zemlje. Na dubini do 10 cm ispod radioaktivnog zrna, koncentracija osiromašenog uranijuma se smanjivala za 2 reda, a na dubini od sledećih 30 cm za dodatna 3 reda veličine. Na osnovu ovih zapažanja zaključuje se da je mobilnost korodiranog osiromašenog uranijuma u trenutnom sastavu zemljišta niska zbog činjenice da je usporena sorpcijom i koprecipitacijom sa mineralima. Kontaminacija podzemnih voda nije verovatna zbog male mobilnosti proizvoda korozije osiromašenog uranijuma.

6) *Kontaminacija vode:*
a) Osiromašeni uranijum bio je jasno identifikovan u jednom od uzoraka vode za piće. Drugi uzorak vode za piće iz bunara pokazao je tragove kontaminacije osiromašenim uranijumom, koje je bilo moguće detektovati samo upotrebom masenih spektrometrijskih merenja. Koncentracije su veoma niske i odgovarajuće doze radijacije beznačajne i ne predstavljaju ikakvu opasnost po zdravlje. To je takodje i slučaj u vezi sa toksičnošću uranijuma kao teškog metala. Medjutim, s obzirom da nisu poznati detalji mehanizma kojim se voda kontaminira, zaključuje se da treba nastaviti sa uzorkovanjem i merenjem vode tokom sledećih nekoliko godina.

b) Kao što je gore zaključeno, verovatno je većina radioaktivnih zrna skrivena u zemlji. Ova radioaktivna zrna bi mogla predstavljati opasnost od kontaminacije podzemnih voda i vode za piće u budućnosti pošto se neki od ovih izvora vode nalaze blizu linije napada. Ovo važi u slučaju uzoraka koji ukazuju na kontaminaciju. Iako je mobilnost osiromašenog uranijuma niska, do kontaminacije može doći ako se radioaktivno zrno nalazi u neposrednoj blizini izvora vode. Ispaljivanje velikog broja zrna sa osiromašenim uranijumom u nekoj oblasti moglo bi da poveća potencijalni izvor kontaminacije uranijumom podzemnih voda za faktor od 10 do 100, u poredjenju sa kontaminacijom koju proizvodi jedno radioaktivno zrno. Mada će doze zračenja biti niske, rezultirajuća koncentracija uranijuma može da premaši zdravstvene standarde WHO ili preporuke vezane za vodu za piće.

7) Kontaminacija bioindikatora:

Prisustvo osiromašenog uranijuma pronadjeno je u uzorcima lišajeva na 3 gore navedene lokacije. To je pokazatelj da su neka radioaktivna zrna pogodila mete i tvrde površine, delom se pretvorila u prašinu koja se rasprostrla po vazduhu. Ovo takodje ilustruje da analiza uzorka lišajeva predstavlja koristan metod monitoringa kvaliteta životne sredine.

8) Uzorci povrća:

Dva uzorka povrća (kupusa) uzeta su u blizini nekadašnjeg objekta za popravku tenkova u Hadžićima. Rezultati analize ova dva uzorka nisu dovoljna za izvodjenje ikakvog naučnog zaključka. Nema razloga za očekivanje osiromašenog uranijuma u hrani zbog male brzine širenja u zemljištu i niskog faktora apsorpcije u hrani.

9) Kontaminacija vazduha:

a) Kontaminacija vazduha osiromašenim uranijumom pronadjena je na dve lokacije gde je potvrdjena upotreba osiromašenog uranijuma. Razlog tome može biti ponovno podizanje u vazduh čestica osiromašenog uranijuma vetrom ili ljudskim aktivnostima sa tačaka kontaminacije, korodiranih radioaktivnih zrna ili fragmenata koji leže na površini tla. Koncentracije su bile veoma niske i rezultirajuće doze zračenja male i beznačajne. Osiromašeni uranijum nije detektovan u vazduhu na razdaljinama većim od 100 m od kontaminiranih oblasti. Razlog tome mogu biti ograničenja instrumenata za detekciju.

b) Kontaminacija vazduha i nekih površina osiromašenim uranijumom utvrdjena je unutar dve zgrade na dve gore navedene lokacije. Razlog tome može biti ponovna suspenzija čestica osiromašenog uranijuma vetrom ili ljudskim aktivnostima od tačaka kontaminacije, korodiranih radioaktivnih zrna ili delova koji leže na površini tla u zgradama, kao i prašine osiromašenog uranijuma koja se zadržala u zgradi još od vremena napada. Iako niski izmereni nivoi rezultiraju u dozama koje su male i beznačajne, UNEP smatra da je izlaganje takvom izvoru nepotrebno. Dakle, preporučuju se mere predostrožnosti čišćenja kontaminiranih delova.

10) Podizanje svesti:

Tokom cele misije, tim UNEP je primetio da radnici i civili koji imaju pristup ovim lokacijama, kao i vojno osoblje i osoblje koje radi na uklanjanju mina, nisu svesni ili pogrešno shvataju rizike i, uopšte, pitanja vezana za municiju sa osiromašenim uranijumom.

11) Metodologija:
Korišćene tehnike, oprema i metodologije veoma su dobro funkcionisale tokom misije a iskustvo stečeno tokom prethodnih misija je doprinelo uspešnim procenama.

12) Zaštita od zračenja i radijaciona sigurnost:

a) Tek nedavno je u BiH uspostavljena infrastruktura sigurnosti od zračenja. U Federaciji BiH, Parlament je 1999.g. odobrio novi *Zakon o zaštiti od zračenja i radijacionoj sigurnosti*, koji je postavio osnovu za novi regulatorni sistem. U Republici Srpskoj je 2001. usvojena legislatura u skladu sa medjunarodnim standardima IAEA u vezi sa zaštitom od jonizujućeg zračenja. Napori učinjeni radi uspostavljanja institucionalnog okvira za zaštitu od zračenja u BiH od kraja konflikta zavredjuju pohvale, imajući u vidu ograničena sredstva na raspolaganju i ohrabrujuće rezultate koji su postignuti, mada je neophodno još rada kako bi se poboljšala zaštita od zračenja.

b) Pored dva nezavisna pravna okvira za zaštitu od zračenja, u Federaciji i Republici Srpskoj su osnovana dva odvojena regulatorna tela i organizacije za zaštitu od zračenja. Ovo rezultira u dupliranju službi i aktivnosti što je naročito nepodesno s obzirom na nedostatak raspoloživih sredstava. Nedostatak saradnje izmedju dve organizacije koje se bave zaštitom od zračenja negativno utiče na uspostavljanje i sprovodjenje efikasnog režima radijacione sigurnosti u Bosni i Hercegovini.

c) Odlagalište za radioaktivni otpad niskog nivoa u Federaciji BiH predstavlja adekvatan objekat za bezbedno skladištenje radioaktivnog otpada na toj teritoriji, uključujući i ostatke osiromašenog uranijuma. Rad na izgradnji objekta za obradu i skladištenje radioaktivnog otpada je započet, ali u poslednjih godinu dana nije načinjen značajan pomak. Ovaj objekat će poboljšati sposobnost Centra za zaštitu od zračenja da skladišti radioaktivni otpad. Nažalost, u Republici Srpskoj ne funkcioniše nikakvo odlagalište za radioaktivni otpad niskog nivoa iako je učinjen napredak ka pronalaženju moguće lokacije gde bi se takvo odlagalište moglo da izgradi.

d) U BiH je pre rata korišćen znatan broj radioaktivnih izvora, kao što su industrijski izvori, gromobrani i javljači požara. Evidencija o njima više nije dostupna. Mnogi od tih izvora su zastareli, ili su izgubljeni ili oštećeni tokom rata i još nisu pronadjeni. Opasnost od potencijalne izloženosti ovim izvorima je znatno veća od izloženosti ostacima osiromašenog uranijuma. Treba razmotriti skladištenje i kasnije odlaganje ovih izvora, a pogotovo pronalaženje i bezbedno skladištenje ili odlaganje takvih izvora koji su izgubljeni ili oštećeni tokom rata.

e) Mada uobičajena kontrola životne sredine nije jedno od najvažnijih prioriteta za BiH tamo gde nema značajnih izvora radioaktivnosti iz objekata zabrinjavajuće je što se nikakve aktivnosti ne sprovode kako bi se obezbedila zaštita stanovništva u oblastima kojima ono ima pristupa, a gde postoji radijacija i/ili opasnost od kontaminacije. Ovo se pogotovo odnosi na one oblasti u kojima se nalaze oštećeni ili napušteni i nekontrolisani izvori, što je posledica ratnih sukoba.

13) Pitanja vezana za zdravlje:

Zbog nedostatka pravilno vodjene evidencije oboljenja od raka i sistema izveštavanja, tvrdnje o povećanju stope negativnih efekata po zdravlje prouzrokovanih osiromašenim uranijumom ne mogu biti potkrepljeni. Ohrabruje što su vlasti BiH započele sprovodjenje sistema registrovanja slučajeva i sistema izveštavanja kako bi otkrile i izvestile o oboljenjima od raka u zemlji. To bi trebalo da omogući utvrdjivanje istinitosti tvrdnji u vezi sa promenama učestalosti oboljevanja od raka. Naučni podaci o uranijumu i efektima osiromašenog uranijuma po zdravlje do kojih se došlo tokom poslednjih pedeset godina i veoma mala izloženost utvrdjena tokom ove misije UNEP ukazuje da postoji veoma mala verovatnoća da osiromašeni uranijum može na bilo koji način biti povezan sa ovim prijavljenim posledicama po ljudsko zdravlje.

14) *Kutija sa osiromašenim uranijumom:*

Jedan od zadataka UNEP bio je da istraži istorijat i lokaciju kutije sa zrnima sa osiromašenim uranijumom, fragmentima, košuljicama i čaurama, koja se prvobitno nalazila u nekadašnjem objektu za popravku tenkova u Hadžićima (videti Poglavlje 7.1). Na osnovu faksa NATO datiranog 3. decembar 2002. god, kutija sa sakupljenim materijalom sa osiromašenim uranijumom preneta je u proleće 2001. god. u nacionalni objekat SAD, izvan Bosne i Hercegovine radi odlaganja.

15) *Teški metali:*

Na tri istražene lokacije izmerena je visoka kontaminacija površine tla teškim metalima (objekat za proizvodnju municije u Vogošći, lokacije za uništenje municije u Kalinoviku i na platou na Bjelašnici). Takva kontaminacija bi u budućnosti mogla da bude opasna po zdravlje. Pošto su već dostignute vrednosti za određene elemente u zemljištu koje zahtevaju intervenciju, potrebno je izvršiti dodatno istraživanje kako bi se situacija pravilno procenila.

Recommendations

1. **Measure contamination and detect possible DU.**
    At all sites in BiH where DU was used, the appropriate authorities should undertake investigations using field measurement equipment suitable for (i) making complementary searches for possible local ground contamination of significance, and (ii) detecting the presence of penetrators, jackets/casings and contamination points on the ground surface. At the same time, the feasibility of any necessary clean-up and decontamination measures should be assessed.

2. **Decontaminate contamination points.**
    All contamination points, including those marked by UNEP and those which may be found in the future, both indoors and outdoors, should be cleaned from loose DU and covered with asphalt, concrete or clean soil depending on the ground surface. The sites should be properly documented for possible future activities.

3. **Handle and dispose of DU material properly.**
    If any penetrators, fragments or jackets are found in the future, the following steps are recommended:
    *   The location of all found penetrators should be properly documented;
    *   Any such material should be collected by authorized personnel;
    *   Once collected, they should be safely stored as decided by responsible authorities;
    *   Proper disposal methods should be developed.

4. **Keep records on the DU sites.**
    There are reasons to believe that many penetrators remain buried deep in the ground at DU-affected sites. It is recommended to the BiH authorities that adequate documentation be kept on each site to inform local populations of the presence of DU at these sites, thereby minimizing any risks in the future, for example from any rebuilding activities that occur at the sites. This documentation should include specific site information concerning DU.

5. **Appropriate planning prior to any soil disturbance.**
    Planning for any future soil disturbance or removal of vegetation should consider the risk of DU dispersion in air and inhalation of DU dust. In addition, the potential for subsequent contamination of land from corroded penetrators should be taken into account. Buried penetrators brought up to the surface and any newly discovered contamination points should be cleaned and/or removed and disposed of safely, as determined by the relevant competent authorities. As a result, appropriate contingency plans should be developed prior to ground-breaking activities when working at sites where DU weapons have been used.

6. **Clean the contaminated buildings.**
    To reduce the risk of resuspension of DU dust inside contaminated buildings, either vacuum-cleaning techniques, with high-quality filters that help contain any DU particles collected, or wet cleaning methods should be used in cleaning the interior of such buildings.

7. **Test the drinking water yearly.**
    Where the presence of DU at a site was confirmed by penetrators, soil or water contamination, sampling and measurements on water at or from the site should be made annually if that water is used for drinking purposes. The same applies to any areas which may source their water or be located in the direction of groundwater flow from a contaminated area.

6

8. Avoid contaminated water.

If tests show that there is DU contamination in the water, for precautionary reasons, other water sources should be used to supply drinking water.

9. Do not transport DU to ammunition destruction sites.

The destruction of ammunition by explosives should not include any DU ammunition or DU-contaminated material, otherwise secondary contamination may occur in the form of DU fragments or dust.

10. Implement the site-specific recommendations.

The site-specific recommendations contained in Chapter 7 of this report should be implemented without delay at the discretion of the relevant and competent authorities.

11. Release the missing DU coordinates.

DU decontamination and protection of the civilian population can only be done when the precise coordinates of a DU-attack are known. The longer time elapses since the time of the attack, the more difficult it is to implement countermeasures, including decontamination. As six NATO DU-attack coordinates in the vicinity of Sarajevo are still missing, these should be disclosed to the BiH authorities without delay.

12. More scientific work needed.

Further scientific work should be carried out to reduce the scientific uncertainties related to the assessment of the environmental impact of DU. This particularly concerns corrosion of DU, dispersion in the ground, uptake by groundwater or drinking water, resuspension and dispersion in air, and possible sources of DU in vegetation.

13. Inform the civilian population and military and mine-clearing personnel.

The responsible authorities should consider awareness-raising activities for the local population in general and both military and mine clearance personnel in particular. A flyer or leaflet, such as that already existing for mine safety, could be produced and distributed. This should include information about DU in general, associated risks, handling and storage, and contact information for relevant authorities.

14. Train experts for DU decontamination.

The responsible authorities should develop a training course for designated personnel to act as authorized persons in the field of DU mitigation. Such a course would ideally include clean-up measures.

15. Investigate all health claims.

The relevant health authorities should continue the development of a cancer reporting system and registry and investigate claims of health effects from exposure to depleted uranium in order to determine if any increased incidences of health issues exist.

16. Develop descriptive and analytical epidemiological studies.

All claims regarding health deterioration allegedly caused by exposure to DU should be addressed by the relevant health authorities. This can be facilitated by:

- developing descriptive epidemiological studies to respond to questions of changes in frequency and distribution of cancers in the population.
- developing analytical epidemiological studies to investigate the potential contribution of risk factors including environmental risks and DU exposure, as well as other risk factors, to specific types of cancer

17. Develop health cooperation between the Federation of BiH and Republika Srpska.

The relevant authorities within the FBiH and Republika Srpska should cooperate further to facilitate the development of the activities between medical researchers, population offices and cancer registries, as exchange of information is likely to be necessary to achieve the above goals. Furthermore, studies of rare cancers generally could benefit from case studies in the FBiH and the Republika Srpska.

18. Strengthen the radiation safety authorities.

The radiation safety infrastructure for the whole of BiH needs to be strengthened. The support provided by the IAEA, through the programme of the Technical Co-operation Department, should help to ensure that this is achieved.

19. Improve radiation safety cooperation between FBiH and Republika Srpska.

The existence of two distinct separate infrastructures and lack of cooperation between the two radiation protection organizations in the FBiH and Republika Srpska are causes of concern. A closer collaboration between the two organizations responsible for radiation safety would be welcome, as it would be beneficial to the establishment and implementation of an efficient radiation safety regime in the whole of BiH. Efforts should be made at the international level to foster this collaboration.

20. Build facilities for radioactive waste treatment and storing.

The FBiH and Republika Srpska authorities should be encouraged in their efforts to build new – or complete ongoing – radioactive waste treatment and storage facilities. Support for these activities could be provided by the IAEA through its Technical Co-operation programme.

21. Mitigation of all radioactive waste.

Storage of depleted uranium residues in BiH should be dealt with within the wider context of the safe disposal of radioactive waste in the country. The authorities of the FBiH and the Republika Srpska should also record, safely store and eventually dispose of the large number of obsolete radioactive sources, such as industrial sources, lightning rods and smoke detectors present on the territory of BiH, and in particular those which were damaged during the war. The risks from potential exposure to these sources are significantly higher than those from exposure to depleted uranium residues.

22. Monitor the targeted sites for radioactivity.

Monitoring of radiation and radioactive contamination in areas affected by the war should be addressed by the authorities in BiH, with particular attention, in view of the risk of potential exposures, to the different sources mentioned above, including depleted uranium.

23. Use proper measures to avoid heavy metal contamination.

Sites where soil contamination by heavy metals was measured, the following recommendations could apply:

- Further chemical analyses, including of soil, rainwater runoff and groundwater, should be undertaken in order to gain a more complete picture of heavy metal contamination;
- The sites should be properly documented;
- Safety measures should be considered, such as fencing off ammunition destruction sites, in order to prevent civilian access;
- Grazing of farm animals should be prevented on these sites.

24. Investigate other regions where DU has been used.

Scientific work should also be conducted in other post-conflict areas where DU has been used. To fully understand how DU behaves in the natural environment, areas with climatic conditions and soil composition other than those which occur in the Balkans region should also be investigated. UNEP, IAEA and WHO should continue to address this issue jointly.

Depleted Uranium in Bosnia and Herzegovina

Preporuke

6

1. Izmeriti kontaminaciju i detektovati mogući osiromašeni uranijum

Na svim lokacijama u BiH gde je korišćen osiromašeni uranijum, nadležne vlasti trebalo bi da preduzmu istraživanje koristeći opremu za terensko merenje koja je adekvatna za (a) komplementarne potrage za mogućom znatnom lokalnom kontaminacijom zemljišta, i (b) detektovanje prisustva radioaktivnih zrna, košuljica, čaura i tačaka kontaminacije površinskog sloja zemljišta. Istovremeno trebalo bi proceniti izvodljivost svih neophodnih mera za čišćenje i dekontaminaciju.

2. Dekontaminirati tačke kontaminacije

Sve tačke kontaminacije, uključujući one koje je obeležio tim UNEP i one koje će eventualno biti pronadjene u budućnosti, kako u unutrašnjosti zgrada tako i napolju, treba da budu očišćene od rasutog osiromašenog uranijuma i pokrivene asfaltom, betonom ili čistom zemljom u zavisnosti od površine tla. Ova mesta trebalo bi da budu pravilno evidentirana zbog eventualnih budućih aktivnosti.

3. Pravilno rukovati i odlagati materijal sa osiromašenim uranijumom

Ukoliko u budućnosti budu pronadjeni nova radioaktivna zrna, fragmenti ili košuljice, preporučuju se sledeći koraci:

- Lokacije svih pronadjenih radioaktivnih zrna treba da bude pravilno dokumentovane;
- Sav takav materijal treba da sakupi ovlašćeno osoblje;
- Pošto je sakupljen, taj materijal treba da bude bezbedno uskladišten, u skladu sa odlukom nadležnih lokalnih vlasti;
- Treba razviti pravilne metode odlaganja takvog materijala.

4. Voditi evidenciju o lokacijama na kojima se nalazi osiromašeni uranijum

Postoje razlozi za verovanje da su mnoga radioaktivna zrna ostala duboko ukopana u zemlji na lokacijama gadjanim osiromašenim uranijumom. Preporučuje se da vlasti BiH vode adekvatnu dokumentaciju o svakoj takvoj lokaciji kako bi lokalno stanovništvo bilo informisano o prisustvu osiromašenog uranijuma na tim lokacijama, čime se minimizuju rizici u budućnosti, npr. tokom gradjevinskih radova na tim lokacijama. Ta dokumentacija bi trebalo da sadrži informacije o osiromašenom uranijumu na toj konkretnoj lokaciji.

5. Pripremiti odgovarajuće planove pre pomeranja zemljišta

Planiranje svakog pomeranja zemljišta ili uklanjanja vegetacije u budućnosti treba da uzima u obzir rizik rasprostiranja osiromašenog uranijuma u vazduhu i udisanja prašine osiromašenog uranijuma. Takodje, treba uzimati u obzir mogućnost kasnijeg zagadjenja zemljišta korodiranim radioaktivnim zrnima. Ukopana radioaktivna zrna koja su izneta na površinu i sve novopronadjene tačke kontaminacije treba da budu bezbedno očišćene, uklonjene i odložene u skladu sa odlukom odgovarajućih nadležnih vlasti. Zato treba razvijati adekvatne alternativne planove pre otpočinjanja aktivnosti pomeranja zemljišta prilikom rada na lokacijama gde je korišćeno naoružanje sa osiromašenim uranijumom.

6. Očistiti kontaminirane zgrade

Kako bi se smanjila opasnost od ponovnog podizanja prašine s osiromašenim uranijumom u kontaminiranim zgradama, za čišćenje unutrašnjosti takvih zgrada treba koristiti ili tehnologiju usisivača sa visokokvalitetnim filterima koji zadržavaju sve čestice osiromašenog uranijuma ili metode vlažnog čišćenja.

7. *Godišnje testirati vodu za piće*

Na lokacijama gde je potvrdjena upotreba osiromašenog uranijuma prisustvom radioaktivnih zrna, kontaminacije vode ili zemljišta od strane misije UNEP, jednom godišnje treba vršiti uzorkovanje i merenje vode na toj lokaciji ili vode koja dotiče od nje ukoliko je ta voda namenjena za piće. Ovo se preporučuje i u slučaju svih oblasti čiji se izvor vode nalazi u kontaminiranoj oblasti, ili koje se nalaze u pravcu toka podzemnih voda koje dolaze iz kontaminiranih oblasti.

8. *Izbegavati kontaminiranu vodu*

Ukoliko testovi pokažu da je voda zagadjena osiromašenim uranijumom, iz predostrožnosti treba koristiti druge izvore vode za piće.

9. *Ne odnositi osiromašeni uranijum na mesta gde se uništava municija*

Prilikom uništavanja municije eksplozijom, u njoj ne treba da se nalazi bilo kakva municija sa osiromašenim uranijumom ili materijal kontaminiran osiromašenim uranijumom, jer može doći do sekundarne kontaminacije u obliku čestica ili prašine sa osiromašenim uranijumom.

10. *Sprovoditi preporuke za konkretne lokacije*

Preporuke za konkretne lokacije koje se nalaze u Poglavlju 7 ovog izveštaja treba da budu sprovedene bez odlaganja po odluci odgovarajućih nadležnih vlasti.

11. *Objaviti koordinate tačaka u kojima je upotrebljen osiromaseni uranijum koje nedostaju*

Proces dekontaminacije prostora od osiromašenog uranijuma i zaštita civilnog stanovništva mogu biti sprovedeni samo ako su poznate koordinate napada oružjem sa osiromašenim uranijumom. Što više vremena prodje od vremena napada, to je teže sprovoditi protivmere, uključujući dekontaminaciju. Pošto i dalje nedostaju koordinate NATO za 6 lokacija koje su napadnute osiromašenim uranijumom, vlasti BiH treba da budu upoznate sa ovim koordinatama bez odlaganja.

12. *Sprovesti dodatni naučni rad*

Dodatni naučni rad trebalo bi da bude sproveden kako bi se smanjile naučne nejasnoće vezane za procenu uticaja osiromašenog uranijuma na životnu sredinu. Ovo se pogotovo odnosi na koroziju osiromašenog uranijuma, širenje u zemlji, apsorpciju u podzemnim vodama ili vodi za piće i ponovno podizanje u vazduh i rasprostiranje njime, kao i na moguće izvore osiromašenog uranijuma u vegetaciji.

13. *Informisati civilno stanovništvo, vojno osoblje i osoblje koje se bavi uklanjanjem mina*

Nadležne vlasti trebalo bi da razmotre aktivnosti za podizanje svesti lokalnog stanovništva uopšte, a pogotovo vojnog osoblja i osoblja koja vrši uklanjanje mina. Mogao bi da se pripremi i razdeli letak ili pamflet kao što je onaj postojeći u vezi sa sigurnošću od mina. U njemu bi se nalazile opšte informacije o osiromašenom uranijumu, rizici koje on donosi, način rukovanja i skladištenja, i informacije o načinu kontaktiranja nadležnih vlasti.

14. *Obučiti stručnjake za dekontaminaciju od osiromašenog uranijuma*

Nadležne vlasti treba da razviju kurs obuke za odabrano osoblje, koje bi bilo ovlašćeno za ublažavanje posledica osiromašenog uranijuma. Takav kurs bi u idealnom slučaju uključivao i mere čišćenja.

6

15. Istražiti sve tvrdnje o posledicama osiromašenog uranijuma po zdravlje

Nadležne zdravstvene vlasti treba da nastave sa razvojem sistema izveštavanja i evidentiranja oboljevanja od raka i i da istražuju sve tvrdnje vezane za posledice izloženosti osiromašenom uranijumu po zdravlje kako bi ustanovile da li postoji povećanje učestalosti zdravstvenih problema.

16. Razviti opisne i analitičke epidemiološke studije

Odgovarajuće zdravstvene vlasti treba da prouče sve tvrdnje vezane za pogoršanje zdravlja koje je navodno prouzrokovano izloženošću osiromašenom uranijumu. To se može olakšati:

- Razvojem opisnih epidemioloških studija kako bi se odgovorilo na pitanja promena u učestalosti i geografske rasprostranjenosti oboljevanja stanovništva od raka.
- Razvojem analitičkih epidemioloških studija kako bi se istražio potencijalni doprinos faktora rizika, uključujući rizik po životnu sredinu, i i doprinos izloženosti osiromašenom uranijumu, kao i drugih faktora rizika, pojavi odredjenih vrsta raka.

17. Razviti saradnju u oblasti zdravstva izmedju Federacije BiH i Republike Srpske

Odgovarajuće vlasti u Federaciji i Republici Srpskoj trebalo bi da dodatno saradjuju kako bi olakšale razvoj gore navedenih aktivnosti izmedju medicinskih istraživača, statističkih službi i registratora lica obolelih od raka, pošto će verovatno biti neophodna razmena informacija, kako bi se postigli gore navedeni ciljevi. Štaviše, studije retkih oblika oboljenja raka će možda zahtevati proučavanje slučajeva u Federaciji BiH i Republici Srpskoj da bi bile u stanju da pronadje odgovor na pitanje studije.

18. Konsolidovati vlasti koje se bave radijacionom sigurnošću

Potrebno je ojačati infrastrukturu radijacione sigurnosti u celoj BiH. Podrška koju pruža IAEA kroz program Odeljenja za tehničku saradnju trebalo bi da obezbedi jačanje nacionalne infrastrukture radijacione sigurnosti.

19. Poboljšati saradnju Federacije BiH i Republike Srpske u oblasti radijacione sigurnosti

Postojanje dve zasebne, odvojene infrastrukture i nedostatak saradnje izmedju dve organizacije za zaštitu od zračenja u Federaciji i Republici Srpskoj izazivaju zabrinutost. Bliža saradnja izmedju dve organizacije zadužene za zaštitu od zračenja bila bi dobrodošla, jer bi doprinela uspostavljanju i sprovodjenju efikasnog režima zaštite od zračenja u celoj Bosni i Hercegovini. Treba uložiti napore na medjunarodnom nivou kako bi se ova saradnja podsticala.

20. Izgraditi objekte za obradu i skladištenje radioaktivnog otpada

Treba podsticati vlasti Federacije BiH i Republike Srpske u naporima da izgrade nove ili dovrše postojeće objekte za obradu i skladištenje radioaktivnog otpada. Podršku ovim aktivnostima mogla bi da pruži IAEA preko svog programa za tehničku saradnju.

21. Sanirati sav radioaktivni otpad

Skladištenje ostataka osiromašenog uranijuma u BiH treba vršiti u širem kontekstu bezbednog odlaganja radioaktivnog otpada u državi. Vlasti Federacije i Republike Srpske takodje treba da vode evidenciju, bezbedno skladište i u neko doba da odlože veliki broj zastarelih izvora radioaktivnosti, kao što su industrijski izvori, gromobrani, i javljači požara prisutni na teritoriji BiH, pogotovo onih koji su oštećeni tokom rata. Opasnost od potencijalne izloženosti ovim radioaktivnim izvorima je znatno veća od rizika izlaganja ostacima osiromašenog uranijuma.

22. Vršiti monitoring pogodjenih lokacija radi uočavanja radioaktivnosti

Vlasti BiH s posebnom pažnjom treba da vrše monitoring radijacione i radioaktivne kontaminacije u oblastima pogodjenim ratom s obzirom na opasnost od mogućeg izlaganja raznim gore opisanim radioaktivnim izvorima, uključujući osiromašeni uranijum.

23. Primenjivati pravilne metode kako bi se izbegla kontaminacija teškim metalima

Sledeće preporuke odnose se na lokacije gde je izmereno zagadjenje zemljišta teškim metalima:

- Preduzeti dodatne hemijske analize, uključujući analize zemlje, izlivene kišnice i podzemnih voda, kako bi se dobila potpunija slika kontaminacije teškim metalima na takvim lokacijama.
- Voditi pravilnu dokumentaciju o tim lokacijama.
- Razmotriti sigurnosne mere, kao što je ogradjivanje lokacija na kojima se uništava municija, kako bi se sprečio pristup civila tim lokacijama.
- Sprečiti napasanje domaćih životinja na tim lokacijama.

24. Istražiti ostale regije u kojima je korišćen osiromašeni uranijum

Naučni rad takodje treba da bude sproveden u drugim post-konfliktnim oblastima u kojima je korišćen osiromašeni uranijum. Kako bi se u potpunosti razumelo ponašanje osiromašenog uranijuma u životnoj sredini, trebalo bi istražiti i oblasti u kojima se klimatski uslovi i sastav zemljišta razlikuju od onih na Balkanu. UNEP, IAEA i WHO trebalo bi da nastave da se zajedno bave ovim pitanjem.

7

Site-specific findings

Detailed results of the sample findings mentioned in this chapter for soil, water, botanical (biota), air, penetrators, special studies and heavy metals can be found respectively in Appendices D, E, F, G, H, I, J and K. Complete investigation and sampling techniques are discussed in Appendix C *'Methodology and Quality Control'*. Lichen samples (identified in this chapter by an asterix) were subdivided into single-species sub-samples. All sub-samples have the same number as the original samples but with an additional letter. The same applies to all lichen samples taken during the mission at various sites.

7.1   HADZICI TANK REPAIR FACILITY, 14-15 OCTOBER 2002

NATO ref:	#9, #14, #15
Coordinates:	34T BP 74100 / 56950
Target:	Two large hard-surface yards where a large number of tanks and vehicles were located at the time of attack, as well as the large buildings near the central yard where tank repair activities took place.
Date of attack:	5 and 9 September 1995
Number of rounds:	1 500
Area:	Large, fenced area with mine warnings around the perimeter. The site has limited access privileges to those working within the local businesses that are presently located within the complex (lumber, storage, car repair, etc.).
Investigated surface area:	325 m x 850 m
Town/Population:	Hadzici municipality currently has a mostly Muslim population of about 20 660 inhabitants. Detached and multi-family houses and flats surround the targeted site. A few hundred people live in the immediate vicinity.
Other information:	The former Hadzici Tank Repair Facility is approximately 1 km from the centre of Hadzici town. It was once a large operating facility with a number of buildings of various sizes, most of which were partly destroyed at the time of attack.

Site description and general information

The former *Hadzici Tank Repair Facility* is situated in an east-west oriented valley. The site is fenced and has limited access privileges, but the area outside of the fence has unlimited public access. Inside the facility area are numerous small and large workshops, storage barns and buildings. Most of these were bombed during the war, and some totally destroyed, with only concrete pads now left. Many of the remaining buildings are still partly destroyed. Repairs are ongoing and several of the bombed buildings are now used as workshops or storage areas.

The western part of the facility was the main target for A-10 attacks with DU ammunition. Penetrators hit tanks and vehicles which were parked in the open yards, and also hit a number of the workshops and buildings.

A large portion of the facility contains hard surfaces such as asphalt, concrete or basalt cobblestones. These surfaces aid rainwater to discharge into a small canalized stream that runs through the facility. Although surface rainwater runoff is probably discharged into the stream, this is unlikely to be the case for the area's groundwater. Although the drainage direction for groundwater is uncertain, it is probably from the sides of the valley towards the stream. Thus, any potential contamination of stream water by DU would have occurred after the attack and may still be continuing.

An overview of the Hadzici Tank Repair Facility from a neighbouring home

The ground consists of clayey soil. There is no exposed rock in the area and the soil layer is believed to be several metres thick. The whole area surrounding the facility was mined during the conflict to prevent access. The mines and unexploded ammunition are only partly cleared.

During the pre-mission, repeated references were made both by SFOR and locals on the site about the existence of a box containing loose DU ammunition, including penetrators, fragments and jackets/casings. The box was studied in detail by a German SFOR troop who had visited the site previously, and it had since been removed from the site. In January 2001, pictures of that very box were published worldwide by the press in articles related to the issue of DU in the Balkans. The history of this box was difficult to follow, especially with regard to its current location. It is discussed in further detail at the end of this chapter.

Field investigation

Due to mines and the risk of unexploded ordnance, all investigations were restricted to hard surface areas. Exceptions included small grassy areas and buildings that the BiH Mine Action Center declared safe. Within the fenced site, most of the surface area and two buildings were searched by on-line survey (this method is described in Appendix C). Random surveys were done over some of the grassy areas and within a few additional buildings. No search for DU contamination was performed outside the fenced perimeter. Special attention was given to the cobblestone lot and the large concrete yard where tanks were positioned during the attack.

One penetrator was collected for detailed analysis. There were also indications from field measurements of a large number of penetrators hidden in the ground (contamination points). Importantly, some may have spread over larger, inaccessible areas within the minefields or have been collected at an earlier date.

Samples taken included:
- 1 penetrator
- 10 surface soil samples to a depth of 5 cm
- 2 surface/grab samples
- 4 water samples (1 well, 2 stream, 1 tap)
- 7 bio-indicators (3 lichen*, 2 moss, 2 bark/lichen*)
- 2 vegetable samples (cabbage)
- 9 air filter samples.

Depleted Uranium in Bosnia and Herzegovina

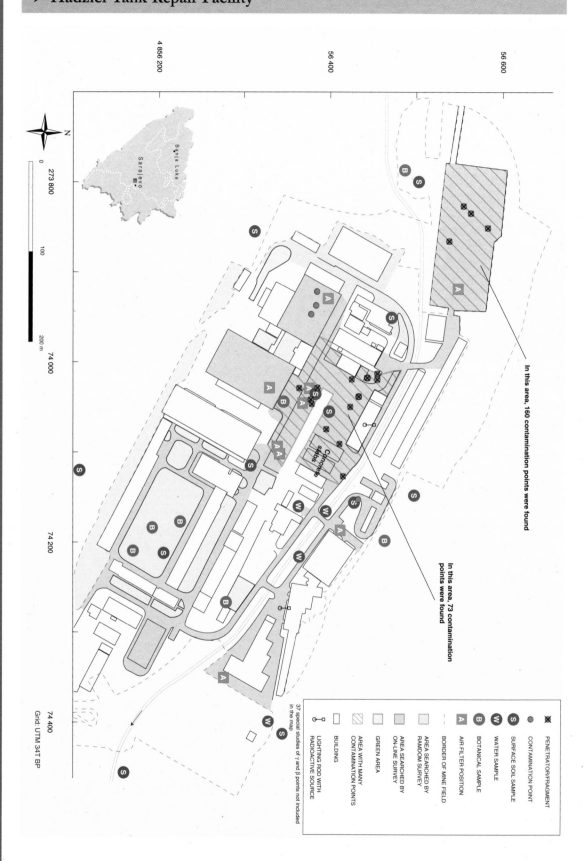

In this area, 160 contamination points were found

In this area, 73 contamination points were found

Concrete slabs

Sarajevo

Banja Luka

N

0   100   200 m

273 800

74 000

74 200

74 400

Grid: UTM 34T BP

4 856 200

56 400

56 600

37 special studies of γ and β points not included in the map

PENETRATOR/FRAGMENT

CONTAMINATION POINT

SURFACE SOIL SAMPLE

WATER SAMPLE

BOTANICAL SAMPLE

AIR FILTER POSITION

BORDER OF MINE FIELD

AREA SEARCHED BY RANDOM SURVEY

AREA SEARCHED BY ON-LINE SURVEY

GREEN AREA

AREA WITH MANY CONTAMINATION POINTS

BUILDING

LIGHTING ROD WITH RADIOACTIVE SOURCE

Post-Conflict Environmental Assessment

69 contamination points were found in the site's central cobblestone yard

■ **General contamination**

In spite of the large number of DU rounds used, there was no detectable widespread surface contamination, either with field measurements or with soil sample measurements. Localized surface contamination was identified in two areas. However, there were a large number of contamination points and penetrators on or hidden beneath the surface.

■ **Measurements of radiation**

Conditions for detecting contamination, penetrators and fragments were favourable. During investigations with both on-line and random surveys, the total gamma and beta radiation was continuously measured by the SRAT and Inspector instruments (for methodology information, see Appendix C). The background gamma radiation on hard surface areas was 0.02-0.04 μSv/h and on soil 0.03-0.05 μSv/h. Beta radiation background was 0-1 cps. This represents very low gamma and beta radiation.

Enhanced gamma radiation was encountered at two locations, with radiation levels at 0.05-0.15 μSv/h. The radiation was emitted from two lightning rods on the roofs of buildings, one of which appeared to be damaged. These rods were equipped with radioactive sources used for the ionization of surrounding air in order to attract lightning.

Special studies of possible contamination of DU by measurements of gamma and beta radiation on metal, concrete and wood surfaces were carried out at 34 locations (see Appendix J).

■ **Penetrators, jackets and localized points of contamination**

During the investigation the team found 233 points with increased radiation caused either by contamination from DU dust formed at the time of impact, fragments or whole penetrators on, close to or under the ground surface. Increased radiation (ß+γ or just γ) was located to contamination points, usually not larger than 10-50 cm in diameter. Radiation levels were usually in the range of ten times normal background, but could also be found as high as

Depleted Uranium in Bosnia and Herzegovina

100 times normal background. All contamination points located were marked by a circle of red paint. Widespread contamination was not encountered.

Sixty-nine contamination points were found in the cobblestone yard near the large workshops in the western part of the facility. A further 160 points were located on the concrete field lot in the northwest corner (see map). Three contamination points were also found inside a workshop building, and only one contamination point was found in soil. No contamination points were found in the eastern part of the facility.

To a large extent, the penetrators that hit the concrete and cobblestone areas are still lying on or just below the hard surfaces, making it favourable to find them. Certainly, many of the penetrators that were fired also hit soft ground and remain in the soil, both inside and outside the fenced area. It is expected that many penetrators and fragments could be found in the soil, although in many cases penetrators will have entered so deeply into the ground as to be undetectable even by gamma sensitive instruments used during the mission. However, few measurements were possible there, and no measurements were made on the railway track that leads into the centre of the concrete yard.

160 contamination points were found on this large concrete surface in the site's northwest corner

Prior to leaving the area, UNEP collected penetrators and fragments lying openly on the ground as they represented a potential health risk were they to be picked up by people working on the site. Contaminated soil, as well as full penetrators and fragments that were buried in the ground, were left to be removed by authorized personnel during later decontamination activities.

■ **Soil**

DU in surface soil was only found close to impact points. Local DU dispersion could be measured at a distance up to a few metres from penetrator impact points. Beyond a distance of 50-100 m, no indications of widespread DU contamination could be found.

In order to define the topsoil concentration of local DU contamination and the approximate magnitude of the contaminated surface, 12 surface soil samples were collected from different locations both within and outside the fenced area. Sampling sites were selected just outside of the immediate vicinity (1-2 m) of visible impact points in order to more accurately measure any local contamination. Six samples were taken inside the fenced area where many impact points were identified. A further six samples were taken outside the fenced area, where no indications of penetrators or impact points could be found.

Samples were taken both inside and outside the fenced facility area

Inside the facility, only one topsoil sample (NUC-2002-024-008) had measurable local DU contamination of 0.2 mg/kg of soil. This value is equivalent to only about 10 per cent of the average natural uranium concentration in soil. The sample was collected on a grass surface at a distance of about 5-10 m to the nearest confirmed penetrator impact point, situated on the edge of a hard surface (concrete, asphalt).

At the edge of the large cobblestone yard near the centre of the facility, two sand samples (NUC-2002-024-011 and NUC-2002-024-012) were collected where rainwater runoff had deposited a 3 cm layer of sand and dust. In this yard, and within a distance of about 50 m, many penetrator impact points were identified. DU concentration in these two samples was 11 and 30 mg/kg, equivalent to roughly ten times the natural uranium concentration in soil. These samples certainly included some material and residues collected directly from the penetrator shot holes as they are known to contain much higher levels of local DU contamination.

No indication of DU contamination exceeding the detection limit could be found in any of the samples taken outside the fenced area. Natural uranium concentration in these samples was in the range of 2.8-4.7 mg/kg of soil, which is in the normal range of natural uranium concentration in soil. The measured isotopic composition of the uranium was indicative of natural uranium.

■ **Water samples**

Four water samples were collected (APAT-BHW01 to -BHW04). The first was taken from a concrete drainage well close to the bank of the small stream that crosses the site. The second was collected directly from the stream. A third was a well-water sample taken near the office buildings. This water is used for cooking purposes once it has been boiled. The last sample was taken from a concrete drainage well on the eastern side of the facility. This water is also used for drinking and cooking.

The $^{234}U/^{238}U$ and $^{235}U/^{238}U$ ratios show DU contamination in one of the well-water samples (BHW03). Mass spectrometric data also indicated contamination in the other well-water sample (BHW01). It should be noted that although the measured uranium values in all samples collected at this site are higher than other water samples collected in Bosnia and Herzegovina, the corresponding radiation doses are lower than 0.1 μSv per year and are therefore insignificant.

■ **Botanical samples**

Four lichen and two moss samples were taken inside the fenced area. The first lichen sample (APAT-BH01a) was collected together with tree bark (probably *Acer* sp.) due to the very small size of the lichen. Moss was also taken on the same tree (APAT-BH01b).

The second moss sample (APAT-BH04) was taken on the soil and showed the presence of DU particles; this confirms the earlier presence of DU in the air. Several penetrators, one jacket and a large number of fragments were also found in this area.

Collecting a bark and lichen sample in Hadzici

However, as the sample lay on soil and it is difficult to clean all soil from such samples, it is likely that there was a contribution of soil particles to the activity found in the sample.

The remaining lichen samples (APAT-BH02a,b,c APAT-BH03a, APAT-BH05) were collected around the site. The presence of DU in all but sample APAT-BH02a indicates the earlier presence of DU in the air, which means that at least some of the penetrators hit hard surfaces, split into dust and dispersed into the air. It is also an indication of possible resuspension of DU from ground contamination.

Depleted Uranium in Bosnia and Herzegovina

Botanical samples (APAT-BH06a, APAT-BH06b and APAT-BH07) were collected from a private garden outside the site. No presence of DU could be detected. In addition, two vegetable samples (V-UBS1, V-UBS2) were collected for uranium isotopic determination. However, results from these two cabbage samples were insufficient to allow for any scientific conclusion (see Appendix F). There are no reasons to expect any DU to occur in food due to the low dispersion rate in the ground and the low uptake factor in food.

- **Air samples**

Four air samples were taken during the first day and five during the second day. The first day's samples were taken at random in order to estimate the average uranium concentration within the entire facility's premises (see map). During the second day, two air samplers were placed inside buildings close to the large cobblestone yard with many contamination points in order to ascertain any possible risk to employees currently working on the site. The three remaining samples were taken from other areas selected in order to get a complete picture of the site.

DU in air was detected in five of the samples, including inside a building in which contamination points were identified, in another building where no DU contamination was found with field instruments, and on the cobblestone area where numerous contamination points and penetrators were found. This was a new finding as it was the first time that contamination of air had been found in the natural environment. It is necessary, however, to question whether the UNEP personnel were responsible for placing any of the DU contaminated dust in the air by digging for penetrators or through resuspension of contaminated dust on the ground. As digging activities on the second day began only after the air samplers were shut off, the positive result from within the buildings supports the latter explanation. Further, it is important to note that any DU resuspension would occur normally through the ongoing daily activities at the site (i.e. resuspension would be caused in circumstances other than field investigations).

Samples that were taken more than 100 m away from attacked areas did not show any DU, nor did the filter sample taken on the first day on the cobblestone area.

The uranium concentrations were in the range of 10-50 picograms per m^3 in all but two of the air samples, which represents very low-level contamination of the air, and of the same order of magnitude as the natural uranium background in air. Only in two air samples was the uranium measured at a level of 0.4-1.0 nanograms per m^3, which is in the upper natural background range. The air resuspension factors for this site were found in the range of $(0.12-2.1)\ 10^{-9}\ m^{-1}$.

- **Box of DU penetrators**

Neither SFOR, the workers on the site, or local authorities could provide information on the location of the DU box. The workers on site mentioned that it had been removed by SFOR in 2001. Further information is provided in section 7.16 below.

- **Residual risks**

The *Tank Repair Facility* was one of the most heavily attacked areas in the region, with 1 500 rounds corresponding to roughly 450 kg of uranium. Of the 1 500 reported rounds, about 15 per cent were identified during the mission based on the number of contamination points identified. The areas searched no longer have penetrators on the surface and all identified contamination points are marked with a circle of red paint. This should reduce the risk that someone might unintentionally pick up a penetrator or touch a marked contamination point and be contaminated by uranium. The risk of uranium intake and the corresponding radiation dose (less than one mSv), as well as heavy-metal toxic effects, are small due to the relatively low concentration of uranium (about 30 mg of uranium - mainly DU - per kg of soil), unless the penetrator is heavily corroded. Further, potential direct intake from contaminated hands is small; it can be higher for children than for adults, but in this instance the area is fenced and is not accessible to children.

It should be mentioned that due to mines and unexploded ordnance, not all areas or buildings of the site were surveyed. Away from the searched area in unpaved parts there may still be many penetrators hidden in the ground. Some may also be on the surface, such that once the area is cleared of mines, penetrators could be picked up by someone and contaminate their hands. In this case, and with conservative assumptions on intake (1 g DU),

The radioactive source from lightning rods is another important issue to address

which also assumes bad hygiene, there is a possibility of contracting radiation doses of the order of 1 mSv (= natural background), exceeding limits protecting against heavy metal effects. If a penetrator or fragment were placed in a pocket and kept close to the body for several weeks, there is a possibility of absorbing a radiation dose to the skin higher than the accepted level of radiation for workers in one year (greater than 500 mSv).

Contamination of soil was found only at and close to the contamination points and therefore there are no foreseen future risks of widespread ground contamination.

With respect to water contamination, the rate of penetrator corrosion can be relatively high depending on the chemical qualities of the surrounding soil. Complete corrosive disintegration can occur in 25-35 years. However, the solubility and – thereby – susceptibility to contamination of groundwater and subsequent drinking water is even more uncertain. In one of the wells there was a clear indication of DU contamination, and a weak indication in one of the concrete drainage wells (see Appendix E). The concentration in both was very low and insignificant from a radiological and chemical-toxicological point of view. This can obviously change with time, and possible future DU contamination of well-water will depend on the dissolution rate and solubility of DU and the well-water uptake area. There are so many uncertain factors governing the possible contamination of water that it is impossible to predict future contamination levels. Enough is known, however, that even after eight years there are still no problems with DU in drinking water from the radiological and chemical risk standpoint.

Contamination of the superficial ground layer can also cause contamination of the air. Although DU contamination of the air could be detected in some cases, the concentrations were very low and insignificant from the point of view of radiological and heavy-metal chemical risk. Nevertheless, the observations are interesting with respect to studies on the relation of ground to air con-

Empty shells and UXO were found at the site

tamination. The measurements and samples taken were unfortunately not numerous enough to make systematic studies on the possible reasons for air contamination. For instance, air contamination could depend on activities that were ongoing simultaneously, or DU contamination indoors (on floors and walls) could also cause air contamination. Irrespective of the reason, the observation that air contamination can still be detected seven years after the attack occurred is important in the overall understanding of the short- and long-term environmental consequences of using DU in military conflicts.

Depleted Uranium in Bosnia and Herzegovina

Need for mitigation - Recommendations

Site investigations revealed low-level DU results based on the measurements achieved. They represent no real risk to individuals at the site. However, as the team was not able to explore the whole site, and as a precautionary measure, the following conclusions and recommendations are proposed:

1. All penetrators and fragments that still might lie on the surface of unmined areas should be removed, with due consideration of all safety aspects in handling and storage.

2. All marked contamination points should be cleaned of loose contamination and contaminated soil.

3. Holes on hard surfaces of still hidden penetrators and non-decontaminated surfaces should be covered by new asphalt or concrete. In grassy areas these should be covered by clean soil.

4. All buildings should be searched for loose contamination, such as penetrators, fragments and DU dust (within reasonable limits of $10 \, g/m^2$). Authorized personnel should remove any such detected contamination and these residues should be handed over to the relevant authorities for proper storage.

5. Water contamination levels on the site were found to be below stated WHO limits. However, given all the uncertainties concerning DU in the ground and possible increased contamination of drinking water in the future, it is recommended that consideration be given by the authorities to reconstructing the water pipeline which was damaged during the war in order to avoid any unnecessary future risks. Nevertheless, any present and future drinking water that might originate from the site area should be checked for possible DU contamination by sampling and measurement once a year.

6. As some buildings are currently in use and additional buildings may be put to future use, it is recommended that authorized personnel properly clean those buildings. Based on current data, such cleaning could be completed through well-filtered vacuum cleaning or wet washing methods.

7. As the UNEP sampling was limited to hard surfaces, it can be expected that a large number of penetrators remain undetected in grassy areas. Throughout future mine clearance activities, all safety aspects should be considered in the handling and storage of penetrators and fragments. In addition, the area should be searched for penetrators and contamination points and measures taken accordingly.

8. Another radiological issue on the site is the radioactive source from the lightning rods. Although it is difficult to estimate the risk associated with the rods, the potential exposure from these sources could be higher than that from DU. The rods should therefore be removed and handed to the relevant authorities for proper storage.

9. Information should be provided to military, civilian and mine clearance personnel, as well as other concerned personnel, on the presence of DU, corresponding risks and how to deal with newly found penetrators.

7.2 LUKAVICA, 16 OCTOBER 2002

NATO ref:	None www.nato.int/du/docu/d010523b.pdf; NATO Unclassified (C-M (2001)43)
Coordinates:	34T BP 8850 / 55800
Target:	Metal workshop and barracks
Number of rounds:	Unknown
Area:	Open area, converted into residences, shops and market place. Very active.
Investigated surface area:	600 m x 500 m
Town/Population:	The community of Lukavica (population 13 000) is a suburban area of Sarajevo belonging to the Republika Srpska. The population surrounding the immediate site can be estimated to be approximately 1 000-1 500.
Other information:	Extensive rebuilding of residences and businesses is now ongoing. Some animals graze on the available grassy surfaces.

Site description and general information

The investigated area lies within *Lukavica* town, a suburb of Sarajevo. During the war, this area was attacked as it housed a military compound. The targets were army barracks, storage areas and workshops, which were heavily hit and partly destroyed. During the fact-finding pre-mission, the Republika Srpska authorities mentioned that the area may have been attacked using DU munitions.

Today, the workshops and several of the barracks have been rebuilt and are now used as workshops, storage areas and shops. The metal workshop is active and employs a small number of people. Between a shop area and the former barracks is a market place selling food and other items for locals living nearby. There are no mines in the area and it has been cleared of unexploded ordnance.

Field investigation

Both on-line and random survey techniques were used on all streets, open places, the market area, within certain destroyed buildings and on grassy areas. The ground surface within and around a large, rebuilt mechanical workshop in the eastern part of the area was also thoroughly investigated.

Samples taken included:
- 4 surface soil samples to a depth of 5 cm
- 1 water sample (tap)
- 6 bio-indicators (2 lichen*, 3 moss, one bark)
- 4 air filter samples.

The SE part of the area has been redeveloped, whereas the NW remains in disarray

Depleted Uranium in Bosnia and Herzegovina

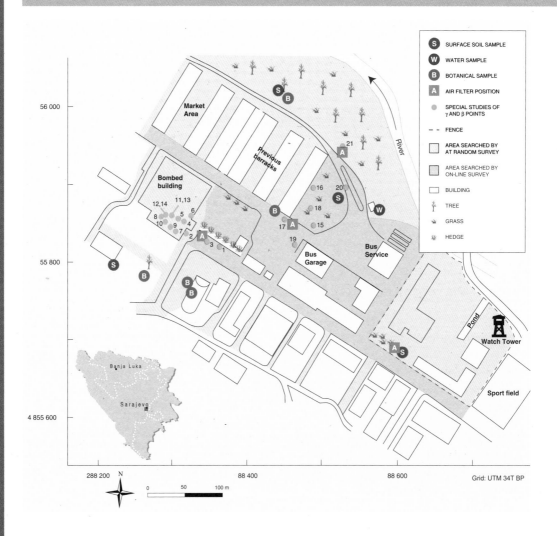

Findings

■ General contamination

No contamination was detected by the field measurements, which means that any contamination on the surface was less than 10 per cent of the *Reference Level* (or less than 1 g DU/m² assuming superficial deposition on the ground but nevertheless 90 per cent absorption). There was also no indication of contamination in soil, water or air samples.

■ Measurements of radiation

The gamma background was low, 0.03-0.10 μSv/h, which was favourable for detecting radiation from possible DU. Increased gamma radiation was measured outside one of the workshop buildings and was shown to be caused by radioactive sources used for gamma radiography (see below).

Special studies of possible DU contamination of surfaces were done by taking measurements of gamma and beta radiation on metal, concrete and wood surfaces carried out at 23 locations (see Appendix J). In all of these locations beta radiation did not exceed 0.2 cps.

■ Penetrators, jackets and localized points of contamination

No penetrators, jackets or contamination points were found.

■ Soil

Four surface soil samples were taken from different parts inside and around the area. Since no indications of penetrator impact points were found, the samples were taken from different places randomly distributed over the whole surface of the site.

No soil contamination was found. The uranium concentration in the samples was in the range of 2.1-3.0 mg/kg of soil. These values are in the normal range of natural uranium concentration in soil. The measured isotopic composition of the uranium was indicative of natural uranium.

A bus repair service and a number of other shops are currently operating in this area of Lukavica

■ Water samples

A public tap water sample was taken from the fuel station. No DU contamination was found.

■ Botanical samples

Lichen and moss samples were taken inside the urbanized area. The selection of the sampling points was made on the basis of information received on the main targets during the bombing. The results indicate that there is no presence of DU at this site.

■ Air samples

Four air samples taken in open areas near residences and public spaces found no presence of DU. Uranium concentration in air was within normal ranges. However, special studies on resuspension revealed, on 5-10 occasions, uranium concentrations higher than at the other sites where no DU contamination was found. It was concluded that the magnitude of the corresponding resuspension factor was in the range of $(3.5\text{-}7.1)\ 10^{-9}\ m^{-1}$.

■ Radiography sources

A measurement taken outside a metal workshop detected a radioactive source emitting gamma radiation inside the workshop. With the assistance of the factory owner, the source was located within a locked shed in the main building and proved to be from radiography equipment used in the examination of metal constructions. It could not be established whether the source was properly licensed or whether any appropriate radiation protection procedures were in place at the site, and should thus be inspected by responsible authorities.

■ Residual risks

There are no additional risks caused by DU in the investigated area.

Need for mitigation - Recommendations

No evidence or indication was found that DU had been used on this site, and neither is there any reason to believe DU was used in the area. Therefore, no specific recommendations relevant to DU are necessary.

However, the presence of the radiographic source in the metal workshop premises is of some concern for employees as the potential risk from exposure is significant. The radiation protection authorities of the Republika Srpska should investigate whether the source is properly registered and licensed, and whether the necessary measures are being taken to ensure the facility is being operated in accordance with the radiation safety legislation.

Depleted Uranium in Bosnia and Herzegovina

7

7.3 HADZICI BARRACKS, 17 OCTOBER 2002

NATO ref:	None www.nato.int/du/docu/d010523b.pdf; NATO Unclassified (C-M (2001) 43)
Coordinates:	34T BP 75300 / 54700
Target:	The area was most likely not targeted by A-10 planes.
Number of rounds:	Unknown.
Area:	The area is a secured, active military site with no civilian access.
Investigated surface area:	200 m x 300 m
Town/Population:	The barracks immediately adjoin the town of Hadzici and are situated alongside a residential area. The population is 20 660.
Other information:	UNEP was informed that the barracks were not heavily attacked (by air). The military authorities do not think DU would have been used here. The site normally holds about 100 soldiers, but is occasionally used for military training with up to 400 soldiers.

Site description and general information

The investigated area is a secured military barracks located on the outskirts of the town of Hadzici, lying at the base of a forested hill. During the war, some of the barracks were attacked, but according to the soldiers now present, the site was not attacked by air. The barracks area leads to the entrance to an ammunition storage depot (see site 7.4) which was quite large at the time of the conflict.

The area has been rebuilt and is used by a small number of soldiers. There are barracks, offices, kitchen and storage facilities, and an area for sports activities. The perimeters of the site are still mined, particularly the forested areas. A stream runs along the western edge of the site.

The central portion of the Hadzici Barracks which is in active use

Post-Conflict Environmental Assessment

➤ Hadzici Barracks

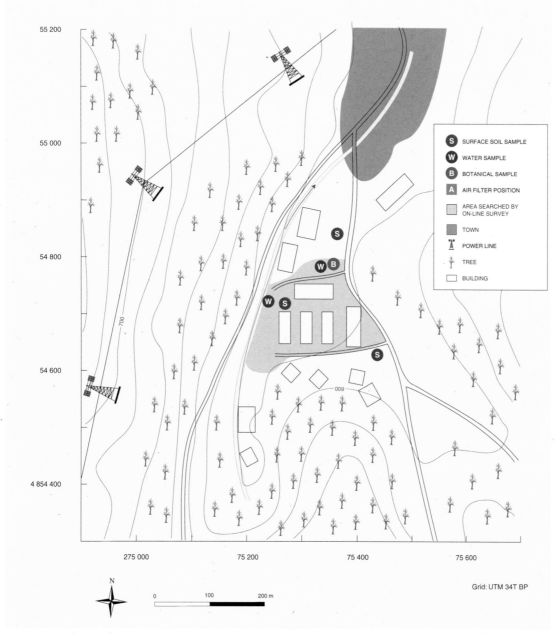

S	SURFACE SOIL SAMPLE
W	WATER SAMPLE
B	BOTANICAL SAMPLE
A	AIR FILTER POSITION
	AREA SEARCHED BY ON-LINE SURVEY
	TOWN
	POWER LINE
	TREE
	BUILDING

Grid: UTM 34T BP

N

0   100   200 m

◆ *Map Approximation*

Field investigation

The site was fully investigated using the on-line survey method on all hard surfaces and between most buildings. Random surveys were completed between any remaining buildings and on the sports field. Only normal background radiation was detected. No mapping was done at the time of the investigation due to time constraints. The site map is an approximation based on NATO maps and UNEP personnel recollections and photographs.

Samples taken included:

- 3 surface soil samples to a depth of 5 cm
- 2 water samples (1 tap, 1 stream)
- 1 bio-indicator (lichen*)
- 2 air filter samples.

Depleted Uranium in Bosnia and Herzegovina

Findings

■ General contamination

No contamination was detected by the field measurements, which means that any contamination on the surface was less than 10 per cent of the *Reference Level* (or less than 1 g DU/m^2 assuming superficial deposition on the ground but nevertheless 90 per cent absorption). There was also no indication of contamination in soil, water or air samples.

■ Measurements of radiation

The gamma background was low, 0.03-0.10 μSv/h, which was favourable for detecting radiation from possible DU. Special studies of possible contamination of DU were carried out by taking measurements of gamma and beta radiation on metal, concrete and wood surfaces at two locations. In all of these locations the beta radiation did not exceed 0.3 cps.

■ Penetrators, jackets and localized points of contamination

No penetrators, jackets or contamination points were found.

■ Soil

Three surface soil samples were taken from different locations inside the fenced area of the Hadzici Barracks. Because there were no indications of penetrator impacts, the samples were taken randomly over the whole surface of the site. No soil contamination was found.

The uranium concentration of the surface soil samples was in the range of 2.6-3.1 mg/kg of soil. These values are in the normal range of natural uranium concentration in soil. The measured isotopic composition of the uranium was indicative of natural uranium.

A stream water sample was taken from the western edge of the site

■ Water samples

Two water samples were taken, one from a stream and one from tap water. The uranium concentrations were low and there was no indication of DU.

■ Botanical samples

One lichen sample was taken inside the area. No contamination was found.

■ Air samples

Two air samples were taken near the military barracks, and indicated uranium concentration within normal ranges. No DU contamination of the air was found. The air resuspension factors for this site were found in the range of $(5.1-6.7)\ 10^{-10}\ m^{-1}$.

■ Residual risks

There are no additional risks caused by DU in the area investigated.

Need for mitigation - Recommendations

No evidence or indication was found that DU had been used on this site, and there is no reason to believe DU was used in the area. Therefore, no specific recommendations relevant to DU are necessary.

7.4 HADZICI AMMUNITION STORAGE DEPOT, 17 OCTOBER 2002

NATO ref:	#16, #17, #18, #19
Coordinates:	34TB BP 76600 / 53480
Target:	The ammunition storage bunkers containing a large amount of varied live ammunition. Possibly anti-aircraft guns.
Date of attack:	11 September 1994
Number of rounds:	1 500
Area:	Fenced, limited access even to military personnel.
Investigated surface area:	1000 m x 1000 m
Town/Population:	The town of Hadzici (population 20 660) lies 1-2 kilometres down the hill from this site. The military barracks 1.5 km from the ammunition depot hold approximately 100 soldiers.
Other information:	Dangerous site and heavily destroyed area. This area will be out of bounds for some time due to the heavy presence of mines and unexploded ordnance.

Site description and general information

The *Hadzici Ammunition Storage Depot* is a restricted site situated in a forested area about 1.5 km southeast of Hadzici Barracks. While the barracks have military access only, access to this site is further restricted due to the state of destruction and large spread of unexploded ordnance. Mines were used to protect the depot and are still present in large numbers within the forested area. Within the depot are many former bunkers and storage barns for ammunition and military equipment. Most were destroyed by precision bombing during which live ammunition was spread widely around the area. After the war, the area was closed and is now mostly overgrown by trees and bushes. It is not yet possible to walk beyond hard surface areas.

The DU targets are unknown, but may have been anti-aircraft guns. DU penetrators were found at a road crossing near a bunker in the eastern part of the site.

Penetrator impact points were found at this overgrown road crossing through on-line surveying

Depleted Uranium in Bosnia and Herzegovina

➤ Hadzici Ammunition Storage Depot

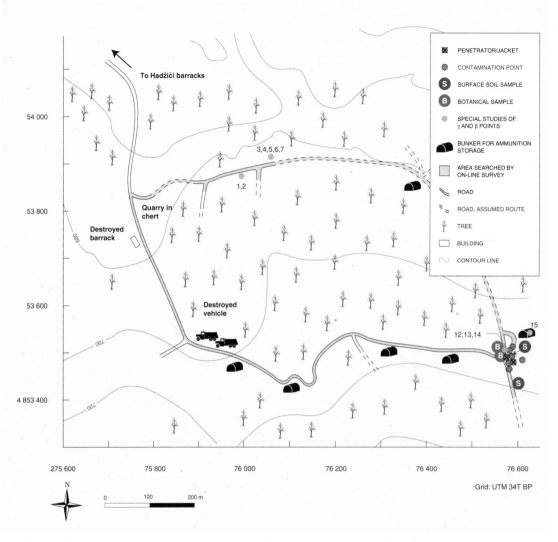

The topography of the area is rugged. The bedrock, where it was exposed along the road, consists of quartzite and chert and the soil cover is relatively thin. There are no occupied homes inside the area, but some farmhouses are situated relatively close to it. Cattle tracks indicate that the site is used for grazing.

Field investigation

The site was investigated by on-line survey on the roads along the path shown in the map. Due to the heavy mine and unexploded ordnance situation, the team kept strictly to the roads. Contamination points were marked and recorded.

Samples taken included:
- 2 surface soil samples to a depth of 5 cm
- 2 bio-indicators (lichen*, bark)
- No water samples
- No air filter samples.

Findings

■ **General contamination**

General widespread surface contamination in the area could not be detected by gamma and beta measurements even though the area had been heavily attacked by DU munitions. Soil and botanical samples confirmed this finding. However, the heavily mined areas limited the search to the roads and therefore no sampling or measurements were possible outside the roads in order to confirm this assumption.

■ Measurements of radiation

Gamma radiation was low, 0.04-0.08 μSv/h. Special studies of possible contamination of DU by measurements of gamma and beta radiation on metal, concrete and wood surfaces were carried out at 12 locations (see Appendix J). In all of these locations beta radiation did not exceed 0.5 cps.

■ Penetrators, jackets and localized points of contamination

One penetrator was found on the surface, as well as 1 jacket (both were covered in soil and left at the site). Five penetrators were located by gamma measurements lying under the asphalt surface of the road. Increased radiation ($\beta+\gamma$ or just γ) was located to contamination points, usually not larger than 10-50 cm in diameter. All points found were marked by a circle of red paint. No contamination points other than those related to penetrators/jackets were found. Widespread contamination was not encountered.

■ Soil

Two surface soil samples were taken on grassy surfaces near a crossroad where a number of impact points on the asphalt were identified. Due to the mine situation, samples could only be collected along the edge of the road. The sampling sites were chosen outside the immediate vicinity (1-2 m) of visible impact points. In both soil samples collected, DU contamination could be detected.

In one case, at a distance of 5-10 m to the nearest confirmed impact point, DU contamination of 3.7 mg/kg of soil could be measured (sample NUC-2002-027-004). The other sample was taken at a distance of 50-100 m from the nearest impact point and showed DU presence of 0.1 mg/kg of soil (sample NUC-2002-027-005). The higher value is equivalent to about the average concentration of natural uranium in soil.

Storage bunkers were completely destroyed

UXO has been strewn across the site

■ Botanical samples

Due to the heavy mine situation, only one bark and one lichen sample on two different trees were collected. The 234U/238U ratio gave indications of DU in these samples (APAT-BH14a, -BH14ba and -BH14bb).

■ Residual risks

There are likely to be penetrators and contamination points beside and beyond the roads. However, the risks from DU are very limited as the site is closed to the public and

Depleted Uranium in Bosnia and Herzegovina

most areas where DU remains in the soil are impossible to approach because of the risk of mines and unexploded ordnance.

Need for mitigation - Recommendations

Due to the limited access and mine situation, at present there is no need for any mitigation other than to pick up any penetrators that are still lying on the road. Those that have been detected but are below the ground surface could be left there permanently. Due to the large amount of DU ammunition used to attack this site, there are reasons to believe that there are many penetrators and contamination points by the side of the road. Consequently, the following recommendations are given:

1. All penetrators that still might lie on the surface of unmined areas should be removed, with due consideration of all safety aspects in handling and storage.

2. As the team was limited to hard surfaces, it can be expected that a large number of penetrators remain undetected in the grassy areas. In any future mine clearing activities, all safety aspects should be considered in the handling and storage of penetrators and fragments.

3. In addition, it is recommended that when the area is cleared of unexploded ordnance and mines, the area should be searched for penetrators and contamination points, and measures taken accordingly.

4. Information should be provided to military, civilian and mine clearance personnel, as well as other concerned personnel, on the presence of DU, corresponding risks and how to deal with newly found penetrators.

7.5 ROSCA, 76 MM AT SELF-PROP GUN, 17 OCTOBER 2002

NATO ref:	#1
Coordinates:	34T BP 86819 / 46649
Target:	76 mm AT Self-Prop Gun
Date of attack:	5 August 1994
Number of rounds:	860
Area:	The targeted area is located on the top of a small mountain but was not accessible.
Investigated surface area:	Unknown
Town/Population:	There is no town or population in the immediate vicinity.
Other information:	UNEP was unable to access the site due to the presence of anti-tank mines. No surveying or samples were possible.

Need for mitigation - Recommendations

This site, confirmed by NATO, was inaccessible due to the presence of anti-tank mines. It is recommended that once the mines have been cleared the site should be fully investigated for any DU contamination.

1. Any loose contamination, such as penetrators and fragments, should be picked up by authorized personnel.

2. Mine clearance and military personnel should be properly informed of the risks associated with DU.

7.6   PJELUGOVICI - T55 TANK, 17 OCTOBER 2002

NATO ref:	#2
Coordinates:	34T BP 81850 / 61770
Target:	T55 Tank that was used for shelling Sarajevo
Date of attack:	22 September 1994
Number of rounds:	120
Area:	Small hill with view onto Sarajevo. Residential, open access.
Investigated surface area:	200 m x 200 m
Town/Population:	There are four homes in the immediate vicinity of the hill
Other information:	The site is located on top of a hill in a civilian area. Foundations of houses that existed before the war were found, as well as an old bunker that has been filled in and is overgrown. A local civilian indicated to UNEP where the tank had been located at the time of the attack.

Site description and general information

This hilltop site is in a civilian area with a good view of Sarajevo and is used to grow apples and for animal grazing. The entire hill is covered with topsoil and there are some old trees and newly planted fruit trees. The concrete foundations of three houses destroyed during the war are also evident. On the edge of the hill is an old bunker which has been filled in and is now overgrown. A bit further on from the former tank position is a farmhouse which is currently occupied. A small village is situated about 200 m from the site at the base of the hill.

Field investigation

The site was investigated by on-line survey and random survey. Studies of possible DU contamination were carried out at seven locations through measurements of gamma and beta radiation on metal, concrete and wood surfaces.

The T55 Tank hilltop site. Sarajevo can be seen in the distance

Depleted Uranium in Bosnia and Herzegovina

➤ Pjelugovici - T55 tank

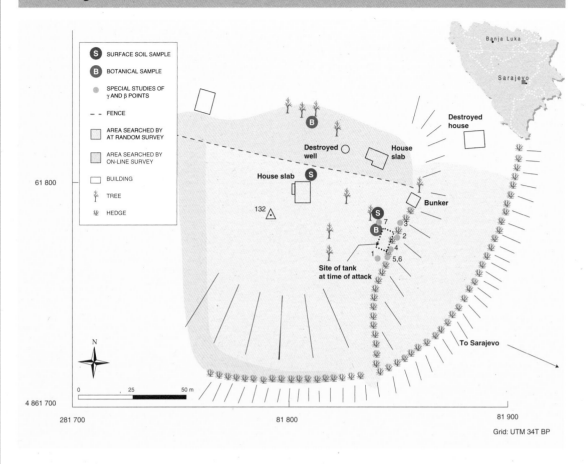

Samples taken included:
- 2 surface soil samples to a depth of 5 cm
- No water samples
- 2 bio-indicator (both lichen*)
- No air filter samples.

Findings

■ General contamination

No general contamination in terms of localized surface contamination could be detected. As many years have elapsed since the military conflict and the area is currently used for planting, the soil may have been farmed, fertilized and turned over several times. As a result, possible DU contamination could have been diluted and dispersed in so much soil that it was no longer discernible by the field instruments used. However, even the more sensitive soil and biota sampling and measurements did not indicate any contamination. It is therefore concluded that there is no localized or widespread contamination of any significance.

■ Measurements of radiation

The gamma background was 0.10-0.12 µSv/h, and ß-background was 0-1 cps. Conditions for detecting DU were favourable. At all locations the beta radiation did not exceed 0.5 cps.

■ Penetrators, jackets and localized points of contamination

No penetrators or jackets were found. Since DU ammunition was used in the area, there are reasons to speculate that some may already have been taken away and some penetrators could be hidden deep in the ground and are not detectable by field measurements. These should not cause any concern as long as any future digging is not too deep.

■ Cesium contamination

No DU contamination points were found. However, at two opposite corners of a concrete foundation of a former house, an enhanced gamma radiation level was detected. The gamma radiation over these respective spots were 0.15 μSv/h and 0.25 μSv/h. Measurements by a portable gamma ray spectrometer revealed that the increased radiation was caused by cesium-137. During the 1986 Chernobyl accident, cesium-137 was dispersed over the whole of Europe, including BiH, causing fallout on the ground, lakes and other surfaces, including the roof of the former household. Over the years, the roof would have been repeatedly washed by rainwater and the cesium-137 would have been transported down through the drainpipes. The outlets of these drainpipes were located above the radioactive spots detected.

■ Soil samples

Two surface soil samples were taken from the area around the former position of a T55 tank. One was taken near the tank at the time of attack, the other about 50 m northeast of the tank near the ruins of a small house. As no indications of penetrator impacts were detectable on the surface, samples were taken from different places distributed over the surface of the site. No contamination of the soil was found.

The uranium concentration of the surface soil samples was in the range of 1.5-1.8 mg/kg of soil. These values are in the normal range of natural uranium concentration in soil. The measured isotopic composition of the uranium was indicative of natural uranium.

■ Botanical samples

Two lichen samples were taken: one from apple trees near the point where the tank would have been located at the time of the attack, and the other from an old tree 50 m northwest of the tank position. No indications of DU contamination could be found.

■ Residual risks

There is no risk of DU contamination from either contamination points or penetrators on the ground. However, hidden penetrators deeper in the soil might be dug up unintentionally in the future and cause a risk of exposure. It is also possible that hidden penetrators could cause some DU contamination of drinking water supplies in the future. However, based on previous experience and the fact that the total amount of DU that was used in the area was relatively small, the risk of significant drinking water contamination is small.

Need for mitigation - Recommendations

No evidence or indication was found that DU munitions had been used on this site. Because nothing was found there is no immediate need for mitigation. However, as there are probably penetrators hidden in the ground that could be dug up in the future and cause some minor contamination, the following recommendations are given:

1. The people living in the area should be properly informed about DU and its risks. All penetrators found in future should be given to the appropriate authorities.

2. Because people are living below the area investigated, it is recommended that, in line with the precautionary principle and as part of scientific research, samples of drinking water should be taken once per year and measured for DU if the drinking water is sourced from the hill.

7.7 HAN PIJESAK ARTILLERY STORAGE AND BARRACKS, 18-19 OCTOBER 2002

NATO ref:	#10, #11, #12, #13
Coordinates:	34T CP 35600 / 84400
Target:	Tanks, vehicles, artillery and potentially an anti-aircraft gun
Date of attack:	7 September 1995
Number of rounds:	2 400
Area:	Large site, military barracks. Also artillery and vehicle storage site.
Investigated surface area:	900 m x 250 m
Town/Population:	The site is approximately 1.5 km north from the town of Han Pijesak (population 5 500). Approximately 50 soldiers remain on the site on a regular basis. A full battalion of 250-400 soldiers come to the site during training periods.
Other information:	The site is a short distance from the town and has secured military access only. The site was heavily attacked and many vehicles were hit. These have all been removed. The site is surrounded by forest in an east-west oriented valley.

Site description and general information

The *Han Pijesak Artillery Storage and Barracks* consists of several barracks, storage barns, garages, parking lots for army vehicles, and training grounds. During the war, the site was heavily attacked and several of the buildings in the western part of the site were destroyed or partly destroyed. The buildings in the eastern part survived. The destroyed buildings have been repaired or replaced by new buildings. Some of the new wooden buildings are used as storage facilities and garages for artillery and army vehicles.

The barracks and storage area are situated in a shallow east-west oriented valley. The northern area borders a steep slope and a small stream runs through the site and disappears into a sinkhole. The bedrock of the area consists of limestone. The bottom of the valley is in

The western part of the site (seen here) was the most heavily attacked during the conflict

Post-Conflict Environmental Assessment

➤ Han Pijesak Artillery Storage and Barracks

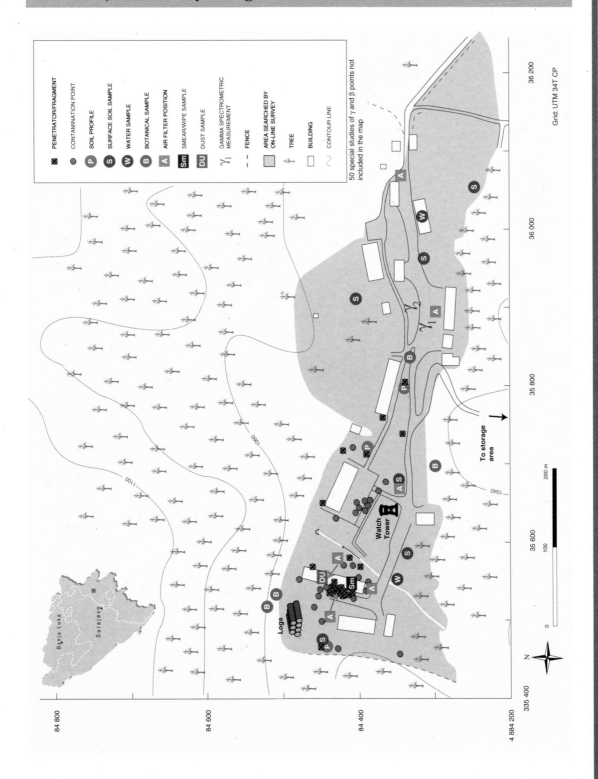

Legend:
- ⌧ PENETRATOR/FRAGMENT
- ● CONTAMINATION POINT
- Ⓟ SOIL PROFILE
- Ⓢ SURFACE SOIL SAMPLE
- Ⓦ WATER SAMPLE
- Ⓑ BOTANICAL SAMPLE
- Ⓐ AIR FILTER POSITION
- Sm SMEAR/WIPE SAMPLE
- DU DUST SAMPLE
- γ₁ GAMMA SPECTROMETRIC MEASUREMENT
- – – FENCE
- ▨ AREA SEARCHED BY ON-LINE SURVEY
- ⋆ TREE
- ▫ BUILDING
- ∿ CONTOUR LINE
- 50 special studies of γ and β points not included in the map

Grid: UTM 34T CP

Watch Tower

Logs

To storage area

Banja Luka
Sarajevo

0   100   200 m

Depleted Uranium in Bosnia and Herzegovina

the central part of the investigated area and is rather damp and wet. The road surfaces are paved by asphalt and concrete. There are no mines in the area and it has been cleared of unexploded ordnance, permitting full access to the site.

No information was available on whether any DU-related material had been collected or removed by SFOR or the local troops.

Field investigation

The site was thoroughly investigated over a two-day period. The whole site was searched by on-line survey, including hard and grassy surfaces, a small part of the forested area at the western edge of the site, adjoining fields, behind all buildings, and over the hill where an anti-aircraft gun was probably positioned at the time of attack. Random surveying was done between vehicles and within certain buildings. One of the barracks now occupied by soldiers was rumoured to have a penetrator lodged in the wall and was thus inspected using gamma spectrometric measurements.

Forty-nine contamination points, penetrators or fragments were found, marked and recorded. One of the penetrator fragments, as well as DU dust contamination, was found in one of the barns used for artillery storage. Radioactive measurements, scratch sampling and smear sampling were also performed in the barn.

Samples taken included:
- 3 penetrators (including one still in its jacket)
- 6 surface soil samples to a depth of 5 cm
- 3 soil profiles of 60 cm in depth
- 4 smear samples (taken from within a contaminated building)
- 2 scratch samples (taken from within a contaminated building)
- 2 water samples (1 tap, 1 stream)
- 4 bio-indicators (lichen*)
- 6 air filter samples (including one inside a contaminated building).

Findings

■ General contamination

Although the area was attacked using 2 400 rounds, indicating up to 730 kg of DU might be deposited within the area, surface contamination was limited. Field measurements did not show any clear indication of widespread contamination. However, a large number of contamination points and penetrators on the surface or hidden in the ground were detected. DU could also be detected in soil, air and lichen samples.

■ Measurements of radiation

Conditions for detecting contamination, penetrators and fragments were favourable. During on-line and random surveys, the total gamma and beta radiation was continuously measured by the SRAT and Inspector instruments. The background gamma radiation on the hard surface areas was 0.02-0.04 μSv/h and on soil 0.05-0.08 μSv/h, while the beta radiation background amounted to 0-1 cps.

Gamma radiation was also encountered on the ground under a drainpipe of a building that had survived the attacks. Gamma spectrometric measurements performed on the spot revealed that this was caused by cesium-137 fallout from the 1986 Chernobyl accident.

Gamma spectrometric measurements were carried out on a concrete pavement at the centre of the area, and on soil. The concentrations within the concrete were: uranium 0.2 mg/kg, thorium 0.4 mg/kg and potassium less than 0.1 per cent; and in the soil were: uranium 1.4 mg/kg, thorium 6.7 mg/kg and 0.8 per cent potassium.

A third measurement was carried out within the occupied barracks as it was rumoured that a penetrator was lodged within the wall. However, measurements ranged within natural background levels and it was thought unlikely that any penetrator would be located there.

Special studies on ß and γ from ground or surface were conducted through measurements on 50 various surfaces. Fourteen measurements were made inside and 36 measurements outside the contaminated building. In ten of these locations the beta radiation exceeded 1 cps. Using these results, it was estimated that the DU contamination density of the concrete floor inside the attacked storage barn was 0.7 g m^{-2} (see Appendix J, Figure J.3).

■ **Penetrators, jackets and localized points of contamination**

On-line surveying in an adjoining field

On-line surveying identified 8 whole penetrators, 2 half penetrators, and 11 penetrator fragments. Most were lying openly on the ground surface. Those on hard surfaces were not outwardly affected by weathering and remained in relatively good condition, whereas those that were covered by soil, even if only by a few centimetres, were usually very corroded. Three penetrators were collected for further studies.

A further 27 points were found with contamination or enhanced radiation caused by DU dust, fragments, or penetrators deeper in the soil. All DU was localized to the western half of the site (see map). All contamination points identified were marked with a red circle of paint. Although the team searched the eastern part of the area carefully, no DU was found there. No widespread contamination was found.

Additional DU contamination was found inside one of the barns used as artillery and vehicle storage. At least one other building, as well as a large garage, was most likely hit as they were positioned in the line of attack; both penetrators and fragments were found close to them. These buildings are very likely contaminated by DU, but they were not accessed.

Before leaving the area, the penetrators and fragments found lying on the ground were collected as they entailed a health risk. Penetrators and fragments which were located but remain buried in the ground were left to be removed at a later date by proper decontamination teams. Contaminated soil was also left on site.

■ **Soil**

Six surface soil samples were collected from different areas of the site. Three samples were taken around the storage barns and the parking lot in the western section. Many penetrator impact points could be detected on both hard (asphalt, gravel, concrete) and soft surfaces. Sampling sites were chosen outside the immediate vicinity (1-2 m) of visible impact points.

Only one topsoil sample from this area (sample NUC-2002-028-003) showed localized DU contamination of 0.2 mg/kg of soil. The sample was collected on a grassy surface approximately 50 m from the nearest confirmed impact points on a hard surface (gravel). This value is equivalent to only 10 per cent of the average concentration of natural uranium in soil and is therefore insignificant from a health point of view. The other two samples from this area, collected on grassy surfaces at distances between 3 m and 30 m from confirmed impact points, showed no indication of localized DU contamination.

Depleted Uranium in Bosnia and Herzegovina

The other three surface soil samples were collected in the eastern section, although no impact points were found nearby. To establish the concentration of local DU contamination of topsoil and the approximate extent of the contaminated surface, samples were collected from different places randomly distributed over the site.

Localized DU contamination of 0.1 mg/kg of soil was measured in one of these samples (NUC-2002-028-001). The sample was collected near the occupied barracks, cantina and the sports field, at a distance of about 170 m from the nearest confirmed impact point. Again, this value is equivalent to less than 10 per cent of the average concentration of natural uranium in soil and is therefore insignificant from a health point of view. This spread of localized contamination over a distance of nearly 200 m is unusually large, but could be due to undetected impact points on the soft ground between the sampling point and the nearest confirmed impact point. The other two samples showed no indication of DU contamination exceeding the limit of detection.

Natural uranium concentration for the uncontaminated surface soil samples was in the range of 1.3-2.6 mg/kg of soil. These values are in the normal range of natural uranium concentration in soil. The measured isotopic composition of the uranium was indicative of natural uranium.

■ Soil profiles

Contamination of subsurface soil directly below two DU penetrators was investigated by taking soil profile samples to a depth of 60-65 cm below the soil surface. The penetrators were lying in undisturbed grass-covered ground at depths of between 3 and 8 cm and were found in two different parts of the site. In the first case, the average contamination in the second layer of soil (5-10 cm) in which the penetrator was lying was 45 g of DU per kilogram of soil (samples NUC-2002-028-101 to 112). In the second profile, the intact penetrator was found still held within its jacket. The average contamination in the upper layer around the penetrator was only 4.7 g of DU per kilogram of soil (samples NUC-2002-028-120 to 132). It is likely that the jacket/casing acted as partial surface protection from corrosive attack. The DU contamination of these samples consists mainly of a thick layer of DU corrosion products, formed on the exposed surfaces of the penetrator in the soil. Penetrators without their jacket/casing had lost approximately 25 per cent of their metallic mass through corrosion.

A large hammer is used to drive the soil profile plate into the ground

Bearing in mind the state of the penetrators when they were found, UNEP established the losses to be 66-93 g more than 7 years after the conflict. Based on these findings, penetrators consisting of metallic DU will no longer be found in the Balkans grounds 25 to 35 years after impact. Instead, only contaminated spots containing DU decomposition products will remain in the ground.

Within the first 10 cm of soil below the penetrators, DU concentration diminished roughly by two orders of magnitude from values of 230 to 69 mg/kg of soil respectively. Within the next 30 cm, the DU concentration diminished by approximately another three orders of magnitude to values less than 0.1 mg/kg of soil (i.e. near the limit of detection). Therefore, within the first 40 cm below the penetrator, DU concentration diminished by almost six orders of magnitude. For layers deeper than 40 cm, no traces of DU were detected.

In conclusion, based on the results from these soil profile analyses, the mobility of DU corrosion products in the type of soil found at Han Pijesak is very low.

A third soil profile was taken by Bristol University and will be studied further in the context of ongoing PhD work on uranium mobility.

■ Surface deposits / Smear samples

Scratch and smear samples were taken from within a wooden storage barn in the western portion of the site. Shot holes on the concrete floor indicated that the building had been heavily hit by DU rounds. Following the attack, the barn was emptied, repaired and used once again to store army material, such as cannons and wooden boxes. All materials that were in the building at the time of attack were removed. It is not known where this equipment has been moved to, nor how long the current equipment has been stored there.

Two scratch samples were taken inside the barn. The first was taken from the concrete floor against the wall; the second was collected from the horizontal surface of a wooden beam. Both scratch samples consisted of sand and dust.

The uranium concentration of the sand and dust material from the first sample (NUC-2002-028-302) was 1 890 mg/kg, representing a surface contamination of 1 070 mg/m^2. This concentration is approximately 1 000 times higher than the natural uranium content of soil. The uranium concentration in the material collected from the wooden beam (sample NUC-2002-028-301) was 92 mg/kg, representing a surface contamination of 11 mg/m^2, approximately 100 times higher than the natural uranium content of soil. The uranium in both samples consisted of almost 100 per cent DU.

These two scratch samples most likely represent primary deposits of debris and dust from the initial impact of DU penetrators on the concrete floor inside the building. It is unlikely that this coarse, sandy material was later resuspended inside the building. These results confirm that primary contamination from penetrator impacts can be higher inside a building than outdoors. As the contamination occurred indoors, there are no weathering effects and the initial superficial contamination will remain on the ground surface for a long time.

Both scratch and smear samples were collected inside the contaminated storage barn

Depleted Uranium in Bosnia and Herzegovina

Two smear samples were taken from smooth, painted horizontal surfaces of a cannon and a wooden box stored in the barn. Both smear samples consisted of fine brown dust. The measured loose surface contamination from the cannon (sample NUC-2002-028-303) was 59 $\mu g/m^2$. The sample from the surface of the wooden box (sample NUC-2002-028-304) measured loose surface contamination of 270 $\mu g/m^2$. The uranium in both samples again consisted of almost 100 per cent DU.

A similar result emerged from the measurement of the DU contamination on the surface of another cannon (sample NSI-smr-07-03). DU contamination density of this surface was 110 $\mu g/m^2$

These smear samples are most likely due to secondary deposits following the resuspension of contaminated dust from the floor. Indeed, the DU concentration was very low, about 1 000 times less than the primary contamination on the floor. Since the detailed history of the management of the building is unknown, it is not possible to know the length of time the deposited dust on the sampled surfaces was left undisturbed. These results show that secondary deposition of resuspended dust can lead to DU contamination of objects brought into a building after an attack.

The forested area was fully investigated

An important result was the detection of DU in two additional smear samples taken from metal surfaces at distances of about 100 m (sample NSI-smr-07-05) and 400 m (sample NSI-smr-07-16) from the attacked storage barn. From these results the estimated total mass of DU used in the attacks was 40-330 kg, or 150 -1100 penetrators (see Appendix J.3)

■ **Water samples**

One sample of tap water was collected from a barracks and another was taken from the stream. No DU contamination was found, which is interesting considering the large number of DU rounds used in the area. However, tap water for this site most likely comes from the nearby town rather than the site itself, and the stream running through the site ran at fast volume.

■ **Botanical samples**

Two lichen samples were collected along the road crossing the site, and another two were taken at the border of the forest at the western edge of the site where indications of an attack were apparent. On the basis of $^{234}U/^{238}U$ ratio, the results give an indication of DU presence in three lichen samples, confirming the earlier presence of DU in the air, which means that at least some of penetrators hit hard surfaces, split into dust and dispersed in the air.

■ **Air samples**

On the first day, four air samples were taken. The air samplers were arranged at approximately equal distances from each other in a parallel line to the main road leading from the entrance of the site to the forest at the western edge. This was done in order to estimate the average uranium concentration in air. On the second day, one air sampler was placed outside the entrance of the contaminated wooden storage barn, and another was placed inside the barn.

Three of the air samples showed significant DU contamination, including one from the first day (NUC-2002-027-204) taken just outside the contaminated storage barn. However, some members of the UNEP team were working around the building while the sampling was going on as this area was found to have many contamination points. Therefore, it is likely that a part of the DU measured may be attributed to resuspension due to walking and digging performed at the time.

Post-Conflict Environmental Assessment

Air samplers were positioned throughout the site for an overall estimation on the presence of DU in air

The two samples taken during the second day both indicate the presence of DU. One sampler was placed inside the contaminated storage barn (NUC-2002-028-202) and the second just outside its entrance on the gravel surface where many contamination points had been identified the previous day (NUC-2002-028-201). Special care was taken not to disrupt the area while the sampling was in progress, and to ensure natural results the samplers were shut down when anyone approached the area. Therefore, the main contribution to the DU measured in the air could be attributed to natural resuspension.

The amount of DU measured in the air inside the building was much higher than that measured outside. The concentration was about 50 times normal value for uranium and consisted of almost 100 per cent DU. The reason for resuspension could be due to air coming through the openings in the building near the floor and blowing the DU dust on the floor. However, as the dust was found to be highly contaminated with DU, it should be noted that any regular activities occurring inside the barn would create further resuspension. The resuspended DU particles outside the storage barn are diluted in the open air, which explains the wide difference.

Breathing that kind of air for a whole year, the resulting radiation dose will be a few μSv and therefore the radiological (as well as the chemical) consequences are insignificant. Nevertheless, it is one of the highest concentrations of DU in air measured during missions to study the presence of DU in the Balkans.

The other sample containing DU was taken just outside the building. The uranium concentration was about normal, but the relative part of DU was high (90 per cent). Further away (40 m) the relative part of DU in air was less than 50 per cent, while at a greater distance still, no DU could be detected.

The outdoor air resuspension factors for this site were found in the range $(4.8-12)\ 10^{-10}\ \text{m}^{-1}$. The average value of resuspension factors inside the bombed storage barn was $5.2\ 10^{-9}\ \text{m}^{-1}$, approximately seven times higher than the average value outside the buildings. The differences are possibly due to the design of the storage barn. There are large openings near the floor surface and the speed of the air passing through these openings could be much higher than outdoors.

■ **Residual risks**

The area was heavily attacked with 2 400 rounds of DU ammunition. Eight penetrators and 49 contamination points were identified. Contamination points indicated hidden penetrators. There are reasons to believe that some penetrators are still lying on the ground in the forested area, most likely covered by grass and soil. In the areas where nothing was found by on-line survey, it is unlikely that anything will be found on the surface in the future, if no digging occurs.

All penetrators laying on the surface present a potential risk of being picked up and improperly handled.

Certain buildings, particularly the wooden storage barn, are still contaminated indoors. By entering and remaining inside these buildings, there is a risk of inhaling DU contaminated air. The related radiological risks are not expected to be of any significance, but nevertheless should be avoided.

In addition, contamination of hands and clothing is possible by coming into contact with the stored materials. The corresponding radiation doses would be low, but again should be avoided.

No contamination of water was found. However, with almost 730 kg of uranium in the ground within a relatively small area, there exists the possibility that DU could dissolve in the future and disperse in the ground and contaminate groundwater. This report demonstrates that penetrators will corrode completely within 25-35 years after impact. It is shown that the only risk for groundwater contamination is the composition of the soil in which the penetrators remain.

There are still some contamination points in the paved area where cars are parked, as well as between the buildings. If not covered, these constitute a potential source of contamination of the air through resuspension of DU dust.

Need for mitigation - Recommendations

Because of the results and potential risks for the future, the following recommendations are given:

1. In order to decontaminate the forest area a full search of the area is recommended. Any penetrator/fragments found should be removed and stored by responsible authorities.

2. Contaminated buildings should be dealt with in the following way by authorized personnel:
   a. All areas, including floors, should be cleaned by vacuum or under water pressure;
   b. Contamination points on hard surface areas should be covered with asphalt or concrete;
   c. Loose contamination needs to be removed by authorized personnel and stored by responsible authorities.

3. Cover all contamination points outdoors with clean soil (for grassy areas), and asphalt or concrete (for hard surfaces).

4. If water is used for drinking purposes, it is recommended that, in line with the precautionary principle and as part of scientific research, sampling and measurements of drinking water should be made once a year.

5. Proper information should be given to military personnel on the appearance and presence of DU ammunition in general, the corresponding risks and how to take care of any penetrators found.

6. Any remaining vehicles that were hit during the attack should be investigated, wherever they may be stored.

Post-Conflict Environmental Assessment

7.8 HAN PIJESAK AMMUNITION STORAGE AREA, 18 OCTOBER 2002

NATO ref:	None www.nato.int/du/docu/d010523b.pdf; NATO Unclassified (C-M (2001) 43)
Coordinates:	34T CP 35750 / 83950
Target:	Equipment storage buildings
Number of rounds:	Unknown; unlikely DU was used for this site
Area:	Small, secluded area removed from rest of site (7.7).
Investigated surface area:	250 m x 100 m
Town/Population:	There are no homes or barracks in the immediate vicinity of the site.
Other information:	The site is situated 400 m south of the Han Pijesak Barracks and is somewhat secluded. Access is by a 400 m long road. One soldier guards the storage area. The area was shelled. Cut trees have shrapnel scars.

Site description and general information

The site is a clearing in the forest and is accessed by a gravel road leading southwards from the Han Pijesak Barracks. In the clearing are three military equipment storage buildings. The bedrock of the area is limestone. The ground is comprised of soil.

Field investigation

The entire site was searched by on-line survey. No enhanced radiation was measured. No samples of any kind were collected and no special studies of possible DU contamination by measurements of gamma and beta radiation were carried out. No information led UNEP to believe that this area had been attacked using DU munitions.

Samples taken:
- None.

The repaired storage facilities are in a secluded area of the site

Findings

■   **General contamination**

No contamination was detected by the field measurements, which means that any contamination on the surface was less than 10 per cent of the *Reference Level* (or less than 1 g DU/m² assuming superficial deposition on the ground but nevertheless 90 per cent absorption).

■   **Measurements of radiation**

Conditions for detecting contamination, penetrators and fragments were favourable. During on-line and random surveys, the total gamma and beta radiation was continuously measured by the SRAT and Inspector instruments. The gamma background radiation was 0.08-0.10 µSv/h.

■   **Penetrators, jackets and localized points of contamination**

No penetrators, fragments, contaminated spots or enhanced radioactivity was found through gamma and beta measurements. However, it is not impossible that penetrators and fragments exist in the area, but these would be buried deep in the soil.

Depleted Uranium in Bosnia and Herzegovina

> ➤ Han Pijesak Storage Area

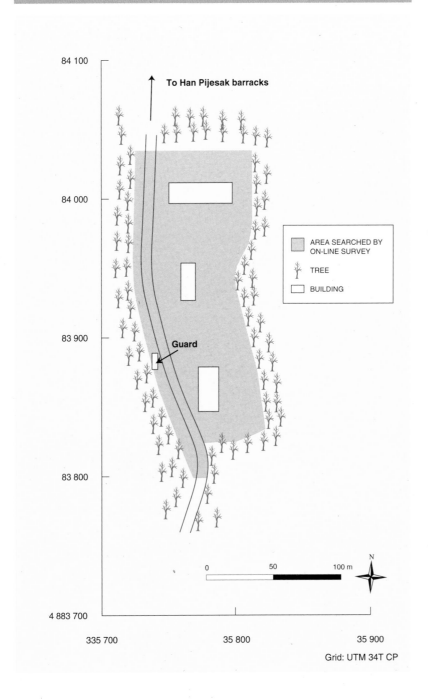

To Han Pijesak barracks

AREA SEARCHED BY
ON-LINE SURVEY

TREE

BUILDING

Guard

Grid: UTM 34T CP

■ **Residual risks**

It is unlikely that any residual risk exists at this site. There is no enhanced gamma or beta radiation and no DU contamination was found on the ground surface. In addition, the site is situated at some distance from inhabited areas.

Need for mitigation - Recommendations

No evidence or indication was found that DU munitions had been used on this site. Neither is there any reason to believe DU was used in the area. Therefore, no specific recommendations relevant to DU are necessary.

7.9 PALE KORAN BARRACKS, 19 OCTOBER 2002

NATO ref:	None www.nato.int/du/docu/d010523b.pdf; NATO Unclassified (C-M (2001) 43)
Coordinates:	34T CP 05530 / 52350
Target:	Barracks and military vehicles
Number of rounds:	Unknown
Area:	The area is a secured military site still in use. No civilian access.
Investigated surface area:	300 m x 150 m
Town/Population:	The population in and around Pale is approximately 30 000. About 30 soldiers reside/work at the site.
Other information:	Rumoured A-10 attack. The site still has a large number of tanks and vehicles, both within and outside the buildings. Some tanks were hit during the attack.

Site description and general information

The barracks are situated about 0.5 km southeast of Pale town. During the war, the site was bombed intensively. Several of the former buildings were wholly destroyed and only concrete slabs remain, while other buildings have since been repaired. The site is currently used by the army as barracks and military storage buildings for tanks, armoured personnel carriers (APCs), guns and army vehicles. The surface of the site is mainly soil.

Field investigation

Most of the site and around the buildings was searched by on-line survey. One building was inspected by random survey, as were areas between most vehicles. No atmospheric aerosol samples were collected as it was raining on site at the time. No mapping was done at the time of the site investigation due to weather and time constraints. The site map is based on NATO maps and the recollections of UNEP personnel.

None of the military vehicles at the Pale Koran Barracks had been hit by DU ordnance

Depleted Uranium in Bosnia and Herzegovina

> **Pale Koran Barracks**

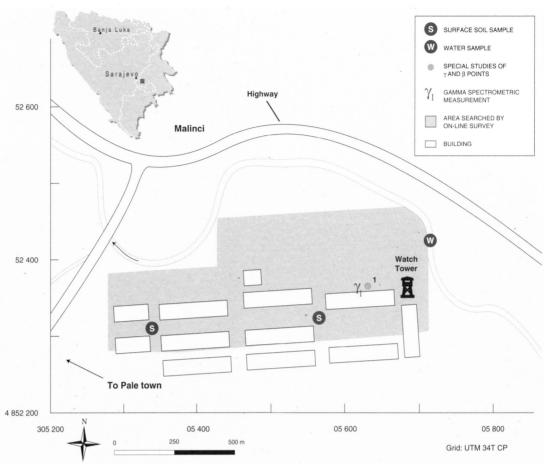

♦ *Map Approximation*

Samples taken included:

- 2 surface soil samples to a depth of 5 cm
- 1 water sample (stream)
- No bio-indicators
- No air filter samples.

Findings

■ **General contamination**

No increased radiation was found other than six contamination spots created by cesium-137 (Chernobyl fallout).

A westward view of the site

■ **Measurements of radiation**

Conditions for detecting contamination, penetrators and fragments were favourable. During on-line and random surveys, the total gamma and beta radiation was continuously measured by the SRAT and Inspector instruments. Background gamma radiation in the areas was 0.04-0.08 µSv/h and the beta radiation background 0-1 cps.

Enhanced gamma radiation was encountered at six spots, all of them beneath drainpipe outlets of buildings that had survived the bombing. Gamma radiation on these spots was up to 0.2 µSv/h. Gamma spectrometric measurements performed on two of the spots revealed that the enhanced gamma radiation was caused by cesium-137, fallout from the 1986 Chernobyl accident. The equivalent uranium concentration at these spots was about 2 mg U/kg.

■ **Penetrators, jackets and localized points of contamination**

No penetrators, fragments or contamination points were found. However, it is not impossible that penetrators and fragments exist in the area, but these would be buried deep in the soil.

■ **Soil samples**

Two surface soil samples were taken from different parts within the fenced site. As there were no indications of impact points on the surface, samples were taken from randomly distributed places over the site surface. No indication of DU contamination was found.

Uranium concentration in the samples was in the range 2.6-3.1 mg/kg of soil. These values are in the normal range of natural uranium concentration in soil. The measured isotopic composition of the uranium was indicative of natural uranium.

Although the site had been attacked during the conflict, no presence of DU was found

■ **Water samples**

One sample was collected from a stream. The uranium concentration was very low and there was no indication of DU.

■ **Residual risks**

It is unlikely that any residual risks exist at this site. There is no enhanced gamma or beta radiation and no DU contamination was found on the ground surface.

Need for mitigation - Recommendations

No evidence or indication was found that DU had been used on this site. Neither is there any reason to believe DU was used in the area. Therefore, no specific recommendations relevant to DU are necessary.

Depleted Uranium in Bosnia and Herzegovina

7.10 VOGOSCA AMMUNITION PRODUCTION FACILITY, 20 OCTOBER 2002

NATO ref:	None www.nato.int/du/docu/d010523b.pdf; NATO Unclassified (C-M (2001) 43)
Coordinates:	34T BP 89300 / 65100
Target:	The Vogosca ammunition production plant. The ammunition production capabilities.
Number of rounds:	Unknown
Area:	Divided into two areas. Front, smaller section is an operational factory with civilian staff. Back, much larger area, with restricted access (not an active part of the factory and heavily destroyed).
Investigated surface area:	The investigated area comprised 400 m x 800 m of the former ammunition production area, which represented the bulk of the facility at the time of attack. Two smaller areas along the road leading to the test range at the far end of the site were also investigated. The full site is roughly 5 km in length.
Town/Population:	The nearby town of Vogosca has a population of 18 000. No residential community is located in the immediate vicinity of the facility, but a small area at the front is operating with an unspecified number of employees.
Other information:	The site, located just north of Sarajevo, can almost be considered a suburb. It is a very extensive (long) site, in a narrow valley, and was heavily hit. The water going through this site also feeds the water supply for Vogosca and possibly Sarajevo. The rear end of the facility contains a former ammunition test range. 13 000 staff worked at the facility during the conflict; only 400 were present at the time of attack.

Site description and general information

The site is a former ammunition production facility. Prior to the war, this complex was one of largest ammunition production plants in this part of the world, with over 13 000 employees. The plant is situated in a narrow valley along the Vogosca River (see map). It occupies a 5 km long area, with factories in the south and storage bunkers along the river. The northern end of the site

This extensive facility once employed over 13 000 people

➤ Vogosca Ammunition Production Plant

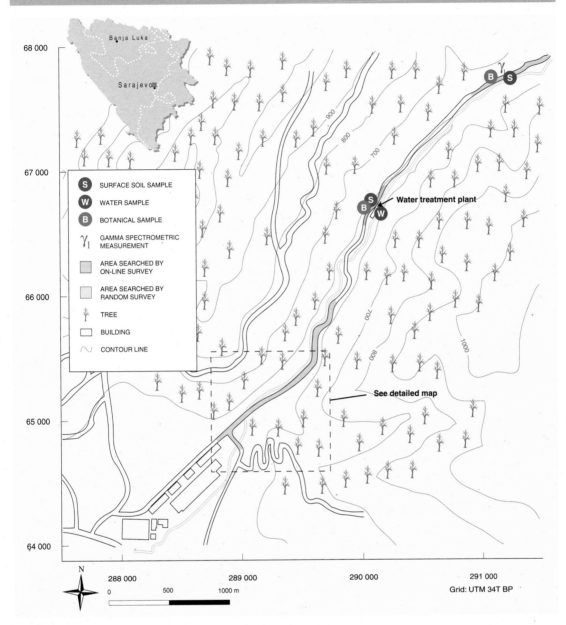

contains a former test range for ammunition. According to local sources, the plant was heavily bombed by A-10 planes during the conflict. Almost all the factories, workshops and bunkers were destroyed. Ammunition in different phases of production was strewn all over the area. Today, only the hard surfaces have been cleared of unexploded ordnance; the rest is inaccessible. The site in its entirety is filled with broken equipment and building materials. The exposed bedrock at the site consists of shale. Otherwise, the ground is covered by soil.

The Federation of Bosnia and Herzegovina (FBiH) authorities, as well as the current facility's Director, were of the belief that DU munitions had also been used as the site had been attacked by A-10 planes. However, A-10 aircraft are also frequently used for bombing.

Field investigation

Due to its large size, the search focused on four different areas. On-line survey investigation was done partially near the operational area accessible to local staff, and fully near the bombed factory, workshops and bunkers (limited access areas - see the detailed map) and at the test range. Random surveys were also done within accessible buildings and on bridges. Random surveys were also conducted on sections of the road leading to the test range, for example at the water treatment plant.

Depleted Uranium in Bosnia and Herzegovina

➤ Vogosca Detailed Map

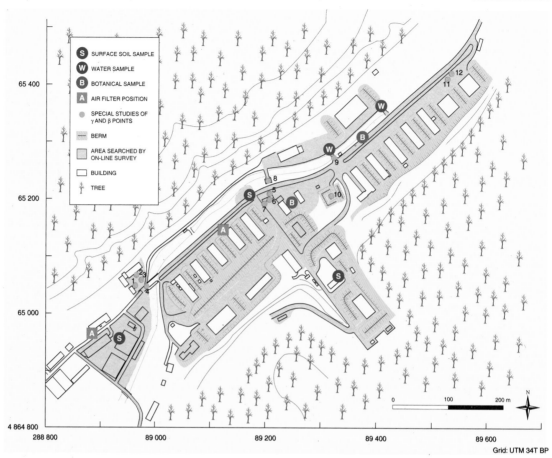

All surveys, with the exception of those on the test range, were restricted to roads and other areas with hard surfaces. On-site analysis of lightning rods showed no radioactivity.

Samples taken included:
- 5 surface soil samples to a depth of 5 cm
- 2 water samples (1 stream and 1 from a former water treatment plant)
- 4 bio-indicators (lichen*, bark, moss, mushroom)
- 2 air filter samples
- (9 smear samples (tape), of which one was studied under Appendix J).

Findings

■ General contamination

No contamination was detected by the field measurements, which means that any contamination on the surface was less than 10 per cent of the *Reference Level* (or less than 1 g DU/m² assuming superficial deposition on the ground but nevertheless 90 per cent absorption).

■ Measurements of radiation

Conditions for detecting contamination, penetrators and fragments were favourable. During on-line and random surveys, total gamma and beta radiation was continuously measured by the SRAT and Inspector instruments. The background gamma radiation was 0.02-0.05 μSv/h and the beta radiation background was 0-1 cps.

One gamma ray spectrometric measurement was performed on soil. The concentrations of natural radioactive elements were: equivalent uranium 0.9 mg U/kg, thorium-232 3.8 mg Th/kg and potassium 1.1 per cent K. A slight contamination by cesium-137 could be detected, fall-out from the 1986 Chernobyl accident.

Special studies of possible DU contamination of surfaces were done by measurements of gamma and beta radiation carried out at 16 locations, on metal, concrete and wood surfaces. In the main part of these locations beta radiation did not exceed 0.3 cps, while two locations were in the range 0.3-1.0 cps.

The many lightning rods throughout the site were used to prevent the live ammunition from being struck

- ■ **Penetrators, jackets and localized points of contamination**

No penetrators, fragments or DU contamination points were found. However, it is not impossible that that penetrators and fragments exist in the area, but if so they are situated within inaccessible parts of the site or buried deep within the soil.

- ■ **Soil samples**

Five surface soil samples were taken from different parts inside and outside the fenced area of the former ammunition factory at Vogosca. As there were no indications of impact points on the surface, samples were taken from randomly distributed places over the site surface. No indication of DU contamination was found.

The uranium concentration of the samples was in the range 1.6-2.0 mg/kg of soil. These values are in the normal range of natural uranium concentration in soil. The measured isotopic composition of the uranium was indicative of natural uranium.

Water samples

Two water samples were collected, one from a stream coming from the water reservoir, and the second directly from the water reservoir. The water flowing through the site is believed to feed the water supply of Vogosca and Sarajevo. The uranium concentration was very low and there was no indication of DU.

Water collected from the former water treatment plant showed no indication of DU

Depleted Uranium in Bosnia and Herzegovina

- **Botanical samples**

The results indicate that there was no presence of DU.

- **Air samples**

Two air samples were taken. Samplers were placed in open areas close to where staff work. No DU was detected in air. The air resuspension factors for this site were found in the range $(5.3\text{-}5.7)\ 10^{-10}\ \text{m}^{-1}$.

- **Heavy metals**

High concentrations of chromium (280-408 mg/kg) and nickel (179-330 mg/kg) were recognized in all selected soil samples from this site. The target values for these metals (based on the Dutch target and intervention values for soil) were exceeded by several factors. Moreover, in most of the samples the intervention values were already reached. Based on these results, a future detailed assessment of the situation concerning heavy metals at this site could be considered (for further information see Appendix K).

Most buildings were completely destroyed during the attack

- **Residual risks**

It is unlikely that any residual risks exist at this site. There is no enhanced gamma or beta radiation and no DU contamination was found on the ground surface.

Need for mitigation - Recommendations

No evidence or indication was found that DU munitions had been used on this site. Neither is there any reason to believe DU was used in the area.

If any evidence appears that DU armaments were used for the attack on the *Vogosca Ammunition Production Plant*, it is recommended that new investigations be carried out to find and clear any DU contamination that may constitute a health risk. However, such an investigation cannot be performed before the site is cleared of unexploded ordnance.

Unexpected high concentrations of chromium and nickel were measured in the soil samples taken. The levels would indicate the necessity of assessing the situation concerning heavy metals in detail. This would allow the whole site or areas of it to be registered as a contaminated site, leading to possible government restrictions on future activities and/or clean-up.

7.11 USTIKOLINA BARRACKS, 21 OCTOBER 2002

NATO ref:	None www.nato.int/du/docu/d010523b.pdf; NATO Unclassified (C-M (2001) 43)
Coordinates:	34T CP 19800 / 28500
Target:	Storage bunkers and one barrack
Number of rounds:	Unknown
Area:	Long and narrow valley. A newly built prison is now on site. Access is not restricted, but due to the mine situation few civilians come through.
Investigated surface area:	2000 m x 150 m
Town/Population:	The population of the on-site prison is 25. The population of Ustikolina is 2 600.

Site description and general information

The site is a former Serb ammunition storage and barracks area roughly 2 km long and situated in a deep valley along the Potok stream. Within the site are many remains of bunkers and storage buildings destroyed during the war. The FBiH authorities believe that DU munitions may possibly have been used.

A newly built FBiH prison is now on the site, housing some 25 people. Along the valley, on both sides, are minefields that have not yet been cleared. Therefore, the investigation was restricted to the hard surface of the dirt track along the stream, the concrete slabs of former buildings, and the open spaces at the prison.

The bedrock of the area is exposed on the sides of the valley and on the dirt track and consists of shale and flysh. The soil is brown, with a mixture of clay, sand and stones.

A new prison is now located on the site which was formerly used to store ammunition

Depleted Uranium in Bosnia and Herzegovina

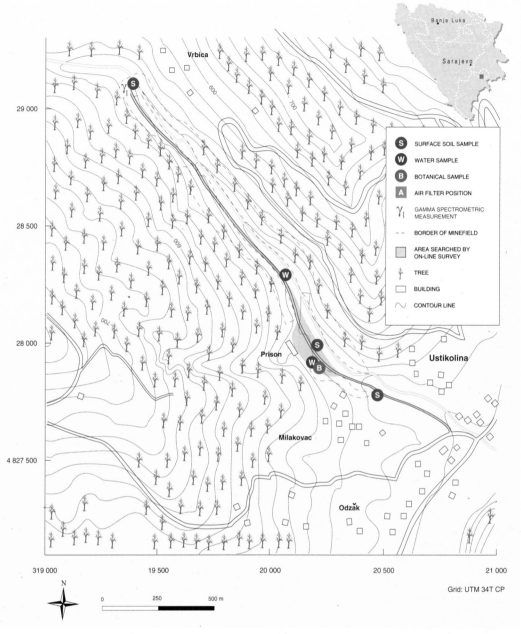

Field investigation

The road surface was searched by on-line survey. Random surveys were carried out along some of the destroyed bunkers and around the existing prison and garden.

Samples taken included:
- 3 surface soil samples to a depth of 5 cm
- 2 water samples (2 tap)
- 1 bio-indicator (lichen*)
- No air filter samples.

Findings

■ General contamination

No contamination was detected by the field measurements, which means that any contamination on the surface was less than 10 per cent of the *Reference Level* (or less than 1 g DU/m² assuming superficial deposition on the ground but nevertheless 90 per cent absorption).

■ **Measurements of radiation**

Conditions for detecting contamination, penetrators and fragments were favourable. During on-line and random surveys, total gamma and beta radiation was continuously measured by the SRAT and Inspector instruments. Background gamma radiation was 0.06 - 0.12 μSv/h and background beta radiation was 0-1 cps.

At the end of the dirt track one gamma ray spectrometric measurement was performed on soil. The concentrations of natural radioactive elements were: equivalent uranium 2.1 mg U/kg, thorium-232 5.7 mg Th/kg and potassium 1.6 per cent K.

No special studies of gamma and beta radiation were made.

■ **Penetrators, jackets and localized points of contamination**

No penetrators, fragments or DU contamination points were found. However, it is not impossible that that penetrators and fragments exist in the area, but if so they are situated within inaccessible parts of the site or buried deep within the soil.

■ **Soil samples**

Three surface soil samples were taken from different areas. As there were no indications of impact points on the surface, samples were taken from randomly distributed places. No indication of DU contamination was found.

The uranium concentration of the surface soil samples was 2.5 mg/kg of soil. This is a value in the normal range of natural uranium concentration in soil. The measured isotopic composition of the uranium was indicative of natural uranium.

A close look at holes in the ground surface

■ **Water samples**

Two tap water samples were collected from taps serving local spring water, the uranium concentrations of which were very low (2.7 mBq/l). There was no indication of DU.

■ **Botanical samples**

A lichen sample was collected from a tree near a small vegetable garden in front of the prison. There was no indication of DU.

■ **Residual risks**

It is unlikely that any residual risks exist at this site. There is no enhanced gamma or beta radiation and no DU contamination was found on the ground surface.

Need for mitigation - Recommendations

No evidence or indication was found that DU munitions had been used on this site. Neither is there any reason to believe DU armaments were used in the area. Therefore, no specific recommendations relevant to DU are necessary.

Depleted Uranium in Bosnia and Herzegovina

7.12 FOCA BRIDGE (SRBINJE), 21 OCTOBER 2002

NATO ref:	None www.nato.int/du/docu/d010523b.pdf; NATO Unclassified (C-M (2001) 43)
Coordinates:	34T CP 20450 / 20480
Target:	Bridge
Number of rounds:	Unknown
Area:	Small bridge on the outskirts of the town. A local Republika Srpska prison is located nearby.
Investigated surface area:	150 m x 150 m
Town/Population:	The population of Foca (Srbinje) is 23 000.
Other information:	The bridge has been repaired since the conflict. Part of the riverbank on the eastern side was filled in with cracked limestone and soil.

Site description and general information

The site is located at the edge of the town of Foca (Srbinje) and includes a bridge spanning the Drina River that was bombed and destroyed during the war. It is suspected that DU munitions may have been used. The bridge was repaired after the war and vehicles can now freely use it. The surrounding abutments were restored, with the land at the eastern abutment filled in by stones, gravel and sand. Any potential penetrators in this area would have been completely covered.

Field investigation

The riverbanks (top and bottom) on both sides of the river were searched by on-line survey. As the water level was low, it was possible to search parts of the riverbed below the bridge. An on-line survey was also completed on the bridge.

The bridge near Foca (Srbinje) spans the Drina river

Post-Conflict Environmental Assessment

➤ Foca Bridge (Srbinje)

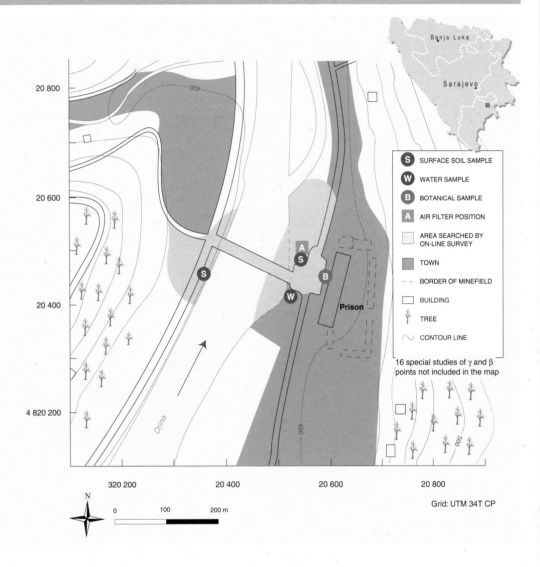

Samples taken included:

- 2 surface soil samples to a depth of 5 cm
- 1 water sample (tap)
- 1 bio-indicator (lichen*)
- 1 air filter sample.

Findings

■ General contamination

No contamination was detected by the field measurements, which means that any contamination on the surface was less than 10 per cent of the *Reference Level* (or less than 1 g DU/m² assuming superficial deposition on the ground but nevertheless 90 per cent absorption).

■ Measurements of radiation

Conditions for detecting contamination, penetrators and fragments were favourable. During on-line and random surveys, total gamma and beta radiation was continuously measured by the SRAT and Inspector instruments. Background gamma radiation was 0.05-0.06 μSv/h and background beta radiation was 0-1 cps.

Depleted Uranium in Bosnia and Herzegovina

Special studies of possible DU contamination of surfaces were done by measurements of gamma and beta radiation carried out at 16 locations, on metal, concrete and wood surfaces. In most areas, beta radiation did not exceed 0.3 cps and at only one location was it in the range 0.3-0.5 cps.

■ Penetrators, jackets and localized points of contamination

No penetrators, fragments or DU contamination points were found. However, it is not impossible that that penetrators and fragments exist in the area, but if so they are situated within inaccessible parts of the site or buried deep within the soil.

■ Soil samples

Two surface soil samples were taken from both sides of the bridge. As there were no indications of impact points on the surface, samples were taken from randomly distributed places. No indication of DU contamination was found.

The uranium concentration of the samples was in the range 2.6-3.1 mg/kg of soil. These values are in the normal range of natural uranium concentration in soil. The measured isotopic composition of the uranium was indicative of natural uranium.

■ Water samples

One tap water sample was collected in a nearby restaurant. No indication of DU was found.

■ Botanical samples

A sample of lichen was taken in front of the prison. No indication of DU could be found.

■ Air samples

One air sampler was placed in the open field near the bridge. No DU was detected. The air resuspension factor for this site is $1.5 \ 10^{-9} \ m^{-1}$.

■ Residual risks

It is unlikely that any residual risks exist at this site. There is no enhanced gamma or beta radiation and no DU contamination was found on the ground surface.

Need for mitigation - Recommendations

No evidence or indication was found that DU munitions had been used on this site. Neither is there any reason to believe DU armaments were used in the area. Therefore, no specific recommendations relevant to DU are necessary.

Special surface contamination studies were undertaken at 16 locations both near and on the bridge

Post-Conflict Environmental Assessment

7.13 KALINOVIK WATER RESERVOIR, 21 OCTOBER 2002

NATO ref:	None www.nato.int/du/docu/d010523b.pdf; NATO Unclassified (C-M (2001) 43)
Coordinates:	34T BP 93330 / 20570
Target:	Water reservoir/pumping station
Number of rounds:	Unknown
Area:	Open area on hilltop used for grazing. Small cemetery nearby.
Investigated surface area:	150 m x 200 m
Town/Population:	The population of Kalinovik at the base of the hill is 3 500.
Other information:	Altitude 1 135 m. The site was probably mistaken for a military site, but could have been a gun or radar position. Access is completely unrestricted and open.

Site description and general information

The site is situated on a hill about 1 km northwest of Kalinovik town centre. Two structures remain from the water reservoirs that were destroyed. The surrounding area is pastureland. A small cemetery is located at the edge of the site. The FBiH authorities believe that DU ammunition was possibly used on this site.

The entire hill is soil covered. Boulders show that the underlying bedrock consists of limestone.

Field investigation

The area around the water reservoirs was searched by on-line survey. Random surveys were carried out around and immediately behind the former water pumping station. No mapping was done at the time of the site investigation due to time constraints. The site map is based on the recollections of UNEP personnel and photographs.

The destroyed water reservoir was most likely mistaken for a bunker

Depleted Uranium in Bosnia and Herzegovina

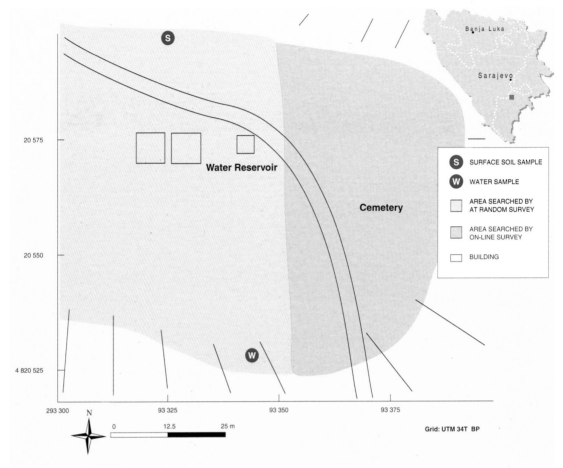

♦ *Map Approximation*

Samples taken included:

- 1 surface soil sample of 5 cm
- 1 water sample (from the small stream running off from the reservoir)
- No bio-indicators
- No air filter samples.

Findings

■ General contamination

No contamination was detected by the field measurements, which means that any contamination on the surface was less than 10 per cent of the *Reference Level* (or less than 1 g DU/m^2 assuming superficial deposition on the ground but nevertheless 90 per cent absorption).

■ Measurements of radiation

Conditions for detecting contamination, penetrators and fragments were favourable. During on-line and random surveys, total gamma and beta radiation was continuously measured by the SRAT and Inspector instruments. Background gamma radiation was 0.05-0.06 µSv/h and background beta radiation was 0-1 cps.

Special studies of possible DU contamination of surfaces were done by measurements of gamma and beta radiation carried out at two locations, on metal and concrete surfaces. In all of these locations beta radiation did not exceed 0.3 cps.

Looking down onto the town of Kalinovik from atop the water reservoir

- **Penetrators, jackets and localized points of contamination**

No penetrators, fragments or DU contamination points were found. However, it is not impossible that that penetrators and fragments exist in the area, but if so they are situated within inaccessible parts of the site or buried deep within the soil.

- **Soil samples**

Only one surface soil sample was taken due to time constraints. As there were no indications of impact points on the surface, the sample was taken from a flat place in a meadow near the position of the ruined target. No DU contamination of soil was found.

The uranium concentration of the surface soil sample was 4.5 mg/kg of soil. This is a value in the normal range of natural uranium concentration in soil. The measured isotopic composition of the uranium was indicative of natural uranium.

- **Water samples**

One water sample was collected from a runoff stream coming from the remains of the water reservoir. The uranium concentration was very low and there was no indication of DU.

- **Residual risks**

It is unlikely that any residual risks exist at this site. There is no enhanced gamma or beta radiation and no DU contamination was found on the ground surface.

Need for mitigation - Recommendations

No evidence or indication was found that DU munitions had been used on this site. Neither is there any reason to believe DU armaments were used in the area. Therefore, no specific recommendations relevant to DU are necessary.

Depleted Uranium in Bosnia and Herzegovina

7.14 KALINOVIK AMMUNITION DESTRUCTION SITE, 21 OCTOBER 2002

NATO ref:	None
Coordinates:	34T BP 91660 / 18330
Target:	None
Number of rounds:	None
Area:	This is a large, open area in a rugged, rocky part of the landscape. Difficult of vehicle access, but not restricted.
Investigated surface area:	300 m x 300 m
Town/Population:	The population of Kalinovik town (some 3 km away) is 3 500.
Other information:	French SFOR uses the site for the destruction of ammunition/unexploded ordnance. There are many large karst holes in the area and some of these have been used for the destruction of the ammunition. Altitude 1 025 m.

Site description and general information

The site is situated on plain about 3 km southeast of Kalinovik town centre and is used for the destruction of ammunition/unexploded ordnance. The site was investigated as it was thought feasible that mine clearing teams could have collected penetrators and fragments and potentially included them among the ammunition and unexploded ordnance destroyed here. UNEP investigated whether this was true and if any remaining DU penetrators were to be found on the site.

The site is comprised of several small and large karst holes. Some have been used for the destruction of ammunition/unexploded ordnance by placing the items at the bottom of the holes and then detonating them. The area is usually cleared of the larger pieces of scattered ammunition. However, some unexploded grenades could still be found and the area was not considered safe. This hindered the search for DU inside the karst holes and surveying was limited to the perimeter of the holes.

The large karst holes in this area are used to detonate ammunition

➤ Kalinovik Ammunition Destruction Site

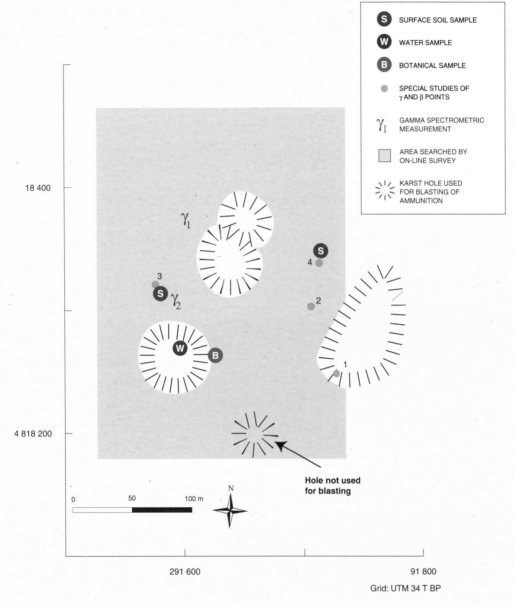

S	SURFACE SOIL SAMPLE
W	WATER SAMPLE
B	BOTANICAL SAMPLE
●	SPECIAL STUDIES OF γ AND β POINTS
γ_1	GAMMA SPECTROMETRIC MEASUREMENT
▢	AREA SEARCHED BY ON-LINE SURVEY
☼	KARST HOLE USED FOR BLASTING OF AMMUNITION

Hole not used for blasting

Grid: UTM 34 T BP

The bedrock of the area is exposed limestone outcrops. The soil layer is thin and is made up of red laterite.

Field investigation

The site was fully searched around the karst holes by on-line survey.

Samples taken included:

- 2 surface soil samples to a depth of 5 cm
- 1 water sample (bottom of karst hole)
- 1 bio-indicator (lichen*)
- No air filter samples.

Depleted Uranium in Bosnia and Herzegovina

Findings

■ General contamination

No contamination was detected by the field measurements, which means that any contamination on the surface was less than 10 per cent of the *Reference Level* (or less than 1 g DU/m^2 assuming superficial deposition on the ground but nevertheless 90 per cent absorption).

■ Measurements of radiation

During on-line surveys, total gamma and beta radiation was continuously measured by the SRAT and Inspector instruments. Background gamma radiation was 0.04-0.08 μSv/h and background beta radiation was 0-1 cps. The conditions for detecting contamination, penetrators and fragments were favourable.

Gamma spectrometric measurements were made on red lateritic soil at the locations of the soil samples. The concentration of the natural radioactive elements were: at BP 91586/18312, equivalent uranium 1.9 mg U/kg, thorium-232 11.4 mg Th/kg and potassium 0.7 per cent K; at BP 91714/18346, equivalent uranium 1.7 mg U/kg, thorium-232 13.1 mg Th/kg and potassium 0.7 per cent K.

Special studies of possible DU contamination of surfaces were done by measurements of gamma and beta radiation carried out at four locations, on metal, concrete and wood surfaces. In all of these locations beta radiation did not exceed 0.5 cps.

■ Penetrators, jackets and localized points of contamination

No penetrators, fragments or contamination points were found. If penetrators had been among the ordnance destroyed, they would have been scattered all around the karst holes and have remained on the ground unless picked up during site cleaning.

■ Soil samples

Two surface soil samples were taken from different parts of the site. As there were no indications of impact points on the surface, samples were taken from randomly distributed places. No presence was found of DU in soil.

The uranium concentration of both surface soil samples was 3.1 mg/kg of soil. This is a value in the normal range of natural uranium concentration in soil. The measured isotopic composition of the uranium was indicative of natural uranium.

■ Water samples

A sample of water was collected from the body of water at the bottom of one of the karst holes. Although the uranium concentration was higher than that found in the sample collected at the *Kalinovik Water Reservoir*, there was still no indication of DU.

■ Botanical samples

A lichen sample was collected from a rock by a crater. No indication of DU was detected.

■ Heavy metals

The soil sample NUC-02-031-002 showed high contamination of zinc (1 900 mg/kg), arsenic (90 mg/kg), cadmium (6 mg/kg) and lead (1 000 mg/kg). The target values for these metals (based on the Dutch target and intervention values for soil) were exceeded by several factors. Moreover, in most of the samples the intervention values were already reached.

The other soil sample (NUC-02-031-003) showed an indication of contamination by heavy metals of the neighbouring environment. The water sample also showed heavy metals contamination.

The overall picture from this analysis suggests a detailed assessment be carried out concerning the heavy metals present at this site, the more so since it is situated in a karstic region and might be the source of streams and rivers supplying drinking water. For more information see Appendix K.

■ **Residual risks**

It is unlikely that DU penetrators were among the ammunition/unexploded ordnance that was destroyed. There was no enhanced gamma or beta radiation and no DU contamination was found on the ground surface.

On-line survey was completed with care to avoid any UXO. No increased radiation was detected

Need for mitigation - Recommendations

It is unlikely that DU penetrators were among the ammunition/UXO that was blasted at the investigated site. However, the whole site was not fully investigated due to its size and the danger of unexploded ordnance. Thus, it is possible that in some places penetrators and fragments may exist. It is not advisable to destroy DU penetrators by blasting them and this situation should be avoided.

With respect to heavy metals, the site should be further investigated and possible mitigation considered. It is recommended that such sites be placed in a restricted environment and away from any water sources.

Depleted Uranium in Bosnia and Herzegovina

7.15 BJELASNICA PLATEAU - AMMUNITION DESTRUCTION SITE, 22 OCTOBER 2002

NATO ref:	None
Coordinates:	34T BP 61950 / 42420
Target:	None
Number of rounds:	None
Area:	High plateau with pine forest cover.
Investigated surface area:	300 m x 600 m
Town/Population:	The population is limited to three houses located approximately 2 km below the plateau. Civilians leave the area during the winter season.
Other information:	Altitude 1 220 m. The site is unguarded, but not easy of access, and is situated at some distance from any large population. A number of craters have been formed due to explosions, and others have been filled in. Ammunition destruction was stopped a few weeks before the UNEP investigation as villagers below the hillside began to complain about poor water quality and health problems. They linked this to the ammunition destruction activities.

Site description and general information

The site is situated on the *Bjelasnica* high plateau. SFOR and the Ministry of Civil Protection have used this site for the destruction of ammunition/unexploded ordnance by blasting. A number of craters have been formed as a result, some of which have subsequently been filled in. Some 220 tons of unexploded ordnance have been destroyed here. The site was investigated as it was thought feasible that mine clearance teams could have collected penetrators and fragments and potentially included these among the munitions destroyed. UNEP investigated whether this was true and if any remaining DU penetrators were to be found on the site.

Craters have been created for the destruction of ammunition on this remote site

➤ Bjelasnica Plateau

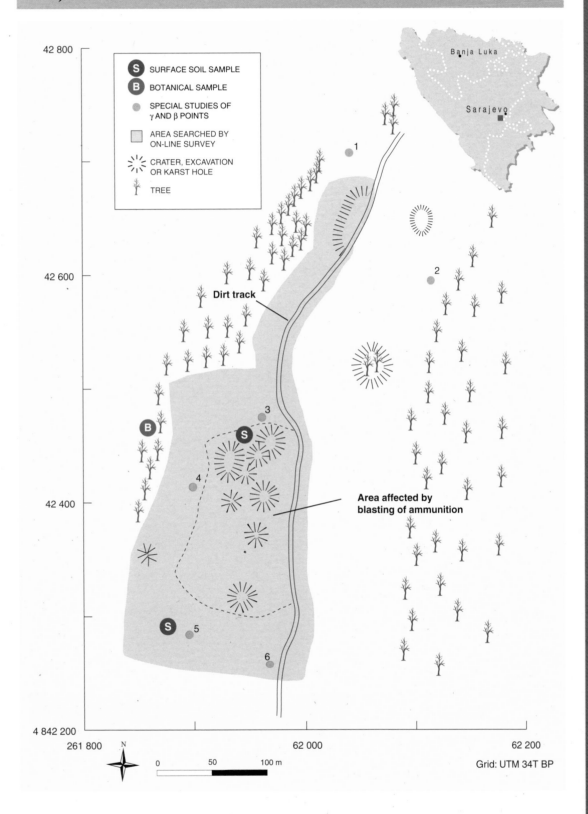

Depleted Uranium in Bosnia and Herzegovina

Several karst holes are situated in the area, two are close to the site where the ammunition was blasted. The area was cleaned of scattered pieces of ammunition after blasting. However, some fragments were still spread around the area and the craters were not considered safe. This hindered the search for DU presence inside the crater holes.

The bedrock of the area is limestone exposed in several outcrops. The soil is brown-red laterite.

Field investigation

The area around the craters was searched by on-line survey.

Samples taken included:
- 2 surface soil samples to a depth of 5 cm
- 2 water samples (1 from a drinking fountain and 1 from a stream some distance from the site)
- 1 bio-indicator (lichen*)
- No air filter samples.

Lichen was readily available onsite

Findings

■ General contamination

No contamination was detected by the field measurements, which means that any contamination on the surface was less than 10 per cent of the *Reference Level* (or less than 1 g DU/m² assuming superficial deposition on the ground but nevertheless 90 per cent absorption).

■ Measurements of radiation

During on-line and random surveys, total gamma and beta radiation was continuously measured by the SRAT and Inspector instruments. Background gamma radiation was 0.05-0.06 μSv/h and background beta radiation was 0-1 cps.

Special studies of possible DU contamination of surfaces were done by measurements of gamma and beta radiation carried out at six locations, on metal, concrete and wood surfaces. In all of these locations beta radiation did not exceed 0.3 cps.

■ Penetrators, jackets and localized points of contamination

No penetrators, fragments or contamination points were found. If penetrators had been among the blasted ordnance, they would have been scattered all around the karst holes and have remained on the ground unless picked up during site cleaning.

■ Soil samples

Two surface soil samples were taken from the ammunition destruction site. As there were no indications of impact points on the surface, the samples were taken from two different places near the craters, one from the north, and the other from the south. No presence of DU was found in soil.

The uranium concentration of the surface soil samples was in the range 1.7-2.6 mg/kg of soil. These values are in the normal range of natural uranium concentration in soil. The measured isotopic composition of the uranium was indicative of natural uranium.

■ Water samples

Both water samples were collected at locations along the road leading uphill from the village of Zovic to the site. One sample was taken from a drinking fountain that supplies spring water and the other from a stream. Uranium concentrations were very low and there was no indication of DU. However, none of the samples are likely to contain water from the destruction site.

■ **Botanical samples**

One lichen sample was taken from a tree in front of one of the craters. There was no indication of DU in the sample taken.

■ **Heavy metals**

In both samples from this site (NUC-02-035-001 and -002), a high contamination of copper (in the range of 2 000 mg/kg), zinc (~460-1 650 mg/kg) and lead (~290-600 mg/kg) could be measured. The situation is similar to the one mentioned above for the Kalinovik Ammunition Destruction Site (7.14). However, what is alarming in the results for this site - in addition to the lead contamination - is the very high copper concentration in the samples taken (for more information see Appendix K).

■ **Residual risks**

It is unlikely that DU penetrators were among the ordnance that was blasted. There was no enhanced gamma or beta radiation and no DU contamination was found on the ground surface.

Need for mitigation - Recommendations

It is unlikely that DU penetrators were among the ammunition/UXO that was blasted at the site. However, all of the site was not fully investigated. Thus, it is possible that in some places penetrators and fragments could exist. It is not advisable to destroy DU penetrators by blasting them and this situation should be avoided.

With respect to heavy metals, the site should be further investigated and possible mitigation should be considered. It is recommended that such sites be placed in a restricted environment and away from any water sources.

7.16 THE BOX OF DU PENETRATORS

One of UNEP's tasks was to investigate the history and location of the box containing DU penetrators, fragments and jackets/casings originally located at the former *Hadzici Tank Repair Facility* site (see 7.1). Workers at the site informed UNEP that the box had been collected by SFOR in the spring of 2001 and they believed that it had been taken to one of the SFOR camps. Despite numerous enquiries, additional information concerning the location of the box was not forthcoming from SFOR, local workers or the authorities.

The box of retrieved DU munitions by SFOR

However, continuing investigations led UNEP to believe that the box could have been taken to one of the ammunition destruction sites and duly destroyed. Field investigations at the two sites mentioned by the authorities (see 7.14 and 7.15) showed no indication of DU.

The mystery surrounding the box continued until a meeting was held at NATO headquarters in Brussels in November 2002. As the box represented a potential health risk, the situation concerning its unknown whereabouts, contents or its disposal was raised with NATO officials who advised that they would look into the matter. Shortly thereafter, NATO indicated by fax that:

> *In April 2001, the Multi National Division (North) collected DU held by Multi National Divisions, with the aim of transferring it to US national facilities outside of Bosnia and Herzegovina for disposal. The transfer was completed at the end of April 2001.*

This note confirms that the box was officially removed from the country and is no longer a risk consideration for Bosnia and Herzegovina.

Depleted Uranium in Bosnia and Herzegovina

APPENDIX A

Risk Assessment

A.1 THE CONCEPT OF 'RISK'

'Risk' is a word which is frequently used, yet holds a variety of different meanings. At times, it can imply the **probability** of occurrence of an event that is understood to be unpleasant or detrimental, such as the risk of getting the flu. Everyone knows what 'flu' implies and is mainly concerned with the 'risk' (i.e. the probability) that they will get it.

Another meaning relates more directly to the **consequence** of an event or situation. For example, in response to the question 'what are the risks of radiation?', a typical answer from the non-scientific community might be 'getting cancer'. Alternatively, in saying that the radiological/radiation risk of a given situation is small, it is usually meant that the radiation doses, and therefore the health consequences in terms of the number of adverse effects, are likely to be small.

A third meaning —and perhaps the most appropriate one— is a combination of assessment of **probability and consequence** used to guide the choice of an appropriate response to a given situation. For instance, if one is judging whether information on an approaching flu epidemic should change travel plans, both the probability of catching the flu, and the likely consequences of doing so, are taken into account in the decision-making process.

For this report, the second meaning of risk is the dominant one when used in connection with a given event, situation or scenario. If probability is also included in the judgement, then the third meaning is used.

To complicate things further, an additional factor is the difference between actual risk and the notion of risk. This is a highly complex issue that will not be developed in detail here. However, it is clear that scientific quantification of a given risk has to be expressed comprehensibly, so that the risk can be conceived in a way that favours appropriate judgement and responses. In a report such as this, it is important that the quantification of a given risk remain as objective as possible. One possible way of judging the consequences of radioactivity levels is to compare findings and measurements with natural levels, given limits and standards, in addition to so-called 'action or intervention levels' (levels above which action is deemed necessary).

Through such comparisons, it should be possible to express the risk as small, significant, or large, having in mind the basis for comparisons. However, technical comparisons alone are not enough to justify decisions and responses. Relevant economic and social factors must also be considered, as well as the probability of occurrence.

In this report, the possible radiological and toxicological consequences (from the chemical toxicity of DU) of events in a given scenario are often dealt with in terms of possible intake of DU by ingestion and inhalation, as well as possible external exposure to radiation from DU.

In the case of radiation risks, the consequences can also be expressed as radiation doses, quantified as 'effective committed dose' or 'annual effective dose'. The name of the unit is sievert (Sv), usually expressed as 'millisieverts' (mSv or 10^{-3} sievert) or 'microsieverts' (μSv or 10^{-6} sievert). The comparisons are made with:

- natural levels of radiation and intakes of uranium;
- limits of radiation doses to the public;
- so-called action levels for an existing contamination or radiation situation;
- doses that are considered to be trivial; and
- with doses that are expected to give deterministic effects.

These values are given in *Appendix O 'Data on Uranium'*.

In the case of chemical risks, the consequences are expressed as resulting concentrations of uranium in air, water and food and as intake by inhalation and ingestion. Comparisons are made with natural concentrations and intakes, with limits and hygiene standards for water, air and food, as well as with concentrations that are expected to give acute biochemical effects in humans. Again, these values are provided in Appendix O.

A.2 METHODS OF RISK ASSESSMENT

The method of risk assessment used and the precision of the assessment should be adjusted to the assessment's objective. If the objective is to estimate the consequences of an event as close to the real conditions as possible, it is necessary to use realistic models, parameters and input data. This translates as special requirements in terms of accuracy and quality of measurements and assessments.

If, on the other hand, the objective is to verify the existence or non-existence of radiation or a radioactive, chemically toxic pollutant above a level that is of concern —DU in this case—, more approximate models may be applicable as long as the assessments are based on conservative assumptions and the models do not underestimate the consequences. If, by chance, the result of a given assessment is ambiguous or close to the level that would trigger concern, a more precise assessment is advisable.

Any assessment will, in some way, be faulty. This is particularly true for those based solely on models. It is therefore always necessary to supplement the theoretical assessments with practical measurements if a high degree of accuracy is needed.

A.3 THE APPLICATION OF THE RISK ASSESSMENT METHODS TO BiH

The objectives of the mission to Bosnia and Herzegovina are defined in Chapter 3. Measurements and collection of samples were planned to support the subsequent risk assessments while keeping in mind the theoretical results given in the October 1999 UNEP/UNCHS Balkans Task Force (BTF) Report – *'A preliminary assessment'*. Assessments in that report were based on conservative safety assumptions with regard to conditions of exposure to DU, but with realistic assumptions about the resulting doses and chemical effects. Some of the theoretical results were ambiguous and the resulting consequences in some parts of the assumed scenario were close to levels of interest from a health viewpoint. More sophisticated models did not help in this case due to poor input data.

In this report, as well in UNEP's 2001 Kosovo and 2002 Serbia and Montenegro reports, the scenario described in the 1999 theoretical assessment is used as the *Reference Case*. The assumed activity levels are translated to corresponding measurement results by calibration and used as input data in the comparison with measured ground contamination. The method is described below.

In the Kosovo and Serbia and Montenegro reports, it was concluded that the measurement values corresponding to the *Reference Case* were well above the level detectable with the field instruments chosen. Thus, zero results imply a sufficient margin of safety before thresholds of possible concern from a health viewpoint are reached.

In the 1999 theoretical assessments of the health consequences in various scenarios, conservative assumptions
were often used and the time during which the DU had
been on/in the ground at a given stage was not relevant.
However, the quality and presence of DU in a defined
part of the environment may have changed over the years
due to the corrosion of DU penetrators, dispersion in
ground, new or re-use of the ground (e.g. construction
building, farming), assuming the same initial contamination of penetrators and DU dust. The results of the
measurements may, accordingly, be different as a function of time. Therefore, any quantitative conclusions
of the initial amount of DU in the area must be made

**Gamma measurement of a cesium
contamination spot**

with caution. However, in the interpretation of the measurement results in terms of risk to
people, the same relations apply as in the *Reference Case*. In particular, the conclusions of zero
measurement results would not be affected.

Therefore, the method of assessment is applied to the use of the *Reference Case*, also for the
current situation in BiH roughly 7 years after the 1994-95 NATO strikes. As DU is the same
as natural uranium in many respects, and all results up to now indicate very low concentrations of DU in the ground, it appears appropriate to make comparisons with natural uranium
in the assessments of radiological and chemical consequences. Theoretical environmental
dispersion models are used only exceptionally because of insufficient measurement data and
knowledge of the local geochemical and geohydrological properties.

A.4 THE APPLICATION OF THE REFERENCE CASE
       IN THE RISK ASSESSMENTS

The *Reference Case* from the UNEP DU Desk Assessment Report (1999) is defined as follows:

> *"It is assumed that an attack includes 3 aircraft and the total DU used in the attack is 10 kg.
> The target is one or several vehicles and the area affected by the subsequent DU contamination
> is 1 000 m². The impact of DU on soldiers and civilians in the vehicles and on the affected
> area during the attack is not specifically considered. The chemical and radiological impact
> during the attack is probably small as compared with the consequences of explosions and fire.
> However, the survivors may have been seriously exposed to depleted uranium, in addition to
> the consequences of explosion and fire.*
>
> *Most of the dust that is caused by explosions and fire is assumed to settle on the ground within the
> area of 1 000 m². It is assumed that someone very close to the target at the time of attack would,
> for a short time, be instantaneously exposed to the DU dust cloud, which probably has a very high
> DU concentration. 100 mg DU/m³ air is assumed.*
>
> *After some time people may enter the area which will then be cultivated. By entering the area
> people cause resuspension of DU dust in the air, breathe contaminated air, are contaminated by
> touching objects in the area, and are externally exposed from solid DU pieces of the ammunition on
> or in the ground that are picked up.*
>
> *Some of the DU will be dissolved in water in the ground and contaminate the groundwater that
> serves a nearby well.*
>
> *Some animals will graze in the area, be contaminated and eventually be used as meat and
> contaminate people.*
>
> *By dispersion, a small part of the DU dust will, in the long-term, be spread over larger areas."*

From these conditions, possible exposures were estimated. These referred to the situation that might have occurred in the time shortly after the attack. In that respect, the conclusions are still valid.

At the time of the October 2002 mission to BiH, over 7 years had elapsed since the end of the military conflict. Rain and snow would have partly washed away the superficial ground contamination; there may have been some DU corrosion and migration into the ground, the groundwater may have been contaminated; people would have – in different ways – disturbed the environmental conditions by moving contaminated soil, objects, etc.

Background radiation at most sites was within normal ranges

The chief purpose of the UNEP mission was to assess the situation from both short- and long-term perspectives based on the current situation. Due to the length of time lapsed since the conflict, many of the possible exposures which occurred in 1994-95 could not be investigated and are irrelevant for the purposes of this report.

Table A.1 summarises the changes concerning issues of interest. The inclusion of 'Same' in the second column does not mean that the risks are quantitatively the same as in 1994-95, but that the means of exposure are the same and have to be considered in the risk analyses. The eight means of exposure to date, and their subsequent consequences, are described below. If the consequences as described in the *Reference Case* are ambiguous or close to limits, standards, or any other value of relevance, the actual values of contamination at the visited sites at the time of visit (i.e. October 2002) must be at least a factor of ten below the *Reference Case* values. The reason for this is that one should be certain that the contamination does not exceed any limits or standards or that the consequences are of no concern.

Table A.1   Comparison of possible means of DU exposure in 1994-95 and from late 2002 onwards

Means of exposure in 1994-95	Means of exposure from late 2002 onwards
(a) Solid pieces of DU picked up	Same
(b) Inhalation of re-suspended DU	Same
(c) Soil in mouth	Same
(d) Contaminated hands	Same
(e) Contaminated water	Same
(f) Contaminated food	Same
(g) External radiation	Same
(h) Activity spread over large areas	Same
(i) Rounds that passed through or missed the target and might contaminate groundwater	Same. The risks refer to (a) or (e)
(j) Instantaneous inhalation of DU dust after an attack	Not applicable
(k) Surface-contaminated vegetables	Not applicable
(l) Open wounds	Not applicable

* Items (a) - (h) are discussed in order of appearance in section A.5. Items (i) - (l) are not discussed here.

Depleted Uranium in Bosnia and Herzegovina

A.5 THE RISKS IN THE REFERENCE CASE

Comparisons to natural levels, limits etc. refer to *Appendix O 'Data on Uranium'*. All radiation doses refer to pre-teenage boys (7-12 years), which means that the doses to children less than one year old may be up to five times higher per unit of intake. In practice, the doses to very young children are less than this due to lower intake. The dose to adults is two times lower than that to pre-teenagers per unit of intake. The means of exposure (a) – (h) refer to Table A.1.

(a) Solid pieces of DU picked up

The only significant external exposure may be by beta radiation. The gamma radiation is very weak and alpha radiation cannot penetrate the skin layer. The surface radiation dose rate is about 2 mSv/h. If a piece of DU is placed in a pocket, the beta radiation is somewhat reduced (50 % reduction is assumed). The exposed skin area will therefore be quite small.

By keeping a piece of DU in a pocket for several weeks, it might be possible that the skin dose will exceed values corresponding to the limit for the public (50 mSv/year) and workers (500 mSv/year). It is not feasible that there will be any deterministic effects (skin burns) even though the skin dose might be high. The gamma radiation may give a radiation dose to tissue close to a piece of DU kept in a pocket. The gamma dose rate at different distances from a penetrator containing roughly 300 g DU has been measured and the approximate dose rates are shown in Table A.2. Considering 0.1 m as the closest distance of significance, it would need more than 1 000 hours of continuous exposure until the organ dose approached the natural annual gamma radiation dose to that organ.

Table A.2 External gamma dose rate from a DU penetrator (300 g DU)

External dose rate (µSv/h)	Distance from the penetrator (m)
2.7	0.05
0.85	0.1
0.25	0.2

Another means of exposure in picking up a piece of DU, such as a penetrator, is contamination of hands from loose activity on the surface of the penetrator. Smear tests have shown that less than 10 mg of DU is lost, which might be a good indicator of possible hand contamination from touching a penetrator. The subsequent possible intake into the mouth would be more dependent on bad hygiene than intentional ingestion. Therefore, the probable intake would be 10 - 100 times less than 10 mg (i.e. 0.1-1 mg of DU).

An intake of 10 mg would lead to a value of about 7 µSv, which is an insignificant dose. An intake of 10 mg DU is considerably above generic standards for daily intake (WHO, 1998) but less than the corresponding annual intake. If the intake is 100 times less, it approaches the WHO limit. Acute heavy metal toxic effects from uranium might occur if the amount of intake is higher by a factor of 10 times or more than 10 mg (see the 1999 UNEP DU Desk Assessment Report).

Penetrator fragments can be easily picked up

The conservative estimation of risk lies in the assumption of an intake of 10 mg DU.

If a penetrator is heavily corroded, there is a risk that in picking it up the hands will be contaminated with more than 10 mg of DU. Assuming very bad hygiene, the highest probable intake would be 1 g of DU (compare point (c) below) which would result in radiation doses up to 1 mSv effective dose, but would lead to acute heavy metal toxic effects. Furthermore, if the penetrator is placed in a pocket and subsequently removed, there is a risk of contamination of the pocket. Consequences would include continuous exposure of the skin under the pocket, although less than with a penetrator in the pocket, a repeated contamination of the hand every time it is put into the pocket, followed by a risk of ingestion and internal contamination. The radiological consequences would be repeated exposures of less than 1 mSv each day, which is an unacceptable scenario, particularly from the toxicological point of view.

The overestimation of risk lies even more in this case in the assumption of an intake of 1 g of DU. The probable intakes would be expected to be much less than 1 g.

Another risk of exposure from a heavily corroded penetrator is by inhalation. One has to be careful in handling such a penetrator to avoid corroded DU from becoming airborne. Inhalation of 10 mg of DU might lead to significant doses (greater than 1 mSv).

The conservative estimation of risk lies in the assumption that the corroded DU is easily airborne and that the amount of inhaled DU is 10 mg

(b) Inhalation of resuspended DU

In the *Reference Case* it is assumed that 10 kg DU is spread over 1 000 m², i.e. 10 g/m². Through wind action, walking around in the area, or digging etc., dust from the ground may become airborne and be inhaled. All DU is assumed to be present in the form of small particles (less than 10 μm) and to be in the form of insoluble oxides (Type S), which are only slowly cleared from the lungs.

DU is mixed with soil on the ground and – for the purpose of assessment – it is assumed that a soil layer 1 mm thick includes all the DU contamination, all of which will become airborne dust. With the assumption of 10 kg DU spread over 1 000 m², the top 1 mm of soil in this area contains 1 m³ of soil, weighing 1 500 kg. The DU concentration in the dust will therefore be 6 μg DU per 1 mg dust.

Normal dust concentration in outdoor air is 50 μg/m³ and under very dusty conditions may reach 5 mg/m³, which would result in DU concentrations of 0.3 μg/m³ and 30 μg/m³ of DU respectively. From a toxicological point of view, these levels are lower than or within the range of given hygiene standards for chronic exposure.

A two-hour stay in a dusty area, such as a field being ploughed, with a respiration rate of 1 m³ per hour, would lead to an intake of 60 μg of DU, corresponding to an effective dose of 7 μSv.

Even a continuous stay night and day for a year under the dustiest of conditions would not lead to a dose of more than a few tens of mSv. Normal dust conditions would result in a dose that is 100 times less, i.e. of the order of 0.1 mSv per year. The heavy metal risks are, in all cases, insignificant.

The conservative estimation of risk lies in the assumptions that all DU is breathable, of Type S (see Appendix O), and that all DU is distributed in the upper first mm of soil. If, for instance, the measurements should indicate that the DU, if any, is distributed to a depth of 10 cm

instead of 1 mm, the radiation doses would again be 100 times less (a few μSv per year) with the same area of deposition (10 kg over 1 000 m²), which is insignificant.

(c) Soil in mouth

The concentration of DU in soil is assumed to be 6 mg DU/g soil (see above). At most, 1 g of soil is assumed to be ingested, leading to an intake of 6 mg DU which corresponds to an effective dose of 4 μSv. Acute heavy-metal toxic effects from uranium might occur with amounts roughly ten times higher than this.

The same conclusions can be drawn in the case of a contamination point containing DU-contaminated soil or sand.

The overestimation of risk lies in two assumptions:

1. In the general case, DU is assumed to be distributed in a 1 mm thick layer of soil. If it is found to be thicker the corresponding doses are proportionally smaller.
2. In the case of a contamination point, the conservative estimation of risk lies in the assumption that someone (a child) would dig soil out of the hole and eat it (a low probability)

(d) Contaminated hands

Hands can be contaminated by touching contaminated objects, clothes etc. The risk then lies in ingesting any contamination during meals, etc. However, as in the case of contamination from a penetrator (see (a)), the intake is further dependent on poor hygiene than intentional ingestion, which is more or less the case of soil in mouth (case (e)). Therefore, the amount is assumed to be 10–100 times less than in case (e), with the doses correspondingly less (i.e. less than 1 μSv). This corresponds with no risk of any acute heavy-metal toxic effect, although it may be close to the Tolerable Daily Intake (TDI) (WHO, 1998). With the same corrected assumptions described above, there is no special overestimation of risk.

(e) Contaminated water

Contamination of drinking water may result from migration of soluble uranium to the groundwater that serves as a water reservoir for small private drinking water and/or irrigation wells or large drinking well-water fields. Due to the complexity of DU mobility in the soil, a valid risk assessment estimation of the short- and long-term impact to the groundwater from the DU contamination can only be meaningful once a number of interrelated factors has been investigated and evaluated:

1. Initial ground-surface contamination, as well as any penetrators buried at each site. The contribution to the total load of uranium to the groundwater will naturally depend on the amount of DU ammunition per m².

2. Information is required on the geochemical and hydrological properties of the relevant soil in order to estimate the rate of oxidation, adsorption, solubility and transport of dissolved DU to the groundwater. Some data and discussion of uranium behaviour in natural environments is provided in *Appendix D 'DU in Soil'* and *Appendix E 'DU in Water'*.

3. Quantitative information is required on the 'water mass balance' including; the yearly rainfall, the surface runoff, evaporation and trans-evaporation in order to evaluate the potential for transporting DU to the groundwater.

4. In order to evaluate a potential impact of DU on groundwater quality, the measurements from potential affected areas must be compared with natural background levels of

uranium in water and in the soil/rock through which the water is passing. A number of measurements of uranium in drinking water and in soil in non-affected DU contaminated areas were made in BiH. The arithmetic mean of U-238 in water is 40 10⁻⁵ mg/L (0.4 µg/L) and in soil 3.34 mg/kg. These values calculate the relation between the concentrations in water compared to the one in soil to be 10⁻⁴, considering that this value might be valid for naturally occurring uranium

To make a first approximation of the risk to groundwater, it is necessary to base the calculations on assumptions which are conservative in nature in order to minimise the possibility of underestimating possible short- and long-term health problems. At the same time, the calculations should not be unrealistic in order to avoid raising unjustified concerns and/or recommending unjustified mitigation measures. From the radioactivity viewpoint, U-238 is the radionuclide of concern for groundwater, and theoretical calculations indicate that this will still be so even after 1 000 years.

In the *Reference Case*, it is assumed that 10 kg of DU is spread over 1 000 m². Assuming 3 m depth to the water table, the total volume of soil that might be contaminated by dissolved DU will be 3 000 m³, which is about 5 000 tons. In this amount of soil the natural uranium content will be 17 kg, corresponding to the measured water uranium concentration of 40 10⁻⁵ mg/L water. 10 kg DU over this area would mean an increase of about 60 % and a corresponding increase of uranium in drinking water assuming DU behaviour is the same as natural uranium.

The uncertainty is the solubility of DU compared with that of natural uranium. If it is more soluble, the uranium concentration in water will increase by more than 60 %. The maximum number of penetrators fired at any specific site within BiH was 2 400, representing 720 kg of

DU. The areas affected were of a maximum size of 800 x 400 m (i.e. 300 times the *Reference Area*). This would lead to a roughly 15 % increase of uranium in drinking water (if DU behaves like natural uranium).

The *Reference Case* in the assumption of the contamination by uranium through rainfall is based on a yearly dissolution of 10 % (1 kg) of DU ammunition and washing out to the groundwater.

Stream water is sampled near Hadzici Barracks

This DU Assessment report reveals that this *Reference Case* is not realistic as penetrators are now known to corrode completely within 25-35 years. A linear approach results in the corrosion of penetrators buried in the ground of about 3-5 % per year. It is now also shown that the corrosion products are not very soluble in the surrounding soil conditions found. Assuming that 1 % of the corrosion products could be dissolved and transported down by rainwater to the groundwater, it would still have to be taken into consideration:

- that 20 % is capillary water and will not contribute to the replenishment of the groundwater; and

- the surface run-off, evaporation and trans-evaporation result in approximately 30 % of rainfall reaching the groundwater.

In a single year, the rainfall is approximately 0.5 m, leading to a total of 500 m³ over the *Reference Area* of 1 000 m². About 150 m³ could therefore reach the groundwater each year. This volume – in the *Reference Case* – if not absorbed by the soil, could carry 3 g of DU. Assuming a groundwater reservoir (aquifer) of 1 000 m³, this would lead to a contamination of this aquifer of 3 μg/L per year. The WHO guideline value of 2 μg/L would then be exceeded.

Field instruments helped identify radioactive sources

These levels were not measured in BiH, indicating that adsorption to the soil takes place resulting in a reduced mobility of DU by a number of decades. The contribution to the total load of uranium to the groundwater will naturally decrease or increase if the amount of DU ammunition per m² varies from the *Reference Case*. Another conservative element is the assumption that the size of the catchments area for rainwater to the groundwater reservoir. The *Reference Case* is limited to the soil column immediately below the affected ground surface. It is more likely that the catchments area is larger, leading to a lower concentration of uranium in the water.

It is shown that the only risk for groundwater contamination is the composition of the soil in which the penetrators remain. In BiH, none of the investigated sites had a greater specific ground contamination (g DU per m²) in average than in the *Reference Case*.

In addition, by comparing natural uranium levels in drinking water, values vary for ground water from 0.0001 to 0.014 mg/L (UNSCEAR, 1993) with exceptionally high values (e.g. in Finland) of up to 10 mg/kg in some drinking water. In comparisons with these, the normal values of uranium in drinking water at the places visited in BiH are low.

Conclusion:

If the amount of DU dispersed over an area of approximately 1 000 m² is much less than 10 kg (the *Reference Case*), depending on the composition of soil, it is improbable that there will be a problem with DU contamination of drinking water.

(f) Contaminated food

Over seven years after DU ground contamination, there may still be an intake of DU (although very small) through ingestion of contaminated food, assuming that there is some cultivation on site. This may be from vegetables, fruits, etc. which are contaminated indirectly by root uptake of DU, or from milk and meat from animals that have eaten contaminated plants and soil. These long-term consequences can be assessed in comparison with natural levels of U-238.

With regard to the contamination of plants (and then meat) by root uptake, the following relationship can be used (UNSCEAR, 2000):

35 Bq/kg soil of U-238 leads to a total intake from food and water of 5.7 Bq of U-238 per year, resulting in an effective dose of 0.25 μSv per year. The contribution from U-234 is about the same. In DU, the relative activity of U-234 is only 20 % of that in equilibrium and the resulting dose from DU in the ground with 35 Bq/kg soil of U-238 and 7 Bq/kg soil of U-234 (corresponding to 3 mg uranium/kg soil) will accordingly be 0.25+0.05 = 0.3 μSv per year.

10 kg DU spread over 1 000 m^2 and distributed in a soil layer 10 cm deep (a reasonable assumption from the measurements in Kosovo) is assumed to be available to plant roots. This corresponds to a concentration of 70 mg DU/kg soil (870 Bq/kg) if the density of soil is 1 500 kg/m^3 and will result in an effective dose by ingestion of 7 μSv per year. The corresponding toxicological risks are insignificant.

An uncertainty is the DU uptake factor. Natural uranium has a plant/soil concentration ratio of 10^{-4} to 10^{-3}. The low resulting dose caused by ingestion (about 10 μSv/year) will allow more than 100 times more effective root uptake for DU than natural uranium before the doses begin to be significant.

If, at some location in BiH, the DU ground contamination is as in the *Reference Case* and remains very close to the surface, the uptake by animals may be substantial (mainly by 'consumption' of soil). A large animal may consume up to 0.5 kg of soil every day. If the DU contamination in this case is distributed in a soil layer only 0.5 cm deep, the worst case is the consumption of 0.5 kg of this layer, corresponding to about 0.1 m^2 contaminated ground. This implies a daily consumption of 1g of DU by the animal, which is most likely unhealthy for the animal. People eating the meat (and drinking milk from cows) will probably be exposed to a higher intake than the 'Tolerable Daily Intake' (TDI). The radiation doses will be less than 1 μSv per day from such meat or milk consumed.

The underlying assumptions are very conservative for this particular case. However, it can be concluded that grazing animals should be kept away from (potentially) contaminated areas (at a level corresponding to the *Reference Case*) where contamination is still close to the surface.

Conclusion:

If the ground contamination is at the level of the *Reference Case* and distributed to a depth of at least 10 cm, there is no problem from either chemical or radiological viewpoints. In the case of close surface contamination of the same order of magnitude, some mitigation measures might be discussed. If the contamination level is less than 10 % of the *Reference Case*, no problem exists.

(g) External radiation

The same deposition is assumed, i.e. 70 mg DU/kg soil over 1 000 m^2. Natural uranium (3 mg/kg soil) in the level of equilibrium that exists in soil, gives 17 nGy per hour or an effective dose of 0.02 mSv per year (corrected for indoor occupancy 0.8 and conversion factor Sv/Gy of 0.7). The gamma radiation from DU is only 0.8 % of that of natural uranium. Therefore, the resulting dose from 10 kg DU over an area of 1 000 m^2 would be (0.02/3) x70 x0.008 mSv per year = 4 μSv per year.

The 'Theoretical assessments of external radiation from DU' was given in an appendix of the 2002 Serbia and Montenegro report (UNEP, 2002) using a computer code RESRAD-6.

Conclusion:

If the ground contamination by DU is the same as in the *Reference Case*, or even increased by a factor of 10, the external radiation will not be a problem to the local population.

(h) Activity spread over large areas

A wider dispersion than assumed in the *Reference Case* means a larger area than assumed and all possible consequences in terms of individual doses will decrease proportionally.

A.6 THE REFERENCE CASE AND CORRESPONDING MEASUREMENT VALUES

Field beta measurement

The assessments are made assuming the *Reference Case* as defined in the October 1999 UNEP DU *Desk Assessment* report (UNEP/UNCHS, 1999). By calibration, the following relations apply (measurements carried out using the 'Inspector' instrument; see *Appendix C 'Methodology and Quality Control'*).

(a) Sensitivity of detection

- No absorption

$$10 \text{ kg DU}/1\,000 \text{ m}^2 = 10 \text{ g/m}^2 = 100 \text{ mg/dm}^2 \text{ gives } 120 \text{ cps}$$

- Absorption

With DU covered by dust, grass etc., there is only slight absorption. Assuming 90 % absorption, the readings will consequently be reduced by a factor of ten and will probably not underestimate the surface contamination. This means that in the 10 kg/1 000 m² from the *Reference Case* gives 12 cps.

(b) Detection limit

- Surface contamination

Random survey at Lukavica site

The detection limit is dependent on the sensitivity and the background of the instrument. With the instrument used, the background with normal natural background radiation is 0.1-1 cps using the count rate meter. The detection limit is defined as double background, i.e. 1 cps.

Assuming no absorption (which might be true for a short time after the initial contamination), the limit of detection would be:

$$1\% \text{ of the Reference Case or } 100 \text{ mg DU/m}^2 = 1\,240 \text{ Bq/m}^2 \text{ corresponding to } 1 \text{ cps (nett)}$$

Assuming some absorption (< 90 %), the limit of detection would be:

$$10\% \text{ of the Reference Case or } 1\,000 \text{ mg DU/m}^2 = 12.4 \text{ kBq/m}^2 \text{ corresponding to } 1 \text{ cps (nett)}$$

- The activity is distributed in a soil layer 10 cm deep.

The *Reference Case* signifies surface contamination of 10 kg DU/1 000 m² or 100 mg DU/dm². If the activity is evenly distributed to a limited depth of 10 cm, the activity in the upper layer will be detected with a field beta measurement. 1 mm efficient depth is used in the assessment (1 mm corresponds to about 150 mg/cm² leading to about 60 % absorption of the beta radiation).

In the 1 mm layer there is 1/100 of the total activity, i.e. 1 mg/dm² = 12.4 Bq/dm² = 1 240 Bq/m² corresponding to 0.5 cps with 60 % absorption, which is just below the detection limit with field beta measurement.

Conclusion:

If the activity is evenly distributed in a soil layer 10 cm deep, not less than a factor of two to five times the activity of the *Reference Case* can be detected (i.e. not less than 20 - 50 kg DU/ 1 000 m² or 20 - 50 g DU/m² or 200 - 500 mg DU/dm²). If the activity is distributed in a deeper layer of soil, the detection limit is proportionally higher. If the activity is covered with thick layer of leaves, dust or soil nothing will be detected.

The contribution of the gamma radiation from DU is still minor, about 1 % of the natural background.

Soil sample measurement sensitivities

The overall sensitivity for detecting DU in a soil sample is dependent on the uncertainties of the laboratory analyses and measurements, and on the uncertainties of the natural background content of uranium in the sample. Background measurements show that the overall uncertainty (variation) for each individual team member and site is around 10 % (1σ).

Using the ratio R = U-235/U-238 by weight as an indicator of DU (see *Appendix O 'Data on Uranium'*) the samples containing DU can be identified. If the detection limit of DU in a sample is defined as 20 % above the average background value, and the background is measured to be 20 Bq U-238/kg soil, the detection limit would be 4 Bq DU/kg soil. By 20 % the R value is clearly DU-indicative.

Assuming the *Reference Case* activity is distributed to a depth of 10 cm means 70 mg DU/kg soil or 830 Bq U-238/kg soil. 4 Bq DU/kg soil means 0.005 or approximately 1 % of the *Reference Case*, or 0.1 g DU/m².

Conclusion:

In laboratory measurements the limit of detection is 0.01 of the *Reference Case* or 0.1 g DU/m².

One penetrator (right) and two penetrators still fixed in their jackets. The left penetrator has partly moved from its position in the jacket.

Depleted Uranium in Bosnia and Herzegovina

A.7 SUMMARY

The results of the risk assessments are summarised in Table A.3.

Table A.3 The risks from different sources and means of exposure

Means of exposure → Source of exposure ↓	Inhalation		Soil in mouth		Contaminated hands		Contaminated water		Contaminated food		External radiation	
	Rad	Chem	Rad	Chem	Rad	Chem	Rad	Chem	Rad	Chem	Rad	Chem
Penetrators etc. (>30)	Na	Na	Na	Na	Ins	S	Ins	→S	Na	Na	S (β) Ins(γ)	Na Na
Contamination spots <10g U/kg soil	Na	Na	Ins	S	Ins	S	Na	Na	Na	Na	Ins	Na
Ground/surface-contamin. ≥ RC On surface In 10cm layer	Ins Ins	Ins Ins	Ins Ins	S Ins	Ins Ins	S Ins	Ins/S* Ins/S	S S	Na Ins	Na Ins	Ins Ins	Na Na
Ground/surface-cont. = 0.1 RC On surface In 10 cm layer	Ins Ins	Ins Ins	Ins Ins	S Ins	Ins Ins	Ins Ins	Ins Ins	S S	Na Ins	Na Ins	Ins Ins	Na Na
Ground/surface-cont. = 0.01 RC On surface In 10 cm layer	Ins Ins	Ins Ins	Ins Ins	Ins Ins	Ins Ins	Ins Ins	Ins Ins	Ins Ins	Na Ins	Na Ins	Ins Ins	Na Na

Comments:
A 'significant' (S) level of exposure or risk does not mean that at that level there are major adverse consequences such as serious illness. On the contrary, at the levels given above there would still be large margins before an unconditionally unacceptable situation was reached.However, by surpassing these levels there should be a degree of concern, since it might be justified and necessary to do something about the situation, at least in the long run. In the case of 'insignificant' (Ins) levels there is no reason whatsoever to be concerned.

Explanations:

Rad =	radiological aspects
Chem =	chemical toxicity aspects
>30 =	greater than 30 penetrators
→S =	may approach a significant level of exposure when number of penetrators increases or the potential exposures increase by other reasons
Na =	not applicable
Ins =	insignificant levels of exposure/risk (less than 1 mSv, less than WHO standards/guidelines)
S =	significant levels of exposure/risk (greater than 1mSv, greater than WHO standards and close to acute risks)
RC =	Reference Case = 10 kg DU/1 000 m² = 10 g DU/m²
On surface =	the contamination is superficial in the upper mm of the ground surface
In 10 cm layer =	the contamination is distributed in the upper 10 cm of the soil layer

APPENDIX B

Prerequisites and Limitations

B.1 THE OBJECTIVES

The objectives of the mission defined the minimum work requirements to be completed (see Chapter 3.1). Some of the tasks were performed during the field mission to Bosnia and Herzegovina (BiH); others were completed in laboratories following the mission, and some through the publication of this report. In short, all of the mission's objectives were met.

Evidently, by setting certain objectives, other tasks had to be excluded by default. The consequences are summarised as follows:

Not all places were visited

NATO air attacks during which DU ammunition was used are known for ten locations in BiH, although only 5 of these sites are identified with full coordinates. Four of these confirmed sites were investigated by UNEP, as one of the sites was inaccessible due to the heavy presence of anti-tank mines leading to the site. During investigations, the sites were surveyed for DU contamination and some of the penetrators, penetrator fragments and jackets found were removed, others were covered in soil. The sites investigated are assumed to be representative for all DU sites. If the results of the mission had varied significantly, it would have been very difficult to make any truly representative conclusions. However, where the results from each site were broadly similar, particularly those related to possible environmental contamination, general conclusions could be drawn. The criteria for site selection applied by the UNEP team are further described in Chapter 3.3.

NATO/SFOR authorities had investigated the sites earlier

Since 1999, significant efforts have been undertaken in the Balkans region by international expert teams with NATO support in order to localize and measure contamination from DU on the ground (see www.nato.int/du/docu/d010523b.pdf). Those teams covered a range of sites that stood under SFOR troop jurisdiction. Dose rate measurements were conducted and, in some cases, different environmental samples such as soil and water were taken. These were analysed in detail mainly by gamma spectrometric measurements and other chemical parameters. The teams essentially detected no risk from DU at the sites. Some of these previously examined sites were also subject to the UNEP assessment presented here.

NATO had previously been involved in limited clean-up activity at an unspecified time to remove loose DU contamination (i.e. penetrators and jackets) from the ground surface at one of the sites visited during the UNEP mission - the former *Hadzici Tank Repair Facility* (see www.nato.int/sfor/indexinf/105/s105p03a/t0101243a.htm). These previously undertaken and important clean-up activities would impact the UNEP assessment in terms of achieving a complete overall scientific picture of contamination at a specific site.

Limited access

In ensuring the safety of the team, the main concern was the risk of mines and unexploded ordnance (UXO) that were still present in many of the sites investigated and adjacent areas. Sometimes the risks of UXO and minefields limited the extent of investigations. To improve safety, UNEP was advised by its own security advisor as well as the local BiH Mine Action Center (MAC).

Food measurements

The only reliable and scientifically correct way to make general conclusions on food safety would be to collect and measure representative 'food baskets' from markets. However, the sites investigated are either restricted military sites or pastureland and not used for arable agriculture, with the exception of Pjelugovici, which had a small crop of apple trees. From earlier assessments it is concluded that it is very unlikely that contamination of food would be a problem or concern. It would be easy, however, to undertake such collection and measurement in the future in order to confirm this conclusion.

No people were measured and no health examination

Until an extensive and credible health examination programme is implemented, it is probable that rumours and suspicions about the health implications of DU exposure will persist, irrespective of statements to the contrary. Due to the lack of a proper cancer registry and reporting system, claims of an increase in the rates of adverse health effects stemming from DU cannot be substantiated.

The question of health studies has been taken up by the WHO in the report Depleted Uranium - Sources, Exposure and Health effects (WHO, 2001). The WHO undertook an assessment of the information on cancer in BiH (see Appendix L).

B.2 POSSIBLE CONSEQUENCES OF A SEVEN-YEAR DELAY

Potential exposure

In the UNEP/UNCHS report of October 1999 'The potential effects on human health and the environment arising from possible use of depleted uranium during the 1999 Kosovo Conflict: A preliminary assessment', it was recommended that:

*   Further measurements should be organised, with highest priority given to finding fragments of DU, heavily contaminated surfaces and other 'hot spots'.
*   DU fragments, heavily contaminated objects and loose contamination should be collected and removed. Authorised personnel should undertake this work under controlled conditions.
*   Any collected DU should be stored in safe conditions under the responsibility of a designated authority.
*   At contaminated sites signs should be posted to forbid public access.
*   Access by grazing animals should be curtailed using fences.
*   Local authorities and people concerned should be informed about the results.
*   A programme of measurements, countermeasures and waste disposal should be developed.

These recommendations had not been implemented at any of the sites visited by UNEP. Since the countermeasures had not been undertaken, and not all site coordinates are known, risks of exposure to DU remain today.

The consequence of changed conditions for the mission

Over the seven-year period between the military conflict and the UNEP mission, the conditions for finding DU had changed significantly. A possible scenario and its consequences are described below:

1. Penetrators and DU fragments on the ground surface could be covered by soil, grass and/or other organic matter. If these are covered by several cm of soil, field measurement instruments cannot detect the solid DU.

2. Penetrators and DU fragments on the ground surface were taken away by members of the local population and/or by military personnel. Consequently, the mission would not find these objects.

3. Soil, grass and/or other organic material cover ground surfaces contaminated by DU dust. If the ground surface is covered by several mm of soil, DU will not be detectable by beta field instruments.

4. DU dust originally dispersed over a specific area has been moved by wind, rain and/or melting snow. If the dust was displaced by wind, contamination would be dispersed over large areas and therefore diluted to a degree that the mission would be unable to detect it. Displacement of DU by rain or melting snow would result in dispersion into the ground. However, DU is expected remain in the top layer of surface soil (e.g. usually 10 cm and less than 15 cm). Contamination would then be found through soil sample analyses.

5. If the ground surface is composed of concrete or asphalt (i.e. hard surfaces), DU dust would likely have been swept away a certain distance and been absorbed by adjacent soil or be carried into a ditch, stream or river. Soil contamination would be found through soil sample analyses. Due to dilution, contamination of ditch, stream or river waters would be low and below the detection limits.

6. Contaminated vehicles were removed and their locations remained unknown.

Depleted Uranium in Bosnia and Herzegovina

APPENDIX C
Methodology and Quality Control

C.1 STRATEGIES

UNEP's strategy for site selection was initially based on NATO information concerning the strike coordinates and target type for locations where DU ordnance was fired (Appendix P). In addition to these NATO confirmed sites, further sites were chosen based on information provided by local authorities, institutions and civilians during a fact finding pre-mission which took place on 5-14 September 2002. See also Chapter 3.3. During the subsequent mission planning stage, final decisions were made by UNEP on which sites to visit and on how to organise the work to reach optimal results.

The selection of specific study areas and central matters of interest on each site, taking into consideration the mine and unexploded ordnance situation for each area, was prepared in Geneva and confirmed by the UNEP team upon arrival in the field. The fieldwork in Bosnia and Herzegovina (BiH) covered sites in both the Federation of Bosnia and Herzegovina (FBiH) and the Republika Srpska (RS).

The field mission in (BiH) had one significant difference to the previous missions: roughly 7 years had elapsed since the military conflict and the subsequent environmental contamination of DU. In that time, DU might have been moved or removed, corroded, hidden by soil, leaves and grass, etc. This had to be kept in mind during planning, in the assessments and, particularly, in drawing conclusions from the results.

The choice of specific study areas at each site was based on the following considerations:
a. Presence of marks on the ground made by penetrators and/or cluster bombs.
b. Probable direction of the air strike.
c. Locations of former destroyed vehicles and gun emplacements.
d. Drinking water sources and other nearby surface waters.
e. Cleared from mines. Minimal risk of unexploded ordnance (UXO).
f. Adjacent settlements and buildings.
g. Information from local people about areas of probable interest (if possible, based on their own observations during the military conflict).
h. Other points of particular interest from a scientific point of view (e.g. a variety of environmental conditions).

The central matters of interest for each site were chosen based on the principle that the mission would concentrate on those areas where it was realistic to expect any evidence and/or results to be available, and where it was possible for the mission to investigate given the mine and UXO situation. In line with this approach, certain matters of interest had to be excluded; for example, deeply buried penetrators could not be investigated due to the impossibility of undertaking major excavations. The main issues examined were:

a. Widespread and localized surface soil contamination;
b. Penetrators/jackets on the surface;
c. Penetrators/jackets covered only by grass or a thin layer of soil/sand/mud;
d. Penetrators/jackets buried somewhat deeper in the ground (i.e. top 15 cm of soil);
e. Contamination points/"hot spots" (contaminated penetrator holes, impact marks);
f. DU transport to deeper soil layers;
g. DU contamination of water;

Post-Conflict Environmental Assessment

h. DU presence in bio-indicators;

i. DU contamination of air (re-suspension); and

j. DU traces found within any buildings, etc.

The specific areas investigated at each site are marked on the site maps contained in Chapter 7.

The organisation of the on-site work was dependent on the tasks to be fulfilled, available resources, safety and time. The strategy was to be as flexible as necessary, in order to maximise the results of the mission as a whole. To that end, short briefings were made upon arrival and in the middle of each site visit (usually around lunch time), so that the organisation of the work could be changed if needed. The UNEP team was organised in sub-teams to proceed as efficiently and competently as possible. These sub-teams included:

- Field Survey sub-team
- Soil sampling sub-team
- Air sampling sub-team
- Water/Vegetation/Bio-indicator sampling sub-team
- Medical/health sub-team.

In addition, the team was supported at all times by the experts from the BiH Mine Action Centre (MAC) with the aim of giving the proper advice concerning the mine situation in certain areas of interest for a specific sub-team. Security was complemented by following strict orders from UNEP's own safety officer to be disciplined, observant and careful during site investigations.

C.2 METHODS AND SURVEY TECHNIQUES

C.2.1 General overview

In choosing both methods and techniques, a major requirement is that these be suited to meet the objectives and strategies decided upon. They also have to match the mission's prerequisites and limitations (Appendix B). Furthermore, field instruments set the boundaries of the techniques that can be used.

Methods and techniques must be adaptable to the specific characteristics of a given area such as:

(a) Topography - different techniques have to be applied - it is not possible to survey irregular or broken ground in the same way as a flat field, village, or garden etc.

(b) Surface conditions - in soft ground, uranium dust may have dispersed into the ground; a penetrator that has missed the target could easily have penetrated deep into the ground; there may be grass and other vegetation shielding the beta radiation etc., but soil sampling is possible and useful. With hard surfaces such as rock or concrete, there are different conditions and possibilities. Thus, methods and techniques have to be adjusted accordingly.

(c) Probability of finding DU at a given location - if it is known with relative certainty that DU has been used in a given area, then the field survey is conducted in a strict and systematic manner. In the other cases, the measurements are made more at random, based on visual observations or indications in 'suspicious' areas.

(d) Presence of mines and unexploded ordnance (UXO) - the only areas examined on site were those declared as safe, meaning that the area had been searched for mines and UXO. Without clearance from the mine experts (MAC), no sampling took place.

C.2.2 Fieldwork

During the fieldwork, experts from the BiH Mine Action Centre (MAC) accompanied UNEP. In certain cases where access to closed/restricted sites was necessary, an SFOR officer also escorted the team. Once on site, a short examination of the area was made. After a detailed briefing by the team leader, security adviser, scientific leader, technical leader and MAC expert, the choice of areas to be investigated and methods to be used was made. Generally, the soil and vegetation/water sub-teams began specific sampling procedures following visual observations and examination of the site in close cooperation with the MAC expert. Within the first hour on site, the air sampling sub-team installed air filter pumps and started air sampling for periods usually exceeding four hours. The remaining team members comprised the field survey sub-team and undertook survey measurements using the different techniques described in sections C.2.3 and C.2.4. The technical leader had the responsibility of mapping the site area, based on positions obtained by Global Positioning System receivers (GPS). The accuracy of these positions was usually better than ± 10 m.

C.2.3 Measurements in the field

■ Methods

For the radiometric measurements during surveys for DU, the following methods are applicable:

● a) Gamma radiation

For a gamma survey with the purpose of identifying radiation slightly higher than the background, the requirement is that:
– the instrument is sensitive enough to measure the gamma background (e.g., NaI crystal detector with channel integrated total counts);
– it is relatively insensitive to varying gamma energies;
– it gives a quick response (a short time constant) to gamma radiation;
– it gives a sound signal the intensity of which increases with the radiation intensity;
– it is insensitive to the direction of radiation;
– it is insensitive to rain, humidity and temperature (down to -20° Celsius);
– it is robust but light.

Gamma spectrometric differential measurements using, for example, solid-state detectors can give information on which radioactive gamma emitting isotopes exist in the surveyed area. Such measurements can also be used to distinguish between natural occurring uranium and depleted uranium. However, gamma spectrometric measurements take several minutes to perform at each position. Therefore they are used to gain information on radioactive isotopes at spots of special interest. For example, solid-state detectors such as HP Ge-detectors need cooling with liquid nitrogen.

In the case of field measurements, such instruments can only be considered as complementary equipment for special measurements. However, if the background of natural radioactive elements (uranium, radium, thorium or potassium) is enhanced, gamma ray spectrometric measurements are needed to distinguish between gamma radiation emitted from DU and that from naturally occurring radioactive elements or gamma radiation from contamination of cesium-137 fallout from the 1986 Chernobyl accident.

The unit of measurement is not decisive, but units of cps and μSv/h (or μGy/h) are preferable. The instrument should meet the ordinary ISO standards, be well calibrated, and its 'normal' background should be known.

The gamma instrument is used to identify penetrators, other solid pieces of DU and highly contaminated surfaces i.e. 'hot spots'. It is normally not sensitive enough to detect slightly contaminated areas (less than 10 Bq/cm^{-2}).

- **b) Beta radiation**

Beta radiation field measurement instruments are normally of the GM (Geiger-Müller) or proportional chamber type with thin windows to permit beta radiation to enter the sensitive detection chamber. The efficiency is high for beta radiation energies above 0.5 MeV, about 30 % up to 2 cm above a small source (the window of the beta instrument).

The purpose of using a beta instrument is to discover surface contamination, contamination points, and penetrators, providing that none are covered by more than a thin layer of grass, leaves or dust. Otherwise, beta radiation will be absorbed and undetected by the instrument. The detection window should not be too small; a diameter of at least 5 cm is recommended.

When necessary, it should be possible to shield the window easily in order to measure gamma radiation only. For example, this may be required in order to determine whether the measured activity is superficial or at some depth. Without a shield, both beta and gamma radiation are measured.

The instrument should be light but robust, give a quick response to beta radiation, give an audible signal which increases in power in line with radiation intensity, and should be insensitive to rain, humidity and temperature. The instrument, particularly the thin window foil, needs to be protected against dirt and DU contamination. Covering the instrument with a thin plastic bag easily accomplishes this and will not reduce the beta response by more than about 10 %.

The unit of measurement recommended is cps (μSv/h or μR/h can be used in case of gamma measurements). The instrument should meet ordinary ISO standards and be well calibrated (cps per Bq cm^{-2} for surface contamination or cps per Bq for contamination spots or sources).

- **c) Alpha radiation**

Although DU emits alpha radiation, it is impractical to measure this radiation using field techniques as it is easily blocked by a thin layer of dust, grass (or similar). Furthermore, its range in air is of only a few cm. Resulting measurements would therefore be unreliable. Consequently, no alpha measurements were carried out.

C.2.4 Instruments and Equipment

■ **Measurements of radiation in the search for DU penetrators and DU contamination**

Because emitted gamma radiation from uranium in general and DU in particular is rather weak (Appendix O), a significant increase above natural background gamma radiation only occurs in the vicinity of intact penetrators or large pieces of DU, and where the ground surface has been heavily contaminated with DU dust. Even with a sensitive gamma meter based on scintillation, it is not possible to measure a significant increase in gamma radiation further than about 50 cm away from a penetrator lying on the ground (depending on the type of instrument used and the gamma-ray background at the location in question).

Beta radiation from DU is rather strong (about 50 % of the beta radiation emitted during the whole of the uranium-238 series emanates from protactinium-234m). However, as the beta radiation is absorbed by air, the radiation from a penetrator or contamination of the ground decreases rapidly with distance. Thus, in order to measure the emitted beta radiation the detector must be close to the object emitting the radiation.

The range of alpha radiation in air is only a few cm, even less if the DU is covered by a thin dust layer or organic matter. For this reason, the detector must be held very close to the object, and it is therefore not practical to search for DU by alpha radiation field measurements.

■ Instruments used

During the mission to BiH three different instruments were used. The mission was supplied with gamma meters and beta counters rented from the Swedish Radiation Protection Authority (SSI).

From the SSI, 15 scintillometers of type Saphymo-SRAT S.P.P.2 NF were used by UNEP for the measurements of gamma radiation. They were selected for the mission due to their high sensitivity, effective sound-alarm and durability. The Saphymo-SRAT S.P.P.2 NF scintillometer is manufactured by Saphymo-PHY, Massy, France (Saphymo-SRAT 1969). It is designed for uranium exploration in rugged conditions. The detector is a 1 x 1.5 inch (15.2 cm³) NaI(Tl) (sodium iodide activated with thallium) scintillation crystal. The operation range for gamma radiation is 0.02 to 30 microsieverts per hour (µSv/h). The instrument has a built in audible alarm that gives a high signal. The

Saphymo-SRAT scintillometers measure gamma radiation

threshold and the frequency of the sound alarm can be varied according to the strength of the radiation. The time constant for the sound alarm is 0.25 seconds. The SRAT's unit of measurement is cps (counts per second). Its size is 32 x 13 x 12 cm and the weight 3.6 kg.

For beta measurements, ten Geiger-Müller Inspector instruments manufactured by Radiation Alert, were used. Each team member was equipped with a SRAT and each group of two members used one or two Inspectors.

The Inspector instrument is manufactured by S.E. International Inc., Summertime, TN 38483, U.S.A. (S.E. International Inc. 1999). The detector is a halogen-quenched Geiger-Müller tube of the pancake type that has an effective diameter of 45 mm. The detector window is covered by a mica foil, which is protected against damage by a metal net. The window has a diameter of 50 mm. It can be covered by a metal lid that, when used, only allows gamma radiation to reach the detector, with beta and alpha rays being unable to penetrate the lid. With the lid removed the Inspector measures gamma, beta and alpha radiation. Units of measurement are cpm, cps, mR/h or µSv/h. The instrument can be used in a direct reading mode or as a counter. The counting time can be set in the range 1 minute to 24 hours. A timer can be set at the desired counting time. The instrument is equipped with a sound alarm, which clicks for each radiation event detected. The Inspector measures 15 x 80 x 30 mm and weighs 272 g.

Inspectors can measure gamma, beta and alpha radiation

The Inspector instrument was chosen for the field mission because of its high sensitivity to beta radiation due to the pancake GM-tube and its rather large window. It is necessary to measure very close to the ground in order to detect beta radiation from DU on the ground or in the upper few millimetres of the soil. As a result, long-handled grippers designed for picking up litter (manufactured by Scan-Motor AS, Denmark) were used for holding the instrument. As the Inspector is not water resistant it had to be placed in a plastic freezer bag to protect it from moisture. The bag also prevented the mica foil from being punctured by grass or twigs and blocked alpha rays as well.

UNEP also rented from SSI a gamma ray spectrometer of the type Exploranium GR-130G/BGO, which was brought on the field mission (manufactured by Exploranium Ltd, Canada). The IAEA expert also provided the same type of spectrometer. These instruments are equipped with a 70 cm³ large detector of bismuth germanate oxide (BiGeO) which has much better resolution than instruments with detectors of sodium iodide (NaI(Tl)). The instruments weigh 2.6 kg, and they are not larger than an ordinary gamma meter that measures the total gamma radiation field. The spectrometers were used for in situ determination of the natural concentrations of uranium, thorium and potassium-40 in the bedrock and soils at some of the investigated sites. These measurements gave rapid information on the concentration of natural nuclides. It indicated whether any enhanced gamma radiation detected was caused by natural radiation or DU contamination. They were also very helpful in detecting that some of the radioactive spots encountered were caused by cesium-137 fallout or americium-241 used as ionisation sources on lightning rods to enhance their ability to attract lightning.

The Exploranium GR-130G/BGO measures the gamma ray spectrum within an interval 0.1 - 3 MeV. The spectrum is divided into 256 channels. The counts received in each channel are shown on a display, but also given in a written form. As the energy of the gamma radiation emitted at decay of radioactive isotopes depends on the type of isotope, this is used to distinguish between isotopes. During measurements, the spectrometer was placed directly on exposed bedrock or on the soil layer. The measuring time used was 400 seconds. As there are usually disequilibria between uranium-238 and radium-226 in weathered rock and in soils, and as the radium-226 concentration is determined by measurement of the gamma emission of bismut-214 at the 1.76 MeV peak, the results obtained do not represent the true uranium concentration (IAEA, 1979). Therefore, the result is given as equivalent uranium concentration (eU), comparing the measurements obtained to a situation when there is equilibrium between uranium-238 and radium-226. DU does not affect the spectrometer much when used in this mode as there is practically no radium-226 in DU. In practice, the spectrometer using this peak will indicate only the natural uranium content of the soil and not a possible DU contamination. As the gamma spectrometer for the determination of eU measures on the peak of Bi-114 at 1.76 MeV, it is therefore not influenced by Pa-234m at 1 MeV. It is not possible to measure the 1 MeV peak of DU with a gamma spectrometer as the Compton slope is too dominant.

■ **Calibration**

The instruments were calibrated and/or tested for their response against sources with known activities of radioactive elements prior to the mission. The Saphymo SRATs were calibrated against sources of radium-226. 1 cps corresponds to a gamma exposure rate of 0.002 μSv/h.

The Inspector instruments were calibrated for the beta response against a (^{90}Sr + ^{90}Y) source with source strength of 432.6 Bq. The response to DU in an area superficially contaminated by 1 mg DU per cm² would result in approximately 120 cps ± 24 cps, when measured 1 cm above the surface. Thus, 1 cps corresponds roughly to ground surface contamination of 0.01 mg DU per cm² or 0.1 g per m². This is the approximate lower detection limit for the Inspector instrument. The beta radiation measured at 10 cm above evenly contaminated ground is 40 % of that measured at 1 cm above the surface. For beta radiation, the shielding effect of a plastic freezer bag around the Inspector instrument results in a ~5 % reduction of the count rate.

Calibration of the Exploranium GR-130G/BGO gamma spectrometer was made on the calibration pads for calibration of airborne gamma-ray spectrometers at Borlänge airport, Sweden. Upon calibration, the instrument was adjusted to withdraw the background caused by cosmic radiation at sea level.

■ **Techniques for surveying the sites**

The objectives of the field measurements were to indicate and identify surface contamination, penetrators, and jackets. For such a purpose, measurements can be more quantitative than qualitative.

During the UNEP's investigations in BiH, field survey techniques which had been successfully applied in the Kosovo and Serbia and Montenegro assessments were used:

A. Method A, referred to in the report as 'line-up survey', means that the members of the team (most often 4-6 people) were lined up with 1-2 metres between each person. The group walked slowly forwards, maintaining their alignment with one another, while sweeping the instruments perpendicularly left and right to the walking direction at ground level in such a way that approximately all of the area was measured. The walking speed was 7 ± 2 metres per minute, depending on the terrain.

B. This method, referred to in the report as 'qualified at random survey', involved sending out team members after a briefing on what to expect, how to conduct the survey and where to search, to make visual observations in combination with the search for radioactivity with instruments in the environment. This method is possible if the team members are highly qualified and experienced.

C. Method C, referred to in the report as 'careful measurements', was often used to complement the measurements derived from method A. It consisted of measurements made with the Inspector beta/gamma instrument, involving careful removal of any covering of dust, grass etc., and measuring over a longer time period, to detect any possible shielded beta radiation from widespread contamination or from small surfaces of particular interest (e.g. corroded metal surfaces).

D. This method, referred to in the report as 'individual survey', meant that single individuals or groups of two individuals conducted surveys by sweeping, as per method A, in predetermined directions and areas. This method was used in very special circumstances when very little was known about the precise areas of a given site.

■ **Views on the instruments and the techniques used in the search for DU**

The team confirmed the SRAT and Inspector instruments to be well suited for the work carried out. The robust construction of the instruments made them easy to handle in the field without any special precautions.

The SRAT's very short time constant and the loud audible signal made it possible to walk quite quickly over the study areas but to maintain good control over the slightest changes in radioactivity. In the search for radioactive objects, high sensitivity is preferred over measurement accuracy. One disadvantage of the Inspector is that it is rather heavy. Not a single instrument failed during the mission.

The Inspector instrument proved to be quite good. It is light, has a fairly good alarm signal and is easy to handle, even for an inexperienced user. The plastic freezer bag protected the window foil well. Only one GM-detector was punctured. There were no problems due to rain. The instrument were reliable in wet conditions, bearing in mind that special attention had been paid to ensure that the plastic bags covering the instruments had not been torn.

The Exploranium GR-130G/BGO gamma spectrometers were very useful. Without them, it would not have been possible to distinguish between gamma radiation from DU contamination and cesium-137 Chernobyl fallout.

■ Concluding remarks on Instruments

All three instrument used on site in the field mission fulfilled the on-site requirements of the mission.

When searching for contamination, it is very important that the instruments are held close to the ground as the gamma radiation measured directly on a penetrator on the ground is 5 μSv/h, and decreases at a 10 cm to 0.8 μSv/h, at 20 cm to 0.3 μSv/h, and at 30 cm to 0.15 μSv/h. As the detection distance in the horizontal plane is rather limited, when searching for DU penetrators and fragments it is necessary to carry out the measurements in a very detailed manner so that no DU objects are missed. Penetrators and pieces of DU that are covered by more than 20 cm of soil or water are almost impossible to detect through their gamma radiation due to the shielding effect of these matters.

At the sites investigated, the gamma and the natural beta radiation was low or very low as the bedrock consisted of limestone, dolomites, quartzite or slate with low concentrations of U, Th and K.

Additionally, in every place where soil samples were taken, the local gamma dose rate at 1 m above ground level was measured with a precise dose rate meter (Automess 6150 ADB) with a measurement uncertainty of +/- 3 %. The gamma dose rate at the sampling sites differed slightly due to different geological situations. The range of measured values was from 75 to 151 nanosievert per hour. These values can be regarded as normal background values.

Low natural radioactivity gives increased possibilities of detecting and finding penetrators and contamination by DU, whereas, for instance, higher natural background will make it difficult or impossible to detect DU contamination The fallout of cesium-137 was noticeable at Han Pijesak, but the gamma and beta radiation from cesium-137 was not so high that it hindered the search for penetrators and fragments.

■ Other Equipment

For the personal use of each team member, UNEP supplied blue overalls designed to protect personal clothing, a warm UNEP jacket and a blue UN cap. Further individual protective equipment was also available on request (disposable full body overalls, rubber gloves, half masks etc.).

Each team member was required to wear rubber gloves when picking up penetrators or jackets, and to wear rubber boots in the field, as it is possible to easily decontaminate them in case of contamination. Due to the team's similar dress attire, it was easy to distinguish them among any onlookers.

The sampling sub-teams provided the necessary equipment to fulfil their tasks: soil sampling tools, air filter equipment, bio indicator/vegetation sampling tools, bags, filters, bottles etc.

Depleted Uranium in Bosnia and Herzegovina

C

Any additional and necessary equipment (e.g. paint to mark a "hot spot" or anything else of interest) was available for the survey sub-team.

Based on the former UNEP DU assessments, in combination with the on-site measurements, there was no reason to suspect any significant airborne/re-suspended DU contamination outside buildings. Therefore, it was not necessary to use special protective clothing or any respiratory protection. The air and soil sub-teams used half masks when investigating the wooden storage barn in Han Pijesak.

Finally, several of the team members also brought GPS instruments, which were used during the mapping of site areas and for determining the exact positions of the samples collected.

C.3 SAMPLING METHODS IN THE FIELD

■ General organisation in the field

At the sites investigated, samples of soil, soil profiles, water, lichen, bark, atmospheric aerosols, plants, surface deposits and penetrators were taken. The collection of the samples, followed by analysis in the laboratories, was organised as follows:

- The soil sub-team (Swiss team) was responsible for the collection and analysis of the soil samples and samples of special interest, e.g. penetrators, fragments, smear samples. In cooperation with the Bristol University experts, soil cores (soil profiles) were taken and prepared and analysed by both teams at Spiez Laboratory.

- The water/vegetation sub-team (Italian team) was responsible for the collection and analysis of botanical and water samples. The collected samples were then analysed by APAT's laboratories.

- The air sub-team (Greek and Russian team member), in cooperation with the Swiss team and other members of the field team, were responsible for air/aerosol sampling. The air filters were analysed at Spiez Laboratory.

C.3.1 Sampling in the field (Spiez Laboratory)

■ Surface Soil samples

Soil samples were taken at each site visited, even if there were no immediate indications of DU ammunition having been used. If possible, the location of the centre and dimensions of the attacked target site were defined first by gamma and beta radiation field measurements (field survey sub-team).

Detailed photographic documentation was taken of all sampled sites.

The following rules were observed when defining the procedures and during field sampling:
- Use proven and standardised sampling procedures.
- Be aware of possibly very uneven deposition of DU on the soil surface.
- Do not take too small a sample mass, or from too small a surface area. Pool (combine) a number of smaller samples.
- Avoid cross-contamination of samples (the DU concentration of typical samples can vary by many orders of magnitude).

The following procedure was used during the soil sampling. Topsoil (layer 0-5 cm) core samples were taken using a manual corer. Usually, 10 core samples were taken at random from a defined area (normally 5 x 5 m). The core samples from an area were pooled in a double plastic bag. The sample code was determined according to standard Spiez Laboratory procedures based on ISO/IEC 17025. In addition, a sample form (NATO AEP 49 Volume 2, Environmental Sample) for each pooled sample was completed immediately at the time of sampling. The typical mass of such pooled soil samples was about 2 kg.

A) Sites with no indication of the use of DU ammunition (e.g. Lukavica)

Sampling areas of 5 x 5 m (i.e. 25 m²) were defined. Some of these were within the expected zone of attack and most symmetrically around the expected target site. Others were up to a distance of several hundred metres away, to make sure that it would be possible to detect the presence and approximate areal extent of any assumed DU contamination, even if it was not detected by field measurements.

All sampling areas were checked by the Mine Action Center (MAC) experts to ensure that there were no mines or unexploded ordnance before sampling took place.

B) Sites with indication of the use of DU ammunition (e.g. Han Pijesak)

Sampling areas of 25 m² were defined. Some of them were within the attacked target and most symmetrically around the expected target site. Others were up to a distance of several hundred metres away, to make sure that it would be possible to detect the presence and approximate areal extent of any DU contamination.

All sampling areas were checked by the Mine Action Center (MAC) experts to ensure that there were no mines or unexploded ordnance before sampling took place.

C) Sites where impact points of penetrators were identified

Having clearly defined the impact point of a penetrator, 10 topsoil cores (layer 0 - 5 cm) were taken along a concentric circle with radius of 3 metres around the central point of impact. These cores were combined to one pooled soil sample.

■ **Samples of special interest**

Samples of special interest included penetrators, fragments, jackets, shot holes (holes clearly indicating that a DU penetrator had hit the ground - in some cases with the penetrator still visible) or smear samples (special alinea below).

A soil sample of special interest was taken from the ground surface around the shot hole or directly from the hole by using a small shovel or the manual corer. The surface dimension and sampling depth were adapted to the specific conditions of each location. The sampling procedure was reported in detail.

Penetrators and jackets were collected methodically and triple packed to make sure that contamination from/of any other sample could be excluded. All relevant information was documented in detail.

■ **Soil cores/Soil profiles**

Profiles of subsurface soil were taken at places where penetrators were found laying at or near the undisturbed ground surface. The soil layer above the penetrator was first collected carefully from a surface of about 15 x 15 cm using a small shovel. Then, the penetrator was taken out of the soil and the soil layer surrounding the penetrator was collected separately using the same procedure. Positioned exactly where the penetrator was found, the core

C

METHODOLOGY

template was driven to a depth of 60 cm using a heavy hammer. The core template consists principally of a heavy U-shape profile of stainless steel with inside dimensions of 10 x 10 cm. The soil profile, isolated inside the core template, was then carefully collected layer by layer from the open side, using a metallic spatula. Normally, the vertical dimension of each layer was 5 cm. Therefore, the volume of a soil layer sample was 500 cm^3. Using this procedure, the cross contamination from higher to lower profile layers is minimized.

■ **Samples of Surface deposits/ Smear Samples**

Surface deposits inside attacked buildings consisting of loose material like sand and dust on rough surfaces like concrete were collected from a defined surface using a metallic spatula.

Surface deposits (dust) on smooth surfaces inside attacked buildings were taken from horizontal areas of about 20 x 20 cm using dry smear sampling kits.

C.3.2 Sampling in the field (APAT Laboratory)

■ **Botanical samples**

Samples of tree bark and lichen growing on trees were collected at each of the investigated sites where these were accessible in order to search for the presence of DU dust particles. Considering that such particles can be dispersed in the environment according to wind direction, and can be deposited on trees, bushes, rocks and soil, the presence of DU in lichen, mosses and tree bark is mainly attributable to:

- Direct deposition of DU dust particles during the attack; and
- deposition of suspended materials in air (originating from resuspension of soil and deposited DU dust particles).

Lichen sampling was carried out according to the "Guidelines for the use of epiphytic lichen as bio-monitors of atmospheric deposition of trace metals" (Nimis and Barbagli, 1999). This methodology identifies the following criteria in order to select the lichen to be sampled:

- sample fruticose or foliose broad-lobed species only;
- use epiphytic species whenever possible;
- collect from trees that satisfy the following conditions:
  - trunk with an inclination not higher than 10°;
  - without evident sign of disturbance;
  - surface without stem-flow tracks;
  - far from wounds of the bark;
  - with growth of bryophytes not higher than 25% ; and
  - preferably a mature tree/bush should be chosen.
- sample lichen from all around the trunk; and
- sample at a height of more than 1 m above the ground to avoid terrigenous contamination.

At each location, thalli of foliose lichen, together with their substrates, were collected from trees and/or bushes using a steel knife and placed in paper envelopes. Tree bark samples were also collected in some sites in order to investigate the relationship between the uranium content of bark and lichen samples.

Where available, lichen growing on rocks or soil, and moss samples were collected as well in order to identify other environmental matrices that can accumulate uranium. After sampling, the botanical samples were air-dried and then stored in paper bags (Rosamilia *et al.*, 2003a).

Post-Conflict Environmental Assessment

■ **Water samples**

The mobilisation of DU in the soil profile and its possible contamination of groundwater will depend on a range of factors such as the chemistry and the structure of the surrounding soil, rainfall and hydrology. In order to verify the presence of DU in drinking water, water samples from private wells and taps were collected.

One litre of water was sampled in each location using a polyethylene bottle. Immediately after sampling, without any water filtering, the pH of all water samples was adjusted by adding HNO_3 in order to ensure that trace elements were kept in solution to inhibit biological growth and to leach uranium from the particles in the water (ASTM, 1999a).

C.3.3 Sampling in the field (Bristol University)

■ **Soil cores/Soil profiles**

The same procedure as Spiez Laboratory was used for the soil profile collected by Bristol University (see above).

C.3.4 Sampling in the field (Air sub-team)

■ **Air /Aerosol Samples**

Under the responsibility of the air sub-team (Greek and Russian experts in strong co-operation with the Swiss team), Spiez Laboratory air filter equipment was used at most of the sites investigated using portable electricity generating units.

Uranium nuclides are present in air as resuspended soil particles. The typical natural uranium concentration in atmospheric aerosols is very low. Normally, the concentration of uranium radionuclides in air is in the range of 0.02 to 18 $\mu Bq/m^3$ (about 0.002 to 1.5 ng/m^3) (UNSCEAR, 2000). 1 $\mu Bq/m^3$ (about 0.08 ng/m^3) is considered as a reference value. To measure such low concentrations, sampling systems equipped with high flow rate air pumps have to be used. During the UNEP mission to BiH, four air filter systems of the type Gravicon VC 25 G were used.

'Schleicher und Schüll AE 99' membrane filters were used. The diameter of the effective filter area is 142 mm, which is equivalent to 158 cm^2. The uranium-238 concentration of the cellulose filter material (filter blank) was 2.68 ± 0.12 ng per filter (equivalent to 3.94 ng/g), according to analysis carried out prior to the mission. The 'Schleicher und Schüll AE 99' filter has good collection efficiency for aerosol particles in the range above 0.05 μm, high particle and mass loading capacity, low flow resistance and high mechanical strength. It is the optimal filter material for the Gravicon VC 25 G.

The instrument was used in configuration to measure total dust. The air inlet was between 90 and 165 cm above ground level. These air pumps operate at a constant airflow of 22.5 m^3/h, which is controlled and regulated at this value, independent of ambient temperature and flow resistance/back pressure. The sampled air volume is calculated from the sampling time, registered by the integrated timer, and the constant flow rate. The airflow of the filter system was calibrated before the mission to an altitude of 620 m above sea level and to standard atmospheric pressure. The estimated combined uncertainty of the sampled air volume due to calibration uncertainty, variable atmospheric pressure and different altitude during the mission is ± 6 %.

For typical sampling times of 6 hours and use of ICP MS analyses, the detection limit for uranium in atmospheric aerosols is around 0.003 ng/m^3. It is therefore possible to measure uranium in atmospheric aerosols even at the lowest range of reported natural concentrations.

Depleted Uranium in Bosnia and Herzegovina

C 3.5 Measurements and smear tests in the field (Russian Expert)

On various surfaces within the sites, studies were conducted to estimate conversion coefficients for the recalculation from count rates of the Inspector instruments (in cps) to the density of DU contamination of surfaces (in Bq cm^{-2} or µg cm^{-2}).

In addition, specific smear samples were taken by using scotch tape to fix the pollution particles to the adhesive. 32 such smear samples were taken and five of these were analysed in detail in Moscow (SIA RADON).

C.4 LABORATORY METHODS

C 4.1 Samples and analyses: Introduction

UNEP visited 15 different sites, of which 5 were NATO confirmed sites. One NATO confirmed site, the 76mm Self-Prop AT Gun, was inaccessible due to mines. Altogether, from the 14 accessible sites the team collected 132 samples (173 including soil core layers). Of these, 46 were surface soil samples and 3 core soil samples composed of 46 layers, 19 water samples, 24 air, 29 botanical (lichen, bark, moss, mushrooms, vegetables), 2 scratch, 5 surface deposits/smear samples, 3 penetrators and 1 full bullet (penetrator still in its jacket). Many of the botanical samples were divided into sub-samples as they contained more than one species. All samples were allocated unique code numbers.

The complete lists of the analysis of the samples, including sample type, location collected and results of analyses are given in Appendices D (soil), E (water), F (biota), G (air) and H (penetrators).

The samples collected by the Swiss and Italian team members were taken back to the laboratories of Spiez Laboratory, Switzerland and the Italian Environmental Protection Agency and Technical Services (APAT) in Rome to be analysed in detail. The Swiss samples included those collected by Bristol University and the air filters collected by the air sub team.

The laboratories have, respectively, provided a report on sample preparation, the analytical methods used and the results of the analyses (Rosamilia *et al.*, 2003a; Test Reports, 2003). The following is a synthesis of these reports.

The analyses included the determination of concentrations by weight and activity of the ^{tot}U, ^{234}U, ^{235}U and ^{238}U. In some cases, the concentration of ^{236}U, Pu and Np were also determined.

The main objectives of sampling in the field were:
- to determine the presence and range of any ground contamination around or within the assumed target areas investigated;
- to determine whether localized, highly contaminated areas or 'contamination points'/ "hot spots" are present and to measure the level of DU activity concentrations;
- to determine the concentrations of uranium isotopes in groundwater;
- to study vegetation (lichen, mosses, etc.) as bio-indicators of environmental DU contamination;
- to study the depth distribution of DU in subsurface soil below a penetrator buried a couple of centimetres below the ground surface;
- to assess the amount of uranium isotope activity that can easily be removed from the surface of a DU penetrator, the effect of weathering on the penetrator, and the possible dissolution in groundwater;
- to study the mobility of DU corrosion products in a core collected for the depth distribution studies by using extraction methods; and
- to upgrade the data on the quality of DU used in DU ammunition.

C.4.2 Preparation of samples and analytical methods

■ Spiez Laboratory procedures

In order to determine radionuclides, chemical and isotopic analyses were performed by an inductively coupled Plasma Mass-Spectrometry (or Alpha Spectrometry) through the implementation of accredited procedures (ISO/IEC 17025) in Spiez Laboratory's STS 028 Testing Laboratory.

Sample preparation

● **Soil samples**

The samples were dried at 40° C in air re-circulating drying ovens until weight constancy was achieved. The dried samples were then crushed and sieved (2 mm/ mesh 10). The sieved materials were homogenised in a TURBULA® mixer for 10 minutes. 50 g of the dried, homogenised soil samples was then ashed in quartz crucibles at 520°C in high temperature furnaces for 16 hours (weight constancy). The ashed soil was milled in a 250 ml Syalon (silicium nitride; SiN_4) ball-mill with silicium nitride balls (15 balls, diameter 20 mm) for 2 minutes at 600 rpm. 5 g of the milled soil ash was fully mixed with 7 g of fluxing agent (Lithium metaborate / Lithium tetraborate 80 % / 20 %). The mixture was transferred in a platinum-gold crucible (Pt/Au; 95/5) and 250 μL of ^{209}Bi solution (1 000 ppm) was added as internal standard. After going through a drying oven for 30 minutes at 70°C, the samples were fused in a high temperature furnace for 20 minutes at 1 100°C. The melt was poured into a 250 mL beaker containing 200 g c (HNO_3) = 4.5 mol/L. 1 mL of polyethylene glycol (c(PEG-2000) = 0.2 mol/L) was added as flocculating agent to precipitate silica gel and boric acid. This mixture was heated to 40° C with constant stirring for 3 hours. After cooling, 3 mL of the upper solution layer was filtered < 0.45 μm (Spartan 30/0.45 RC; Schleicher & Schüll). 1.4 mL of the filtrate was diluted with w(HNO_3) = 2 % to 40 mL to form the master solution.

● **Smear samples**

Smear samples were leached in 50 ml c(HNO_3) = 8 mol/L for 5 hours at a temperature of 50 °C. During this process, the samples were also held in an ultrasonic bath 4 times for 1 minute. The solutions were transferred to a 100 mL measuring flask. The beakers were washed 3 times with 15 mL c(HNO_3) = 8mol/L and then the measuring flask was filled with distilled water. Aliquots of these solutions were further diluted for the analysis by ICP-MS.

● **Scratch samples**

Scratch samples were treated like soil samples.

● **Seaweed and Lichen**

Aliquots of 500 mg of the materials (as delivered by IAEA) were digested in the microwave system like water filters.

● **Water samples**

The water samples were diluted 1:10 with w(HNO_3) = 2 % . 50 ppb of ^{209}Bi was added as internal standard for the ICP-MS measurements.

● **Air filters**

Air filters were cut in half. Half was then brought into a teflon beaker and a mixture of 5 mL HNO_3 conc., 2mL w(HF) = 40% and 2 mL w(H_2O_2) = 30% was added. 100 μl of ^{209}Bi-solution (250 ppm) was added as the internal standard. The samples were then digested in a temperature controlled microwave system by heating to 180°C in 5 minutes and holding the temperature for a further 10 minutes. After cooling, the solutions were diluted with $c(HNO_3)$ = 2mol/L to 11 mL master solution.

- **Penetrators**

Penetrators were carefully handled in the laboratories in order to avoid any contamination and were weighed directly after unpacking. The samples were then cleaned mechanically with a sharp knife to remove corrosion products and dirt. The material thus removed was stored separately. Remaining surface corrosion (yellow/black) was washed off with $c(HNO_3)$ = 5 mol/L HNO_3 in an ultrasonic bath, followed by washing with water and ethanol. The samples were air dried and then weighed. After the cleaning procedure, the penetrators were held for 60 minutes in 100 mL hot concentrated HNO_3 (14 mol/L) for partial digestion. The solutions containing the digested DU were diluted with water to a final concentration of $c(HNO_3)$ = 5-7 mol/L. The penetrators were washed with water and ethanol, dried and re-weighed.

- **Plutonium separation**

Tracer was added to 5 mL of each solution containing 0.2 g of the penetrator material and diluted with 45 mL $c(HNO_3)$ = 5 mol/L. This solution was introduced into a TEVA-Spec® column. Uranium was eluted with 100 mL $c(HNO_3)$ = 5 mol/L and 10 ml $c(HNO_3)$ = 2 mol/L. The column was then washed with 20 mL $c(HCl)$ = 6 mol/L. Plutonium was eluted with 30 mL $c(HCl)$ = 0.5 mol/L. 250 µL of concentrated sulphuric acid were added to the plutonium fraction. The fraction was put in a sand bath and brought to dryness. Any residual organic material was destroyed by heating with sulphuric acid to fuming temperatures on a hotplate. Some drops of nitric acid were then added. Plutonium was electro-deposited from a sulphuric acid ammonium-sulphate system on a steel plate and determined with alpha spectrometry.

- **Neptunium separation**

45 mL 5 M HNO_3 containing 0.2 g of the penetrator, 0.1 M Fe^{2+} and Np-tracer was loaded on a TEVA-Spec® column. Uranium was eluted with 50 mL 5 M HNO_3/0.1 M Fe^{2+}. Neptunium was eluted with 20 mL 0.1 M HNO_3. The Np-tracer was measured with gamma-spectrometry in order to determine the chemical yield. The Np-237 concentration was measured with ICP-MS.

Chemical and isotopic analyses using ICP-MS analysis

All analyses were performed on a FINNIGAN Element 2 HR-ICP-MS (high resolution inductively coupled plasma mass spectrometer) in the low-resolution mode. In this configuration, the response for 1 ppb U-238 was about 1 200 000 cps.

Quantitative Determination of Uranium-238

All calibration and master solutions contained Bi-209 as an internal standard. The master solutions were diluted with 2 % nitric acid until no matrix suppression of the U and Bi signal occurred. A five-point calibration with U was performed in the expected U concentration range. Only U-238 and Bi-209 isotopes were measured. The U calibration was verified with two independent U standards. In order to check the sensitivity and the calibration during the measurement procedure, a U standard was measured after every ten samples.

Determination of the isotopic composition of uranium.

The dissolved soil samples were diluted with 2 % nitric acid to a concentration of about 0.5 ng/mL U-238. The uranium isotopes U-234, U-235, U-236 and U-238 were measured.

Furthermore, in order to correct for interferences, the isotopes Pt-195 and Th-232 were measured. The performance of the ICP-MS was checked with natural and certified U solutions. After every 6 -10 samples, a natural uranium standard was measured to correct for mass discrimination of the ratio U-235/U-238. The mass discrimination was < 1%.

Measurements of blanks and detection limits

The U-238 concentrations are determined by external calibration. The U-238 concentration from the chemical reagents can be neglected. Despite careful cleaning of the equipment after each sample, a uranium background can be measured. The background of U-238 per fusion is about 10 ng and per microwave digestion about 0.1 ng. The U-238 concentration of an air filter-blank was 2.68 ng, whereas the U-238 concentration of a water filter-blank could be neglected. The isotope concentrations of U-234, U-235 and U-236 are calculated with the measured ratio relative to U-238. Thus, the detection limits for the isotopes U-234, U-235 and U-236 depend on the U-238 concentration in the sample. For low U concentrations interfering PtAr-species can cause higher detection limits. Typical detection limits for the samples investigated in this report are given in Table C.1.

Table C.1 Detection limits

	U-234	U-235	U-236	U-238	Isotope ratio[%]
Soil	30 ng/kg	30 ng/kg	30 ng/kg	2 µg/kg	0.001
Air	2 fg/m³	2 fg/m³	2 fg/m³	0.005 ng/m³	0.002
Water	0.01 ng/L	0.01 ng/L	0.01 ng/L	1 ng/L	0.001
Sea weed, lichen	1 ng/kg	1 ng/kg	1 ng/kg	0.5 µg/kg	0.001

Calculation of the percentage of DU of the total uranium concentration.

The difference of the average weight of a U atom in natural and depleted U can be neglected. Hence, the mole fraction of DU of the total U is equal to the mass fraction of DU of the total U and can easily be calculated from the ratio R_m = U-235/U-238 of the sample. The ratio R_m = U-235/U-238 was corrected for mass discrimination. The ratio U-235/U-238 for natural and depleted U is assumed to be $R_{U\text{-}nat}$ = 0.00725 and R_{DU} = 0.00200, respectively.

$$DU[\%] = 100 \cdot \frac{R_{U-nat} - R_m}{R_{U-nat} - R_{DU}} = 100 \cdot \frac{0.00725 - R_m}{0.00525}$$

Statistical and measurement uncertainties at the ICP-MS analysis

The combined relative standard deviations (k-values) were calculated by propagation of errors from the relative standard deviations (rsd). The relative standard deviations of the variables were either experimentally determined or estimated.

- ## Quantitative Determination of Plutonium and Neptunium

Alpha spectrometry (plutonium and neptunium analyses) was performed using high-vacuum alpha chambers with 1-inch PIPS detectors.

The energy calibration of the alpha spectrometer was performed with Pu-239, Am-241 and Cm-244. The efficiency calibration was performed with the same nuclides to determine the chemical recovery of the tracer. A known amount of tracer (Pu-236; not present in the sample) was added to each solution. By evaluating the spectra, the count rate of the tracer can be directly compared with the count rate of the unknown amount of the sample. Any loss of sample will be compensated by this technique. Based on the count rates of the tracer and the unknown, the content in Bq/g can be calculated.

There are no reference materials available for DU penetrators. The described method was applied to reference soil samples. The results were inside the confidence interval of the reference values.

■ APAT - Laboratory work

Lichen species identification

The lichen species of each sample have been identified in the Botany of the Environmental Sciences Department of Tuscia University in Viterbo, Italy (Laboratorio di Botanica - Dipartimento di Scienze Ambientali) laboratory. The following macroscopic characters have been used for a first identification:
- the thallus growth form and its colour under dehydrate condition;
- the presence/absence of structures on upper and/or lower surface (apothecia, perithecia, soredia, isidia, pycnidia, rhizine etc.).

Afterward, microscopic analyses, both using a stereomicroscope and chemical spot-tests, have been conducted. Chemical spot-tests are based on reactions occurring between some chemical lichenic substances, such as weak phenols or fatty acids, and specific reagents.

In some cases, the use of a light microscope permitted the distinction of microscopic characters, which are clearly visible exclusively through the observation of thin sections of lichen's reproductive structures. The type of ascocarps and asci and the shape and size of ascospores are the main elements observed.

The micro- and macroscopic characters observations have been supported by analytical dichotomic keys, and in some cases, by the use of reference books concerning the European taxa (Clauzade & Roux, 1985; Nimis, 1987; Purvis *et al.*, 1992; Dobson, 2000); the Internet Lichen Database of Italy (http://dbiodbs.univ.trieste.it) was also used.

Some specimens are preserved in Laboratory of Botany of the Tuscia University in Viterbo (Italy) and in the APAT Laboratory in Rome (Italy). They are available for any future consultation.

Preparation of samples

● Lichen

In the laboratory, the samples were dried at 40° C at constant weight. The lichen samples were subdivided according to species identification made by the laboratory of Botany of the Dipartimento di Scienze Ambientali of the Tuscia University in Viterbo (Italy).

Samples were not washed as the aim was to measure the elements that were physically trapped on the surface of the thallus, as well as chemically bound to cell walls. The lichen samples were separated from the bark substratum using a steel knife and extraneous materials such as mosses and large soil particles were removed under a binocular microscope.

The fine powder (= 250 μm) of lichen samples was obtained by grinding in a Planetary Ball Mill (Retsch PM4), using grinding jars of 500 mL in agate and 20-agate ball of 20 mm diameter.

The samples were stored in polyethylene containers. A Teflon ball was put into each container when initially filled, to facilitate subsequent re-homogenisation (Rosamilia *et al.* 2003a).

- **Mosses**

In the laboratory the extreme apices of the shoots were cut in order to eliminate older parts of the shoots and soil. The green parts of unwashed mosses were dried to a constant weight (40° C).

The fine powder (= 125 μm) of moss samples was obtained by grinding in a Planetary Ball Mill (Retsch PM4), using grinding jars of 500 mL in agate and 20-agate ball of 20 mm diameter. The samples were stored in polyethylene containers. A Teflon ball was put into each container when initially filled, to facilitate subsequent re-homogenisation.

- **Tree barks**

Soil, insects or any other solid pollutants were removed from bark samples. Using a hard steel knife, the external surface (about 3 mm) of bark was cut and dried at 40° C for 24 h. The samples were crushed and ground in a Planetary Ball Mill (Retsch PM4), using grinding jars of 500 mL in agate and 20-agate ball of 20 mm diameter. The samples were stored in polyethylene containers. A Teflon ball was put into each container when initially filled, to facilitate subsequent re-homogenisation.

- **Radiochemical analysis**

^{238}U, ^{234}U and ^{235}U concentration in all samples were determined by alpha-spectrometry following total dissolution (U. Sansone *et al.*, 2001; Jia *et al.* 2002a; Jia *et al.*, 2002b). The alpha-spectrometry system (CANBERRA) is controlled by Genie-2000 software. Genie-2000 is a comprehensive set of capabilities for acquiring and analysing from Multichannel Analyzers (MCAs). Its functions include MCA control, spectral display and manipulation, basic spectrum analysis and reporting.

The energy calibration of the alpha spectrometer was performed with ^{241}Am, ^{244}Cm and ^{237}Np. The efficiency calibration was performed with ^{232}U or ^{236}U. A known amount of tracer (^{232}U not present in the sample) was added to each solution. By evaluating the spectra, the count rate of the tracer can be directly compared with the count rate of the unknown amount of the sample. Any loss of sample will be compensated by this technique. Based on the count rates of the tracer and the unknown, the content can be calculated in Bq/kg.

Sample preparation

- **Botanical samples**

Usually the analytical procedure to leach botanical samples is different from the procedure used to dissolve soil/sediment samples.

As reported above, lichens mosses and tree bark can accumulate DU by trapping also soil particles. Considering that this investigation was aimed at detecting the presence of DU, the soil leaching procedure was also applied to these botanical samples to be able to detect any DU presence in these samples also attributable to soil particles.

On this basis, the milled and homogenised samples were screened by gross beta measurements using a low-level planchet counter with proportional gas flow counter tubes. This procedure was selected to decide the order for processing and analysing the samples.

A platinum crucible containing 3 g of botanical sample was put in a muffle. To avoid burning the sample, the muffle was heated very slowly (over 10 hours) starting from the room temperature to 600° C. After 14 hours at 600° C, the temperature of the muffle slowly decreases (about 8 hours.)

Depleted Uranium in Bosnia and Herzegovina

After cooling to room temperature, 2 g of Na_2O_2 and 2 g sodium carbonate are added in the platinum crucible containing the sample. The crucible is heated at 600 °C for 15-20 min in a muffle. The melted sample is cooled to room temperature and transferred to a 100 mL teflon beaker by distilled water and concentrated HNO_3. 0.03 Bq of ^{232}U, 5 mL of concentrated HNO_3, 5 mL of HCl (37%), 5 mL of 40% HF and 1 mL of 30% H_2O_2 is added, evaporation is carried out at 250 °C. Before drying, the sample is further intervened with 5 mL of concentrated HNO_3, 5 mL of HCl (37%) and 5 mL of 40% HF in order to eliminate the majority of silicates. The residue is changed into nitric form by two time evaporations with 4 mL of concentrated HNO_3. The residue obtained is dissolved again with 5 mL of concentrated HNO_3 and 10 mL of distilled water and filtered through a 0.45 μm Millipore filter paper in a 150 mL beaker, the teflon beaker is washed with 10 mL 2M HNO_3 and filtered into the 150 mL beaker. Further separation is carried out following the uranium determination procedure provided below.

- **Water samples**

No particular preparation was needed for water samples. One ml of Fe^{3+} (40 mg Fe^{3+}/mL) as carrier, 0.03 Bq of ^{232}U as tracer and 20 mL of concentrated HNO_3 is added to one litre of water sample. After boiling for 30 min, the solution is removed to an electric-magnetic stirrer and adjusted to pH 9.5-10 with concentrated ammonia solution to co-precipitate uranium with iron (III) hydroxide. The solution is stirred for another 30 minutes and the precipitate is allowed to settle down for at least 4-6 h (preferably overnight). The supernatant is carefully syphoned off and the hydroxide slurry is centrifuged at 3 500 rpm. The supernatant is discarded, the precipitate is dissolved with 5 mL of concentrated HNO_3 and 0.3 mL of 40 % HF and transferred to a 150 mL beaker. The solution obtained is evaporated to incipient dryness and the residue is dissolved with 4 mL of concentrated HNO_3, 26 mL of distilled water and 0.3 mL of 40 % HF by heating at 100 °C. Further separation is carried out following the uranium determination procedure provided below.

- **Column preparation**

A solution (50 mL) of 0.3 M TOPO (Trioctylphosphine oxide 99 %) in cyclohexane was added to 50 g of Microthene; the mixture was stirred for several minutes until homogeneity was reached and then evaporated to eliminate cyclohexane at 50° C. The porous powder thus obtained contained about 10.4 % TOPO. A portion (1.6 g) of the Microthene-TOPO powder, slurred with 3 mL concentrated HCl and 10 mL of distilled water, was transferred to a chromatographic column; after conditioning with 30 mL of 2 M HNO_3, the column was ready for use.

- **Separation and determination of uranium**

The solutions, obtained from the aforementioned procedures, were passed through a preconditioned Microthene-TOPO column at a flow rate of 0.6-0.8 mL/min. After washing with 30 ml 6M HNO_3, 60 mL 1M HCl and 5 mL of distilled water at the same flow rate, uranium is eluted with 30 mL of 0.025 M $(NH_4)_2C_2O_4$ at a flow rate of 0.1 mL/min. The first 3.5 mL of eluant are discarded and the remains directly collected in an electro-deposition cell. 0.61 mL of 8M HNO_3 was added to the cell and the solution was adjusted to pH 1-1.5 with 1:4 ammonia solution. Uranium was electro-deposited on a stainless steel disk at a current density of 400 mA/cm² for 4 hours and counted by alpha spectrometry.

- **Lower limits of detection**

The lower limits of detection were assessed using Currie's method (1968). Taking into account the blank count rates, the counting efficiencies of the instruments, the radiochemical yields and the sample quantity, the lower detection limits of the method are 0.37 Bq/kg (soil or lichen) and 0.22 mBq/L (water) for ^{238}U and ^{234}U, and 0.038 Bq/kg (soil or lichen) and 0.022 mBq/L (water) for ^{235}U if 0.5 g of soil and 1 litre of water are analysed.

- **Statistical and measurement uncertainties**

The analytical uncertainty associated with the activity concentration was estimated following steps as reported on EURACHEM/CITAC Guide [Eurachem/Citac Guide, 2000]. Activity concentration can be expressed as:

$$C = \frac{\left(\dfrac{N}{T} - BK\right)}{\left(\dfrac{N_t}{T_t} - BK_t\right)} * \frac{V_t}{P}$$

where:

N   =   Number of sample counts;
T   =   Time of sample counting (s);
BK   =   Count per second of background of reagent and counting system;
Nt   =   Number of tracer counts;
Tt   =   Time of tracer counting (s);
BK t =   Count per second of tracer background;
Vt   =   Tracer activity (Bq);
P   =   weight (kg) or volume (lm^3).

The cause-effect diagram (sometimes called fish-bone) shown below highlights the significant uncertainty in avoiding over-counting (Barbizzi S. et al., 2002). The uncertainty components have been expressed as standard deviations and amalgamated according to the appropriate rules to give a combined standard uncertainty. The uncertainty associated with time is neglected.

With respect to the uncertainty associated with weight (P), the following contributions are considered: linearity of the balance, repeatability and reproducibility.

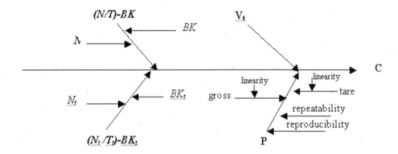

With respect to the water sample, the volume was measured using a graduated cylinder, so the uncertainty associated with the volume has been evaluated on the basis of its characteristics. With regard to the air samples, the air volume collected by each air sampler has been estimated as the air pumping speed multiplied by the time duration of each measurement. The uncertainty in the measurement of air speed was calculated by the fluctuation of the indications of the measuring instrument during the operation and is estimated at 3 %. The uncertainty associated with time duration was neglected.

The tracer uncertainty activity (Vt) includes the uncertainty due to two dilutions of the tracer, the uncertainty reported on the tracer certificate and associated with the addition of the tracer to the sample.

The uncertainty associated with the ratios $^{234}U/^{238}U$, $^{235}U/^{238}U$ has been calculated according to the appropriate rules of the uncertainty propagation. In the tables the uncertainty is reported as 1 standard deviation.

$$\frac{\partial C}{C} = \sqrt{\left(\frac{\partial((N/T) - BK)}{(N/T) - BK}\right)^2 + \left(\frac{\partial((N_t/T_t) - BK_t)}{(N_t/T_t) - BK_t}\right)^2 + \left(\frac{\partial P}{P}\right)^2 + \left(\frac{\partial V_t}{V_T}\right)^2}$$

$$\partial C = \frac{\partial C}{C} * C$$

- **Sequential Extraction Procedure (Bristol University)**

A sequential extraction procedure was used to investigate the chemical phase associations of uranium, present in a 60 cm soil profile collected at Han Pijesak. Each extractant used in sequence is intended to target a specific geochemical phase (e.g. organic matter, type of mineral(s)) and thereby indicate the geochemical sites to which uranium has bound within the soil. This should give a better understanding of the ultimate sites of uptake of uranium in soil and the ease with which uranium may be removed from these sites (e.g. by the percolation of rainwater). The analysis of soil sections down a 60 cm soil profile should also provide information on the mobility of uranium with depth and the resulting change of physical parameters (i.e. pH, Eh, p_{CO2}) experience with increased depth.

The extractants used are chosen to target six specific geochemical phases (exchangeable cations, carbonate bound, iron and manganese oxide/hydroxide bound, organic matter, amorphous silica and refractory minerals). However, as each geochemical phase varies considerably in its properties, no single extractant is able to attack any one specific phase in entirety and isolation, and thus overlap of attacked phases will occur. Therefore, the results obtained from this method are strictly extractant defined.

Much work has been carried out in the last forty years to match the extractants employed with the extraction of metals from specific phases (Tessier et al, 1979; Schultz et al. 1997). The method used in this investigation was based on a six-step extraction procedure, developed for the extraction of actinides in river sediment (Klemt, 2001). The extraction procedure is summarized below.

Table C.2 Sequential Extraction Procedure

Extraction step	Targeted Phase	Chemical Reagent	Treatment
1	Exchangeable cations	NH4-Ac (1 mol/l)	Stirring for 24hrs
2	Carbonate minerals	NH_4-Ac (1 mol/l) + HNO_3 (1 mol/l)	Stirring with the addition of nitric acid until the pH stabilises at pH 5
3	Oxides and hydroxides of iron and manganese	NH_2OH-HCl (0.2 mol/l) in HAc (25%)	Stirring for 3 hrs
4	Organic matter	H_2O_2 (35%) + HNO_3 (1 mol/l) up to 0.05 mol/l.	Stirring for 3 hrs at 85°C
5	Amorphous silica	(i) NaOH (0.2 mol/l) (ii) HNO_3 (0.3 mol/l)	Stirring for 40 min at 90°C
6	Refractory material	HNO_3 (7 mol/l)	Stirring for 4hrs at 85°C

In this study required changes to the experimental method above included the introduction of a defined extraction time of 4 hours in the carbonate extraction and the addition of 15mL of H_2O_2 (35%) per sample in the organic matter extraction step (necessary due to the higher organic content of the soils).

This study should therefore provide information on the dominant geochemical phase to which the uranium present within the soil is bound, and therefore also an indication of how mobile the uranium is within the soil. In addition to the sequential extraction procedure, total ^{238}U concentration measurements down the profile were also performed in order to establish an estimate of the uranium recovery during the sequential extraction procedure.

Sequential extraction method

The sequential extraction of uranium from the soil samples was performed according to Klemt (2001) with slight modifications. The extractions were performed in series, in plastic centrifuge bottles, with 20 g of soil sample to 200 g of extraction agent. A magnetic stirring bead was placed in each bottle, and VARIOMAC® Thermoblocks were used to heat and stir samples as required in each extraction step. Two sample blanks were used throughout the extraction procedure.

(i) Readily exchangeable ions: 20 g of soil was treated with 200 mL of 1M ammonium acetate (NH_4OAc) at room temperature for 24 hours, at a stirring speed of 800 rpm (to ensure a suspension of all the soil). The samples were subsequently centrifuged for 12 minutes at 4 000 rpm using a Dupont RC5C® centrifuge. After centifugation, 50 mL of extraction solution was decanted, of which approximately 6 mL was filtered using Becton Dickenson 5ml Syringes and 0.45 μm SPARTAN 30/0.45 RC filters. The sample filtrates were then diluted for storage to give a 1:10 dilution, using subboiling 2% HNO_3. After the removal of an aliquot of extraction solution for filtration, dilution and analysis, the remaining extraction solution was carefully removed from the centrifuge bottles using a vacuum pump, which was cleaned between samples with nanopure water. The last few millilitres of solution on the surface of the solid material layer were removed using a plastic pasture pipette. (A portion of the extraction solution will remain in the pore system within the soil residue in the bottle. This residual solution was considered to be negligible in comparison with soil mass losses and uranium losses that would incur if complete filtration of the extraction solutions and soil residues, using filter papers, was carried out between each extraction step.)

(ii) Bound to Carbonates: The soil residues from extraction step (i) were treated with 200 mL of 1M-ammonium acetate (NH_4OAc), which had been adjusted to pH 5 with HNO_3 (69%). The samples were then stirred in the thermoblock for 4 hours at room temperature. The solution pH was monitored to ensure that it remained above pH 5 (to minimise premature attack to manganese oxides). The subsequent extraction procedure was performed as above.

(iii) Fe/Mn oxides and hydroxides: The soil residues from extraction step (ii) were treated with 200 mL of 0.2M hydroxyl amine hydrochloride ($NH_2OH·HCl$ in 25 % (v/v) HAc) and stirred for 3 hours. The subsequent extraction procedure was performed as in (i).

(iv) Bound to organic matter: The residues from above were treated with 200 mL of H_2O_2 (30%, adjusted to 0.05M with 1M HNO_3), heated to 85°C, and stirred for 3 hours. 15 mL of H_2O_2 (30%) was added to each sample bottle during the 3-hour treatment period. The volume of concentrated hydrogen peroxide is unlikely to have caused the complete oxidation of the organic material, and should be increased for future sequential extraction studies on soils. The subsequent extraction procedure was performed as in (i).

(v) Amorphous silicates: The residues from (iv) were treated with two extraction solutions in succession. Firstly, with 200 mL of 0.2M sodium hydroxide (NaOH) (extraction (v)a), and then by 200 mL of 0.3M HNO_3 (extraction (v)b). Both treatments involved the samples being stirred at 80°C for 40 minutes. The subsequent extraction procedure was performed as in (i).

(vi) Residual: The residues from (v)b were treated with 200 mL of 7M HNO_3 and stirred for 4 hours at 85°C. The subsequent extraction procedure was performed as in (i).

■ **IBRAE RAS (Russian Expert) samples in cooperation with SIA "Radon" Laboratory**

Radioactive contamination of different surfaces

To estimate conversion coefficients for recalculations from the Inspector instruments count rate (in cps) to density of radioactive contamination of surfaces (in Bq cm^{-2} or μg cm^{-2}), two methods were used:

1. the creation of a computer model for the Inspector device; and

2. calibration of the Inspector by using standard point sources, and by specially prepared surface sources of γ- and β-radiation.

Smear samples analysis

Smear samples of dust were fixed at the sampling point on a scotch tape. The tape width was 44 mm, the length of samples ranged from 120 to 190 mm. The fixed pollution was isolated by sticking a second layer of scotch tape. All 32 samples were studied with the Inspector instrument and by non-destructive radioactivity measurement techniques. In addition, 5 of these samples were analysed in detail through radiochemical procedures.

Research Direction

● **Beta- radiometry**

Instrumentation

For sample activity measurements, a low-background alpha-beta radiometer HT-1000 (Canberra Inc.) with four gas-flow detectors was applied. A typical background count rate in beta-particles registration channels is near 0.01 counts/sec.

Preparation of counting sources

Samples were cut in four piece fragments of about equal length. Each fragment was measured with a separate detector. For sample calculations, the measurement values of clean scotch tape fragments were used as background. Fragments of about 40 mm were stuck together with the sticky sides to completely reproduce the real geometry of samples.

A calibration source for the HT-1000 radiometer was prepared via drop by drop dispensing of a weighed amount of standard solution of ^{238}U in equilibrium with daughter products ^{234}Th/^{234m}Pa on the gluing surface of a "Scotch"-film (45x45 mm) (i.e. a calculated volume of standard solution of ^{238}U (in equilibrium with daughter products ^{234}Th/^{234m}Pa) was selected by pipette and weighed. The selected solution was uniformly dispensed drop by drop by a pipette on the gluing surface of adhesive tape). Total activity of ^{238}U was 13.9 Bq. After liquid evaporation under and infrared lamp, the prepared film with ^{238}U was covered by another piece of film with the same dimensions. Determined efficiency for registration of the ^{234}Th/^{234m}Pa emission with HT-1000 radiometer ranged from 0.182 ± 0.013 up to 0.200 ± 0.014 for different detectors.

● **Gamma-spectrometry measurements**

Instrumentation

A gamma-spectrometer based on HPGe Coaxial Detector (EG&G ORTEC GEM-110210-P, 112.1 % relative efficiency, resolution - 2.1 keV at 1 332 keV FWHM ^{60}Co peak) was applied to determine gamma-emitting radionuclides. The average duration of measurements neared 20 000 seconds.

Sample pre-treatment for alpha-/beta-emitting radionuclides analysis

Samples were ashed in a muffle furnace at 550° C. The ashes were then handled with concentrated HNO_3 and a periodic addition of H_2O_2 before obtaining a light colour solution and a solid residue (the complete decomposition of organic compounds). The liquid phase was decanted, sediments were washed with HNO_3 and solutions were combined. Solid residues were completely decomposed in a mixture of concentrated HNO_3 and HF in a microwave digestion unit "MLS 1200 mega" (Milestone) equipped with HPR1000/6 rotor and high-pressure TFM vessels. The obtained solutions were treated by multiple evaporations with concentrated HNO_3 to eliminate fluorine. Finally, the obtained residue was dissolved in 7.5 M HNO_3.

- **Alpha/beta spectrometry via liquid scintillation technique**

Instrumentation

A TRI-CARB 2550 TR/AB (Packard Inc.) liquid scintillation analyzer was applied for the analysis of beta-emitting radionuclides as well as for the evaluation of composition and activity of alpha-emitters in submitted samples. ULTIMA GOLD AB® was used for the preparation of counting sources.

Identification and activity calculations of radionuclides in samples according to their LS-spectra

Identification and calculation of radionuclide activities were fulfilled in compliance with the algorithm, including the optimised convolution of the spectrum into groups, and modelling the spectra by a set of single library spectra, which were corrected for sample quenching parameters (Kashirin, 2000). During the calculations, the basic spectra are fitted to the quenching parameters by means of interpolation between two reference spectra. The library of quenched spectra for each radionuclide was obtained for at least 10 quench levels.

Preparation of the counting sources for LS-spectrometry

Aliquots of sample solutions, equal to 1/5 were prepared in the previous steps. These aliquots were evaporated, transferred into hydrochloric form by evaporation with concentrated hydrochloric acid. Phosphoric acid was then added periodically. After this operation, the solutions became colourless, since colourless iron complexes (phosphates) were formed instead of the yellow coloured chloride complexes.

- **Analysis of the Uranium isotope composition in samples by alpha-spectrometry**

Instrumentation

For the determination of uranium isotope activity ratios an alpha-spectrometer consisting of four units model 7401 (CANBERRA Inc.) was used. Detectors with an active area of 600 mm^2, type passivated implanted planar silicon (PIPS), were used. The resolution of theses detectors is better than 18 keV. The duration of measurements ranged from 30 000 to 45 000s.

Radiochemical separation of Uranium

After selecting the aliquots for LS-spectrometry, the known activity of chemical yield radioisotope tracer ^{232}U was introduced into residual sample solutions. Solutions were evaporated and converted into 7.5M HNO_3 form. From the specified solution, uranium was extracted with a 30% solution of tributhylphosphate in toluene. After purification of the organic phase by means of double washing with 7.5M HNO_3 and back-extraction of thorium with 0.04M HF in 0.5M HNO_3, the final solution containing uranium was obtained by extraction with distilled water. The solution obtained was evaporated and, after destroying organic traces, uranium was electroplated onto stainless discs from an ammonia oxalate-chloride solution.

Depleted Uranium in Bosnia and Herzegovina

C.4.3 Quality Control

During the mission, the team members decided to organise a quality control exercise based on an inter-laboratory comparison between APAT Laboratory (Italy) and Spiez Laboratory (Switzerland) in order to verify the precision and comparability of the analytical results obtained in the two laboratories.

Since most samples collected were soils, lichen and water, the team decided to run the comparison on these sample types. Furthermore, the respective laboratory teams decided to use IAEA reference materials in order to compare results for homogenous sample materials with recommended reference values and recommended confidence intervals for the concentration of uranium isotopes. In this framework, IAEA Laboratories in Seibersdorf made available reference samples of lichen (IAEA-336), seaweed (IAEA-140TM), sea water (IAEA-381), and soil (IAEA-326) for the two laboratories. These were the best available uranium standard samples. The uranium in all these samples is in its natural isotopic composition. Unfortunately, certified standards for DU contaminated environmental samples are not available. The laboratories applied their established methodologies; APAT analysed the samples by an alpha-spectrometry system, while Spiez Laboratory used the ICP-MS system.

APAT laboratory made three analyses on each reference material. Spiez Laboratory made two analyses on each reference material. The mean values are reported in Table C.3. The mean values are in good agreement with the recommended and/or informal values.

Table C.3 Data of the inter-laboratory comparison between APAT Laboratory (Italy) and Spiez Laboratory (Switzerland)

IAEA 326 Soil Sample ID	^{238}U Bq/kg	^{234}U Bq/kg	^{235}U Bq/kg
APAT-Mean	29.5 ± 1.45	28.0 ± 1.16	1.53 ± 0.32
SPIEZ Mean	28.02 ± 0.59	27.49 ± 5.22	1.31 ± 0.04
% 95 Confidence Interval	28.1 - 30.7	26.5 - 29.3	1.21 - 1.75

IAEA 381 Sea water Sample ID	^{238}U mBq/kg	^{234}U mBq/kg	^{235}U mBq/kg
APAT Mean	37.8 ± 1.22	42.7 ± 1.71	2.06 ± 0.24
SPIEZ Mean	40.67 ± 0.87	43.23 ± 0.87	1.86 ± 0.15
% 95 Confidence Interval	38 - 48	43 - 58	1.4 - 2.4

IAEA 140/TM Seaweed Sample ID	^{238}U Bq/kg	^{234}U Bq/kg	^{235}U Bq/kg
APAT-Mean	9.3 ± 0.37	10.6 ± 0.36	0.48 ± 0.08
SPIEZ Mean	9.29 ± 0.17	10.86 ± 1.52	0.43 ± 0.04
% 95 Confidence Interval	8.02 - 10.08	(these values refer only to U-tot)	

IAEA 336 Lichen Sample ID	^{238}U Bq/kg	^{234}U Bq/kg	^{235}U Bq/kg
APAT-Mean	0.62 ± 0.04	0.59 ± 0.04	0.031 ± 0.009
SPIEZ Mean	0.60 ± 0.013	0.65 ± 0.11	0.028 ± 0.0015
% 95 Confidence Interval	0.37 - 0.62	(these values refer only to U-tot)*	

* The IAEA [IAEA, 1999] does not give an information value for the U concentration. In the section "Elements which failed both Recommended and Information Value Acceptance Criteria" in the paragraph regarding Uranium it is written: "Ten laboratories reported results for U and none was rejected as an outlier. The relative standard deviation of the mean was 36%, which exceeds the criterion for it to be classified as an information value. If a t-test had been performed in addition to the four standard outlier tests, one laboratory mean which was very low would have been rejected which would have reduced the relative standard deviation of the nine remaining laboratories to 26.2%. This would have led to uranium qualifying as an information value of 0.04 mg/kg with a confidence interval of 0.03 - 0.05 mg/kg for U."

Post-Conflict Environmental Assessment

Figures C.2a to C.2d report all data from the comparison. In the following, the comments refer only to ^{238}U determination, considered as an indicator of result comparability.

Figure C.2a   Data of the inter-laboratory comparison between APAT Laboratory (Italy) and Spiez Laboratory (Switzerland) and recommended value of IAEA-326 soil. The interval of IAEA value represents the 95 % interval of confidence.

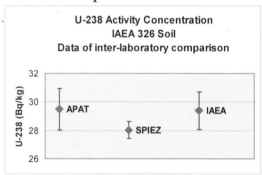

Figure C.2a reports the comparison between the IAEA recommended value and APAT and Spiez data of ^{238}U activity concentrations in the IAEA-326 soil. These results confirm the good agreement between methods applied on totally dissolved samples. The importance of dissolution was already focused in the NAT-9 quality control exercise organised by the IAEA in the framework of the UNEP mission in Kosovo [NAHRES-60, 2001, UNEP, 2001].

Figure C.2b   Data of the inter-laboratory comparison between APAT Laboratory (Italy) and Spiez Laboratory (Switzerland) and recommended value of IAEA-381 Seawater. The interval of IAEA value represents the 95 % interval of confidence .

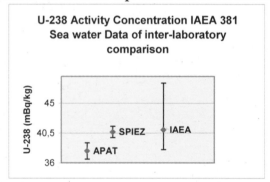

These results of IAEA-381 Seawater confirm the good agreement between the two different methods applied for measuring the uranium isotopes in water samples.

Figure C.2c   Data of the inter-laboratory comparison between APAT Laboratory (Italy) and Spiez Laboratory (Switzerland) and recommended value of IAEA-140/TM Sea weed. The interval of IAEA value represents the 95 % interval of confidence.

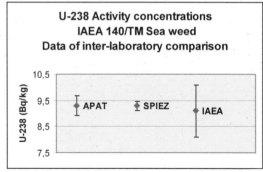

The results on the inter-laboratory made on the IAEA 140/TM Sea-weed show that both laboratories have an accurate procedure for U-analysis on biological samples.

The results on the inter-laboratory comparison made on the IAEA 336 lichen show that both laboratories have accurate procedures for uranium analysis on biological samples.

Figure C.2d **Data of the inter-laboratory comparison between APAT Laboratory (Italy) and Spiez Laboratory (Switzerland) and recommended value of IAEA-336 Lichen. The interval of IAEA value represents the 95 % interval of confidence.**

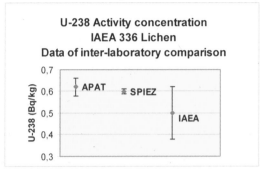

Isotopic ratios

Spiez laboratory evaluates the DU concentration of environmental samples using the 235/238 isotopic ratio because, using a mass-spectrometric technique, the 235/238 isotopic ratio is measured faster and with higher precision than the 234/238 isotopic ratio. On the other hand, APAT laboratory evaluates the DU concentration of environmental samples using the 234/238-activity ratio because using alpha spectrometry, the 234/238-activity ratio is measured faster and with higher precision than the 235/238-activity ratio.

Table C.4 Uranium activity ratios 234/238 and isotopic ratios 235/238 of the reference samples analysed by APAT Laboratory (Italy) and Spiez Laboratory (Switzerland)

	APAT Activity ratio^{234}U/^{238}U	SPIEZ Isotopic ratio^{235}U/^{238}U
IAEA 326 Soil		
Mean	0.95 ± 0.06	0.00724 ± 0.00006
Reference value for natural Uranium	from 0.5 to 1.2*	0.00725
IAEA 381 Sea water		
Mean	1.13 ± 0.05	0.00722 ± 0.00008
Reference value for natural Uranium	from 0.8 to 10 (Goldstein et al., 1997)	0.00725
IAEA 140/TM Seaweed		
Mean	1.13 ± 0.07	0.00725 ± 0.00011
Reference value for natural Uranium	from 0.5 to 1.2*	0.00725
IAEA 336 Lichen		
Mean	0.95 ± 0.08	0.00726 ± 0.00008
Reference value for natural Uranium	0.95 ± 0.08**	0.00725

* Natural composition of uranium in soil is characterized by 234U/238U ratio activity of about 1 and 0.046 respectively: Particularly 234U/238U activity ratio in soil typically range from 0.5 to 1.2 [Bou-Rabee, 1995; Goldstein et al., 1997; UNEP, 2001; 2002; Sansone et al., 2001, 2001a, 2001b]. This value can be considered also for the botanical samples considering that the presence of U could be mainly due to soil addition.

** There are no reference values for natural uranium in lichen reported in literature. Considering that the IAEA-336 lichen is not affected by DU contamination, we can consider the mean value of the APAT-SPIEZ inter-lab exercise, made on IAEA-336, as the reference value for natural uranium in lichen.

Post-Conflict Environmental Assessment

Table C.4 reports the mean values of the uranium isotopic ratios 234/238 for APAT Laboratory and 235/238 for Spiez Laboratory of the reference samples analysed by both laboratories. The ratios were near the theoretical values for isotopic composition of natural uranium.

These results indicate that the two laboratories are able to differentiate DU from natural uranium in environmental samples, and that the derived DU concentrations are analysed with satisfactory precision.

Calculation of measuring errors

Measurement uncertainties for Spiez Laboratory data were calculated by propagation of errors from the relative standard deviations. The relative standard deviation of the variables were either experimentally determined or estimated, as described in the test reports. In the case of APAT data, the uncertainties reported are the combination of the contributions to the uncertainty assessed, as reported in the paragraph Statistical and measurement uncertainties and the repeatability, experimentally obtained analysing three different replicates. For this reason, the uncertainties associated with APAT also take into consideration the contribution due to the inhomogeneity of the sample and are consequently higher than those reported for Spiez Laboratory.

Conclusions

The results of the quality control exercise based on an inter-laboratory comparison between APAT laboratory (Italy) and Spiez Laboratory (Switzerland) showed good agreement for all the reference materials.

Appendix D
DU in Soil

D.1 BACKGROUND

Uranium in bedrock and soils

Without the presence of uranium, the Earth would be a rather different planet as heat produced by the radioactive decay of uranium is partly responsible for keeping the planet's core and mantle hot enough for convective flow to occur (in addition to other naturally occurring radionuclides). When measuring isotopic ratios in environmental samples, it is important to realise that uranium may sometimes become depleted (or enriched) in some of its isotopes due to natural processes such as chemical weathering.

Uranium is ubiquitous in all rocks, soils, rivers and groundwaters on the Earth's surface. Average values for uranium in rocks are about 2-3 mg/kg (ppm, parts per million) and concentrations usually vary slightly (1-30 ppm) according to rock type. Granites, acid volcanic and carbonatitic rocks often have higher uranium content than other rocks. Certain types of black shales have higher uranium concentrations, such as Chattanooga shale (50-100 ppm), alum shales (50-400 ppm) and phosphor containing sediments (up to 200 ppm). These types of rocks cover large areas. A rock containing 3 ppm uranium holds 8.1 g of uranium per cubic metre of rock (1 m^3). If a single penetrator is added, the concentration of uranium increases to 308 g or 115-ppm uranium. For natural waters, uranium is much lower in concentration than in natural rocks and the variations are higher, typically from less than 1 µg/kg (ppb, parts per billion) to 100 ppb or more.

Plutonium, which can be present in DU ammunition in very low concentrations depending on its fabrication process, is also found worldwide in surface soil, air and water mainly as a result of contamination (delayed stratospheric fallout) from nuclear weapons tests carried out in the atmosphere until the 1960s.

Uranium in surface and subsurface soil

10-35 % (up to a maximum of 70 %) of a DU penetrator piercing through an armoured vehicle will aerosolise into a uranium oxide on impact when the uranium metal dust catches fire (Rand 1999). Most dust particles formed are smaller than 5 micrometers in size and, when released into the atmosphere, spread according to wind direction. By sedimentation, DU particles are deposited on the ground and other various surfaces. Pieces or fragments of metallic DU can also be formed and scattered around. According to reports from the

A corroded penetrator fragment in surface soil

Nellis Air Force Range, a US training range for DU ordnance, most DU dust is deposited within a distance of 100 metres from the target (Nellis, 1997). This dust consists mainly of uranium oxides.

It is estimated that in a real attack scenario, only about 10 % of the fired rounds will hit a hard target. Most of the penetrators hitting soft ground will probably penetrate intact more than

Post-Conflict Environmental Assessment

50 cm into the ground and remain there for a long period of time, depending on the weathering/geochemical conditions. Penetrators that impact on a hard ground surface such as concrete, rock or stony soil are, after dispelling their kinetic energy into the superficial ground layer, often found lying on or near the soil surface. They are usually found almost intact, or split into large fragments, and have lost only a small part of their mass through the formation of dust or small uranium particles.

Analysis results of surface soil samples taken during the earlier UNEP missions showed that topsoil contamination which was equal or higher than the soil's natural uranium content could only be found at distances less than a few metres from penetrator impact points in the ground (UNEP, 2001). Around impact points on soft ground, localized DU contamination higher than the detection limit (i.e. about 30 µg per kg soil) could be found for distances less than 20 metres. For impact points on hard ground surfaces, this distance grew to a maximum range of 50 to 100 meters. No widespread DU contamination of topsoil for distances exceeding approximately 100 metres from the impact points was detected.

Uranium or uranium oxide dust as well as fine fragments will initially be deposited on the ground surface. Over time, these will be gradually transported down into the upper soil layer, mostly through physical weathering (rain and wind). Through the dissolution of corrosion products, uranium can also be transported to deeper ground layers. Nevertheless, it is expected that even after many years at least part of the initially deposited uranium could still be found in the surface soil layer.

Various impact points from DU munitions

This explains why sampling of surface soil and subsurface soil profiles is very important in order to analyze and understand the distribution of DU contamination at and around identified or assumed attack sites. Through the use of transfer models, results from soil sample analyses are important input parameters in order to estimate doses to inhabitants living at and around contaminated soil surfaces. The results of inductively coupled plasma mass spectrometry (ICP MS) analyses allow us to identify and measure DU to very low limits and to differentiate it from natural uranium always present in soil (see Appendix C). Soil profile analyses provide insight into the downward transport of DU in subsurface soil.

With respect to the food-to-human ingestion pathway, reports state that due to the very low transfer factors of DU from soil into biological material (i.e. vegetables) and from food stuffs to human, the expected doses due to ingestion would only be a few microsieverts per year (EU, 2001; WHO, 2001). Even in very conservative scenarios with high consumption of vegetables grown in highly contaminated soils, doses to local inhabitants are insignificant.

Inhalation of resuspended DU from contaminated soil in the zone adjacent to the target area (e.g. where a tank was hit by DU) could result in an annual DU intake of a maximum of 0.6–60 µg (UNEP, 1999; UNEP, 2001; EU, 2001; Keller et al., 2001). The resulting effective dose of 0.07–7 µSv per year is negligible, compared to the typical dose from natural radiation sources, which for most populations worldwide is in the range of 1-10 mSv per year.

Geochemical aspects of uranium in soil

Most of the 3 tons of depleted uranium penetrators introduced into the BiH environment are buried in soils, not rocks. Consequently, the most likely harm that DU could cause to the local population would be through the dissolution of penetrators by soil water and subsequent transport of the dissolved uranium down through the profile and into the groundwater table. The uranium could in turn enter water for drinking wells and be a possible cause of radiation and chemical toxicity.

UNEP observed that A-10 attacks introduced one penetrator into the ground at an interval of 1-3 m along target lines. In addition, US test range data indicate that penetrators entering soft soil can go as deep as 6-7 m depending on velocity and angle of impact and can sometimes fragment. Therefore, as available data are reviewed, it is assumed that each penetrator can contaminate a minimum of $1 m^3$ of soil.

Sampled groundwater wells had depths to the groundwater table of ~2 m. Hence, if we imagine in this analysis a column down to the groundwater table with a surface of $1 m^2$, each penetrator has the capacity to contaminate $2 m^3$ of soil before the groundwater is affected. The average concentration of uranium in $1 m^3$ of soil (natural uranium plus one 300 g penetrator with a density of the soil of $1 600 kg/m^3$) will be 115 ppm (i.e. a 38 fold increase over natural uranium in most soils). A penetrator can only slightly contaminate rock, but would more likely contaminate the water in its pore spaces or fractures. The available scientific data for the behaviour of uranium in the natural environment is summarised below:

Uranium metal is unstable when in contact with oxygen and water. Therefore, uranium oxides form on the penetrator or fragment surfaces according to the following reaction, in which uranium is in its tetravalent form:

$$U \quad + \quad O_2 \quad = \quad UO_2$$

Metal   **Uraninite**

However, in contact with the atmosphere, uraninite is unstable and oxidizes to its hexavalent form:

$$UO_2 + 0.5O_2 = UO_3$$

In the presence of water these oxides are hydrated (contain water). The maximum solubility of oxidised uranium phases forming surface layers on penetrators (e.g. schoepite, $UO_3 nH_2O$) at near-neutral pH is about 10 mg/L (ppm). Waters in BiH were found to have near-neutral pH. In this case, the dissolved uranium was in the uranyl ion form (UO_2^{2+}). However, there are many processes in nature which can retard the transport of uranium (sorption to minerals and organics in the soil, co-precipitation with calcite) and reduce (iron-II-bearing minerals, bacteria, organic matter) the uranium from its hexavalent soluble form to its tetravalent insoluble form (UO_2 - solubility at neutral pH (pH7) = 0.1 μg/L). Some confusion about the solubility of uranium oxide still persists today. Here, aqueous uranium is on the form of U^{4+}.

Before evaluating the dissolution and transport of penetrators, it is important to consider the composition of soils and rocks. The rocks that make up the visited areas were largely limestone and dolomites. Soil thickness varied from tens of centimetres in some areas, to only a few centimetres in others. Again, depth to the groundwater table was measured to be ~2 m when water was collected from private wells. These wells can thus be considered to be in unconfined (or surface) aquifers with no confining layer that can protect the aquifers from DU. The climate in BiH is humid-continental with precipitation close to 75 cm/yr. This precipitation value represents the infiltration rate into surface aquifers.

Retrieved penetrators had clear signs of two alteration phases, one black and the other yellow. They had been present in soil for 7-8 years and had grown in size by roughly 100% through the formation of uranium oxides at the penetrators' surface. Analysis of the penetrators from Kosovo using spectroscopy (Raman spectroscopy and X-ray Photoelectron spectroscopy (XPS)) and scanning electron microscopy with energy dispersive spectrometer (SEM/EDS)

Post-Conflict Environmental Assessment

DU corrosion products are left behind in the soil

indicated that the alteration phases contain only uranium and oxygen, in addition to low levels of other metals known to be present in DU ordnance (iron, titanium, chromium, silicon and aluminium) (UNEP, 2000). XPS analyses of a penetrator fragment show uranium in these oxides in both its U(6+) and U(4+) state. The yellow and black alteration phases are thus uranium oxides. A French study of DU metal found in a test site in Southern France used X-ray diffraction studies of the alteration phases observed (also black and yellow) to show that these two phases are $UO_2(OH)_2(s)$ and $UO_3 2H_2O$ (schoepite) (Crançon, 2001). The former is likely to be the black alteration phase and the latter the yellow. Since the yellow phase is more abundant on the surface, it is concluded that the black phase (U^{4+}) is an intermediary step in the alteration from uranium metal (U^0) to the fully oxidised yellow phase (U^{6+}). The alteration phases of the penetrators collected in BiH had the same colours and were considered to be in the same phases as those found in Kosovo.

Investigation of oxidation rates of penetrators found in Kosovo indicated that, in soil solutions, the rate of schoepite dissolution is about the same as that of oxidation. This can be concluded by comparing laboratory dissolution studies of schoepite in the presence of CO_2 from the atmosphere (Duro, 1996), which is 32 g/300 g of schoepite assuming that the surface area of the penetrator is 27 cm². If the penetrator fragments into smaller pieces, its surface area is increased and the dissolution rate increases accordingly. It is thus considered likely that all of the penetrators will completely corrode in 25-35 years. Studies of the retrieved penetrators buried in soil from this mission show that roughly 50% of the penetrator had transformed to oxides at the surface. Therefore, it is likely that total corrosion of the penetrator will take longer than estimated from the Kosovo data.

As the uranium-metal penetrators oxidize, the soils and rocks will initially contain elevated concentrations of schoepite rather than solid uranium metal penetrators. With time, the schoepite will dissolve and uranium will move downward through the soil. How far the uranium will be transported is limited, however, if the penetrator is embedded in organic-rich soil. Once the uranium comes into contact with organic matter and minerals (less than 100 μm), the uranium will initially be sorbed to these minerals (Waite *et al.*, 1994) and organic matter (Nash *et al.*, 1981). This is particularly the case if the pH of the soil is intermediate (pH 6-8). At low pH, no sorption occurs to mineral surfaces as they are positively charged by H^+ sorption and the aqueous uranium is in the form of the uranyl ion (UO_2^{2+}). At high pH, no sorption occurs either because the dissolved uranyl ion forms negatively charged aqueous complexes with carbonate (CO_3^{2-}) and hydroxide (OH^-) and the mineral surfaces are also negatively charged. Due to the presence of divalent iron in soil minerals (Liger *et al.*, 1999) and bacteria (e.g. Loveley *et al.*, 1991), uranium can be reduced to its insoluble quatrovalent form (see for example Ragnarsdottir and Charlet, 2000 for a summary of uranium behaviour in the natural environment). However, this will only occur where soil profiles have reductive conditions. Such conditions were not observed in the soil profiles sampled.

Depleted Uranium in Bosnia and Herzegovina

D.2 RESULTS OF MEASUREMENTS

D.2.1 Uranium in surface soil

Natural uranium levels at the investigated sites

The natural uranium concentration of the uncontaminated soils that were sampled at the investigated sites during the UNEP mission was in the range of 1.3 to 4.8 mg U/kg soil. These values are within the normal range of natural uranium concentration of soil. The results of the measurements of the isotopic composition of uranium in these samples were indicative for natural uranium. They proved that, in these samples, there was no DU contamination present above the detection limit, which is in the range of about 2 % of the natural uranium content of the soil (equivalent to about 30 µg DU per kilogram topsoil).

Contamination points

The soil directly at DU penetrator impact points and in their immediate vicinity is the most contaminated. At *Han Pijesak's Artillery Storage and Barracks*, for example, the soil around two penetrators lying in undisturbed, grass covered ground at a depth between 3 - 8 cm below the soil surface was investigated. The average contamination in the top 10 cm of the soil was 24 g of DU per kilogram of soil on a surface of 15 x 15 cm immediately surrounding an undamaged penetrator without its jacket (samples NUC-2002-028-101 and NUC-2002-028-102), whereas the average contamination around a whole penetrator still in its jacket was 2.6 g of DU per kilogram of soil (samples NUC-2002-028-120 and NUC-2002-028-121). A dominant part of the DU contamination of these samples consists of the thick layer of DU corrosion products. These had formed on the exposed surface of the penetrators over the 7 years in which they had been present in the soil. These corrosion products remained partly in the ground after removing the DU penetrator.

Localized DU contamination of surface soil

The analyses of surface soil samples taken from areas targeted by DU weapons show that there exists local soil contamination around DU penetrator impact points. This localized DU contamination was measurable at the target areas of the former *Hadzici Tank Repair Facility* (sample NUC-2002-024-008), *Hadzici Ammunition Storage* site (samples NUC-2002-027-004 and NUC-2002-027-005) and the *Han Pijesak Artillery Storage and Barracks* (samples NUC-2002-028-001 and NUC-2002-028-003). At all other sites where surface soil samples were collected, no indication of DU contamination exceeding the detection limit could be found. The detection limit for soil samples is noted above.

Inside DU target areas, at distances under 10 - 20 m to the nearest visible penetrator impact points on hard surfaces (concrete, asphalt, rocks, stony ground), localized DU contamination of topsoil

Surface soil sampling near Hadzici

Post-Conflict Environmental Assessment

not exceeding 3.8 milligrams per kilogram could be measured in some of the collected samples. This value is roughly equivalent to the average concentration of natural uranium in soil. The existence of DU in the visible impact holes was confirmed by measuring the Beta radiation of DU in the field with portable instruments.

In certain places, at distances greater than 50 - 100 m from confirmed hard surface impact points, the DU concentration was normally less than 0.3 milligrams per kilogram of soil. In most samples, however, it was even lower than the detection limit. These values are equivalent to less than 10 % of the average concentration of natural uranium in soil. Localized DU contamination was measured at 0.1 milligram per kilogram of soil in only one soil sample from the eastern area of the Han Pijesak military barracks (sample NUC-2002-028-001) at a distance of about 170 m to the nearest confirmed impact point. This unusually large distance for localized ground contamination may be explained by local contamination coming from potential undetected penetrator impact points on the soft ground between the sampling point and the nearest confirmed impact points. The two other samples taken from the same area of the site showed no indication of DU contamination exceeding the detection limit.

Outside the restricted area of the former *Hadzici Tank Repair Facility*, where public access is unlimited, no signs of DU topsoil contamination could be detected. Localised contamination at the *Hadzici Ammunition Storage* site and *Han Pijesak Artillery Storage and Barracks* was limited to the attacked areas of the sites.

No indication of widespread DU contamination could be found at distances exceeding 100 - 200 m from confirmed penetrator impact points. It is assumed that this is probably true even at distances greater than about 50 to 100 m. The short distribution distances of DU contamination is thus defined as localized ground contamination.

Around impact points on soft surfaces (e.g. soil without stones), localized DU contamination of topsoil was generally less intense, reaching even smaller distances. For example, in a topsoil sample (NUC-2002-028-004) from *Han Pijesak*, the DU concentration was below the detection limit at a distance of only 3 m from an impact point on soft ground.

At the edge of a large cobblestone square/yard at the centre of the former *Hadzici Tank Repair Facility*, two sand samples were collected on a surface where rainwater runoff had deposited a roughly 3 cm thick layer of sand and dust from the yard (samples NUC-2002-024-011 and NUC-2002-024-012). Within a distance of about 30 m, a lot of penetrator impact points were identified on this cobblestone surface. Under these circumstances, a certain local enrichment of DU combined with the deposited sand at some distance from the surface of the original deposition can be anticipated. The DU concentration of this material was 30 milligrams per kilogram, or equivalent to approximately 10 times the natural uranium concentration.

D.2.2 DU in subsurface soil

Contamination of subsurface soil immediately below the impact points of three DU penetrators at *Han Pijesak* was investigated by taking soil profile samples down to a depth of 60 – 65 cm below the soil surface. The penetrators were lying in undisturbed, grass covered ground at a depth of 3 - 8 cm below the soil surface. The average contamination in the 5 cm layer of soil around an intact penetrator without its jacket was measured at 45 g of DU per kilogram of soil on a surface of 15 x 15 cm immediately surrounding it (samples NUC-2002-028-101 to -112). The average contamination in the layer around a whole penetrator remaining in its jacket was only 4.7 g of DU per kilogram of soil (samples NUC-2002-028-120 to -132). The difference is probably due to the penetrator's surface being partly protected from corrosive attack by the jacket. The contamination of these samples consists mainly of the thick layer of DU corrosion products, which formed at the exposed surface of the penetrators over the last 7 years in the soil. Penetrators without their jackets have, in that period, lost roughly 25 % of their metallic mass by corrosion.

Within the first 10 cm of soil below the penetrator, DU concentrations diminished by about two orders of magnitude to values of 230 and 69 mg/kg soil respectively (Figure D.1, Profile 1 and 2 respectively). Within the next 30 cm, this concentration diminished by roughly another three orders of magnitude to values of 0.09 mg/kg of soil and below the detection limit (less than 0.06 mg/kg of soil) respectively. Finally, the DU concentration diminished by almost six orders of magnitude to values at or below the detection limit of the analytical method for soil within 40 cm below the penetrators. No traces of DU could be detected in layers deeper than 40 cm. Based on these results, it is concluded that the mobility of DU corrosion products is very low in the type of soil found at Han Pijesak.

A full DU bullet was retreived from Han Pijesak

Figure D.1   Concentration of DU in soil profiles from Han Pijesak

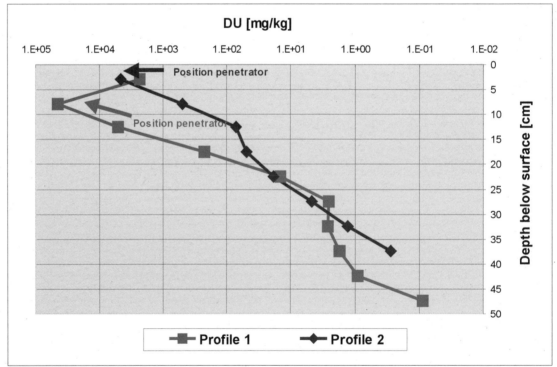

D.3   URANIUM DEPTH DISTRIBUTION AND EXTRACTION EXPERIMENTS

Soil Profile Description

One of the sampled profiles from Han Pijesak was analysed through extraction experiments. The sampled soil profile consisted of three distinct soil horizons, which may have been disturbed prior to the intrusion of the penetrator, as it was adjacent to a built up road track. The profile consisted of a surface organic layer (L), an organic rich silty sand layer (A); a clay horizon (Bs_1); and a horizon of silty sand textured matrix, with downward coarsening clastic content (Bs_2). Ochre coloured iron oxidation and organic matter smearing was evident in the clay and sand horizons. Clasts were dominantly calcareous.

D.2　　　　　　　　**D.3**　　　　　　　　**D.4**

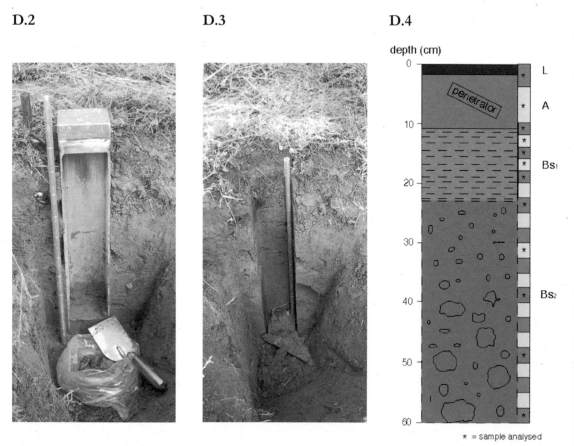

Figure D.2 shows the soil profile midway through the sample collection, figure D.3 shows the soil profile after sample collection and figure D.4 shows the soil description log, the depths at which samples were collected and those samples which were later analysed.

Total uranium (^{238}U)

Total Fusion and Residue Fusion

In order to measure the total uranium content of the soil samples collected, total fusions were performed. In addition, to evaluate the recovery of uranium throughout the extraction experiment procedure, the soil residue remaining at the end of the six extraction stages was also fused.

Fusion method and measurements by HR-ICP-MS are outlined under Spiez Laboratory in Appendix C.

Depth Distribution Results

The quantitative analysis for total fusion ^{238}U concentration indicates that the uranium predominantly occurs within the top 10 cm of the soil profile. Of the total ^{238}U measured in the profile, 87 % occurs within the top 10 cm. However, the ^{238}U concentration remains above the average soil uranium concentration (1-10 mg/kg) down to a depth of 40 cm. As uranium isotope ratio studies have not yet been performed on this particular soil profile, it is not possible by this means to confirm the elevated uranium concentrations as depleted uranium.

Depleted Uranium in Bosnia and Herzegovina

However, using the assumption that measured uranium concentrations exceeding the average soil uranium concentration of 1-10 mg/kg are due to uranium mobilization from the penetrator, it is possible to infer that depleted uranium has been mobilized down to a depth of 40 cm. The uranium mobility may in fact extend down below this depth, however, as Figure D.3 shows, the samples collected from 40 - 47.5 cm were not analysed.

Given the uranium mobilization to a depth of 40 cm within a period of 7 years, the rate of movement of uranium can be estimated as ~5 cm/yr. This rate of mobility varies with soil composition, for example, the porosity and permeability of the soil (i.e. dense clay horizons have reduced permeability, while a horizon with a sand matrix has higher permeability) as well as the organic matter content and mineralogical composition (provide binding sites for the uranium).

Loss-on-ignition (LOI) measurements were performed to establish the organic content down the profile. As Figure D.5 illustrates, the organic content of the soil varies between 1-7 %, with the highest content occurring within the top layers (15 cm) of the soil, as expected. This depth corresponds with the depth of maximum uranium concentration. However, organic matter may also increase the mobility of uranium, through the formation of humic acid complexes, which can be mobilised down the profile. The movement of trace metals by this means tends to occur in acidic soils. As this soil was neutral, it is unlikely that the formation of organo-uranium metal complexes are a significant cause of uranium mobility.

Figure D.5 Total uranium measured in soil profiles

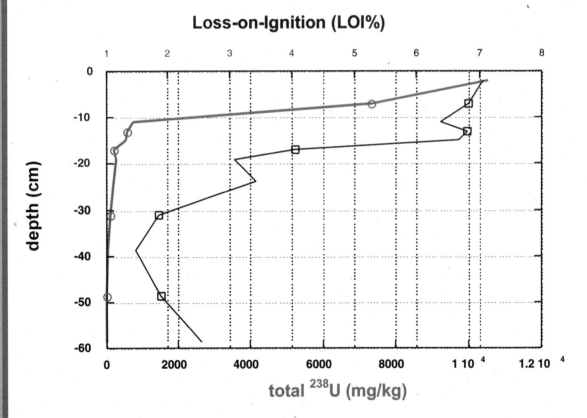

Sequential Extraction Results

As the results from the measurement of total ^{238}U concentration confirm, the ^{238}U concentration decreases with depth. However, the sequentially extracted uranium concentrations infer that the proportion of uranium associated with each geochemical phase varies down the profile. As Figure D.5 shows, in the near surface horizons where the penetrator was embedded, the dominant fraction is the readily exchangeable fraction. At lower levels in the profile, for example, at 37.5 - 40 cm, the carbonate bound uranium dominates. This change in proportion down the profile is seen more clearly in Figures (E) - (I).

Post-Conflict Environmental Assessment

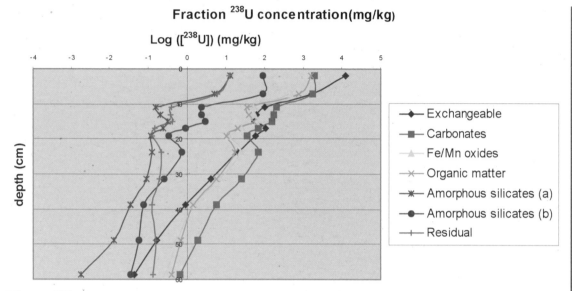

Figure (E)

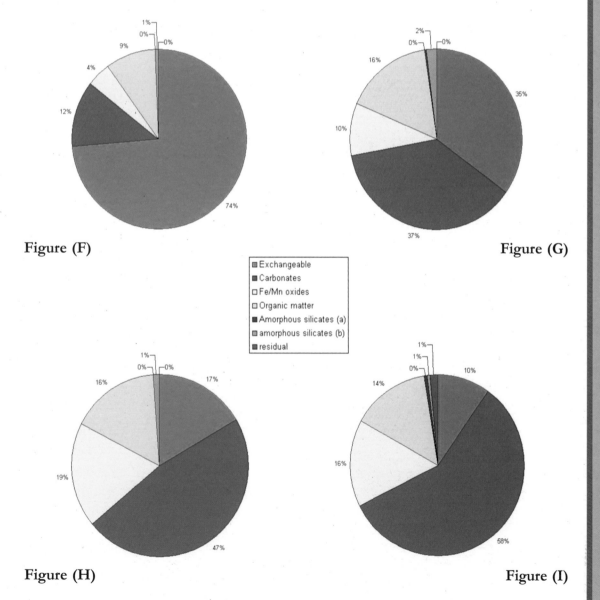

Figure (F)

Figure (G)

Figure (H)

Figure (I)

Figures (F)-(I) show the proportion of ^{238}U recovered from each extraction step at depths of (F) 0-4cm, (G) 4-10cm, (H) 14-16cm and (I) 37.5-40cm

Depleted Uranium in Bosnia and Herzegovina

The dominance of the readily exchangeable fraction in the upper layers of the soil is most likely due to the constant replenishment of uranium from the penetrator to the exchange sites at the surfaces of organic matter and clay minerals, countering the removal of uranium from these sites by leaching as water infiltrates down through the soil. At lower levels in the soil, further from the penetrator, where the concentration of uranium is considerably lower (Figures (D) and (E)), this replenishment does not occur to the same degree. Therefore, larger proportions of uranium are associated with the geochemical phases that bind uranium more strongly, *i.e.* carbonates and organic matter. Uranium held by these binding sites is not so easily removed by percolating groundwater.

Soil pH is neutral and remains fairly constant throughout the profile (between pH 7.4-7.8). These conditions favour the sorption of uranium to the surfaces of soil organic matter, iron oxides and other minerals.

The organic content in the upper layers of the profile (~7%, down to 15 cm depth) contributes significantly to the cation exchange capacity (CEC) of these soil layers (i.e. a measure of the number of exchange sites to which the readily exchangeable fraction is bound). Between 25-90 % of the total CEC of the top layers of mineral soils is thought to be associated with the organic matter content (Stevenson, 1985). Therefore, the organic content within the top layers of the profile plays an important role in providing sites to which uranium can bind. The CEC contribution by organic matter increases with pH, and is therefore greater in a neutral soil, such as the one studied here compared to a more acidic soil, *eg.* a forest soil. Such soils of lower pH are more likely to result in the downward mobilisation of uranium through the formation of uranium-humic complexes.

Finally, the profile appeared fairly well oxidised, as indicated by the visible presence of ochre coloured Fe^{3+} oxidation products throughout the 60 cm profile. Therefore, the immobilisation of uranium through reduction of U^{6+} to U^{4+} is unlikely. However, this may occur during fluctuations of the water table, causing more reduced conditions.

D.4 SUMMARY OF THE FINDINGS:

- Penetrators hitting the ground result in contamination points of several grams per kilogram of soil. However, the extent and distribution of the contamination is low (roughly 15 x 15 cm) and restricted to a mass of a few kilograms of soil in the shothole.

- An additional contamination of tens of grams DU per kilogram of soil can occur after a number of years through the corrosion of penetrators laying in soil. Due to the rather low mobility of DU corrosion products in the type of soil sampled to date in BiH, the extent and distribution of the major part of subsurface contamination is expected to remain restricted to a volume of about 20 kilograms of soil in the shothole.

- Penetrators hitting a hard ground surface (concrete, asphalt, rocks, stony ground) give rise to localized DU contamination of the topsoil around the site of impact with concentrations decreasing as distance increases. Concentrations of DU in topsoil exceeding ten times the natural concentration of uranium in soil are generally not observed outside the immediate surroundings of the impact points (1 – 2 m). Concentrations exceeding the natural concentration of uranium in soil are not expected at distances greater than about 10 to 20 m from impact points. Measurable DU contamination of topsoil is generally restricted to a maximum distance of about 150 metres from confirmed penetrator impact points.

- Widespread DU contamination at distances of more than 200 m from confirmed impact points of penetrators is not expected (i.e. ground contamination remains localized).

- Around penetrator impact points on soft ground surfaces, localized DU contamination of topsoil is expected to be less intense and have a lower distribution than on hard surfaces.

- Although current literature states that widespread DU contamination occurs once penetrators have hit heavily armoured vehicles at attacked sites, no signs of such contamination could be found based on the sampling procedure used on this mission or previous UNEP studies.

- Outside the fenced area of the former *Hadzici Tank Repair Facility*, no signs of a DU contamination of the topsoil could be detected. The localized contamination at the *Hadzici Ammunition Storage* and *Han Pijesak Military Barracks* is clearly limited to below 200 m from the attacked areas of the sites.

- These results generally confirm the major findings of the earlier UNEP missions to Kosovo and Serbia and Montenegro.

- Due to the very limited extent of the contamination zones, defined by DU concentrations in topsoil above the natural uranium concentrations, a health risk for the local population can hardly be expected, either from living close to the aforementioned sites or by visiting these areas.

- Based on the results from the measurement of total ^{238}U concentration, it is clear that the ^{238}U concentration decreases with depth. However, the sequentially extracted uranium concentrations infer that the proportion of uranium associated with each geochemical phase varies down the profile. Figure D.5 shows, in the near surface horizons where the penetrator was embedded, the dominant fraction is the readily exchangeable fraction. While at lower levels in the profile, for example, at 37.5-40 cm, the carbonate bound uranium dominates.

- The soil pH is neutral and remains fairly constant down through the profile, between pH 7.4-7.8. These conditions favour the sorption of uranium to the surfaces of soil organic matter, iron oxides and minerals.

- The organic content in the upper layers of the profile (~7%, down to 15 cm depth) contributes significantly to the cation exchange capacity (CEC) of these soil layers (i.e. a measure of the number of exchange sites to which the readily exchangeable fraction is bound). Between 25-90% of the total CEC of the top layers of mineral soils is thought to be associated with the organic matter content (Stevenson, 1985). Therefore, the organic content within the top layers of the profile plays an important role in providing sites to which uranium can bind. The CEC contribution by organic matter increases with pH, and is therefore greater in a neutral soil, such as this compared to a more acidic soil, *e.g.* a forest soil. Such soils of lower pH are more likely to result in the downward mobilisation of uranium through the formation of uranium-humic complexes.

- The profile appeared fairly well oxidised, as indicated by the visible presence of ochre coloured Fe^{3+} oxidation products. Therefore, the immobilisation of uranium through reduction of U^{6+} to U^{4+} is unlikely. However, this may occur during fluctuations of the water table, causing more reduced conditions.

Depleted Uranium in Bosnia and Herzegovina

DU IN SOIL

D

Table D.1 Surface soil samples

Sample code	Sampling site	Coordinates UTM 34T	Sample type	Depth
NUC-2002-024-001	Hadzici, tank repair facility	BP 74 418 / 56 345	Soil, 10 cores, 25 sqm	0 - 5 cm
NUC-2002-024-002	Hadzici, tank repair facility	BP 74 141 / 56 496	Soil, 10 cores, 25 sqm	0 - 5 cm
NUC-2002-024-003	Hadzici, tank repair facility	BP 74 456 / 56 161	Soil, 10 cores, 25 sqm	0 - 5 cm
NUC-2002-024-004	Hadzici, tank repair facility	BP 73 850 / 56 303	Soil, 10 cores, 25 sqm	0 - 5 cm
NUC-2002-024-005	Hadzici, tank repair facility	BP 73 797 / 56 502	Soil, 10 cores, 25 sqm	0 - 5 cm
NUC-2002-024-006	Hadzici, tank repair facility	BP 74 117 / 56 107	Soil, 10 cores, 25 sqm	0 - 5 cm
NUC-2002-024-007	Hadzici, tank repair facility	BP 74 115 / 56 310	Soil, 10 cores, 25 sqm	0 - 5 cm
NUC-2002-024-008	Hadzici, tank repair facility	BP 74 154 / 56 426	Soil, 10 cores, 25 sqm	0 - 5 cm
NUC-2002-024-009	Hadzici, tank repair facility	BP 74 208 / 56 207	Soil, 10 cores, 25 sqm	0 - 5 cm
NUC-2002-024-010	Hadzici, tank repair facility	BP 73 945 / 56 470	Soil, 10 cores, 25 sqm	0 - 5 cm
NUC-2002-024-011	Hadzici, tank repair facility	BP 74 025 / 56 386	Sand, shovel	0 - 3 cm
NUC-2002-024-012	Hadzici, tank repair facility	BP 74 051 / 56 398	Sand, shovel	0 - 3 cm
NUC-2002-025-001	Lukavica, former barracks	BP 88 222 / 55 799	Soil, 10 cores, 25 sqm	0 - 5 cm
NUC-2002-025-002	Lukavica, former barracks	BP 88 439 / 56 016	Soil, 10 cores, 25 sqm	0 - 5 cm
NUC-2002-025-003	Lukavica, former barracks	BP 88 608 / 55 676	Soil, 10 cores, 25 sqm	0 - 5 cm
NUC-2002-025-004	Lukavica, former barracks	BP 88 527 / 55 883	Soil, 10 cores, 25 sqm	0 - 5 cm
NUC-2002-026-001	Pjelugovici ; T55 tank	BP 81 838 / 61 784	Soil, 10 cores, 25 sqm	0 - 5 cm
NUC-2002-026-002	Pjelugovici ; T55 tank	BP 81 811 / 61 800	Soil, 10 cores, around ruin	0 - 5 cm
NUC-2002-027-001	Hadzici, barracks	BP 75 285 / 54 682	Soil, 10 cores, 25 sqm	0 - 5 cm
NUC-2002-027-002	Hadzici, barracks	BP 75 434 / 54 623	Soil, 10 cores, 25 sqm	0 - 5 cm
NUC-2002-027-003	Hadzici, barracks	BP 75 367 / 54 840	Soil, 10 cores, 25 sqm	0 - 5 cm
NUC-2002-027-004	Hadzici, ammunition storage area	BP 76 577 / 53 496	Soil, 10 cores, 25 sqm	0 - 5 cm
NUC-2002-027-005	Hadzici, ammunition storage area	BP 76 603 / 53 432	Soil, 10 cores, 5 sqm	0 - 5 cm
NUC-2002-028-001	Han Pijesak, barracks	CP 35 969 / 84 314	Soil, 10 cores, 25 sqm	0 - 5 cm
NUC-2002-028-002	Han Pijesak, barracks	CP 35 595 / 84 331	Soil, 10 cores, 25 sqm	0 - 5 cm
NUC-2002-028-003	Han Pijesak, barracks	CP 35 681 / 84 350	Soil, 10 cores, 25 sqm	0 - 5 cm
NUC-2002-028-004	Han Pijesak, barracks	CP 35 468 / 84 445	Soil, 10 cores, 3m around penetrator	0 - 5 cm
NUC-2002-028-006	Han Pijesak, barracks	CP 36 060 / 84 244	Soil, 10 cores, 25 sqm	0 - 5 cm
NUC-2002-028-007	Han Pijesak, barracks	CP 35 909 / 84 409	Soil, 10 cores, 25 sqm	0 - 5 cm
NUC-2002-030-001	Vogosca, ammunition production site	BP 88 927 / 64 949	Soil, 10 cores, 25 sqm	0 - 5 cm
NUC-2002-030-002	Vogosca, ammunition production site	BP 89 334 / 65 067	Soil, 10 cores, 25 sqm	0 - 5 cm
NUC-2002-030-003	Vogosca, ammunition production site	BP 89 185 / 65 195	Soil, 10 cores, 25 sqm	0 - 5 cm
NUC-2002-030-004	Vogosca, ammunition production site	BP 90 088 / 66 734	Soil, 10 cores, 25 sqm	0 - 5 cm
NUC-2002-030-005	Vogosca, ammunition production site	BP 91 215 / 67 689	Soil, 10 cores, 25 sqm	0 - 5 cm
NUC-2002-031-001	Kalinovik, water reservoir	BP 93 325 / 20 622	Soil, 10 cores, 25 sqm	0 - 5 cm
NUC-2002-031-002	Kalinovik, ammunition destruction zone	BP 91 586 / 18 312	Soil, 10 cores, 25 sqm	0 - 5 cm
NUC-2002-031-003	Kalinovik, ammunition destruction zone	BP 91 714 / 18 349	Soil, 10 cores, 25 sqm	0 - 5 cm
NUC-2002-032-001	Foca, bridge (Srbinje)	CP 20 345 / 20 444	Soil, 10 cores, 25 sqm	0 - 5 cm
NUC-2002-032-002	Foca, bridge (Srbinje)	CP 20 545 / 20 492	Soil, 10 cores, 25 sqm	0 - 5 cm
NUC-2002-033-001	Ustikolina, barracks	CP 19 356 / 29 118	Soil, 10 cores, 25 sqm	0 - 5 cm
NUC-2002-033-002	Ustikolina, barracks	CP 20 198 / 28 000	Soil, 10 cores, 25 sqm	0 - 5 cm
NUC-2002-033-003	Ustikolina, barracks	CP 20 470 / 27 780	Soil, 10 cores, 25 sqm	0 - 5 cm
NUC-2002-034-001	Pale, koran barracks	CP 05 514 / 52 297	Soil, 10 cores, 25 sqm	0 - 5 cm
NUC-2002-034-002	Pale, koran barracks	CP 05 304 / 52 293	Soil, 10 cores, 25 sqm	0 - 5 cm
NUC-2002-035-001	Bjelasnica plateau, ammunition destruction zone	BP 61 932 / 42 464	Soil, 10 cores, 25 sqm	0 - 5 cm
NUC-2002-035-002	Bjelasnica plateau, ammunition destruction zone	BP 61 877 / 42 288	Soil, 10 cores, 25 sqm	0 - 5 cm

Table D.2 Concentration of Uranium isotopes and DU in surface soil samples [mg/kg]

Sample code	U-238 [mg/kg]			U-234 [mg/kg]			U-235 [mg/kg]			U-236 [mg/kg]			Utot [mg/kg]			U-235/U-238 ratio	%DU of total U
NUC-2002-024-001	4.43E+00	±	7.68E-02	2.18E-04	±	3.71E-05	3.22E-02	±	8.68E-04		<	4.00E-05	4.47E+00	±	7.68E-02	7.273E-03	<2
NUC-2002-024-002	4.74E+00	±	8.61E-02	2.32E-04	±	3.79E-05	3.43E-02	±	7.89E-04		<	4.00E-05	4.77E+00	±	8.61E-02	7.247E-03	<2
NUC-2002-024-003	2.77E+00	±	5.62E-02	1.54E-04	±	3.18E-05	2.01E-02	±	5.11E-04		<	3.00E-05	2.79E+00	±	5.62E-02	7.264E-03	<2
NUC-2002-024-004	3.77E+00	±	6.47E-02	1.92E-04	±	3.45E-05	2.72E-02	±	6.42E-04		<	3.00E-05	3.79E+00	±	6.47E-02	7.247E-03	<2
NUC-2002-024-005	3.81E+00	±	7.32E-02	1.83E-04	±	3.41E-05	2.76E-02	±	6.44E-04		<	4.00E-05	3.83E+00	±	7.32E-02	7.251E-03	<2
NUC-2002-024-006	4.01E+00	±	6.68E-02	2.03E-04	±	3.53E-05	2.92E-02	±	6.51E-04		<	4.00E-05	4.04E+00	±	6.68E-02	7.278E-03	<2
NUC-2002-024-007	3.87E+00	±	6.52E-02	2.01E-04	±	2.88E-05	2.77E-02	±	7.26E-04		<	4.00E-05	3.90E+00	±	6.52E-02	7.152E-03	<2
NUC-2002-024-008	3.72E+00	±	6.57E-02	1.83E-04	±	3.05E-05	2.58E-02	±	5.99E-04		<	4.00E-05	3.74E+00	±	6.57E-02	6.954E-03	6
NUC-2002-024-009	3.41E+00	±	6.41E-02	1.77E-04	±	3.03888E-05	2.47E-02	±	1.77E-03		<	4.00E-05	3.44E+00	±	6.41E-02	7.218E-03	<2
NUC-2002-024-010	3.67E+00	±	5.81E-02	1.82E-04	±	3.33E-05	2.65E-02	±	7.70E-04		<	4.00E-05	3.70E+00	±	5.81E-02	7.205E-03	<2
NUC-2002-024-011	1.26E+01	±	2.12E-01	1.61E-04	±	2.55E-05	3.37E-02	±	7.73E-04	3.04E-04	±	3.71E-05	1.26E+01	±	2.12E-01	2.683E-03	87
NUC-2002-024-012	3.20E+01	±	6.74E-01	2.99E-04	±	3.93E-05	7.41E-02	±	2.05E-03	8.61E-04	±	1.09E-04	3.21E+01	±	6.74E-01	2.317E-03	94
NUC-2002-025-001	2.11E+00	±	3.85E-02	1.12E-04	±	1.81154E-05	1.53E-02	±	3.40E-04		<	3.00E-05	2.13E+00	±	3.85E-02	7.244E-03	<2
NUC-2002-025-002	2.98E+00	±	5.24E-02	1.64E-04	±	2.2268E-05	2.16E-02	±	4.95E-04		<	3.00E-05	3.00E+00	±	5.24E-02	7.236E-03	<2
NUC-2002-025-003	2.76E+00	±	4.89E-02	1.47E-04	±	2.28499E-05	2.00E-02	±	4.63E-04		<	3.00E-05	2.78E+00	±	4.89E-02	7.251E-03	<2
NUC-2002-025-004	2.52E+00	±	4.91E-02	1.36E-04	±	1.95353E-05	1.82E-02	±	4.39E-04		<	3.00E-05	2.53E+00	±	4.92E-02	7.244E-03	<2
NUC-2002-026-001	1.78E+00	±	3.18E-02	9.14739E-05	±	1.9308E-05	1.29E-02	±	3.73E-04		<	2.00E-05	1.79E+00	±	3.18E-02	7.265E-03	<2
NUC-2002-026-002	1.51E+00	±	3.72E-02	7.63188E-05	±	1.56208E-05	1.10E-02	±	3.22E-04		<	2.00E-05	1.52E+00	±	3.72E-02	7.284E-03	<2
NUC-2002-027-001	2.97E+00	±	4.65E-02	1.54E-04	±	2.15589E-05	2.15E-02	±	4.95E-04		<	3.00E-05	3.00E+00	±	4.65E-02	7.233E-03	<2
NUC-2002-027-002	2.60E+00	±	5.26E-02	1.35E-04	±	2.33E-05	1.88E-02	±	4.39E-04		<	3.00E-05	2.62E+00	±	5.26E-02	7.244E-03	<2
NUC-2002-027-003	3.08E+00	±	5.16E-02	1.63E-04	±	2.58E-05	2.23E-02	±	4.52E-04		<	3.00E-05	3.10E+00	±	5.16E-02	7.238E-03	<2
NUC-2002-027-004	6.75E+00	±	1.07E-01	1.84E-04	±	3.43E-05	2.95E-02	±	6.86E-04	1.11E-04	±	1.85226E-05	6.78E+00	±	1.07E-01	4.362E-03	55
NUC-2002-027-005	3.40E+00	±	5.61E-02	1.69E-04	±	2.89E-05	2.41E-02	±	5.58E-04		<	3.00E-05	3.43E+00	±	5.61E-02	7.084E-03	3
NUC-2002-028-001	2.51E+00	±	4.28E-02	1.30E-04	±	2.16E-05	1.77E-02	±	3.75E-04		<	3.00E-05	2.53E+00	±	4.28E-02	7.043E-03	4
NUC-2002-028-002	2.41E+00	±	4.47E-02	1.35E-04	±	2.15E-05	1.75E-02	±	4.44E-04		<	3.00E-05	2.43E+00	±	4.47E-02	7.246E-03	<2
NUC-2002-028-003	2.08E+00	±	3.46E-02	1.12E-04	±	1.82E-05	1.42E-02	±	3.78E-04		<	3.00E-05	2.09E+00	±	3.46E-02	6.829E-03	8
NUC-2002-028-004	2.56E+00	±	4.31E-02	1.35E-04	±	2.03E-05	1.84E-02	±	5.24E-04		<	3.00E-05	2.57E+00	±	4.31E-02	7.216E-03	<2
NUC-2002-028-006	2.43E+00	±	4.12E-02	1.28E-04	±	2.26E-05	1.75E-02	±	3.64E-04		<	3.00E-05	2.45E+00	±	4.12E-02	7.208E-03	<2
NUC-2002-028-007	1.34E+00	±	2.54E-02	6.57E-05	±	1.46E-05	9.70E-03	±	2.68E-04		<	3.00E-05	1.35E+00	±	2.54E-02	7.256E-03	<2
NUC-2002-030-001	1.78E+00	±	3.86E-02	9.69E-05	±	1.96E-05	1.30E-02	±	3.96E-04		<	2.00E-05	1.80E+00	±	3.86E-02	7.329E-03	<2
NUC-2002-030-002	1.79E+00	±	4.90E-02	9.81E-05	±	1.64E-05	1.30E-02	±	4.42E-04		<	2.00E-05	1.80E+00	±	4.90E-02	7.268E-03	<2
NUC-2002-030-003	2.01E+00	±	4.02E-02	1.09E-04	±	1.74E-05	1.47E-02	±	4.01E-04		<	2.00E-05	2.02E+00	±	4.02E-02	7.313E-03	<2
NUC-2002-030-004	1.56E+00	±	3.90E-02	8.45E-05	±	1.74E-05	1.14E-02	±	3.37E-04		<	2.00E-05	1.57E+00	±	3.90E-02	7.332E-03	<2
NUC-2002-030-005	1.80E+00	±	3.14E-02	8.84E-05	±	1.92E-05	1.31E-02	±	3.10E-04		<	2.00E-05	1.81E+00	±	3.14E-02	7.278E-03	<2
NUC-2002-031-001	4.52E+00	±	7.63E-02	2.10E-04	±	4.56E-05	3.27E-02	±	7.08E-04		<	4.00E-05	4.55E+00	±	7.63E-02	7.249E-03	<2
NUC-2002-031-002	3.14E+00	±	6.14E-02	1.67E-04	±	3.28E-05	2.29E-02	±	5.64E-04		<	3.00E-05	3.16E+00	±	6.14E-02	7.300E-03	<2
NUC-2002-031-003	3.11E+00	±	5.05E-02	1.59E-04	±	3.37512E-05	2.26E-02	±	5.28E-04		<	3.00E-05	3.13E+00	±	5.05E-02	7.287E-03	<2
NUC-2002-032-001	3.10E+00	±	5.43E-02	1.68E-04	±	2.69E-05	2.26E-02	±	5.77E-04		<	3.00E-05	3.13E+00	±	5.44E-02	7.293E-03	<2
NUC-2002-032-002	2.56E+00	±	4.41E-02	1.39E-04	±	2.02E-05	1.87E-02	±	3.95E-04		<	3.00E-05	2.58E+00	±	4.41E-02	7.310E-03	<2
NUC-2002-033-001	2.50E+00	±	4.55E-02	1.39E-04	±	2.20E-05	1.81E-02	±	4.69E-04		<	3.00E-05	2.52E+00	±	4.55E-02	7.245E-03	<2
NUC-2002-033-002	2.50E+00	±	4.02E-02	1.38E-04	±	2.96E-05	1.82E-02	±	3.77E-04		<	3.00E-05	2.52E+00	±	4.02E-02	7.285E-03	<2
NUC-2002-033-003	2.49E+00	±	4.26E-02	1.42E-04	±	2.06E-05	1.81E-02	±	3.82E-04		<	3.00E-05	2.51E+00	±	4.26E-02	7.280E-03	<2
NUC-2002-034-001	3.10E+00	±	5.00E-02	1.59E-04	±	2.25E-05	2.25E-02	±	6.06E-04		<	3.00E-05	3.12E+00	±	5.00E-02	7.279E-03	<2
NUC-2002-034-002	2.63E+00	±	5.16E-02	1.43E-04	±	2.54E-05	1.92E-02	±	5.27E-04		<	3.00E-05	2.65E+00	±	5.16E-02	7.303E-03	<2
NUC-2002-035-001	1.71E+00	±	4.51E-02	8.07E-05	±	1.76E-05	1.25E-02	±	4.69E-04		<	3.00E-05	1.73E+00	±	4.51E-02	7.278E-03	<2
NUC-2002-035-002	2.57E+00	±	7.03E-02	1.29E-04	±	2.36E-05	1.87E-02	±	7.95E-04		<	3.00E-05	2.59E+00	±	7.03E-02	7.267E-03	<2

D

DU IN SOIL

Table D.3 Activity of Uranium isotopes and DU in surface soil samples [Bq/kg]

Sample code	U-238 [Bq/kg]	±	U-234 [Bq/kg]	±	U-235 [Bq/kg]	±	U-236 [Bq/kg]	±	Utot [Bq/kg]	±	U-235/ U-238 ratio	%DU of total U
NUC-2002-024-001	5.52E+01	± 9.56E-01	5.04E+01	± 8.56E+00	2.58E+00	± 6.94E-02		< 9.59E-02	1.08E+02	± 8.61E+00	7.273E-03	<2
NUC-2002-024-002	5.90E+01	± 1.07E+00	5.35E+01	± 8.76E+00	2.74E+00	± 6.31E-02		< 9.59E-02	1.15E+02	± 8.83E+00	7.247E-03	<2
NUC-2002-024-003	3.44E+01	± 7.00E-01	3.56E+01	± 7.33E+00	1.60E+00	± 4.09E-02		< 7.19E-02	7.16E+01	± 7.37E+00	7.264E-03	<2
NUC-2002-024-004	4.68E+01	± 8.05E-01	4.43E+01	± 7.96E+00	2.18E+00	± 5.13E-02		< 7.19E-02	9.33E+01	± 8.00E+00	7.247E-03	<2
NUC-2002-024-005	4.74E+01	± 9.10E-01	4.22E+01	± 7.87E+00	2.21E+00	± 5.16E-02		< 9.59E-02	9.18E+01	± 7.92E+00	7.251E-03	<2
NUC-2002-024-006	4.99E+01	± 8.31E-01	4.70E+01	± 8.15E+00	2.33E+00	± 5.21E-02		< 9.59E-02	9.92E+01	± 8.20E+00	7.278E-03	<2
NUC-2002-024-007	4.81E+01	± 8.11E-01	4.65E+01	± 6.65E+00	2.21E+00	± 5.81E-02		< 9.59E-02	9.68E+01	± 6.70E+00	7.152E-03	<2
NUC-2002-024-008	4.62E+01	± 8.17E-01	4.23E+01	± 7.05E+00	2.07E+00	± 4.79E-02		< 9.59E-02	9.06E+01	± 7.10E+00	6.954E-03	6
NUC-2002-024-009	4.25E+01	± 7.97E-01	4.09E+01	± 7.02E+00	1.97E+00	± 1.42E-01		< 9.59E-02	8.54E+01	± 7.06E+00	7.218E-03	<2
NUC-2002-024-010	4.56E+01	± 7.23E-01	4.20E+01	± 7.70E+00	2.12E+00	± 6.16E-02		< 9.59E-02	8.98E+01	± 7.73E+00	7.205E-03	<2
NUC-2002-024-011	1.56E+02	± 2.63E+00	3.72E+01	± 5.90E+00	2.69E+00	± 6.18E-02	7.30E-01	± 8.88E-02	1.97E+02	± 6.46E+00	2.683E-03	87
NUC-2002-024-012	3.98E+02	± 8.38E+00	6.89E+01	± 9.08E+00	5.93E+00	± 1.64E-01	2.06E+00	± 2.62E-01	4.75E+02	± 1.24E+01	2.317E-03	94
NUC-2002-025-001	2.63E+01	± 4.78E-01	2.59E+01	± 4.18E+00	1.23E+00	± 2.72E-02		< 7.19E-02	5.34E+01	± 4.21E+00	7.244E-03	<2
NUC-2002-025-002	3.71E+01	± 6.52E-01	3.79E+01	± 5.14E+00	1.73E+00	± 3.96E-02		< 7.19E-02	7.67E+01	± 5.18E+00	7.236E-03	<2
NUC-2002-025-003	3.43E+01	± 6.08E-01	3.40E+01	± 5.28E+00	1.60E+00	± 3.71E-02		< 7.19E-02	6.99E+01	± 5.31E+00	7.251E-03	<2
NUC-2002-025-004	3.13E+01	± 6.11E-01	3.15E+01	± 4.51E+00	1.46E+00	± 3.52E-02		< 7.19E-02	6.42E+01	± 4.55E+00	7.244E-03	<2
NUC-2002-026-001	2.21E+01	± 3.96E-01	2.11E+01	± 4.46E+00	1.03E+00	± 2.99E-02		< 4.79E-02	4.43E+01	± 4.48E+00	7.265E-03	<2
NUC-2002-026-002	1.88E+01	± 4.63E-01	1.76E+01	± 3.61E+00	8.82E-01	± 2.58E-02		< 4.79E-02	3.73E+01	± 3.64E+00	7.284E-03	<2
NUC-2002-027-001	3.70E+01	± 5.79E-01	3.57E+01	± 4.98E+00	1.72E+00	± 3.96E-02		< 7.19E-02	7.44E+01	± 5.01E+00	7.233E-03	<2
NUC-2002-027-002	3.23E+01	± 6.55E-01	3.11E+01	± 5.38E+00	1.51E+00	± 3.51E-02		< 7.19E-02	6.49E+01	± 5.42E+00	7.244E-03	<2
NUC-2002-027-003	3.83E+01	± 6.42E-01	3.76E+01	± 5.95E+00	1.79E+00	± 3.61E-02		< 7.19E-02	7.77E+01	± 5.99E+00	7.238E-03	<2
NUC-2002-027-004	8.39E+01	± 1.33E+00	4.24E+01	± 7.92E+00	2.36E+00	± 5.49E-02	2.66E-01	± 4.44E-02	1.29E+02	± 8.03E+00	4.362E-03	55
NUC-2002-027-005	4.23E+01	± 6.98E-01	3.90E+01	± 6.67E+00	1.93E+00	± 4.46E-02		< 7.19E-02	8.32E+01	± 6.71E+00	7.084E-03	3
NUC-2002-028-001	3.13E+01	± 5.32E-01	2.99E+01	± 4.99E+00	1.42E+00	± 3.00E-02		< 7.19E-02	6.26E+01	± 5.02E+00	7.043E-03	4
NUC-2002-028-002	3.00E+01	± 5.56E-01	3.11E+01	± 4.96E+00	1.40E+00	± 3.55E-02		< 7.19E-02	6.25E+01	± 5.00E+00	7.246E-03	<2
NUC-2002-028-003	2.58E+01	± 4.30E-01	2.58E+01	± 4.21E+00	1.13E+00	± 3.02E-02		< 7.19E-02	5.27E+01	± 4.24E+00	6.829E-03	8
NUC-2002-028-004	3.18E+01	± 5.37E-01	3.12E+01	± 4.70E+00	1.48E+00	± 4.19E-02		< 7.19E-02	6.45E+01	± 4.73E+00	7.216E-03	<2
NUC-2002-028-006	3.02E+01	± 5.13E-01	2.96E+01	± 5.21E+00	1.40E+00	± 2.91E-02		< 7.19E-02	6.12E+01	± 5.24E+00	7.208E-03	<2
NUC-2002-028-007	1.66E+01	± 3.16E-01	1.52E+01	± 3.37E+00	7.76E-01	± 2.14E-02		< 7.19E-02	3.26E+01	± 3.38E+00	7.256E-03	<2
NUC-2002-030-001	2.22E+01	± 4.81E-01	2.24E+01	± 4.53E+00	1.04E+00	± 3.17E-02		< 4.79E-02	4.56E+01	± 4.56E+00	7.329E-03	<2
NUC-2002-030-002	2.22E+01	± 6.09E-01	2.26E+01	± 3.79E+00	1.04E+00	± 3.53E-02		< 4.79E-02	4.59E+01	± 3.84E+00	7.268E-03	<2
NUC-2002-030-003	2.50E+01	± 5.01E-01	2.51E+01	± 4.01E+00	1.17E+00	± 3.21E-02		< 4.79E-02	5.13E+01	± 4.04E+00	7.313E-03	<2
NUC-2002-030-004	1.94E+01	± 4.85E-01	1.95E+01	± 4.01E+00	9.13E-01	± 2.70E-02		< 4.79E-02	3.98E+01	± 4.04E+00	7.332E-03	<2
NUC-2002-030-005	2.24E+01	± 3.90E-01	2.04E+01	± 4.43E+00	1.05E+00	± 2.48E-02		< 4.79E-02	4.38E+01	± 4.45E+00	7.278E-03	<2
NUC-2002-031-001	5.62E+01	± 9.49E-01	4.84E+01	± 1.05E+01	2.62E+00	± 5.67E-02		< 9.59E-02	1.07E+02	± 1.06E+01	7.249E-03	<2
NUC-2002-031-002	3.91E+01	± 7.64E-01	3.85E+01	± 7.58E+00	1.83E+00	± 4.51E-02		< 7.19E-02	7.94E+01	± 7.62E+00	7.300E-03	<2
NUC-2002-031-003	3.87E+01	± 6.28E-01	3.67E+01	± 7.79E+00	1.81E+00	± 4.23E-02		< 7.19E-02	7.72E+01	± 7.82E+00	7.287E-03	<2
NUC-2002-032-001	3.86E+01	± 6.76E-01	3.87E+01	± 6.22E+00	1.81E+00	± 4.62E-02		< 7.19E-02	7.91E+01	± 6.25E+00	7.293E-03	<2
NUC-2002-032-002	3.19E+01	± 5.48E-01	3.20E+01	± 4.67E+00	1.50E+00	± 3.16E-02		< 7.19E-02	6.54E+01	± 4.71E+00	7.310E-03	<2
NUC-2002-033-001	3.11E+01	± 5.66E-01	3.21E+01	± 5.07E+00	1.45E+00	± 3.75E-02		< 7.19E-02	6.46E+01	± 5.11E+00	7.245E-03	<2
NUC-2002-033-002	3.11E+01	± 5.01E-01	3.18E+01	± 6.83E+00	1.45E+00	± 3.02E-02		< 7.19E-02	6.44E+01	± 6.84E+00	7.285E-03	<2
NUC-2002-033-003	3.10E+01	± 5.30E-01	3.27E+01	± 4.76E+00	1.45E+00	± 3.06E-02		< 7.19E-02	6.51E+01	± 4.79E+00	7.280E-03	<2
NUC-2002-034-001	3.85E+01	± 6.22E-01	3.68E+01	± 5.20E+00	1.80E+00	± 4.85E-02		< 7.19E-02	7.71E+01	± 5.24E+00	7.279E-03	<2
NUC-2002-034-002	3.27E+01	± 6.42E-01	3.29E+01	± 5.86E+00	1.53E+00	± 4.22E-02		< 7.19E-02	6.72E+01	± 5.89E+00	7.303E-03	<2
NUC-2002-035-001	2.13E+01	± 5.61E-01	1.86E+01	± 4.07E+00	9.97E-01	± 3.76E-02		< 7.19E-02	4.09E+01	± 4.11E+00	7.278E-03	<2
NUC-2002-035-002	3.20E+01	± 8.75E-01	2.98E+01	± 5.46E+00	1.49E+00	± 6.36E-02		< 7.19E-02	6.33E+01	± 5.53E+00	7.267E-03	<2

Post-Conflict Environmental Assessment

Table D.4 Profile soil samples

Sample code	Sampling date	Coordinates UTM 34T	Sample type, sample tool	Depth
NUC-2002-028-101	10/18/2002	CP 35 468 / 84 445	Soil, shovel, above penetrator	0 - 6 cm
NUC-2002-028-102	10/18/2002	CP 35 468 / 84 445	Soil, shovel, around penetrator	6 - 10 cm
NUC-2002-028-103	10/18/2002	CP 35 468 / 84 445	Soil, profile template	10 - 15 cm
NUC-2002-028-104	10/18/2002	CP 35 468 / 84 445	Soil, profile template	15 - 20 cm
NUC-2002-028-105	10/18/2002	CP 35 468 / 84 445	Soil, profile template	20 - 25 cm
NUC-2002-028-106	10/18/2002	CP 35 468 / 84 445	Soil, profile template	25 - 30 cm
NUC-2002-028-107	10/18/2002	CP 35 468 / 84 445	Soil, profile template	30 - 35 cm
NUC-2002-028-108	10/18/2002	CP 35 468 / 84 445	Soil, profile template	35 - 40 cm
NUC-2002-028-109	10/18/2002	CP 35 468 / 84 445	Soil, profile template	40 - 45 cm
NUC-2002-028-110	10/18/2002	CP 35 468 / 84 445	Soil, profile template	45 - 50 cm
NUC-2002-028-111	10/18/2002	CP 35 468 / 84 445	Soil, profile template	50 - 55 cm
NUC-2002-028-112	10/18/2002	CP 35 468 / 84 445	Soil, profile template	55 - 60 cm
NUC-2002-028-120	10/19/2002	CP 35 795 / 84 340	Soil, shovel, around penetrator	0 - 5 cm
NUC-2002-028-121	10/19/2002	CP 35 795 / 84 340	Soil, shovel, below penetrator	5 - 10 cm
NUC-2002-028-122	10/19/2002	CP 35 795 / 84 340	Soil, profile template	10 - 15 cm
NUC-2002-028-123	10/19/2002	CP 35 795 / 84 340	Soil, profile template	15 - 20 cm
NUC-2002-028-124	10/19/2002	CP 35 795 / 84 340	Soil, profile template	20 - 25 cm
NUC-2002-028-125	10/19/2002	CP 35 795 / 84 340	Soil, profile template	25 - 30 cm
NUC-2002-028-126	10/19/2002	CP 35 795 / 84 340	Soil, profile template	30 - 35 cm
NUC-2002-028-127	10/18/2002	CP 35 795 / 84 340	Soil, profile template	35 - 40 cm
NUC-2002-028-128	10/19/2002	CP 35 795 / 84 340	Soil, profile template	40 - 45 cm
NUC-2002-028-129	10/19/2002	CP 35 795 / 84 340	Soil, profile template	45 - 50 cm
NUC-2002-028-130	10/19/2002	CP 35 795 / 84 340	Soil, profile template	50 - 55 cm
NUC-2002-028-131	10/19/2002	CP 35 795 / 84 340	Soil, profile template	55 - 60 cm
NUC-2002-028-132	10/19/2002	CP 35 795 / 84 340	Soil, profile template	60 - 65 cm

Table D.5 Concentration of uranium isotopes and DU in profile soil samples [mg/kg]

Sample code	U-238 [mg/kg]			U-234 [mg/kg]			U-235 [mg/kg]			U-236 [mg/kg]			Utot [mg/kg]			U-235/U-238 ratio	%DU of total U
NUC-2002-028-101	2.31E+03	±	4.32E+01	1.56E-02	±	3.10E-03	4.56E+00	±	2.46E-01	6.35E-02	±	9.90E-03	2.31E+03	±	4.32E+01	1.967E-03	101
NUC-2002-028-102	4.52E+04	±	9.82E+02	2.96E-01	±	4.67E-02	8.96E+01	±	4.14E+00	1.22E+00	±	1.54E-01	4.53E+04	±	9.82E+02	1.974E-03	100
NUC-2002-028-103	5.15E+03	±	9.63E+01	3.05E-02	±	4.03E-03	1.02E+01	±	3.93E-01	1.47E-01	±	2.52E-02	5.16E+03	±	9.63E+01	1.976E-03	100
NUC-2002-028-104	2.28E+02	±	3.92E+00	1.73E-03	±	5.82E-04	4.68E-01	±	1.31E-02	6.28E-03	±	8.09E-04	2.28E+02	±	3.92E+00	2.053E-03	99
NUC-2002-028-105	1.76E+01	±	3.29E-01	2.74E-04	±	5.82E-05	5.20E-02	±	1.29E-03	4.08E-04	±	5.26E-05	1.76E+01	±	3.29E-01	2.958E-03	82
NUC-2002-028-106	5.74E+00	±	1.05E-01	1.93E-04	±	3.11E-05	2.84E-02	±	9.04E-04	7.34E-05	±	1.44E-05	5.77E+00	±	1.05E-01	4.936E-03	44
NUC-2002-028-107	5.81E+00	±	1.64E-01	1.91E-04	±	2.85E-05	2.84E-02	±	1.39E-03	7.15E-05	±	1.42E-05	5.84E+00	±	1.64E-01	4.875E-03	45
NUC-2002-028-108	4.97E+00	±	1.61E-01	1.90E-04	±	3.15E-05	2.69E-02	±	9.74E-04	4.98E-05	±	1.22E-05	5.00E+00	±	1.61E-01	5.403E-03	35
NUC-2002-028-109	4.19E+00	±	7.88E-02	1.87E-04	±	2.7E-05	2.57E-02	±	6.80E-04		<	4.00E-05	4.22E+00	±	#REF!	6.118E-03	22
NUC-2002-028-110	3.57E+00	±	7.00E-02	1.87E-04	±	2.80E-05	2.54E-02	±	5.92E-04		<	4.00E-05	3.59E+00	±	#REF!	7.121E-03	2
NUC-2002-028-111	3.64E+00	±	1.92E-01	1.99E-04	±	3.60E-05	2.64E-02	±	1.43E-03		<	4.00E-05	3.66E+00	±	#REF!	7.248E-03	<2
NUC-2002-028-112	3.38E+00	±	6.66E-02	1.87E-04	±	3.08E-05	2.45E-02	±	7.23E-04		<	4.00E-05	3.40E+00	±	#REF!	7.232E-03	<2
NUC-2002-028-120	4.66E+03	±	3.09E+02	2.82E-02	±	7.73E-03	9.23E+00	±	7.32E-01	1.29E-01	±	1.95E-02	4.67E+03	±	3.09E+02	1.974E-03	100
NUC-2002-028-121	4.93E+02	±	9.43E+00	3.34E-03	±	5.06E-04	9.89E-01	±	2.52E-02	1.27E-02	±	2.22E-03	4.94E+02	±	9.43E+00	2.001E-03	100
NUC-2002-028-122	7.14E+01	±	1.37E+00	5.83E-04	±	1.34E-04	1.54E-01	±	4.05E-03	1.89E-03	±	2.65E-04	7.16E+01	±	1.37E+00	2.153E-03	97
NUC-2002-028-123	4.97E+01	±	7.55E-01	4.28E-04	±	7.1E-05	1.10E-01	±	3.58E-03	1.27E-03	±	1.69E-04	4.98E+01	±	7.55E-01	2.210E-03	96
NUC-2002-028-124	2.03E+01	±	3.41E-01	2.33E-04	±	3.2E-05	5.04E-02	±	1.42E-03	5.14E-04	±	7.3E-05	2.04E+01	±	3.41E-01	2.475E-03	91
NUC-2002-028-125	6.99E+00	±	1.09E-01	1.61E-04	±	2.5E-05	2.65E-02	±	1.34E-03	1.24E-04	±	1.9E-05	7.02E+00	±	1.09E-01	3.780E-03	66
NUC-2002-028-126	3.95E+00	±	7.09E-02	1.61E-04	±	2.6E-05	2.19E-02	±	5.00E-04	4.1E-05	±	1.1E-05	3.97E+00	±	7.09E-02	5.534E-03	33
NUC-2002-028-127	3.14E+00	±	5.50E-02	1.59E-04	±	3.12E-05	2.14E-02	±	4.85E-04		<	3.00E-05	3.16E+00	±	5.50E-02	6.785E-03	9
NUC-2002-028-128	3.15E+00	±	1.25E-01	1.77E-04	±	3.03E-05	2.26E-02	±	9.60E-04		<	3.00E-05	3.17E+00	±	1.25E-01	7.160E-03	<2
NUC-2002-028-129	3.10E+00	±	5.50E-02	1.71E-04	±	2.78E-05	2.24E-02	±	4.70E-04		<	3.00E-05	3.12E+00	±	5.50E-02	7.199E-03	<2
NUC-2002-028-130	2.84E+00	±	6.14E-02	1.57E-04	±	2.67E-05	2.06E-02	±	5.55E-04		<	3.00E-05	2.86E+00	±	6.14E-02	7.240E-03	<2
NUC-2002-028-131	2.32E+00	±	3.91E-02	1.22E-04	±	2.44E-05	1.69E-02	±	4.21E-04		<	3.00E-05	2.34E+00	±	3.91E-02	7.269E-03	<2
NUC-2002-028-132	1.97E+00	±	4.45E-02	1.07E-04	±	2.13E-05	1.44E-02	±	3.74E-04		<	3.00E-05	1.98E+00	±	4.45E-02	7.263E-03	<2

Table D.6 Activity of Uranium isotopes and DU in profile soil samples [Bq/kg]

Sample code	U-238 [Bq/kg]	±	U-234 [Bqkg]	±	U-235 [Bq/kg]	±	U-236 [Bq/kg]	±	Utot [Bq/kg]	±	U-235/U-238 ratio	%DU of total U
NUC-2002-028-101	2.87E+04	5.38E+02	3.60E+03	7.15E+02	3.65E+02	1.97E+01	1.52E+02	2.37E+01	3.28E+04	8.95E+02	1.967E-03	101
NUC-2002-028-102	5.63E+05	1.22E+04	6.85E+04	1.08E+04	7.17E+03	3.31E+02	2.93E+03	3.70E+02	6.41E+05	1.63E+04	1.974E-03	100
NUC-2002-028-103	6.40E+04	1.20E+03	7.05E+03	9.31E+02	8.17E+02	3.14E+01	3.53E+02	6.03E+01	7.22E+04	1.52E+03	1.976E-03	100
NUC-2002-028-104	2.83E+03	4.87E+01	3.99E+02	1.34E+02	3.74E+01	1.05E+00	1.51E+01	1.94E+00	3.28E+03	1.43E+02	2.053E-03	99
NUC-2002-028-105	2.19E+02	4.10E+00	6.33E+01	1.34E+01	4.16E+00	1.03E-01	9.79E-01	1.26E-01	2.87E+02	1.40E+01	2.958E-03	82
NUC-2002-028-106	7.14E+01	1.30E+00	4.46E+01	7.17E+00	2.27E+00	7.23E-02	1.76E-01	3.46E-02	1.18E+02	7.29E+00	4.936E-03	44
NUC-2002-028-107	7.23E+01	2.04E+00	4.40E+01	6.58E+00	2.27E+00	1.11E-01	1.71E-01	3.40E-02	1.19E+02	6.89E+00	4.875E-03	45
NUC-2002-028-108	6.19E+01	2.00E+00	4.38E+01	7.26E+00	2.16E+00	7.79E-02	1.19E-01	2.93E-02	1.08E+02	7.53E+00	5.403E-03	35
NUC-2002-028-109	5.22E+01	9.81E-01	4.32E+01	6.30E+00	2.05E+00	5.44E-02	< 9.59E-02		9.75E+01	#REF!	6.118E-03	22
NUC-2002-028-110	4.44E+01	8.71E-01	4.33E+01	6.46E+00	2.03E+00	4.74E-02	< 9.59E-02		8.98E+01	#REF!	7.121E-03	2
NUC-2002-028-111	4.52E+01	2.39E+00	4.59E+01	8.30E+00	2.11E+00	1.14E-01	< 9.59E-02		9.33E+01	#REF!	7.248E-03	<2
NUC-2002-028-112	4.20E+01	8.29E-01	4.31E+01	7.10E+00	1.96E+00	5.79E-02	< 9.59E-02		8.71E+01	#REF!	7.232E-03	<2
NUC-2002-028-120	5.80E+04	3.85E+03	6.52E+03	1.79E+03	7.39E+02	5.86E+01	3.10E+02	4.66E+01	6.56E+04	4.24E+03	1.974E-03	100
NUC-2002-028-121	6.13E+03	1.17E+02	7.70E+02	1.17E+02	7.91E+01	2.01E+00	3.04E+01	5.33E+00	7.01E+03	1.66E+02	2.001E-03	100
NUC-2002-028-122	8.88E+02	1.70E+01	1.35E+02	3.09E+01	1.23E+01	3.24E-01	4.53E+00	6.34E-01	1.04E+03	3.53E+01	2.153E-03	97
NUC-2002-028-123	6.18E+02	9.40E+00	9.88E+01	1.64E+01	8.80E+00	2.87E-01	3.04E+00	4.05E-01	7.29E+02	1.89E+01	2.210E-03	96
NUC-2002-028-124	2.53E+02	4.24E+00	5.38E+01	7.44E+00	4.03E+00	1.14E-01	1.23E+00	1.76E-01	3.12E+02	8.57E+00	2.475E-03	91
NUC-2002-028-125	8.69E+01	1.36E+00	3.73E+01	5.87E+00	2.12E+00	1.07E-01	2.98E-01	4.56E-02	1.27E+02	6.02E+00	3.780E-03	66
NUC-2002-028-126	4.91E+01	8.82E-01	3.71E+01	5.92E+00	1.75E+00	4.00E-02	9.78E-02	2.54E-02	8.81E+01	5.99E+00	5.534E-03	33
NUC-2002-028-127	3.90E+01	6.84E-01	3.68E+01	7.20E+00	1.71E+00	3.88E-02	< 7.19E-02		7.75E+01	7.23E+00	6.785E-03	9
NUC-2002-028-128	3.91E+01	1.55E+00	4.09E+01	7.01E+00	1.81E+00	7.68E-02	< 7.19E-02		8.19E+01	7.18E+00	7.160E-03	<2
NUC-2002-028-129	3.86E+01	6.84E-01	3.95E+01	6.42E+00	1.79E+00	3.76E-02	< 7.19E-02		7.99E+01	6.46E+00	7.199E-03	<2
NUC-2002-028-130	3.53E+01	7.64E-01	3.63E+01	6.16E+00	1.65E+00	4.44E-02	< 7.19E-02		7.32E+01	6.21E+00	7.240E-03	<2
NUC-2002-028-131	2.89E+01	4.86E-01	2.83E+01	5.63E+00	1.35E+00	3.37E-02	< 7.19E-02		5.85E+01	5.65E+00	7.269E-03	<2
NUC-2002-028-132	2.45E+01	5.54E-01	2.46E+01	4.92E+00	1.15E+00	2.99E-02	< 7.19E-02		5.03E+01	4.96E+00	7.263E-03	<2

Table D.7 Extracted ^{238}U concentrations

NUC-2002-028-	Exchangeable ^{238}U [mg/kg]	k [%]	Carbonates ^{238}U [mg/kg]	k [%]	Fe/Mn oxides ^{238}U [mg/kg]	k [%]	organic matter ^{238}U [mg/kg]	k [%]	amorphous silicates (a) ^{238}U [mg/kg]	k [%]	amorphous silicates (b) ^{238}U [mg/kg]	k [%]	residual ^{238}U [mg/kg]	k [%]
140	12575.2	4.5	2024.5	4.8	760.2	9.6	1609.7	8	12.985	1.7	90.425	54.0	12.015	14.1
141	1683.5	2.7	1781.4	5.9	460.5	7.8	788.2	6.7	5.038	1.8	90.463	43.6	6.041	12.8
142	97.7	4.4	205.2	7.0	50.5	2.6	34.2	2.5	0.152	2.4	2.295	8.4	0.401	2.4
143	60.0	9.9	173.6	1.8	53.8	4.6	38.7	2.2	0.200	2.7	2.294	5.8	0.374	5.2
144	53.8	5.0	152.3	2.0	59.9	1.9	52.6	2	0.313	27.9	2.944	1.9	0.414	8.7
145	105.1	1.7	69.2	2.2	25.2	3.3	20.3	10	0.236	14.1	0.917	3.8	0.151	3.7
146	57.4	2.1	34.8	3.1	11.3	6.7	10.3	5.9	0.115	3.5	0.347	6.3	0.123	13.9
148	19.7	13.4	69.8	6.9	23.3	22.6	17.5	14.3	0.123	29.0	0.729	15.0	0.213	2.3
151	4.1	1.8	25.5	5.1	7.0	1.8	5.6	6.6	0.091	89.4	0.250	2.3	0.199	11.5
154	0.9	1.9	5.6	2.1	1.5	2.8	1.4	3.7	0.035	5.8	0.074	6.5	0.126	3.1
158	0.2	2.7	1.9	3.9	0.5	5.2	0.7	6.6	0.013	79.0	0.057	13.2	0.153	6.5
162	0.0	3.8	0.6	37.1	0.3	7.1	0.4	3.9	0.002	26.3	0.036	5.7	0.131	2.9

Table D.8 Fusion of the residual

NUC-2002-028-	^{238}U [mg/kg]	rsd [%]
140a rf	3.78	0.47
141a rf	3.01	0.50
142a rf	2.24	0.78
143a rf	2.54	0.75
144a rf	2.20	0.87
145a rf	1.37	1.05
146a rf	1.13	0.49
148a rf	1.32	0.98
151a rf	1.11	1.33
154a rf	0.86	1.52
158a rf	0.94	0.95
162aii rf	1.15	1.95
162 ai rf	0.97	1.58

Table D.9 Fusion of the starting

NUC-2002-028-	^{238}U [mg/kg]	rsd [%]
140 ssf	10,529	0.51
141 ssf	7,334	0.32
142 ssf	742	0.26
143 ssf	559	0.29
144 ssf	535.5	0.36
145 ssf	211.6	0.21
146 ssf	256.9	0.22
148 ssf	217.3	0.23
151 ssf	90.6	0.65
154 ssf	19.4	0.40
158 ssf	4.2	0.99
162 ssf	2.5	0.26

Appendix E
DU in Water

E.1 GENERAL ASPECTS

During an A-10 plane attack using DU ammunition, most of the munitions miss the primary target, e.g. the tanks or armoured personnel carriers (APC), and therefore pass more or less intact into the ground.   Once there, the DU penetrators may corrode, gradually dissolve and the depleted uranium may contaminate the groundwater.   This contamination has to be understood as a certain contribution to an already existing natural concentration of uranium in natural waters.   Wells using groundwater within or close to the sites may be affected, and the total uranium concentration in the water may reach concentrations that are above recommended international limits for uranium in drinking water.

As this Appendix also relates to information in both *Appendix D 'DU in soil'* and *Appendix O 'Data on Uranium'*, partial repetition is necessary to allow the reader to follow the subject.

E.2 URANIUM IN GROUNDWATER

A French study from a DU test site in Southern France recently concluded that DU is fairly immobile (Crançon, 2000 and *Appendix D*).   It was found that uranium had moved down the soil profile to a depth of 30 cm in approximately 30 years, and is held entirely within the 'A1' fraction of the soil (Crançon, 2001).   The 'A' mineral horizon is defined as containing less than 17 % organic carbon by mass that has formed at or near the soil surface in the zone of leaching or eluviation of organic materials in solution or suspension, or of maximum *in situ* accumulation of organic matter, or both. The thickness of the A.1 soil horizon depends on the local situation, but it does not usually exceed 30 cm.

Complementary experimental studies show that the distribution coefficient (K_d=concentration of U in the soil ('solid') divided by the concentration of U in water) is 3 000 in the presence of humic acid colloids, i.e. uranium moves 3 000 times slower (retardation factor, R_f= 3 000) than the water that percolates through the soil.

It concludes, however, that about 10% of the uranium is able to move further down the soil profile and reach the underlying groundwater through the formation of uranium-humic acid colloids which aid in the transport of uranium.   This could be the cause of somewhat elevated uranium levels, which reach 25 µg/L (ppb) in the groundwaters and canal waters of the French DU test site during extreme droughts.   The regional maximum concentration does usually not exceed 8 µg/L (ppb).

Groundwater uranium values at the site in Southern France are likely to be higher than in some areas of

Stream water sample near the Bjelasnica Plateau

BiH due to the different rock types in that area. In France, the soil pH is somewhere between 3.5 and 4.5 for the A1 soil fraction, whereas the soil pore water pH for most of the sites in BiH is expected to be higher due to the presence of carbonate minerals from limestone, which increases the pH. In areas where penetrators are embedded in soil in BiH, one could conclude that in future years the maximum concentration of uranium in groundwater would not exceed 25 μg/L.

By comparing the uranium concentrations found at the French DU test site with the acceptable drinking water values, it emerges that the latter values vary according to the different regulating agencies around the world (see also *Appendix O*). The drinking water standards for public waters set by the WHO is 2 μg/L, whereas the US Environmental Protection Agency defined the standard of 30 μg/L, Canadian Health has defined the standard of 10 μg/L and SSK in Germany states 300 μg/L (but in the German territory of Hessen it is set 2 μg/L). EU drinking water directives give an indicative limit expressed as a dose of 0.1 mSv per year for radioactive substances in water. This corresponds to an average daily water intake with a uranium concentration of 100 μg per litre (U-238+234 in equilibrium, but no daughter products). Of note is that many bottled mineral waters have naturally high uranium contents of up to about 100 μg/L. The WHO is currently revising their value of 2μg/L because it is thought to be too low. The reference for WHO's new suggested guideline value for uranium in water is 9 μg/L (WHO, 2002).

Uranium concentrations in groundwater may increase as more of the penetrators corrode and their corrosion products (alteration phase) dissolve. From the observations in the Crançon study mentioned above, it could be concluded that uranium mobility will be retarded if penetrators are trapped in soil. According to UNEP's observations during the last three assessments, the majority of the penetrators are most likely buried within a few cm of soil. Where the penetrators had hit rock, they bounced off and lay on the surface as fragments, whereas where they hit asphalt, penetrators were found in superficial holes and sometimes visible from the surface. The capacity for uranium retardation within surface soils and rocks is thus affected by the thickness of soil, its composition and the presence of man-made surface materials (e.g. asphalt).

Further, where groundwaters are over-saturated with respect to calcite, uranium can sorb with the calcite (Kitano and Oomori, 1971; Carroll and Bruno, 1991; Meece and Benninger, 1993). Finally, it is also important to consider the depth to the groundwater table.

The study of the literature on DU to date would allow to conclude that:

1. Transport of dissolved DU is limited as most of the uranium will stay in the soil;

2. In some cases, under the worst geochemical conditions, DU can be expected to contaminate the groundwater;

3. The concentration of DU in groundwater will depend on thickness and type of soil, type of bedrock, and depth to groundwater, keeping in mind that the naturally arising uranium in the specific groundwater is already a product of these parameters;

4. Since the dissolution kinetics of schoepite is still not established, it is difficult to evaluate the volumes of groundwater that may be affected at the DU sites in BiH;

5. Similarly, it is not possible to state exactly how large the areas are around a targeted site that can significantly be affected by DU;

6. Further, it is impossible to accurately predict how far from a site DU contaminated groundwater can be transported in the flow direction of groundwater. Dilution, dispersion as well as retardation of the uranium concentration will take place;

7. Surface waters are assumed to not be seriously affected by DU widespread or localized contamination (DU dust created due to the impact of penetrators and spread over a large area);

8. Surface waters may be affected by a relevant quantity of penetrators sticking in the surface soil, the bed of the surface water aquifer. The Serbia and Montenegro DU Assessment (UNEP, 2001) showed that penetrators sticking in soil are heavily corroded and result in different corrosion products. Similar observations were made in BiH.

In evaluating what is known about schoepite dissolution kinetics, it emerged that further study is necessary in order to evaluate the rate of dissolution of this mineral with respect to mineral crystallinity, pH, conductivity Eh, soil composition and partial pressure of CO_2. Such a study is currently under way at the University of Bristol.

To evaluate the possible link between contaminated soils and waters with the food chain and the subsequent intake of uranium by people, a study is currently under way in both Kosovo and Serbia as a collaborative effort between the Universities of Middlesex and Bristol and the German Radiation Protection Institute (GSF).

At those sites where contamination of DU was found in water, knowledge of local hydrogeology would be useful in order to understand how such contamination is possible.

Tap water from a fresh water source at Ustikolina

E.3 RESULTS OF THE WATER SAMPLES COLLECTED

The main objectives of water sampling were:

1. the possible contamination of the underground aquifer due to the migration along the soil profile of uranium radioisotopes originating from depleted uranium ammunitions;

2. the presence of any contamination of surface water bodies due to the erosion of contaminated areas; and if the intake of uranium isotopes originating from DU ammunition could represent radiation exposure of any significance to the local population; and

3. as a secondary objective, to measure and assess the potential heavy metals content at certain sites.

In order to distinguish between natural and anthropogenic uranium, $^{234}U/^{238}U$ and $^{235}U/^{238}U$ activity ratios can be used. Goldstein *et al.* (1997) report that these ratios in natural waters range typically from 0.8 to 10 for $^{234}U/^{238}U$, while $^{235}U/^{238}U$ activity ratio is thought to have a relatively uniform value of about 0.045. The high variability of $^{234}U/^{238}U$ activity ratio is due to the "recoil effect" which occurs when the recoil energy, given to the ^{234}Th daughter during the ^{238}U decay, breaks the bond between ^{234}Th (and the subsequent daughters ^{234}Pa and ^{234}U) and the crystal matrix so that the ^{234}U atom is freer and easily leached, thus more ready to enter the solution than the remaining ^{238}U atoms (Mook and de Vries, 2001), considering fixed pH and redox conditions. Values of these ratios below these natural limits may be indicative of an anthropogenic source of uranium in the considered samples (Sansone *et al.*, 2001; 2001b).

Water samples were collected by the APAT team at the locations reported in Table E.1. Sampling procedures are described in *Appendix C*.

Table E.1 Water samples collection sites

Sample (APAT)	Sampling Site	Code	Coordinates	Sample Type
BHW01	Hadzici, Tank repair facility	UA-2003-003-001	34TBP 74215 / 56365	Water form concrete drainage well
BHW02	Hadzici, Tank repair facility	UA-2003-003-002	34TBP 74172 / 56387	Stream water
BHW03	Hadzici, Tank repair facility	UA-2003-003-003	34TBP 74172/ 56370	Well water
BHW04	Hadzici, Tank repair facility	UA-2003-003-004	34TBP 74395 / 56319	Water form concrete drainage well
BHW05	Lucavíca	UA-2003-003-005	34TBP 88560 / 55870	Public tap water
BHW06	Hadzici, Barracks	UA-2003-003-006	34TBP 75321/ 54761	Streem water
BHW07	Hadzici, Barracks	UA-2003-003-007	34TBP 75351/ 54720	Tap water
BHW08	Han Pijesak, Barracks	UA-2003-003-008	34TBP 36022 / 84309	Tap water
BHW09	Han Pijesak, Barracks	UA-2003-003-009	34TBP 35540 / 84380	Stream water
BHW10	Pale, Barracks	UA-2003-003-010	34TCP 05663 / 52318	River water
BHW11	Vogosca	UA-2003-003-011	34TBP 89407 / 65357	River water
BHW12	Vogosca	UA-2003-003-012	34TBP 90083 / 66656	Water reservoir
BHW13	Ustikolina, barracks	UA-2003-003-013	34TCP 20059 / 28289	Spring water collected from tap
BHW14	Ustikolina, barracks	UA-2003-003-014	34TCP 20245 / 27886	Spring water collected from tap
BHW15	Foca Bridge (Srbinje)	UA-2003-003-015	34TCP 20390 / 20510	Public water from tap
BHW16	Kalinovik, Water reservoir	UA-2003-003-016	34TBP 93344/ 20528	Spring water
BHW17	Kalinovik, Ammunition destruction site	UA-2003-003-017	34TBP 91610/ 18277	Pond on the bottom of a karst hole used for blasting of ordnance
BHW18	Bjelasnica Plateau	UA-2003-003-018	34TBP 65667/ 46257	Spring water collected from tap
BHW19	Bjelasnica Plateau	UA-2003-003-019	34TBP 66591/ 45775	Stream water

E.3.1 Water Sample Results

The activity concentrations of ^{238}U, ^{234}U, ^{235}U and the values of ^{234}U/^{238}U and ^{235}U/^{238}U activity ratios measured by APAT in the water samples are reported in Table E.2. In Table E.3, APAT reports the concentrations of ^{238}U, ^{234}U, ^{235}U and the values of ^{234}U/^{238}U and ^{235}U/^{238}U concentration ratios calculated on these same samples. HR-ICP-MS analyses by Spiez were performed on the same samples, results are presented in Tables E.4 and E.5.

Well water from Hadzici showed traces of DU

The ^{234}U/^{238}U activity ratios (Bq/Bq) in the water samples collected range from 0.58 ± 0.04 to 2.29 ± 0.37 with a mean value of 1.48 ± 0.47, while the concentration ratios range (mg/mg) from 3.12E-05 $\pm$ 2.88E-06 to 1.23E-04 $\pm$ 1.02E-05 with a mean value of 7.96E-05$\pm$2.53E-05 with a variation coefficient of 32%. The ^{235}U/^{238}U based on ICP-MS measurements lie in the natural uranium ratio, with the exception of samples BHW01 and BHW03, showing no evidence of DU. The DU percentage of total uranium for BHW01 was measured

Post-Conflict Environmental Assessment

at 14±2% and for BHW03 at 73.4±1%. In addition, the presence of U-236 (18±9 pg/L) could be indetified in BHW03 showing clear evidence of the presence of DU.

Data reported in both Tables E.2 and E.3 indicate that ^{235}U data have high uncertainties as a result of the technique used (alpha-spectrometry). This is attributable to the lower ^{235}U activity concentrations in the water. This isotope is more accurately estimated using mass-spectrometric techniques (Bou-Rabee, 1995) rather than an alpha pulse-height analysis. On the other hand, the former technique is weaker in determining ^{234}U. Results by mass-spectrometry are provided in Tables 4 and 5 showing that ^{235}U concentrations were easily measured.

The evaluation of the alpha-spectrometric results was made only with the activity concentration data on ^{238}U and ^{234}U due to higher sensitivity of this method for these isotopes (UNEP, 2001; Sansone et al., 2001). Comparing the results obtained from the measurements of water samples collected (Tables 2 and 3) with the reference values for natural waters (Goldstein et al., 1997), there is evidence of DU contamination of drinking water in only one collected sample at the former *Hadzici Tank Repair Facility* (BHW03). The result obtained by mass-spectrometry of the U-235/U238 ratio confirms the presence of DU in the sample BHW03. Traces of ^{236}U were also detected in this sample. In addition, using this same technique, a small indication of DU was revealed in the water sample BHW01.

This contamination may be due to the fact that the drinking wells are located directly in what was the line of attack of the A-10 planes. Consequently, a number of penetrators can be expected to be found buried in the soil in the near proximity to the wells. These penetrators are most likely the contamination source of these wells. However, the DU concentration levels were very low and no adverse health effects can occur.

The uranium concentration of the waters collected are consistent with the results obtained from the water samples collected by the UNEP DU Mission to Kosovo (UNEP, 2001) and Serbia and Montenegro (UNEP, 2002). Activity concentrations of naturally occurring radionuclides in drinking water vary widely because of the differing background levels, climate and agricultural conditions that prevail. In the UNSCEAR 2000 Report, the ^{238}U activity concentration in drinking water measured in Europe ranges from 5.0E-04 to 150 Bq/L. The values measured in the water samples collected during the field studies are all within that range. However in BiH two of the water samples show contamination by DU.

Based on the measurements of uranium in drinking water presented in this report, the arithmetic mean of U-238 in water is 40 10^{-5} mg/L (0.4 µg/L) and in soil 3.34 mg/kg. These values calculate the relation between the concentrations in water compared to the one in soil to be 10^{-4}. Respectively the distribution coefficient K_d is 10 000.

Based on the information currently available, uranium isotopes in water in BiH do not constitute a health risk from a radiological point of view. In some cases, the aquifers' depth is very near the upper ground surface, so that the filtering action of the soil could be reduced (Sansone *et al.*, 2001b) and DU corrosion products from the penetrators could reach the groundwater system. A previous study (Sansone *et al.*, 2001; 2001a) indicates that depleted uranium, when found in small fragments or dust particles, is more easily dissolved than uranium from mineral

Collecting a water sample from a drainage well

lattices. Thus, the migration of dissolved DU along the soil profile could represent a potential risk of contamination to the underground aquifers in the future. Since only a limited number of samples were collected in the areas where DU ammunition was used, groundwater used for drinking should be monitored in the future to increase the certainty with the results observed during the three UNEP DU Assessment field studies in the Balkans.

Based on the measurements of uranium in drinking water presented in this report, the arithmetic mean of U-238 in water is 40 10-5 mg/l (0.4 µg/L) and in soil 3.34 mg/kg. These values calculate the relation between the concentrations in water compared to the one in soil to be 10^{-4}. Respectively the distribution coefficient K_d is 10 000.

In the *Reference Case*, it is assumed that 10 kg of DU as dust is spread over 1 000 m^2. Assuming 3 m depth to the water table, the total volume of soil that might be contaminated by dissolved DU will be 3 000 m^3, which is about 5 000 tons. In this amount of soil the natural uranium content will be 17 kg, corresponding to the measured groundwater uranium concentration of 40 10^{-5} mg/L water. 10 kg DU over this area would mean an increase of about 60 % and a corresponding increase of uranium in ground water assuming DU behaviour is the same as natural uranium.

The uncertainty is the solubility of DU compared with that of natural uranium. If it is more soluble, the uranium concentration in water will increase by more than 60 %. The maximum number of penetrators fired at any specific site within BiH was 2 400, representing 720 kg of DU. The areas affected were of a maximum size of 800 x 400 m (i.e. 300 times the *Reference Area*). This would lead to a roughly 15 % increase of uranium in ground water (if DU behaves like natural uranium).

The *Reference Case* in the assumption of the contamination by uranium through rainfall is based on a yearly dissolution of 10 % (1 kg) of DU ammunition and washing out to the groundwater.

This DU Assessment report reveals that this *Reference Case* is not realistic, as penetrators are now known to corrode completely within 25-35 years. A linear approach results in the corrosion of penetrators buried in the ground of about 3-5 % per year. It is now also shown that the corrosion products are not very soluble in the surrounding soil conditions found. Assuming that 1 % of the corrosion products could be dissolved and transported down by rainwater to the groundwater, it would still have to be taken into consideration:

1) that 20 % is capillary water and will not contribute to the replenishment of the groundwater; and
2) the surface run-off, evaporation and trans-evaporation result in approximately 30 % of rainfall reaching the groundwater.

In a single year, the rainfall is approximately 0.5 m, leading to a total of 500 m^3 over the *Reference Area* of 1 000 m^2. About 150 m^3 could therefore reach the groundwater each year. This volume – in the *Reference Case* – if not absorbed by the soil, could carry 3 g of DU. Assuming a groundwater reservoir (aquifer) of 1 000 m^3, this would lead to a contamination of this aquifer of 3 µg/L per year. The WHO guideline value of 2 µg/L would then be exceeded.

These levels were not measured in BiH, indicating that adsorption to the soil takes place resulting in a reduced mobility of DU by a number of decades. The contribution to the total load of uranium to the groundwater will naturally decrease or increase if the amount of DU ammunition per m^2 varies from the *Reference Case*. Another conservative element is the assumption that the size of the catchments area for rainwater to the groundwater reservoir. The *Reference Case* is limited to the soil column immediately below the affected ground surface. It is more likely that the catchments area is larger, leading to a lower concentration of uranium in the water.

It is shown that the only risk for groundwater contamination is the composition of the soil in which the penetrators remain. In BiH, none of the investigated sites had a greater specific ground contamination (g DU per m^2) in average than in the *Reference Case*.

Table E.2 Activity concentrations (mBq/L) of ^{238}U, ^{234}U, ^{235}U in water samples collected by APAT and analysed with alpha pulse-height spectroscopy

Sample ID	U-238 mBq/L	U-234 mBq/L	U-235 mBq/L	ratio U234/U238	ratio U235/U238
BHW01	16.24 ± 0.80	14.83 ± 0.76	0.57 ± 0.14	0.91 ± 0.06	0.04 ± 0.01
BHW02	4.81 ± 0.24	5.34 ± 0.26	0.29 ± 0.06	1.11 ± 0.08	0.06 ± 0.01
BHW03	12.21 ± 0.57	7.09 ± 0.43	0.41 ± 0.11	0.58 ± 0.04	0.03 ± 0.01
BHW04	12.05 ± 0.46	15.61 ± 0.54	0.69 ± 0.10	1.30 ± 0.07	0.06 ± 0.01
BHW05	0.66 ± 0.11	0.95 ± 0.12	0.06 ± 0.03	1.44 ± 0.31	0.10 ± 0.05
BHW06	1.30 ± 0.14	2.44 ± 0.18	0.16 ± 0.05	1.87 ± 0.25	0.13 ± 0.04
BHW07	1.29 ± 0.13	1.81 ± 0.15	0.10 ± 0.04	1.41 ± 0.18	0.08 ± 0.03
BHW08	0.60 ± 0.09	1.02 ± 0.10	0.06 ± 0.03	1.70 ± 0.31	0.10 ± 0.05
BHW09	0.33 ± 0.06	0.41 ± 0.06	0.01 ± 0.02	1.24 ± 0.29	0.04 ± 0.07
BHW10	4.29 ± 0.24	5.13 ± 0.26	0.36 ± 0.07	1.20 ± 0.09	0.08 ± 0.02
BHW11	1.30 ± 0.12	2.95 ± 0.16	0.07 ± 0.03	2.27 ± 0.24	0.05 ± 0.02
BHW12	1.52 ± 0.21	3.48 ± 0.29	0.07 ± 0.06	2.29 ± 0.37	0.05 ± 0.04
BHW13	2.63 ± 0.16	4.14 ± 0.20	0.21 ± 0.05	1.57 ± 0.12	0.08 ± 0.02
BHW14	0.82 ± 0.10	1.45 ± 0.11	0.07 ± 0.03	1.77 ± 0.25	0.09 ± 0.04
BHW15	0.84 ± 0.10	1.90 ± 0.12	0.08 ± 0.03	2.26 ± 0.30	0.09 ± 0.04
BHW16	0.27 ± 0.10	0.46 ± 0.11	0.04 ± 0.02	1.70 ± 0.75	0.14 ± 0.09
BHW17	2.11 ± 0.16	2.19 ± 0.16	0.17 ± 0.05	1.04 ± 0.11	0.08 ± 0.02
BHW18	4.05 ± 0.28	4.67 ± 0.30	0.28 ± 0.08	1.15 ± 0.11	0.07 ± 0.02
BHW19	3.87 ± 0.19	5.23 ± 0.22	0.23 ± 0.05	1.35 ± 0.09	0.06 ± 0.01

Table E.3 Concentrations (mg/L) of ^{238}U, ^{234}U, ^{235}U in water samples collected and analysed with alpha pulse-height spectroscopy

Sample ID	U-238 mg/L	U-234 mg/L	U-235 mg/L	Ratio U-234/U-238	Ratio U-235/U-238
BHW01	1.31E-03 ± 6.49E-05	6.42E-08 ± 3.28E-09	7.17E-06 ± 1.71E-06	4.90E-05 ± 1.85E-05	5.48E-03 ± 1.33E-03
BHW02	3.88E-04 ± 1.95E-05	2.31E-08 ± 1.10E-09	3.64E-06 ± 7.55E-07	5.96E-05 ± 5.38E-06	9.39E-03 ± 2.00E-03
BHW03	9.85E-04 ± 4.57E-05	3.07E-08 ± 1.86E-09	5.17E-06 ± 1.35E-06	3.12E-05 ± 2.88E-06	5.25E-03 ± 1.39E-03
BHW04	9.72E-04 ± 3.69E-05	6.76E-08 ± 2.36E-09	8.68E-06 ± 1.27E-06	6.95E-05 ± 4.12E-06	8.93E-03 ± 1.35E-03
BHW05	5.34E-05 ± 9.26E-06	4.13E-09 ± 5.34E-10	8.03E-07 ± 4.15E-07	7.72E-05 ± 9.99E-06	1.50E-02 ± 8.19E-03
BHW06	1.05E-04 ± 1.14E-05	1.05E-08 ± 7.64E-10	2.05E-06 ± 6.01E-07	1.01E-04 ± 7.28E-06	1.95E-02 ± 6.11E-03
BHW07	1.04E-04 ± 1.07E-05	7.85E-09 ± 6.40E-10	1.21E-06 ± 4.59E-07	7.56E-05 ± 6.16E-06	1.16E-02 ± 4.57E-03
BHW08	4.80E-05 ± 7.17E-06	4.40E-09 ± 4.34E-10	7.37E-07 ± 3.26E-07	9.15E-05 ± 9.04E-06	1.54E-02 ± 7.16E-03
BHW09	2.69E-05 ± 4.68E-06	1.79E-09 ± 2.68E-10	1.49E-07 ± 2.83E-07	6.67E-05 ± 9.96E-06	5.54E-03 ± 1.06E-02
BHW10	3.46E-04 ± 1.90E-05	2.22E-08 ± 1.12E-09	4.51E-06 ± 8.69E-07	6.42E-05 ± 3.22E-06	1.30E-02 ± 2.61E-03
BHW11	1.05E-04 ± 9.46E-06	1.28E-08 ± 6.89E-10	8.86E-07 ± 3.92E-07	1.22E-04 ± 6.58E-06	8.45E-03 ± 3.81E-03
BHW12	1.23E-04 ± 1.70E-05	1.51E-08 ± 1.25E-09	8.95E-07 ± 6.94E-07	1.23E-04 ± 1.02E-05	7.30E-03 ± 5.76E-03
BHW13	2.12E-04 ± 1.32E-05	1.79E-08 ± 8.68E-10	2.66E-06 ± 5.90E-07	8.45E-05 ± 4.09E-06	1.25E-02 ± 2.89E-03
BHW14	6.59E-05 ± 7.78E-06	6.26E-09 ± 4.89E-10	9.22E-07 ± 3.56E-07	9.50E-05 ± 7.42E-06	1.40E-02 ± 5.65E-03
BHW15	6.78E-05 ± 7.86E-06	8.21E-09 ± 5.38E-10	9.94E-07 ± 3.62E-07	1.21E-04 ± 7.94E-06	1.47E-02 ± 5.61E-03

BHW16	2.18E-05 ± 8.17E-06	1.99E-09 ± 4.63E-10	4.57E-07 ± 2.32E-07	9.13E-05 ± 2.12E-05	2.09E-02 ± 1.32E-02
BHW17	1.70E-04 ± 1.30E-05	9.47E-09 ± 7.08E-10	2.10E-06 ± 5.99E-07	5.58E-05 ± 4.17E-06	1.24E-02 ± 3.65E-03
BHW18	3.26E-04 ± 2.27E-05	2.02E-08 ± 1.30E-09	3.53E-06 ± 1.00E-06	6.19E-05 ± 3.98E-06	1.08E-02 ± 3.16E-03
BHW19	3.12E-04 ± 1.49E-05	2.26E-08 ± 9.35E-10	2.93E-06 ± 5.91E-07	7.26E-05 ± 3.00E-06	9.40E-03 ± 1.95E-03

Table E.4 Concentrations of ^{238}U, ^{235}U, ^{234}U and ^{236}U per litre in water samples collected by APAT and analysed with HR-ICP-MS

APAT Code	^{238}U		^{235}U		^{234}U		^{236}U	
	[µg/L]	k [%]	[ng/L]	k [%]	[pg/L]	k [%]	[pg/L]	k [%]
BHW01	2.68	4.1	17.4	5.0	147	14	<30	-
BHW02	0.994	2.5	7.14	3.3	66	12	<10	-
BHW03	0.749	3.0	2.53	3.9	19	27	18	49
BHW04	1.04	3.9	7.57	4.5	79	11	<10	-
BHW05	0.077	4.2	0.57	5.2	<10	-	<10	-
BHW06	0.176	4.1	1.27	5.8	19	24	<10	-
BHW07	0.111	5.0	0.83	6.9	<10	-	<10	-
BHW08	0.059	5.9	0.44	8.1	<10	-	<10	-
BHW09	0.022	10.9	0.16	17.6	<10	-	<10	-
BHW10	0.402	2.2	2.93	3.8	32	16	<10	-
BHW11	0.131	4.1	0.96	5.1	19	31	<10	-
BHW12	0.117	3.8	0.86	4.5	17	28	<10	-
BHW13	0.225	2.2	1.64	5.1	22	31	<10	-
BHW14	0.086	5.1	0.62	6.6	8.5	53	<10	-
BHW15	0.076	5.8	0.55	8.4	<8	-	<8	-
BHW16	0.036	5.9	0.26	9.6	<8	-	<8	-
BHW17	0.221	17.8	1.63	18.4	<14	-	<14	-
BHW18	0.289	4.0	2.09	4.6	21	24	<6	-
BHW19	0.410	3.7	3.02	4.4	33	24	<8	-

Table E.5 $^{235}U/{}^{238}U$ Isotope ratio of the water samples collected by APAT: Results of HR-ICP-MS measurements

APAT Code	Isotopic ratio $^{235}U/{}^{238}U$	k [%]	Percentage DU of total Uranium [%]	k [%]
BHW01	0.00651	1.6	14.0	14.5
BHW02	0.00721	1.3	<2	-
BHW03	0.00340	1.6	73.4	1.4
BHW04	0.00729	1.1	<2	-
BHW05	0.00742	3.3	<10	-
BHW06	0.00728	4.2	<7	-
BHW07	0.00750	4.5	<8	-
BHW08	0.00747	4.2	<11	-
BHW09	0.00728	11.2	<20	-
BHW10	0.00732	2.2	<4	-
BHW11	0.00736	2.0	<8	-
BHW12	0.00736	1.7	<8	-
BHW13	0.00731	3.9	<6	-
BHW14	0.00726	4.6	<10	-
BHW15	0.00726	3.2	<10	-
BHW16	0.00738	4.4	<13	-
BHW17	0.00740	4.4	<6	-
BHW18	0.00726	1.9	<5	-
BHW19	0.00739	1.1	<4	-

Post-Conflict Environmental Assessment

Appendix F
Bio-Indicators

F.1 BACKGROUND

The natural environment today is increasingly affected by a growing number of pollutants. These may include any natural or artificial composition of matter capable of being airborne and may occur as solid particles, liquid droplets, gases, or in various combinations of these forms. Anthropogenic sources of air pollution include emissions due to industrial activities, vehicular traffic, agricultural activities, waste incineration, and war.

Conflicts such as war have serious long-term consequences on the environment and, subsequently, on human beings. Deforestation, water contamination, erosion, fire, pollution via damaged buildings and industries, and the destruction of plant and animal habitat are all potential consequences.

In Bosnia and Herzegovina (BiH), serious concerns were raised over potential health and environmental impacts caused by the bombing of industrial sites and the possible use of weapons containing depleted uranium (Bleise et al., 2003). Due to its high density -about twice that of lead- and its ability to 'self-sharpen', depleted uranium (DU) is used in munitions designed to penetrate armour and as protective plates in military vehicles such as tanks. Upon impact, the DU penetrators create a radioactive cloud of debris that can easily be inhaled or suspended in the air (Sansone et al., 2001a; Jia et al., 2002a; Jia et al., 2002b).

The analysis of soils for the evaluation of an area's contamination levels is essential. However, geological rock composition should be taken into account to avoid any potentially incorrect conclusions. On the other hand, the use of bio-indicators, due to their morpho-physiological characteristics, produces reliable results. (Cenci, 1998; Jovanovic, 1995). Therefore, the analysis of soils alone may be insufficient in order to determine the complete picture of any site investigated.

The studies completed in Kosovo and Serbia and Montenegro showed that a number of years following the the conflict, DU dust particles can still be detected in soil samples and sensitive bio-indicators used in bio-monitoring techniques (i.e. lichen, moss, tree bark).

Bio-monitoring, in a general sense, may be defined as the use of bio-organisms/materials to obtain information on certain characteristics of the biosphere. Relevant information in bio-monitoring (e.g. using plants or animals) is commonly deduced from either changes in the behaviour of the monitor organism (species composition and/or richness, ecological performance, morphology) or from the concentrations of specific substances in the monitored tissues. For monitoring purposes, appropriate organisms should be selected which are generally and permanently available in the field. These organisms may be selected on the basis of their accumulative and time-integrative behaviour towards the atmospheric compounds of interest. Providing these prerequisites, the general advantage of using a bio-monitoring approach is the ease of sampling and that no complicated or expensive technical equipment is required (IAEA-TECDOC-1152, June 2000).

The employment of organisms for the evaluation of the quality of the air has, in the last few decades, become a procedure widely used in monitoring studies (Piervittori, 1998).

Lichen

Lichen are slow-growing, stable combinations between a fungus (the mycobiont) and green algae and/or cyanobacteria (the photobio-nt). This symbiotic association forms the lichen thallus. Normally the fungus is formed of up to 95% lichen, with algae contained in a thin inner layer. These lichen features, combined with their extraordinary capability to grow over large geographical ranges and accumulate mineral elements far above their needs, make them one of the best air quality bio-indicators (Richardson *et al.*, 1980; Richardson and Nieboer, 1980; Nieboer and Richardson, 1981; Boileau *et al.*, 1982; Sloof and Wolterbeek, 1991; Ribeiro Guevara *et al.*, 1995; Haas *et al.*, 1998; McLean *et al.*, 1998; Garty, 2001; Sansone *et al.*, 2001).

Lichen are excellent bio-indicators of mineral elements

Lichen can be used following two strategies:

1. as bio-indicators; comparing different intensity of environmental pollutants changing their morphology and frequency; and

2. as bio-accumulators; using their capacity to absorb pollutants from the local atmosphere and measuring such concentrations in the lichen thalli.

Many countries, particularly France, Germany, Italy, Switzerland, The Netherlands and the USA, are currently using lichen to monitor the effects of gaseous and metal pollution at both local and national levels. There are several reasons why lichen are so extraordinarily useful in this field:

- they are ubiquitous;

- they lack a protective outer cuticle and absorb both nutrients and pollutants over much of their outer surface from predominantly aerial sources;

- they are symbiotic in nature. The fungus is obligate; if either partner is damaged by pollution this will result in a breakdown of the symbiosis, and ultimately in the death of the lichen;

- they are perennial organisms available for monitoring throughout the year;

- many lichen species accumulate high metal contents without exhibiting damage, thereby permitting monitoring over wide areas (Nimis, Purvis, 2002); and

- large areas can be sampled and mapped. Repeated measures can also be used to show changes over time.

Studies have shown that lichen have a high capacity to accumulate uranium under both moist and dry conditions from airborne particles and dust. Even tiny fragments of lichen may contain concentrations that can be readily detectable (Garty *et al.*, 1979; Becket *et al.*, 1982; Trembley *et al.*, 1997; Sansone *et al.*, 2001b). Lichen are efficient accumulators of many elements, particularly heavy metals and radionuclides that are released into the atmosphere from both natural and human activities (Jeran *et al.*, 1995). They accumulate metallic elements by trapping insoluble particulates (usually metal oxides, sulphates, sulphides and soil particles). A large body of research has been carried out in order to monitor the radionuclides from the 1986 Chernobyl accident (Adamo *et al.,* 1989; Biazrov, 1994; Feige *et al.*, 1990; Hoffman *et al.,* 1993; Triulzi *et al.*, 1996; Kirchner and Daillant, 2002). In addition, the distribution patterns of uranium and other associated elements in lichen growing in the vicinity of uranium mining/milling operations have been extensively studied (Boileau *et al.*, 1982; Jeran *et al.*, 1995, Loppi *et al.*, 2001).

Moss

Moss (Division Bryophyta) are relatively unspecialised plants, lacking true roots. In many moss, the stems have a central strand of water-conducting cells (hydroids) with thin end walls, which are highly permeable to water. Moss usually grow in low, dense, carpet-like masses on tree trunks, rocks, or moist ground.

There are approximately 14 500 moss species. They are found worldwide at sea level as well as the highest altitudes. Mosses are often abundant in relatively moist areas where a variety of species can be found. However, they can also grow in deserts or be submerged in water.

A number of studies have shown the ability of bryophytes to intercept, retain and accumulate pollutants including metals. They also have the ability to accumulate metals to levels far greater than their expected

Mosses can accumulate pollutants. Their cell walls are easily penetrable by metal ions.

physiological needs. Thus, moss seem to be suitable long-term integrators of atmospheric pollution, and some moss species have been used to monitor atmospheric metal deposition since the 1980's (Galsomies *et al.*, 2000).

Moss, as sensitive bio-indicators of heavy metal contamination, have several advantages as indicator organisms (Grodziñska and Szarek-Lukaszewska, 2001):

- many species have a vast geographical distribution, and they grow abundantly in various natural habitats;
- they have no epidermis or cuticle, their cell walls are easily penetrable by metal ions;
- they have no organs for uptake of minerals from substrate, they obtain them mainly from precipitation;
- some species have a layered structure and annually produced organic matter forms distinct segments;
- the transport of minerals between segments is poor because of lack of vascular tissues;
- moss accumulate metals in a passive way, acting as ion exchangers; and
- moss show the concentration of the most metals as a function of the amount of atmospheric deposition.

Tree Bark

It is necessary to base studies on other bio-monitors as well in order to cross check data. Tree barks can be considered as an alternative bio-monitor to lichens and mosses and are widely employed as a passive monitor for airborne trace metals and radionuclide contamination (Biazrov, 1994).

Tree bark are excellent absorbers of airborne pollutants, including anthropogenic heavy metals. The bark surface is very porous, and the absence of any metabolic processes makes it almost inert in the presence of inorganic and organic substances.

Tree bark is less sensitive than lichen but is ubiquitous. Moreover, concentrations of most elements have been found in both bark and lichen from the same tree that were of the same order of magnitude. These only differed by a factor of two or three. Finally, sample volumes are more easily attained by bark than by lichen, which can potentially lead to better statistics on the results (Musílek *et al.*, 2000).

The literature shows that bark can provide data on occurrence and magnitude of airborne uranium contamination (Bellis *et al.*, 2001).

Porous tree bark surfaces easily absorb pollutants

F.2 APAT BIOLOGICAL SAMPLES RESULTS

Throughout the field mission, lichen, moss and tree bark samples were collected at the investigated sites in BiH and the uranium isotopes were determined on all the samples. Table F.1 reports the sites where the botanical samples were collected.

Tables F.2 - F.6 report the activity concentration of ^{238}U, ^{234}U, ^{235}U and the values of ^{234}U/^{238}U and ^{235}U/^{238}U activity ratios measured in lichen, tree bark and moss. Tables F.7 - F.11 report the concentration of ^{238}U, ^{234}U, ^{235}U and the values of ^{234}U/^{238}U and ^{235}U/^{238}U concentration ratios calculated for the same samples.

The uncertainties reported in the tables include:

- the uncertainty associated with the weighing of the sample;
- the uncertainty associated with the activity of the tracer (^{232}U), as well as the uncertainty associated with the addition of the tracer to the sample; and
- the uncertainty associated with the counting statistics of the sample and the blank.

The data reported in Tables F.2 – F.11 indicate that ^{235}U data have very high uncertainties This is attributable to the low ^{235}U activity concentrations measured in the biological samples. This isotope is more accurately estimated using mass-spectrometric techniques (Bou-Rabee, 1995) rather than an alpha pulse-height analysis. On this basis, the evaluation of the results was made with only the ^{238}U and ^{234}U activity concentration data obtained by alpha spectrometry due to the enhanced sensitivity of this method for these measurements (UNEP, 2001; Sansone *et al.*, 2001).

The ^{234}U/^{238}U activity concentration ratios can be used as a fingerprint of natural vs. anthropogenic sources of uranium. The inter-laboratory exercise carried out between APAT and Spiez Laboratories, using the Reference Material IAEA-336 Lichen (RM IAEA, see Appendix C.4.3) pointed out that the composition of uranium in lichen samples is respectively characterised by ^{234}U/^{238}U and ^{235}U/^{238}U mean activity ratios of about 0.95±0.08 and 0.051±0.016. As the IAEA lichen was not affected by DU contamination, considering the lowest value of the inter-comparison activity ratio (^{234}U/^{238}U: 0.92±0.08 and ^{235}U/^{238}U: 0.041±0.012), it is possible to claim that ^{234}U/^{238}U activity concentration ratio values (measured on the botanical samples collected in BiH) below 0.84 could be indicative of anthropogenic contributions of uranium.

The ^{238}U activity concentrations in the lichen samples collected (Table F.2) range from 0.93±0.06 to 29.74±1.08 Bq/kg, with a mean value of 3.91±5.62 Bq/kg (coefficient of variation, CV=143%). The ^{238}U concentration (Table F.7) range from 7.48E-02±4.60E-03 to 2.40E+00±8.70E-02 mg/kg with a mean value of 3.27E-01±4.90E-01 mg/kg.

The high variability of ^{238}U data could be attributed to different factors:

- the different locations of the sampling sites;
- the different levels of DU contamination on each sampling sites;
- the different exposure of lichen to DU radioactive dusts or aerosol micro particles generated at the time of the conflict by the impact of DU penetrators on targets and hard surfaces;
- the different exposure of lichen due to the position of trees with respect to the soil particles dispersed in the air in relation to prevailing wind directions; and
- the different mechanisms of uranium bio-accumulation in different species of lichens (McLean *et al.*, 1998).

The ^{234}U/^{238}U activity ratios in the lichen samples (Table F.2) range from 0.19±0.01 to 1.14±0.09 (Bq/Bq) while the concentration ratios (Table F.7) range from 1.04E-05±7.98E-07 to 6.10E-05±4.84E-06 (mg/mg). Comparing these ratios (Table F.2) with those observed naturally in the RM IAEA, it is possible to distinguish 13 samples in 3 locations where DU is detectable.

The ^{238}U activity concentrations in the vegetable samples (cabbage) collected near the former *Hadzici Tank Repair Facility* (Table F.4) range from 0.54±0.03 to 1.11±0.04 Bq/kg, with a mean value of 0.83±0.40 Bq/kg (coefficient of variation, CV=49%). The ^{238}U concentration (Table F.9) range from 4.35E-02±2.32E-03 to 8.96E-02±3.19E-03 mg/kg with a mean value of 6.66E-02±3.26E-02 mg/kg.

The ^{234}U/^{238}U activity ratios in the vegetable samples (Table F.4) range from 0.64±0,04 to 0.97±0.07 (Bq/Bq), while the concentration ratios (Table F.9) range from 3.46E-05±1.91E-06 to 5.09E-05±3.88E-06 (mg/mg). One sample exhibits ^{234}U/^{238}U activity ratio consistent with DU. However, the contribution of potential soil contamination must be taken into account for the activity found in this sample.

The ^{238}U activity concentrations on the tree bark and tree bark & lichen samples (Table F.5) range from 0.35±0.02 to 1.83±0.08 Bq/kg, with a mean value of 1.15±0.51 Bq/kg (coefficient of variation, CV=44%). The ^{238}U concentration (Table F.10) ranges from 2.86E-02±1.75E-03 to 1.48E-01±6.26E-03 mg/kg with a mean value of 9.30E-02±4.11E-02 mg/kg.

The ^{234}U/^{238}U activity ratios in the tree bark samples (Table F.5) range from 0.67±0,06 to 1.02±0.06 (Bq/Bq), while the concentration ratios (Table F.10) range from 3.59E-05±3.43E-06 to 5.46E-05±3.37E-06 (mg/mg). There is evidence of DU presence in only one of the samples collected at the *Hadzici Ammunition Storage Area* on the basis of ^{234}U/^{238}U activity concentration ratios.

The ^{238}U activity concentrations in the moss samples (Table F.6) range from 2.46±0.09 to 35.74±0.73 Bq/kg, with a mean value of 8.98±11.97 Bq/kg (coefficient of variation, CV=133%). The ^{238}U concentration (Table F.11) range from 1.98E-01±7.22E-03 to 2.88E+00±5.85E-02 mg/kg with a mean value of 7.24E-01±9.65E-01 mg/kg.

The ^{234}U/^{238}U activity ratios in the moss samples (Table F.6) range from 0.63±0,03 to 1.01±0.04 (Bq/Bq), while the concentration ratios (Table F.11) range from 2.53E-05±7.59E-07 to 5.69E-05±2.91E-06 (mg/mg). The samples, collected on a tree at the *Hadzici Ammunition storage area* and on soil in the former *Hadzici Tank Repair Facility*, exhibit ^{234}U/^{238}U activity ratios consistent with DU. For the sample collected on soil, the contribution of soil to the activity must again be taken into account.

A large quantity of lichen is required for analyses

F.3 CONCLUSION

On the basis of ^{234}U/^{238}U activity concentration ratios, the data reported in Table F.2 indicate the earlier presence of DU in the air in almost all samples collected at the former *Hadzici Tank Repair Facility* (vegetables, lichens, tree barks and mosses) and the *Hadzici Ammunition Storage Area* (tree barks and lichens) as well as lichens collected at the *Han Pijesak military barracks*.

The botanical samples collected in all the other sites show values within the natural limits of ^{234}U/^{238}U activity concentration ratios and are indicative of natural contributions of uranium.

In conclusion, the main outcome of this field investigation is that lichens, barks and mosses are sensitive bio-indicators of past airborne contamination for depleted uranium dusts or aerosol particles generated at the time of attack. The presence of DU at three sites in lichen, bark and mosses samples indicates the earlier presence of DU in the air, which implies that at least some of the penetrators hit hard targets and surfaces and fragmented into dust and dispersed into the air.

The results achieved from the UNEP field surveys in the Balkans has clearly confirmed the possibility of using lichens as indicators of past airborne contamination, including depleted uranium (Rosamilia S. *et al.*, 2002). The high variability found in the ^{238}U activity concentration requires, however, additional studies to define the distribution patterns of uranium radioisotopes and associated elements in lichens, as well as identifying the most appropriate lichen species to be used as bio-indicators for depleted uranium air pollution.

Table F.1 Botanical samples collection sites in Bosnia and Herzegovina

Sample ID	Sampling Date	Site	Coordinate	Sample type	Substrate
APAT-BH01a	14/10/02	Hadzici, Tank repair facility	34TBP 74270/ 56275	bark+lichen	tree
APAT-BH01b	14/10/02	Hadzici, Tank repair facility	34TBP 74270/ 56275	moss	tree
APAT-BH02a	14/10/02	Hadzici, Tank repair facility	34TBP 74200/ 56166	lichen	tree
APAT-BH02b	14/10/02	Hadzici, Tank repair facility	34TBP 74200 / 56166	lichen	tree
APAT-BH02c	14/10/02	Hadzici, Tank repair facility	34TBP 74204 / 56166	lichen	tree
APAT-BH03a	14/10/02	Hadzici, Tank repair facility	34TBP 74181 / 56187	lichen	tree
APAT-BH04	14/10/02	Hadzici, Tank repair facility	34TBP 74033 / 56344	moss	soil
APAT-BH05	14/10/02	Hadzici, Tank repair facility	34TBP 74175 / 56222	lichen	tree
APAT-BH06a	15/10/02	Hadzici, Tank repair facility	34TBP 74197 / 56460	bark	
APAT-BH06b	15/10/02	Hadzici, Tank repair facility	34TBP 74197 / 56460	bark+lichen	tree
APAT-BH07	15/10/02	Hadzici, Tank repair facility	34TBP 73780 / 56479	bark+lichen	tree
APAT-BH08a	16/10/02	Lukavica	34TBP 88260 / 55790	bark	
APAT-BH09a	16/10/02	Lukavica	34TBP 88316/ 55770	lichen	tree
APAT-BH09b	16/10/02	Lukavica	34TBP 88316 / 55570	moss	tree
APAT-BH10	16/10/02	Lukavica	34TBP 88320 / 55760	moss	on roof
APAT-BH11	16/10/02	Lukavica	34TBP 88445 / 558666	lichen	tree
APAT-BH12	16/10/02	Lukavica	34TBP 88447 / 56020	moss	tree
APAT-BH13a	17/10/02	Hadzici, Barracks	34TBP 75321/ 54760	lichen	tree
APAT-BH13b	17/10/02	Hadzici, Barracks	34TBP 75321/ 54760	lichen	tree
APAT-BH14α	17/10/02	Hadzici, Ammunition storage area	34TBP 76586 / 53480	bark	
APAT-BH14βa	17/10/02	Hadzici, Ammunition storage area	34TBP 76586 / 53480	lichen	tree
APAT-BH14βb	17/10/02	Hadzici, Ammunition storage area	34TBP 76586 / 53480	lichen	tree
APAT-BH15	17/10/02	Pjelugovici, T55 tank	34TBP 81838 / 61779	lichen	tree
APAT-BH16a	17/10/02	Pjelugovici, T55 tank	34TBP 81809 / 61827	lichen	tree
APAT-BH16b	17/10/02	Pjelugovici, T55 tank	34TBP 81809 / 61827	lichen	tree
APAT-BH17a	18/10/02	Han Pijesak, barracks	34TBP 35832 / 84327	lichen	tree
APAT-BH17b	18/10/02	Han Pijesak, barracks	34TBP 35832 / 84327	lichen	tree
APAT-BH17c	18/10/02	Han Pijesak, barracks	34TBP 35832 / 84327	lichen	tree
APAT-BH18	18/10/02	Han Pijesak, barracks	34TBP 35693 / 84298	lichen	tree
APAT-BH19	18/10/02	Han Pijesak, barracks	34TBP 35519 / 84520	lichen	tree
APAT-BH20a	18/10/02	Han Pijesak, barracks	34TBP 35534 / 84509	lichen	tree
APAT-BH20b	18/10/02	Han Pijesak, barracks	34TBP 35534 / 84509	lichen	tree
APAT-BH21a	20/10/02	Vogosca	34TBP 89360 / 65203	mushroom	tree
APAT-BH21b	20/10/02	Vogosca	34TBP 89360 / 65203	moss	tree
APAT-BH22	20/10/02	Vogosca	34TBP 89386 / 65308	bark	
APAT-BH23	20/10/02	Vogosca	34TBP 90061 / 66641	moss	soil
APAT-BH24a	20/10/02	Vogosca	34TBP 91031 / 67677	lichen	tree
APAT-BH24b	20/10/02	Vogosca	34TBP 91031 / 67677	lichen	tree
APAT-BH25	21/10/02	Ustikolina	34TCP 20209 / 27891	lichen	tree
APAT-BH26a	21/10/02	Foca Bridge (Srbinje)	34TBP 20590/ 20483	lichen	tree
APAT-BH27a	21/10/02	Kalinovik, ammunition destruction	34TBP 91622/ 18251	lichen	rock
APAT-BH28a	21/10/02	Bjelasnica Plateau	34TBP 61840/ 42462	lichen	tree
APAT-BH28b	21/10/02	Bjelasnica Plateau	34TBP 61840/ 42462	lichen	tree
APAT-BH28c	21/10/02	Bjelasnica Plateau	34TBP 61840/ 42462	lichen	tree

Table F.2 Activity of ^{238}U, ^{234}U, ^{235}U lichen samples

Sample ID	Species	^{238}U Bq/kg	^{234}U Bq/kg	^{234}U/ ^{238}U	^{235}U Bq/kg	^{235}U/ ^{238}U
Hadzici, Tank repair facility						
APAT-BH02a	*Hypogymnia physodes*	1,89 ± 0,10	1,78 ± 0,09	0,94 ± 0,07	0,08 ± 0,02	0,042 ± 0,012
APAT-BH02b	*Parmelia subanriferie*	2,65 ± 0,11	2,57 ± 0,11	0,97 ± 0,06	0,19 ± 0,03	0,074 ± 0,013
APAT-BH02c	*Parmelia sulcata Taylor*	2,29 ± 0,09	2,02 ± 0,08	0,88 ± 0,05	0,12 ± 0,02	0,055 ± 0,010
APAT-BH03a	*Parmelia sulcata Taylor*	2,17 ± 0,09	1,67 ± 0,08	0,77 ± 0,05	0,08 ± 0,02	0,038 ± 0,009
APAT-BH05	*Parmelia sulcata Taylor*	3,6 2 ± 0,12	2,44 ± 0,10	0,67 ± 0,03	0,15 ± 0,023	0,041 ± 0,007
Lukavica						
APAT-BH09ab	*Parmelia sulcata Taylor*	2,41 ± 0,09	2,31 ± 0,09	0,96 ± 0,05	0,15 ± 0,02	0,064 ± 0,010
APAT-BH11	*Physcia adscendens*	2,94 ± 0,14	2,77 ± 0,13	0,94 ± 0,06	0,16 ± 0,03	0,054 ± 0,011
Hadzici Barracks						
APAT-BH13a	*Parmelia sulcata Taylor*	1,86 ± 0,08	1,72 ± 0,08	0,93 ± 0,06	0,10 ± 0,02	0,056 ± 0,012
APAT-BH13b	*Hypogymnia physodes*	1,20 ± 0,07	1,36 ± 0,07	1,14 ± 0,09	0,07 ± 0,02	0,062 ± 0,019
Hadzici, Ammunition storage area						
APAT-BH14βa	*Hypogymnia physodes*	10,20 ± 0,34	2,54 ± 0,15	0,25 ± 0,02	0,26 ± 0,06	0,026 ± 0,006
APAT-BH14βb	*Parmelia sulcata Taylor*	29,74 ± 1,08	5,75 ± 0,39	0,19± 0,01	0,70 ± 0,16	0,024 ± 0,006
Pijesak, T55 tank						
APAT-BH15	*Hypogymnia physodes*	1,20 ± 0,06	1,26 ± 0,06	1,05 ± 0,07	0,07 ± 0,02	0,055 ± 0,014
APAT-BH16a	*Parmelia sulcata Taylor*	1,97 ± 0,10	1,92 ± 0,10	0,97 ± 0,07	0,12 ± 0,03	0,060 ± 0,015
APAT-BH16b	*Hypogymnia physodes*	1,21 ± 0,08	1,31 ± 0,08	1,08 ± 0,09	0,05 ± 0,02	0,041 ± 0,017
Han Pijesak, barracks						
APAT-BH17a	*Parmelia sulcata Taylor*	2,71 ± 0,08	1,97 ± 0,07	0,73 ± 0,03	0,09 ± 0,02	0,035 ± 0,006
APAT-BH17b	*Evernia prunastri*	1,37 ± 0,10	1,26 ± 0,10	0,91 ± 0,10	0,05 ± 0,03	0,035 ± 0,023
APAT-BH17c	*Hypogymnia physodes*	1,54 ± 0,08	1,11 ± 0,06	0,72 ± 0,05	0,07 ± 0,02	0,046 ± 0,013
APAT-BH18	*Platismatia glauca*	1,23 ± 0,05	1,05 ± 0,04	0,85 ± 0,05	0,07 ± 0,01	0,053 ± 0,011
Han Pijesak, ammunition storage area						
APAT-BH19	*Hypogymnia physodes*	1,30 ± 0,06	0,74 ± 0,04	0,57 ± 0,04	0,08 ± 0,02	0,058 ± 0,013
APATBH20a	*Hypogymnia physodes*	1,36 ± 0,06	0,94± 0,05	0,69 ± 0,05	0,07 ± 0,02	0,051 ± 0,013
APAT-BH20b	*Parmelia saxatilus*	2,36 ± 0,09	1,29 ± 0,06	0,55 ± 0,03	0,05 ± 0,02	0,021 ± 0,007
Vogosca						
APAT-BH24a	*Hypogymnia tubulosa*	1,07 ± 0,07	1,06 ± 0,07	0,99 ± 0,09	0,06 ± 0,02	0,056 ± 0,023
APAT-BH24b	*Hypogymnia physodes*	0,93 ± 0,06	0,94 ± 0,06	1,01 ± 0,09	0,02 ± 0,01	0,020 ± 0,015
Ustikolina barracks						
APAT-BH25	*Xantoria parietina*	2,58 ± 0,09	2,48 ± 0,09	0,96 ± 0,05	0,15 ± 0,02	0,058 ± 0,009
Foca Bridge						
APAT-BH26a	*Physcia adscendens*	9,91 ± 0,23	9,78 ± 0,23	0,99 ± 0,03	0,47 ± 0,04	0,048 ± 0,004
Kalinovik, ammunition destruction						
APAT-BH27a[1]	*Sqamarina cfr. stella petraea Poelt*	15,93±0,61	15,34±0,59	0,96 ± 0,05	0,79 ± 0,09	0,049 ± 0,006
Bjelasnica Plateau						
APAT-BH28a	*Ramalina fraxinca*	1,11±0,05	1,11±0,05	1,00±0,06	0,05±0,01	0,048±0,013
APAT-BH28b	*Parmelia sulcata Taylor*	3,39±0,10	3,41±0,10	1,01±0,04	0,19±0,02	0,058±0,007
APAT-BH28c	*Parmelia saxatilis*	4,85±0,17	4,63±0,16	0,96±0,05	0,24±0,03	0,051±0,007

(1)= The substrate's sample is the rock

Table F.3 Activity of ^{238}U, ^{234}U, ^{235}U in mushroom sample

Sample ID	^{238}U Bq/kg	^{234}U Bq/kg	$^{234}U/$ ^{238}U	^{235}U Bq/kg	$^{235}U/$ ^{238}U
Vogosca					
APAT-BH21a	0,27±0,02	0,26±0,02	0,97±0,11	0,02±0,01	0,091±0,038

Table F.4 Activity of ^{238}U, ^{234}U, ^{235}U in vegetable samples

Sample ID	^{238}U Bq/kg	^{234}U Bq/kg	$^{234}U/$ ^{238}U	^{235}U Bq/kg	$^{235}U/$ ^{238}U
Hadzici, Tank repair facility					
V-UBVS1	1,11 ± 0,04	0,72 ± 0,03	0,64 ± 0,04	0,03 ± 0,01	0,031 ± 0,007
V-UBVS2	0,54 ± 0,03	0,51 ± 0,03	0,95 ± 0,07	0,02 ± 0,01	0,045 ± 0,016

Table F.5 Activity of ^{238}U, ^{234}U, ^{235}U in tree bark and tree bark+lichen samples

Sample ID	^{238}U Bq/kg	^{234}U Bq/kg	$^{234}U/$ ^{238}U	^{235}U Bq/kg	$^{235}U/$ ^{238}U
Hadzici, Tank repair facility					
APAT-BH01a[1]	1,83 ± 0,08	1,59 ± 0,07	0,87 ± 0,05	0,10 ± 0,02	0,053 ± 0,011
APAT-BH06a	0,99 ± 0,04	0,84 ± 0,04	0,85 ± 0,05	0,04 ± 0,01	0,045 ± 0,011
APAT-BH06b[2]	1,10 ± 0,05	0,93 ± 0,05	0,85 ± 0,06	0,05 ± 0,01	0,043 ± 0,013
APAT-BH07[3]	1,73 ± 0,07	1,45 ± 0,07	0,84 ± 0,05	0,11 ± 0,02	0,063 ± 0,012
Lukavica					
APAT-BH08a	0,84 ± 0,04	0,67 ± 0,03	0,80 ± 0,06	0,06 ± 0,01	0,067 ± 0,014
Hadzici, Ammunition storage area					
APAT-BH14β	0,35 ± 0,02	0,24 ± 0,02	0,67 ± 0,06	0,02 ± 0,01	0,044 ± 0,020
Vogosca					
APAT-BH22	1,22 ± 0,05	1,24 ± 0,05	1,02 ± 0,06	0,03 ± 0,01	0,029 ± 0,009

(1)= Bark + lichen sample, the specie identified is Phaesphyscia orbicularis
(2)= Bark + lichen sample, the specie identified is Arthopyrenia specie
(3)= Bark + lichen sample, the specie identified is Arthopyrenia specie

Table F.6 Activity of ^{238}U, ^{234}U, ^{235}U in moss samples

Sample ID	^{238}U Bq/kg	^{234}U Bq/kg	$^{234}U/$ ^{238}U	^{235}U Bq/kg	$^{235}U/$ ^{238}U
Hadzici, Tank repair facility					
APAT-BH01b	7,34 ± 0,31	5,78 ± 0,27	0,79 ± 0,05	0,29 ± 0,06	0,039 ± 0,008
APAT-BH04[1]	35,74 ± 0,72	16,85 ± 0,37	0,47 ± 0,01	1,11 ± 0,063	0,031 ± 0,002
Lukavica					
APAT-BH09b	3,03 ± 0,12	2,74 ± 0,11	0,90 ± 0,05	0,14 ± 0,03	0,046 ± 0,009
APAT-BH10[2]	7,18 ± 0,25	6,97 ± 0,25	0,97 ± 0,05	0,36 ± 0,05	0,050 ± 0,007
APAT-BH12	2,46 ± 0,09	2,61 ± 0,09	1,06 ± 0,05	0,15 ± 0,02	0,060 ± 0,009
Vogosca					
APAT-BH21b	3,01 ± 0,15	2,86 ± 0,14	0,95 ± 0,07	0,20 ± 0,04	0,067 ± 0,015
APAT-BH23	4,08 ± 0,13	4,23 ± 0,13	1,04 ± 0,05	0,24 ± 0,03	0,060 ± 0,008

(1)= The substrate's sample is the soil
(2)= The substrate's sample is the roof of a building

F

BIO-INDICATORS

Depleted Uranium in Bosnia and Herzegovina

Table F.7 Concentration of ^{238}U, ^{234}U, ^{235}U in lichen samples

Sample ID	Species	^{238}U mg/kg	^{234}U mg/kg	^{234}U/ ^{238}U	^{235}U mg/kg	^{235}U/ ^{238}U
Hadzici, Tank repair facility						
APAT-BH02a	Hypogymnia physodes	1,52E-01 ± 7,76E-03	7,70E-06 ± 4,02E-07	5,06E-05 ± 3,69E-06	9,83E-04 ± 2,88E-04	6,46E-03 ± 1,92E-03
APAT-BH02b	Parmelia subanriferie	2,13E-01 ± 8,93E-03	1,11E-05 ± 4,71E-07	5,21E-05 ± 3,10E-06	2,44E-03 ± 4,29E-04	1,14E-02 ± 2,07E-03
APAT-BH02c	Parmelia sulcata Taylor	1,85E-01 ± 7,34E-03	8,77E-06 ± 3,64E-07	4,74E-05 ± 2,72E-06	1,56E-03 ± 2,84E-04	8,45E-03 ± 1,57E-03
APAT-BH03a	Parmelia sulcata Taylor	1,75E-01 ± 7,22E-03	7,22E-06 ± 3,29E-07	4,12E-05 ± 2,53E-06	1,03E-03 ± 2,43E-04	5,89E-03 ± 1,41E-03
APAT-BH05	Parmelia sulcata Taylor	2,92E-01 ± 1,01E-02	1,06E-05 ± 4,14E-07	3,62E-05 ± 1,89E-06	1,87E-03 ± 2,91E-04	6,40E-03 ± 1,02E-03
Lukavica						
APAT-BH09a	Parmelia sulcata Taylor	1,94E-01 ± 7,08E-03	10,00E-06 ± 3,70E-07	5,15E-05 ± 2,68E-06	1,93E-03 ± 2,86E-04	9,97E-03 ± 1,52E-03
APAT-BH11	Physcia adscendens	2,37E-01 ± 1,11E-02	1,20E-05 ± 5,72E-07	5,06E-05 ± 3,37E-06	1,97E-03 ± 4,11E-04	8,30E-03 ± 1,77E-03
Hadzici Barracks						
APAT-BH13a	Parmelia sulcata Taylor	1,50E-01 ± 6,59E-03	7,46E-06 ± 3,37E-07	4,97E-05 ± 3,13E-06	1,30E-03 ± 2,70E-04	8,62E-03 ± 1,84E-03
APAT-BH13b	Hypogymnia physodes	9,69E-02 ± 5,58E-03	5,91E-06 ± 3,22E-07	6,10E-05 ± 4,84E-06	9,26E-04 ± 2,73E-04	9,56E-03 ± 2,87E-03
Hadzici, Ammunition storage area						
APAT-BH14βa	Hypogymnia physodes	8,22E-01 ± 2,72E-02	1,10E-05 ± 6,32E-07	1,34E-05 ± 8,87E-07	3,26E-03 ± 7,46E-04	3,97E-03 ± 9,17E-04
APAT-BH14βb	Parmelia sulcata Taylor	2,40E+00 ± 8,70E-02	2,49E-05 ± 1,69E-06	1,04E-05 ± 7,98E-07	8,81E-03 ± 2,07E-03	3,67E-03 ± 8,72E-04
Pijesak, T55 tank						
APAT-BH15	Hypogymnia physodes	9,65E-02 ± 4,63E-03	5,46E-06 ± 2,56E-07	5,66E-05 ± 3,80E-06	8,20E-04 ± 2,09E-04	8,49E-03 ± 2,20E-03
APAT-BH16a	Parmelia sulcata Taylor	1,59E-01 ± 8,15E-03	8,32E-06 ± 4,30E-07	5,23E-05 ± 3,80E-06	1,49E-03 ± 3,69E-04	9,38E-03 ± 2,37E-03
APAT-BH16b	Hypogymnia physodes	9,75E-02 ± 6,11E-03	5,66E-06 ± 3,43E-07	5,80E-05 ± 5,06E-06	6,24E-04 ± 2,54E-04	6,40E-03 ± 2,64E-03
Han Pijesak, barracks						
APAT-BH17a	Parmelia sulcata Taylor	2,19E-01 ± 6,81E-03	8,54E-06 ± 2,97E-07	3,91E-05 ± 1,82E-06	1,17E-03 ± 2,03E-04	5,36E-03 ± 9,44E-04
APAT-BH17b	Evernia prunastri	1,11E-01 ± 8,25E-03	5,44E-06 ± 4,22E-07	4,91E-05 ± 5,29E-06	5,97E-04 ± 3,92E-04	5,40E-03 ± 3,57E-03
APAT-BH17c	Hypogymnia physodes	1,24E-01 ± 6,12E-03	4,81E-06 ± 2,72E-07	3,88E-05 ± 2,92E-06	8,92E-04 ± 2,51E-04	7,20E-03 ± 2,06E-03
APAT-BH18	Platismatia glauca	9,90E-02 ± 3,92E-03	4,54E-06 ± 1,91E-07	4,58E-05 ± 2,65E-06	8,18E-04 ± 1,64E-04	8,26E-03 ± 1,69E-03
Han Pijesak, ammunition storage area						
APAT-BH19	Hypogymnia physodes	1,05E-01 ± 4,63E-03	3,22E-06 ± 1,79E-07	3,06E-05 ± 2,17E-06	9,39E-04 ± 2,01E-04	8,92E-03 ± 1,95E-03
APAT-BH20a	Hypogymnia physodes	1,10E-01 ± 5,11E-03	4,07E-06 ± 2,21E-07	3,71E-05 ± 2,65E-06	8,74E-04 ± 2,12E-04	7,98E-03 ± 1,97E-03
APAT-BH20b	Parmelia saxatilus	1,90E-01 ± 7,63E-03	5,57E-06 ± 2,82E-07	2,93E-05 ± 1,89E-06	6,11E-04 ± 1,96E-04	3,21E-03 ± 1,04E-03
Vogosca						
APAT-BH24a	Hypogymnia tubulosa	8,63E-02 ± 5,75E-03	4,59E-06 ± 3,07E-07	5,32E-05 ± 5,02E-06	7,51E-04 ± 2,98E-04	8,71E-03 ± 3,51E-03
APAT-BH24b	Hypogymnia physodes	7,48E-02 ± 4,60E-03	4,06E-06 ± 2,48E-07	5,42E-05 ± 4,70E-06	2,35E-04 ± 1,71E-04	3,14E-03 ± 2,30E-03
Ustikolina barracks						
APAT-BH25	Xantoria parietina	2,08E-01 ± 7,26E-03	1,07E-05 ± 3,79E-07	5,16E-05 ± 2,56E-06	1,88E-03 ± 2,74E-04	9,02E-03 ± 1,35E-03
Foca Bridge						
APAT-BH26a	Physcia adscendens	7,99E-01 ± 1,85E-02	4,23E-05 ± 9,83E-07	5,30E-05 ± 1,74E-06	5,90E-03 ± 4,77E-04	7,38E-03 ± 6,21E-04
Kalinovik, ammunition destruction						
APAT-BH27a[1]	Sqamarina cfr. stella petraea Poelt	1,28E+00 ± 4,92E-02	6,64E-05 ± 2,56E-06	5,17E-05 ± 2,81E-06	9,84E-03 ± 1,18E-03	7,66E-03 ± 9,64E-04
Bjelasnica Plateau						
APAT-BH28a	Ramalina fraxinca	8,95E-02 ± 4,12E-03	4,83E-06 ± 2,22E-07	5,40E-05 ± 3,52E-06	6,62E-04 ± 1,74E-04	7,40E-03 ± 1,97E-03
APAT-BH28b	Parmelia sulcata Taylor	2,73E-01 ± 8,14E-03	1,48E-05 ± 4,40E-07	5,41E-05 ± 2,28E-06	2,44E-03 ± 2,91E-04	8,95E-03 ± 1,10E-03
APAT-BH28c	Parmelia sulcata saxatilis	3,91E-01 ± 1,36E-02	2,01E-05 ± 7,05E-07	5,13E-05 ± 2,54E-06	3,07E-03 ± 4,05E-04	7,85E-03 ± 1,07E-03

(1)= The substrate's sample is the rock

Table F.8　Concentration of ^{238}U, ^{234}U, ^{235}U in mushroom sample

Sample ID	^{238}U mg/kg	^{234}U mg/kg	$^{234}U/$ ^{238}U	^{235}U mg/kg	$^{235}U/$ ^{238}U
Vogosca					
APAT-BH21a	2,16E-02 ± 1,72E-03	1,13E-06 ± 9,12E-08	5,23E-05 ± 5,93E-06	3,05E-04 ± 1,25E-04	1,41E-02 ± 5,89E-03

Table F.9　Concentration of ^{238}U, ^{234}U, ^{235}U in vegetable samples

Sample ID	^{238}U mg/kg	^{234}U mg/kg	$^{234}U/$ ^{238}U	^{235}U mg/kg	$^{235}U/$ ^{238}U
Hadzici, Tank repair facility					
V-UBVS1	8,96E-02 ± 3,19E-03	3,10E-06 ± 1,31E-07	3,46E-05 ± 1,91E-06	4,29E-04 ± 1,01E-04	4,79E-03 ± 1,14E-03
V-UBVS2	4,35E-02 ± 2,32E-03	2,21E-06 ± 1,21E-07	5,08E-05 ± 3,88E-06	3,02E-04 ± 1,04E-04	6,94E-03 ± 2,43E-03

Table F.10　Concentration of ^{238}U, ^{234}U, ^{235}U in tree bark and tree bark + lichen samples

Sample ID	^{238}U mg/kg	^{234}U mg/kg	$^{234}U/$ ^{238}U	^{235}U mg/kg	$^{235}U/$ ^{238}U
Hadzici, Tank repair facility					
APAT-BH01a[1]	1,48E-01 ± 6,26E-03	6,90E-06 ± 3,09E-07	4,67E-05 ± 2,88E-06	1,22E-03 ± 2,56E-04	8,25E-03 ± 1,77E-03
APAT-BH06a	7,96E-02 ± 3,40E-03	3,65E-06 ± 1,66E-07	4,58E-05 ± 2,86E-06	5,61E-04 ± 1,32E-04	7,05E-03 ± 1,69E-03
APAT-BH06B[2]	8,88E-02 ± 4,30E-03	4,05E-06 ± 2,10E-07	4,55E-05 ± 3,23E-06	5,98E-04 ± 1,81E-04	6,74E-03 ± 2,06E-03
APAT-BH07[3]	1,40E-01 ± 5,96E-03	6,28E-06 ± 2,87E-07	4,50E-05 ± 2,81E-06	1,36E-03 ± 2,54E-04	9,72E-03 ± 1,86E-03
Lukavica					
APAT-BH08a	6,81E-02 ± 3,20E-03	2,92E-06 ± 1,50E-07	4,28E-05 ± 2,99E-06	7,02E-04 ± 1,47E-04	1,03E-02 ± 2,21E-03
Hadzici, Ammunition storage area					
APAT-BH14β	2,86E-02 ± 1,75E-03	1,03E-06 ± 7,52E-08	3,59E-05 ± 3,42E-06	1,96E-04 ± 8,65E-05	6,86E-03 ± 3,05E-03
Vogosca					
APAT-BH22	9,83E-02 ± 4,30E-03	5,37E-06 ± 2,33E-07	5,46E-05 ± 3,37E-06	4,38E-04 ± 1,34E-04	4,46E-03 ± 1,38E-03

(1)= Bark + lichen sample, the specie identified is Phaesphyscia orbicularis
(2)= Bark + lichen sample, the specie identified is Arthopyrenia specie
(3)= Bark + lichen sample, the specie identified is Arthopyrenia specie

Table F.11　Concentration of ^{238}U, ^{234}U, ^{235}U in moss samples

Sample ID	^{238}U mg/kg	^{234}U mg/kg	$^{234}U/$ ^{238}U	^{235}U mg/kg	$^{235}U/$ ^{238}U
Hadzici, Tank repair facility					
APAT-BH01b	5,92E-01 ± 2,54E-02	2,50E-05 ± 1,16E-06	4,23E-05 ± 2,67E-06	3,59E-03 ± 7,49E-04	6,05E-03 ± 1,29E-03
APAT-BH04[1]	2,88E+00 ± 5,85E-02	7,29E-05 ± 1,61E-06	2,53E-05 ± 7,59E-07	1,39E-02 ± 7,91E-04	4,81E-03 ± 2,91E-04
Lukavica					
APAT-BH09b	2,45E-01 ± 9,48E-03	1,18E-05 ± 4,70E-07	4,84E-05 ± 2,70E-06	1,74E-03 ± 3,20E-04	7,11E-03 ± 1,34E-03
APAT-BH10[2]	5,79E-01 ± 2,04E-02	3,02E-05 ± 1,07E-06	5,21E-05 ± 2,60E-06	4,49E-03 ± 6,01E-04	7,76E-03 ± 1,07E-03
APAT-BH12	1,98E-01 ± 7,22E-03	1,13E-05 ± 4,03E-07	5,69E-05 ± 2,91E-06	1,84E-03 ± 2,81E-04	9,30E-03 ± 1,46E-03
Vogosca					
APAT-BH21b	2,43E-01 ± 1,19E-02	1,24E-05 ± 6,19E-07	5,10E-05 ± 3,56E-06	2,51E-03 ± 5,36E-04	1,03E-02 ± 2,26E-03
APAT-BH23	3,29E-01 ± 1,06E-02	1,83E-05 ± 5,84E-07	5,56E-05 ± 2,53E-06	3,05E-03 ± 3,84E-04	9,29E-03 ± 1,21E-03

(1)= The substrate's sample is the soil
(2)= The substrate's sample is the roof of a building

F

BIO-INDICATORS

APPENDIX G

DU in Air

G.1 GENERAL ASPECTS

Normal concentrations and radiation doses

Uranium-series radionuclides are permanently present in air as a result of resuspension of soil particles, exhalation of radon (^{222}Rn) into the air, and its subsequent decay products to so-called 'radon daughters'. A dust loading of 50 µg m^{-3} is generally assumed. With a ^{238}U concentration in soil of 10-50 Bq kg^{-1}, the corresponding and estimated concentration of this nuclide in air is expected to be 0.5-2.5 µBq m^{-3}.

Observed values of uranium concentration in air vary widely. Concentrations of uranium in sea air may be an order of magnitude lower than in continental or industrial areas. Reported values of ^{238}U concentration are 0.9-5 µBq m^{-3} in the United States and 0.02-18 µBq m^{-3} in Europe (UNSCEAR, 2000). The given reference value is 1 µBq m^{-3} of ^{238}U, which corresponds to 8 10^{-5} µg ^{238}U per m^3 air or 0.08 ng m^{-3}. Most natural levels of uranium are in the range of 0.1-10 µBq m^{-3} ((1-100)· 10^{-5} µg m^{-3} or 0.01-1 ng m^{-3}). Concentrations of ^{235}U in air are much lower (i.e. 0.04 µBq m^{-3} in the United States) (UNSCEAR, 2000). For this radionuclide, the given reference value is 0.05 µBq m^{-3}. As ^{234}U quickly enters into radioactive equilibrium with ^{238}U, the UNSCEAR 2000 report recommends using 1 µBq m^{-3} as a reference value for ^{234}U concentration in air.

The effective dose caused by inhalation of uranium and its radioactive daughter products as they are present in air is estimated to be 4.7, 5.6 and 5.4 µSv per year for infants, children and adults, accordingly. Age-weighted effective dose is 5.4 µSv per year. The major part is from ^{210}Pb+^{210}Po (98%). From ^{238}U alone it is 0.02 µSv per year, from ^{234}U 0.03 µSv per year. If all U-238 daughters except radon and its daughter product are included, the dose is 0.3 µSv per year. The dose from ^{235}U and its daughter products can be neglected.

The concentration ratios ^{234}U/^{238}U and ^{235}U/^{238}U

The two uranium isotopes ^{234}U and ^{238}U are in the same decay chain (i.e. the ^{238}U series -see Appendix O) and if not disturbed by any selective chemical or physical effect they should be in radioactive equilibrium. In case of equilibrium, natural uranium contains 99.2745 % of ^{238}U by weight and 0.0054% of ^{234}U, which in terms of activity corresponds to about 12.4 Bq each per mg of natural uranium. However, it has been observed that by chemical effects (different leaching rate) and physical effects (alpha recoil) as reported in the WHO study *Depleted Uranium, Sources, Exposures and Health effects*, (WHO, 2001), the ratio can vary by a factor of 1-7 in favour of ^{234}U (i.e. there is an excess of ^{234}U in the dust in air). However, the real variation of the ^{234}U and ^{238}U ratio in air at a given place or region reflects the variation of the ratio in soil at that location, as is discussed below.

In the case of depleted uranium, the concentration of ^{234}U decreases somewhat more than ^{235}U. If the concentration of ^{235}U decreases from 0.72 % to 0.20 % by weight (i.e. a factor of 3.6), the concentration of ^{234}U decreases from 0.0054 % to 0.0010 % (i.e. a factor of 5.4). If DU is mixed with natural uranium in varying proportions the mass ratio as well as the activity ratio will vary accordingly.

Assuming that in a sample containing some DU the mass proportion of DU is X and the part of natural uranium is (1-X) the mass ratio M for ^{234}U/^{238}U is given from the formula:

$$M = [(1-X) \cdot 0.0054 + X \cdot 0.001] / [(1-X) \cdot 99.2745 + X \cdot 99.8] \qquad \text{(G.1)}$$

The activity ratio R is given by:

$$R = M \cdot 2.31 \cdot 10^5 / 12.4 \qquad \text{(G.2)}$$

For X=0 the R-value is 1, for X=0.5 the R-value is 0.6 and for X=1 the R-value is 0.19, etc. Corresponding formulas also apply for $^{235}U/^{238}U$ ratio. In that case, if the mass proportion of DU is X and the part of natural uranium is (1-X) the mass ratio M for $^{235}U/^{238}U$ is given from the formula:

$$M = [(1-X) \cdot 0.72 + X \cdot 0.2] / [(1-X) \cdot 99.2745 + X \cdot 99.8] \quad \text{(G.3)}$$

The activity ratio R is given by:

$$R = M \cdot 80/12.4 \qquad \text{(G.4)}$$

For X=0 the R-value is 0.047, for X=0.5 the R-value is 0.03 and for X=1 the R-value is 0.013, etc.

The percentage of DU in the air samples with measured mass concentration of ^{234}U and ^{238}U ($^{234}C_{air}$ and $^{238}C_{air}$ in pg m^{-3}) can be estimated as:

$$DU\ [\%] = 100 \cdot (0.000054 - {}^{234}C / {}^{238}C) / 0.000044 \qquad \text{(G.5)}$$

For measured mass concentration of ^{235}U and ^{238}U in air ($^{235}C_{air}$ and $^{238}C_{air}$ in pg m^{-3}) this formula becomes:

$$DU\ [\%] = 100 \cdot (0.00725 - {}^{235}C / {}^{238}C) / 0.00525 \qquad \text{(G.6)}$$

Depleted uranium in air

By taking measurements and subsequent chemical analyses on dust that has been sampled with air filters, it is possible to estimate the concentration of total uranium in air, as well as the concentration of ^{238}U, ^{235}U and ^{234}U. By using the previous formulas, it is also possible to estimate the quantity of DU in the sample. How much DU could possibly be expected in air in normal and extreme conditions if there is DU-dust contamination of the ground? What is the relation to the beta/gamma-measurement directly on the ground surface? However, from a health point of view, it is the concentration of uranium as such that is of interest.

Relation 1. The normal situation

Assuming that there is some correlation between the concentration of uranium in air pollution (dust) and that of the soil, the following applies:

A concentration of uranium in air of 8 10^{-5} mg m^{-3} and a normal dust concentration of 50 mg m^{-3} result in 1.6 mg uranium/kg dust, which corresponds with the concentration in soil of 1-4 mg ^{238}U per kg of soil.

Relation 2. DU contaminated ground surface

Assuming 10 kg of DU dust is distributed over the Reference Area of 1 000 m^2 (i.e. the *Reference Case* in this report), the corresponding area contamination would be 10 g m^{-2}. The detection limit with β/γ-instruments used would be 0.01 times the reference value (i.e. 0.1 g m^{-2}). If some absorption occurs and the activity is distributed in the upper 1 mm of soil, the detection limit would be 10 times higher (i.e. 1 g m^{-2}).

Depleted Uranium in Bosnia and Herzegovina

G

Resuspension is normally divided into two types: natural (wind driven), and anthropogenic (vehicular movement, agricultural activities, etc). Wind-driven resuspension assumes that the only disturbance to the surface is a result of natural weathering, while anthropogenic or mechanical resuspension includes mechanical disturbances by pedestrians or vehicles and agricultural operations.

10 g m^{-2} in 1 mm depth corresponds to 8 g DU per kg soil. Assuming that the first mm of soil is the part that chiefly contributes to dust in the air, the concentration in normal dusty air would be 400 ng DU per m³ of air (50 μg m^{-3} · 8 ng DU per μg soil, dust) corresponding to 5 mBq m^{-3} in air, or roughly 5 000 times higher than normal. This distribution model can be considered as representative for a short time period (days – weeks) following the contaminating event. This air concentration would result in an annual effective dose of less than 1 mSv (about 0.5 mSv) caused by continuous inhalation of that air for a full year, and is therefore insignificant. The Wilkins et al (1994) report for this type of estimation recommends using the dust concentration of 100 μg m^{-3} as a reasonably cautious dust loading, but does not change the assessments stated above.

For the worst case assuming desert conditions with vehicular movement and intensive agricultural activities, the dust concentration can reach 30 000 μg m^{-3} based on measurements from Maralinga and Emu nuclear test sites in Australia (Haywood and Smith, 1990), which quoted values from 370 to 65 000 μg m^{-3} for sitting in or near a moving vehicle. A mid-range value can be used for estimates assumed, as the no persons will spend their entire working day close to the vehicles. In that case, the DU concentration in air can be 0.24 mg m^{-3} (30 000 μg m^{-3}· 8 ng DU per μg soil, dust). This value is roughly equal to the recommended limit by the U.S. National Institute for Occupational Safety and Health (NIOSH) for insoluble uranium of 0.2 mg m^{-3} for chronic occupational exposure, and is approximately 3 times lower than a limit 0.6 mg m^{-3} for short-term exposure. When NIOSH occupational guidelines are converted for exposure of the general public, they are 0.05 mg m^{-3} for chronic exposure and 0.15 mg m^{-3} for short-term exposure. For soluble uranium, the levels are 0.5 mg m^{-3} and 10 mg m^{-3}, respectively (NIOSH, 1994).

Considering that people would be in similar conditions no more than 1 working day (8 hours), the total intake of resuspended DU to a male heavy worker outdoors would be at the level of 2.1 mg. This intake corresponds to a committed effective dose at a level 0.26 mSv (see Appendix O) that is approximately 2.5 times higher than the total effective dose 110 μSv per year caused by all uranium daughters in the body from ingestion and inhalation (except inhaled radon daughters).

In the worst case, assuming desert conditions and normal living conditions, dust concentration can be at a level of 2 000 μg m^{-3}. This value is based on measurements from the Maralinga and Emu nuclear test sites in Australia (Haywood and Smith, 1990) for children playing. In that case, the DU concentration in air could be 16 μg m^{-3} (2 000 μg m^{-3} · 8 ng DU per μg soil, dust), or 2 times higher than stated by the U.S. Agency for Toxic Substances and Disease Registry (ATSDR) as a Minimal Risk Level (MRL) for chronic inhalation exposure of 8 μg m^{-3} (ATSDR, 1999).

The intake of DU can be estimated by using the formula (UK, 2002):

$$\text{Intake}_{DU} = [C_{air} \cdot I_{inh} \cdot (1-Occ_{rate})] + [C_{air} \cdot I_{inh} \cdot Occ_{rate} \cdot I/O], \quad (G.7)$$

Where:

- C_{air} is the integrated air concentration due to wind-driven or anthropogenic resuspension.

Post-Conflict Environmental Assessment

- I_{inh} is the inhalation rate, as recommended by the International Commission on Radiological Protection (ICRP, 1994) (see Table G.1). For the best estimate, the outdoor worker rate is used. For the worst case, the heavy worker rate is used.

- Occ_{rate} is the indoor occupancy, assumed to be 50%, i.e. the outdoor worker value from habit surveys (Robinson, 1996). For a one-year-old infant, ten year old child and adult housewife Occ_{rate} is assumed to be 0.9 (UK, 2002).

- I/O is the indoor/outdoor concentration ratio. It is known that small particles can penetrate effectively into buildings, and the degree of equilibrium between indoor and outdoor air is dependent on particle size. For this report, a value of 0.5 is chosen on the basis of a dose-conversion factor suggested in Brown (1989).

Table G.1 Generalised inhalation rates (24-hour averages)

Group	Inhalation rate, $(m^3 \, s^{-1})$
Infant (one year old)	6.02E-05
Child (ten years old)	1.76E-04
Adult housewife	2.04E-04
Heavy worker	3.10E-04
Outdoor worker	2.92E-04

A worst case calculation for total DU intake in the 1st year following initial deposit is shown in Table G.2. While undertaking these calculations, it was assumed that the DU had been dispersed in the upper 1 cm soil layer:

- concentration of DU in top soil box = 0.71 g kg^{-1}, which corresponds to an initial concentration of 0.8 g kg^{-1} in a layer of 0-1 cm with allowance for the averaged value of vertical migration coefficient for the 1st year equal to 0.89;

- dust loading – 2 000 µg m^{-3}.

Table G.2 Intakes of DU for all age groups calculated using the worst case of dust-loading approach

Exposed age group	DU intake, mg
Infant	1.5
Child	4.4
Adult (female)	5.0
Adult (male outdoor worker)	9.8

The maximum value of DU intake in the first year after contamination is equal to 10 mg for adult (male outdoor worker), which corresponds to a committed effective dose at a level of 1.2 mSv. This value, a shade higher than the dose limit for members of the public (1 mSv/year), refers to exposure to artificial sources (EU, 1996). For a housewife remaining 90 % of the time indoors, the corresponding dose is about 0.6 mSv. On the other hand, the aforementioned situation is very conservative and hardly realistic.

Relation 3. DU contaminated ground and distributed to a depth of 10 cm.

Evidently, DU dust may have been distributed to a deeper layer than 10 mm. If it was distributed to a depth of 100 mm, the concentration of DU in soil would be 10 times less. Assuming the same amount of DU (10 kg over 1 000 m²), and the same pattern of suspension of dust from ground, the resulting DU concentration in air would be 10 times less and the actual detection limit would be 10 times the assumed ground contamination (10 g m⁻²). In this case, all values introduced in Relation 2 assessments should be reduced by a factor of 10, and problems related to DU intake by dust resuspension, both for professional workers and for the population, will not arise. This distribution model can be considered as more probable and representative following a long time period (7 years) since the contaminating event.

Conclusions

1. Normal uranium concentration in air is 1 µBq m⁻³ (8 10⁻⁵ µg m⁻³, 0.08 ng m⁻³ respectively) ± factor of 10 upwards and downwards.

2. Resulting effective doses by inhalation are 0.02 - 0.03 µSv per year from ^{238}U and ^{234}U respectively.

3. The ratio ^{234}U/^{238}U in air can normally vary as a result of natural causes, depending on the corresponding ratio in the soil at the location investigated.

4. From measurements, it is possible to estimate the proportion of possible DU in a sample by assessing the activity ratio ^{234}U/^{238}U if it is lower than 1. However, many uncertainties exist and a non-indicative value of ^{234}U/^{238}U does not necessarily imply that no DU is present in the air.

5. The ratio ^{235}U/^{238}U cannot be influenced by any physical or chemical process in nature, it is thus expected to be constant and independent of the origin of the sample. Any statistically significant difference from the natural ratio must be attributed to the existence of artificially processed uranium.

6. If field measurements show no indication of DU contamination on the ground surface, there can still be an easily detectable concentration of DU in air if the DU on the ground is superficial. However, this could only be detected by using extremely sensitive and sophisticated analytical methods. On the other hand, if there is no detectable air contamination, there can still be a ground contamination above the reference level (10 g per m²). This would occur if the nearby ground does not contribute significantly to the dust in air at the area under investigation.

7. From the radiation dose viewpoint, it is concluded that in normal conditions the DU intake and effective doses from airborne uranium are very small, even if the concentration is several hundred times higher than normal. Heavy metal risks are also insignificant in these cases.

8. For the worst (and unrealistic) case assuming desert conditions with vehicular movement, etc. the DU concentration in air can approach the limits for chronic occupational exposure and exceed the limit for short-term exposure of the general public.

9. In the same worst case assuming desert conditions and normal living conditions, DU concentration can be higher than a Minimal Risk Level (MRL) for chronic inhalation exposure of uranium as a toxic metal.

G.2 AIR MEASUREMENT RESULTS

Sampling sites

Air samples were collected at a number of sites in BiH during the mission (Table G.3).

Table G.3 Air-filter samples collection sites in Bosnia and Herzegovina

Code	Sampling site	Coordinates UTM 34T	Sampled volume [m³]
NUC-02-023-201	Hadzici ; [1]	BP 74 353 / 56 272	100.6
NUC-02-023-202	Hadzici; [1]	BP 74 185 / 56 407	100.1
NUC-02-023-203	Hadzici; [1]	BP 74 096 / 56 339	96.8
NUC-02-023-204	Hadzici; [1]	BP 74 098 / 56 338	98.3
NUC-02-024-201	Hadzici; [1]	BP 74 041 / 56 365	131.6
NUC-02-024-202	Hadzici; [1]	BP 74 024 / 56 372	131.9
NUC-02-024-203	Hadzici; [1] inside a former workshop	BP 74 030 / 56 340	61.0
NUC-02-024-204	Hadzici; [1] inside a former workshop	BP 73 920 / 56 398	126.5
NUC-02-024-205	Hadzici; [1]	BP 73 915 / 56 543	67.5
NUC-02-025-201	Lukavica; Barracks	BP 88 332 / 55 825	113.0
NUC-02-025-202	Lukavica; Barracks	BP 88 623 / 55 691	103.1
NUC-02-025-203	Lukavica; Barracks	BP 88 536 / 55 932	85.3
NUC-02-025-204	Lukavica; Barracks	BP 88 473 / 55 844	85.3
NUC-02-026-201	Hadzici; [2]	BP 75 265 / 54 739	79.7
NUC-02-026-202	Hadzici; [2]	BP 75 430 / 54 668	63.7
NUC-02-027-201	Han Pijesak; Barracks	CP 36 070 / 84 360	138.4
NUC-02-027-202	Han Pijesak; Barracks	CP 35 890 / 84 308	136.4
NUC-02-027-203	Han Pijesak; Barracks	CP 35 679 / 84 362	133.9
NUC-02-027-204	Han Pijesak; Barracks	CP 35 542 / 84 386	131.9
NUC-02-028-201	Han Pijesak; Barracks	CP 35 546 / 84 432	75.6
NUC-02-028-202	Han Pijesak; Barracks (inside storage barn)	CP 35 546 / 84 429	67.7
NUC-02-029-201	Vogosca; [3]	BP 88 893 / 64 964	99.9
NUC-02-029-202	Vogosca; [3]	BP 89 132 / 65 128	98.3
NUC-02-030-201	Foca Bridge (Srbinje)	CP 20 545 / 20 476	96.1

1) Tank repair facility 2) Barracks 1 km from ammunition storage area 3) Ammunition production site

To note:

- On the first day at the former *Hadzici Tank Repair Facility*, two air filter samplers were placed in selected positions 150 m (sample NUC-02-023-202) and 300 m (-023-201) respectively away from the areas known to have been attacked with DU ammunition (see map in Chapter 7.1). This was done in order to try to sample the average uranium concentration at a certain distance from the areas that had been hit directly by DU bullets. A further two air filter samplers were placed at the cobblestone square/yard at the centre of the site. This yard and the adjacent workshops had been intensely hit by DU ammunition. One air filter sampler (-023-203) was placed 1.6 metres above the ground surface, whereas the sampler (-023-204) was placed at 0.9 metres, in order to study the effect of DU at different heights.

- On the second day at the former *Hadzici Tank Repair Facility*, two air filters samplers (samples NUC-02-024-201 and NUC-02-024-202) were placed in the middle of the intensely attacked cobblestone square/yard. A further two samplers (NUC-02-024-203 and

NUC-02-024-204) were placed inside two different buildings near the yard. DU contamination was found inside one of these buildings (NUC-02-024-204). Finally, one air filter sample (NUC-02-024-205) was collected at the location of the former tank parking lot in the western-most part of the site. The tanks parked there had been strongly attacked by A-10 planes. 160 DU contamination points were found on this parking lot.

An air filter sampler continues to run while the UNEP team takes a lunch break

- On the first of two days at the *Han Pijesak Artillery Storage and Barracks,* four air filter samplers were arranged roughly 150 m apart in a parallel line to the main road leading from the entrance of the campus to the forest (see map in Chapter 7.7).

- On the second day at the *Han Pijesak Artillery Storage and Barracks,* one sampler (sample NUC-02-028-201) was placed on the west side of the entrance to one of the intensely attacked storage barns and another sampler (NUC-02-028-202) was placed inside the building. Both these samples showed traces of DU.

- Air samples were also collected at *Lukavica, Vogosca, Foca Bridge* (Srbinje) and the *Hadzici Army Barracks.*

Analyses

The $^{234}U/^{238}U$ and $^{235}U/^{238}U$ mass concentration ratios depend on the extent of the enrichment process, which cause depletion in the lighter uranium isotopes and can be used to distinguish natural from anthropogenic uranium. By measurements of dust collected by air filters and by analysing the uranium concentrations in the filters, the total uranium concentration in air, as well the isotopic concentrations of ^{234}U, ^{235}U and ^{238}U, can be determined.

The analyses of the uranium isotopes in the samples collected were made at Spiez laboratory by ICP-MS (see *Appendix C 'Methodology and Quality Control'*). The minimum detection limits for the ^{235}U and for ^{238}U, using ICP-MS is well bellow the concentrations of these nuclides in the air. The $^{235}U/^{238}U$ mass ratio is constantly equal to 0.007, and there is no physicochemical phenomenon occurring in nature that can cause any variation in this value. Consequently, any statistically significant difference from the naturally expected ratio must be attributed to technologically treated uranium. The conclusion on the existence of DU contamination in the air or not was based on the $^{235}U/^{238}U$ activity ratio that varies from 0.0452 (0% DU) to 0.0129 (100% DU).

Results and Discussions

Results from the air filter analyses made on the samples from the UNEP mission are presented in Tables G.4 – G.7. The total uranium concentrations measured in the air varies from 9.7 to 3 600 pg/m³.

DU was detected in air samples collected at two sites: *Hadzici Tank Repair Facility*, and the *Han Pijesak Artillery Storage and Barracks*. Uranium was also detected on air filters collected at other sites where filter samples were taken during the mission, however, no DU was found in these samples.

Air samplers in the Hadzici cobblestone yard

- At the *Hadzici Tank Repair Facility* during the first day, 4 air samplers (samples NUC-02-023-201, -023-202, -023-203, and -023-204) were placed in randomly selected positions. Only one of these samples had an indication of DU contamination (-023-201). This sample was collected at the eastern corner of the facility. The percentage of DU over the total uranium is estimated to be 9 %, but the statistical uncertainty of this measurement is rather high (41 % in k=1). We cannot therefore conclude with any certainty the existence of DU.

- Five samples were taken during the second day (NUC-02-024-201 to -024-205) which all detected the presence of DU.

  - Samples -024-201 and -024-202 were collected from samplers placed on the densely attacked cobblestone square/yard in the centre of the site. Many penetrators, fragments and 'hot-spots' were detected in this area. However, special care was taken during the measurements to avoid any resuspension due to human activities (digging, walking, etc.). The highest DU percentage was detected in this area.

  - Sample -024-023 was collected within a large workshop building bordering the aforementioned cobblestone square. No DU contamination was detected by field measurements.

Samplers were placed in a parallel line at Han Pijesak

  - Sample -024-204 was collected inside the neighbouring workshop west of the square. Three contamination points were found in the building using field measurements.

  - Sample -024-205 was collected on the tank parking lot in the northwest part of the facility where tanks had been parked at the time of attack. A large number of contamination points (160) were detected in this area.

Depleted Uranium in Bosnia and Herzegovina

- At the *Han Pijesak Artillery Storage and Barracks,* the maximum ^{238}U concentration (3.6 ng/m^3) was detected in an air sample collected inside one of the attacked storage barns (sample NUC-02-028-202). Of the total uranium concentrations, 99.6% of it is attributed to DU. The ^{238}U concentration in the air just outside the barrack (sample NUC-02-028-201) was 54.9 pg/m^3 and 90.4% of this is attributed to DU. For an air sample collected the day before (NUC-02-027-204) and 46 m away from this point, the concentration of ^{238}U in air was approximately 2.5 times lower (22.1 pg/m^3). The content of DU in this sample was 43 %. The differences between the measurements inside and outside the barrack can be explained by a disparity in density of soil and floor contamination inside the structure, as well as discrepancies in the resuspension factors R outside of and inside the building. One of the causes for the distinctions in the resuspension factors R could be the different speed of ground wind inside and outside and between different sampling days (see *Appendix I*). On the second day, special care was taken not to disrupt the area while the sampling was in progress, and to ensure natural results the samplers were shut down when anyone approached the area. The air samples which were collected at distances over 200 m from the affected area showed no presence of DU.

No DU was detected in air at Lukavica

Cumulative probability distribution of uranium concentration in air samples collected in BiH is shown in Figure G.1. This figure shows that the major number of measurements (17 of 24) can be found in the range of concentrations from 10 to 60 pg/m^3. This range of data with high-scale of reliability (R^2 is equal 0.96) is subject to the lognormal law with a median value of

Figure G.1   Cumulative distribution of ^{238}U concentrations in air samples

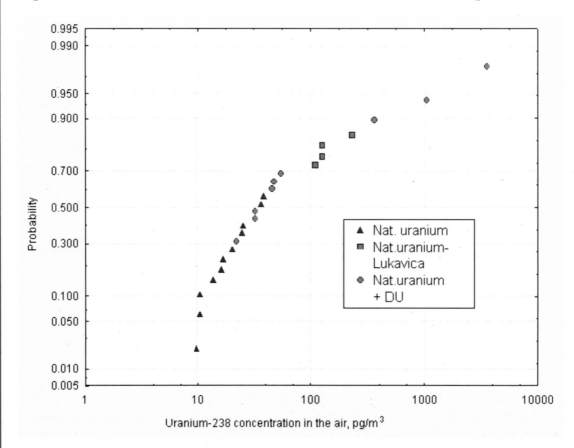

Post-Conflict Environmental Assessment

^{238}U concentration in air equal to 35 pg/m^3 and the standard deviation s - 0.7. Some of the results fall out of this distribution. These are the samples with heightened DU concentrations (green circuits), and all 4 samples from *Lukavica* (site 7.2). *Lukavica*, however, showed rather high contents of natural uranium (red squares).

The doses due to the existence of DU in the air at the measured levels are negligible, as demonstrated by the following facts:

- The total uranium concentrations in places where DU contamination in the open air were detected were in the range of values expected due to natural sources.
- The specific activity of depleted uranium is less than the specific activity of naturally occurring uranium.

The committed effective dose due to the existence of DU in air as calculated on a worst-case scenario assuming that a person works continuously for one year (8 hours for 250 days) in the place where the maximum concentration of DU was detected (1 ng/m^3 – *Hadzici Tank Repair Facility*) is in the order of 0.3 µSv per year. One also has to consider that the air samples were collected under dry, warm weather conditions at moderate wind speed. At higher wind speeds, DU concentrations in air may be higher. In damp, rainy weather, DU particles are washed out from the air and deposited onto the ground. However, DU concentrations in air at the sites investigated will never be high enough that any resulting doses will be significant.

Conclusions

- DU was detected in air samples collected from two sites: *Hadzici Tank Repair Facility*, and the in *Han Pijesak Artillery Storage and Barracks*.
- The total uranium concentrations in places where DU contamination in the open air were detected are comparable with the values expected due to natural origin.
- The radiological significance of the contamination is negligible (three orders of magnitude less than that expected due to other naturally occurring sources).
- There is no widespread DU contamination in the air. No DU contamination was detected in samples collected over one hundred meters away from heavily attacked areas.
- Dose estimations must be based on the air concentration measurements and not on models alone, which lead to great uncertainties because of the numerous unknown parameters involved in such estimations.
- The clarification and verification of the mechanisms causing the existence of DU in air seems to be an interesting scientific problem and should be subject for further research. It may be interesting for researchers to try to further clarify the mechanisms that explain the air contamination as related to the ground contamination. However, it does not influence the conclusions on possible future risks because there is no possible natural way that there will be any increased risk from air contamination. The results presented in this report are three orders of magnitude below those doses which would justify an immediate clarification.

Table G.4 shows the measured isotopic composition of the dissolved filters (filter blank + aerosol). The rsd values (1 sigma) are the relative standard deviations of the ICP-MS measurements.

Table G.5 shows the isotope concentrations of the aerosols, which result after subtraction of the filter blank. The U-238 concentration of the dissolved filter (filter blank + aerosol) was measured quantitatively, and the U-235, U-234 and U-236 concentrations were calculated by using the isotopic compositions from Table G.4. The uranium isotope concentrations of the filter blank were similarly analysed. The average U-238 concentration of the filter blank was 2.68 ng/filter (k = 4.6 %). The average U-235 and U-234 concentrations of the filter blank were calculated by using the natural composition of 0.71 % for U-235 (there was no significant difference between

G

the natural and the measured isotopic composition) and the measured composition of 0.011 % for U-234 (the measured isotopic composition deviated significantly from the natural composition). The k values (1 sigma) are the combined procedure errors.

The isotope concentrations per m^3 air were calculated with the values from Table G.5 and the sampled volume from Table G.3. The procedure error for the sampled volume was estimated to be 6%, including uncertainties of calibration, variable atmospheric pressure and measurements at different altitudes. The k values (1 sigma) are the combined procedure errors.

The percentage of DU was calculated from the measured $^{235}U/^{238}U$ isotope ratio (filter blank + aerosol) and corrected by the ratio of the U-238 concentration in the aerosol to the concentration in the dissolved filter (filter blank + aerosol). The k values (1 sigma) are the combined procedure errors. High detection limits for DU [%] were obtained in some samples due to the low U concentrations and the small differences between the U concentrations of the samples and the filter blank.

Table G.4   Uranium isotopic compositions of the dissolved filters (filter blank + aerosol)

CODE NUC-02-	^{238}U percentage [mass%]	rsd [%]	^{235}U percentage [mass%]	rsd [%]	^{234}U percentage [mass%]	rsd [%]	^{236}U percentage [mass%]	rsd [%]
023-201	99.305	0.47	0.688	1.78	0.0071	11.1	<0.002	-
023-202	99.291	0.97	0.698	0.86	0.0105	5.19	<0.002	-
023-203	99.282	1.10	0.707	1.52	0.0109	2.53	<0.002	-
023-204	99.273	0.25	0.717	2.32	0.0099	10.6	<0.002	-
024-201	99.688	0.42	0.307	0.83	0.0023	13.3	0.0022	6.36
024-202	99.762	0.38	0.234	0.47	0.0013	9.60	0.0026	4.08
024-203	99.328	0.55	0.662	1.64	0.0095	20.8	<0.002	-
024-204	99.423	0.66	0.569	0.90	0.0078	1.99	<0.002	-
024-205	99.381	1.30	0.611	1.23	0.0072	17.1	<0.002	-
025-201	99.279	0.08	0.715	0.35	0.0059	5.11	<0.002	-
025-202	99.277	0.27	0.716	1.32	0.0067	5.20	<0.002	-
025-203	99.267	0.24	0.726	1.51	0.0066	8.63	<0.002	-
025-204	99.268	1.06	0.725	1.22	0.0069	12.2	<0.002	-
026-201	99.284	1.14	0.707	0.99	0.0088	9.01	<0.002	-
026-202	99.287	1.59	0.704	2.85	0.0087	11.3	<0.002	-
027-201	99.292	0.25	0.701	1.07	0.0068	2.77	<0.002	-
027-202	99.287	0.38	0.705	2.84	0.0068	12.2	<0.002	-
027-203	99.290	1.37	0.701	1.00	0.0083	4.44	<0.002	-
027-204	99.388	1.75	0.602	1.47	0.0087	14.6	<0.002	-
028-201	99.560	0.83	0.434	2.02	0.0053	10.2	<0.002	-
028-202	99.789	0.92	0.207	1.38	0.0009	7.75	0.0027	3.61
029-201	99.312	1.13	0.680	2.16	0.0077	20.3	<0.002	-
029-202	99.289	0.90	0.701	2.20	0.0104	19.5	<0.002	-
030-201	99.265	0.59	0.725	1.89	0.0100	4.09	<0.002	-

Table G.5   Isotope concentrations of the aerosols

CODE NUC-02-	^{238}U [ng/filter]	k [%]	^{235}U [ng/filter]	k [%]	^{234}U [pg/filter]	k [%]	^{236}U [pg/filter]	k [%]
023-201	4.80	4.1	0.033	5.3	0.24	33.5	<0.2	-
023-202	1.70	8.9	0.012	10.0	0.17	31.3	<0.2	-
023-203	0.94	14.1	0.007	16.2	0.10	40.2	<0.2	-
023-204	1.04	13.2	0.008	15.2	0.08	69.2	<0.2	-
024-201	47.50	1.7	0.136	2.5	0.84	22.5	1.10	11.9
024-202	138.2	1.5	0.311	2.0	1.56	16.5	3.67	10.9
024-203	2.00	7.5	0.012	10.0	0.15	66.9	<0.2	-
024-204	4.13	4.1	0.020	6.2	0.24	22.9	<0.2	-
024-205	3.11	5.2	0.017	7.9	0.12	66.5	<0.2	-
025-201	14.08	1.9	0.102	2.3	0.71	15.9	<0.3	-
025-202	23.63	1.7	0.171	2.5	1.48	13.5	<0.5	-
025-203	10.63	3.2	0.078	3.9	0.59	19.9	<0.3	-

CODE								
025-204	9.27	2.5	0.068	3.4	0.53	24.4	<0.2	-
026-201	1.62	8.9	0.012	10.1	0.09	59.6	<0.2	-
026-202	1.60	9.1	0.011	12.9	0.08	69.4	<0.2	-
027-201	5.09	4.0	0.036	4.6	0.24	23.6	<0.2	-
027-202	3.45	5.6	0.025	7.7	0.13	52.4	<0.2	-
027-203	2.17	7.2	0.015	8.5	0.11	40.1	<0.2	-
027-204	2.92	5.2	0.015	8.8	0.19	44.5	<0.2	-
028-201	4.15	4.0	0.011	11.3	0.07	76.4	<0.2	-
028-202	243.4	1.4	0.492	2.5	1.81	14.8	6.70	10.7
029-201	1.37	11.4	0.009	15.1	<0.1	-	<0.2	-
029-202	1.02	14.0	0.007	17.1	0.09	89.7	<0.2	-
030-201	3.73	4.4	0.028	5.6	0.35	19.9	<0.2	-

Table G.6 Isotope concentrations of uranium in the air

CODE NUC-02-	^{238}U		^{235}U		^{234}U		^{236}U	
	[pg/m³]	k [%]	[pg/m³]	k [%]	[fg/m³]	k [%]	[fg/m³]	k [%]
023-201	47.7	7.2	0.33	8.0	2.37	34.0	<2	-
023-202	17.0	10.7	0.12	11.7	1.69	31.9	<2	-
023-203	9.68	15.3	0.07	17.2	1.06	40.7	<2	-
023-204	10.5	14.5	0.08	16.3	0.80	69.4	<2	-
024-201	361	6.2	1.03	6.5	6.38	23.2	8.33	13.4
024-202	1048	6.2	2.36	6.3	11.8	17.6	27.8	12.4
024-203	32.8	9.6	0.20	11.7	2.53	67.2	<2	-
024-204	32.6	7.3	0.16	8.6	1.91	23.6	<2	-
024-205	46.1	7.9	0.24	9.9	1.84	66.8	<2	-
025-201	125	6.3	0.90	6.4	6.25	17.0	<2	-
025-202	229	6.2	1.66	6.5	14.3	14.8	<2	-
025-203	125	6.8	0.92	7.1	6.95	20.8	<2	-
025-204	109	6.5	0.80	6.9	6.26	25.2	<2	-
026-201	20.3	10.8	0.14	11.7	1.08	59.9	<2	-
026-202	25.1	10.9	0.18	14.3	1.29	69.7	<2	-
027-201	36.8	7.2	0.26	7.5	1.70	24.4	<2	-
027-202	25.3	8.2	0.18	9.8	0.94	52.7	<2	-
027-203	16.2	9.4	0.11	10.4	0.84	40.5	<2	-
027-204	22.1	7.9	0.11	10.7	1.47	44.9	<2	-
028-201	54.9	7.2	0.14	12.8	0.90	76.7	1.09	25.0
028-202	3596	6.2	7.26	6.5	26.8	16.0	99.0	12.3
029-201	13.7	12.8	0.09	16.2	<1	-	<2	-
029-202	10.4	15.2	0.07	18.2	0.96	89.9	<2	-
030-201	38.8	7.4	0.29	8.2	3.68	20.8	<2	-

Table G.7. Isotopic ratio $^{235}U/^{238}U$ of the dissolved filters (filter blank + aerosol) and calculated percentage of DU in the aerosol

CODE NUC-02-	isotope ratio $^{235}U / ^{238}U$ (filter + aerosol)	k [%]	DU of total U [%] aerosol	k [%]
023-201	0.00694	1.87	9.3	41.6
023-202	0.00704	0.47	<17	-
023-203	0.00713	1.94	<27	-
023-204	0.00724	2.44	<25	-
024-201	0.00309	1.00	83.8	0.74
024-202	0.00235	0.22	95.2	0.10
024-203	0.00668	1.39	25.6	16.2
024-204	0.00573	0.31	47.7	1.17
024-205	0.00616	1.28	38.8	7.21
025-201	0.00721	0.29	<3	-
025-202	0.00723	1.23	<2	-
025-203	0.00733	1.52	<3	-
025-204	0.00731	0.98	<4	-
026-201	0.00713	0.28	<17	-
026-202	0.00710	1.71	<17	-
027-201	0.00708	1.14	<7	-
027-202	0.00712	2.82	<11	-
027-203	0.00708	1.06	<15	-
027-204	0.00607	0.48	43.0	2.46
028-201	0.00437	1.34	90.4	2.03
028-202	0.00208	0.75	99.6	0.30
029-201	0.00686	2.74	<22	-
029-202	0.00707	2.54	<27	-
030-201	0.00731	2.28	<10	-

APPENDIX H
Analysis of DU Penetrators, Fragments and Jackets

During the UNEP DU mission to Bosnia and Herzegovina (BiH), 3 unbroken penetrators and one full bullet (penetrator still sticking in its jacket) were collected for further studies and analyses of the specific composition of the DU, as well as of the uranium oxide layer covering the surfaces. A number of penetrators and fragments were found during field investigations but not collected for analysis. Those found on the surface were collected and handed over to the competent local governmental organisation (Federal Administration for Radiation Protection and Radioactive Security) for safe storage. Similar studies were carried out on penetrators and fragments collected during the previous Kosovo and Serbia and Montenegro missions (UNEP, 2001; 2002).

H.1 STUDIES ON DU PENETRATOR MATERIAL COLLECTED DURING EARLIER MISSIONS

Studies on the soil samples collected during the 2000 UNEP mission to Kosovo revealed that some of the soil samples contained traces of ^{236}U, a non-natural uranium isotope formed when uranium is used as nuclear reactor fuel (UNEP, 2001). This indicated that some of the depleted uranium came from reprocessed uranium. This finding was confirmed by smear test analyses of prepared from found penetrators and jackets and, at a later stage, by analyses carried out on material from four of the penetrators and fragments collected.

The presence of ^{236}U in the penetrators triggered further studies of transuranic elements in the penetrators. These additional studies showed that the penetrators also contained trace amounts of plutonium. The plutonium concentration was very low - near the detection limit - and could be considered as DU impurity. In 2000, the Bristol University laboratory also analysed some of the penetrators for other elements formed in nuclear reactors, such as ^{99}Tc, ^{237}Np, ^{241}Am, ^{243}Am and ^{244}Cm. However, the concentrations of these elements were all below their respective detection limits.

The analysis and studies on penetrators collected during the mission to Serbia and Montenegro showed very similar results for the isotopic composition of uranium and the presence of plutonium. Neptunium (^{237}Np) measurements were below the detection limit. Due to the longer time spent in the soil, these penetrators showed much heavier signs of corrosion than those from Kosovo.

H.2 STUDIES OF THE PENETRATORS COLLECTED IN BiH

Similar studies were also conducted on penetrators collected during the UNEP mission to BiH. These analyses and studies were performed at Spiez Laboratory in Switzerland.

Isotopic analyses

Using ICP-Mass Spectrometry, analyses were performed of the isotopic composition of DU in the penetrators. Analyses showed a rather constant isotopic composition for the uranium isotopes ^{238}U, ^{235}U, ^{234}U and ^{236}U (Tables H.5 and H.6). All three samples analysed contained ^{236}U, which shows that the depleted uranium was contaminated by reprocessed uranium. The mean value for the $^{235}U/^{238}U$ isotopic ratio of the DU penetrators was 0.00198 ± 0.00001, and the

^{236}U concentration was 0.0028 ± 0.0002 %. These values are almost identical to those analysed from the two previous UNEP missions. In addition, this matches the isotopic uranium composition for DU in weapons published in US military and non-confidential literature.

The content of the transuranic elements Plutonium-239/240 in DU was analysed by radiochemical procedures, followed by alpha-spectrometric measurements. To determine the contents of Neptunium-237, radiochemical separation methods were also used, followed by analyses with high-resolution ICP mass spectrometry (HR-ICP-MS). The radiochemical analyses showed that the concentration of plutonium in the penetrators is very low (Tables H.7 and H.8). The range analysed was from 0.0050 to 0.0878 [Bq/g], which corresponds to 2.2E-12 to 38.2E-12 [g/g]. This is equivalent to the very low content of roughly one Pu atom per 100 billion uranium atoms. Again, the results confirm the findings on penetrators from the two previous UNEP missions as well as information provided by the US DOE in open literature (DOE, 2000).

The radiochemical analyses showed that the concentration of Neptunium-237 in the DU penetrators is from less than 0.004 to 0.0162 [Bq/g], which corresponds to less than 1.5E-10 to 6.2E-10 [g/g].

These results establish that the DU found in the Balkans region at some point during its fabrication process came in contact with reprocessed uranium. However, the concentration of the contaminating nuclides is so low, that their contribution to the total radiation dose of DU for all intake paths is insignificant and can be neglected.

Studies of corrosion

Studies of the corrosion on the DU penetrators began by weighing and measuring them in the same state as when they were collected in the field, and again after removing the surface layer of soil and uranium oxide by both mechanical and mild chemical cleaning. After lying in the ground for over 7 years, the penetrators were heavily corroded and intensive pitting (corrosion attack producing small holes) of the DU surface had taken place. According to US military literature, a penetrator's original weight is ~292 g. Thus, the penetrators studied had lost 66 - 93 g due to corrosion.

Penetrator corrosion products were removed from the surface and analysed in the laboratory

These findings differ from the results of penetrator studies from Kosovo, which were only slightly corroded after 1.5 years in the ground. These new findings show that the level of corrosion increases dramatically with time. Once corrosion starts, the exposed surface tends to increase and the pitting effect will thus accelerate. Penetrators laying on the ground surface were much less corroded than those buried below the ground surface. Bearing in mind the state of the penetrators when they were found, UNEP established the losses to be 2-5 g in Kosovo after 1.5 years; 11-38 g in Serbia and Montenegro after 2.5 years; and 66-93 g in BiH over 7 years after the conflict (not corrected for loss of weight due to formation of DU dust during the

Depleted Uranium in Bosnia and Herzegovina

impact). In conclusion, based on these findings, no more penetrators consisting of metallic DU will be found in the Balkans grounds after 25 to 35 years. Instead of metallic penetrators, contaminated spots in the ground will be found containing DU decomposition products.

Transuranic elements

Both ^{236}U and plutonium in the penetrators originate from the reprocessing of nuclear fuel. In order to be used in a nuclear reactor, the concentration of ^{235}U in uranium needs to be enriched

Once cleaned, signs of pitting from corrosion become much more visible

from 0.7 to about 4%. Once the reactor fuel is spent, the removed fuel still contains a quantity of ^{235}U. During the chemical reprocessing of spent reactor fuel, transuranic elements and fission products can be separated from the uranium. The ^{235}U can again be concentrated up to 4 % through enrichment of this reprocessed uranium, and the uranium is again used as recycled reactor fuel. However, during the reprocessing step, a small part of the transuranic elements and fission products will remain in the uranium fraction. If this reprocessed reactor uranium is enriched, both the enriched reactor fuel as well as the DU will contain small amounts of these transuranium nuclides. Some of the transuranics may even contaminate the technical equipment of the enrichment plant (DOE, 2000). Consequently, uranium that is later processed in the plant will be contaminated with tiny traces of transuranics, even if it is received directly from uranium mines.

In January 2000, the US Army reported that investigations on DU used as tank armour had shown that it did contain some transuranics (U.S. Army Material Command, 2000). The concentrations were very low (the average $^{239/240}$Pu activity concentration was 85 Bq/kg and the highest found was 130 Bq/kg). Since the uranium for both DU armour and ammunition likely originates from the same source, contaminations in the same range can be expected in both armour and ammunition. However, the plutonium activity concentration in the collected penetrators from Kosovo, Serbia and Montenegro and now from BiH was in the broad range from less than 0.8 to a maximum of 87.8 Bq/kg, with a mean value around 18 Bq/kg.

The analytical procedures chosen to determine the concentration of ^{237}Np in DU penetrators resulted in very low detection limits. For ^{237}Np, a maximum concentration of 16.2 Bq/kg, or 6.2 E-10 g/g respectively could be measured in the penetrators analysed from BiH.

Table H.1 Sample identification

Code	Coordinates UTM 34T	Sample
NUC-02-024-401	BP 74 050 / 56 362 (Hadzici Tank Repair Facility)	Penetrator, sticking in cobblestone pavement
NUC-02-028-401	CP 35 468 / 84 445 (Han Pijesak Barracks)	Penetrator in soil in depth of 7 cm
NUC-02-028-402	CP 35 795 / 84 340 (Han Pijesak Barracks)	Penetrator with jacket in depth of 3 cm
NUC-02-028-403	CP 35 716 / 84 384 (Han Pijesak Barracks)	Penetrator in soil in depth of 5 cm

Post-Conflict Environmental Assessment

Table H.2 Mass of the penetrators as collected

Code	Sample	Weight [g]
NUC-02-024-401	Penetrator	213.99
NUC-02-028-401	Penetrator	246.46
NUC-02-028-402	Penetrator	414.15
NUC-02-028-403	Penetrator	242.91

Table H.3 Penetrator mass after mechanical surface cleaning (scraping)

Code	Sample	Weight after mechanical cleaning [g]	Loss of weight [g]
NUC-02-024-401	Penetrator	207.35	6.64
NUC-02-028-401	Penetrator	224.85	21.61
NUC-02-028-402	Penetrator	412.65	1.50
NUC-02-028-403	Penetrator	235.39	7.52

Table H.4 Penetrator mass and dimension after weak chemical cleaning

Code	Sample	Weight after chemical cleaning [g]	Loss of weight [g]	Diameter smallest / largest [mm]	Length [mm]
NUC-02-024-401	Penetrator	198.80	8.55	14.5 - 15.2	78
NUC-02-028-401	Penetrator	212.73	12.12	12.2 - 15.8	83
NUC-02-028-402	Penetrator	409.80	2.85		
NUC-02-028-403	Penetrator	225.66	9.73	13.6 - 15.9	74

Table H.5 Isotopic compositions of uranium

NUC-2002-	^{238}U		^{235}U		^{234}U		^{236}U	
	percentage [mass%]	rsd [%]	percentage [mass%]	rsd [%]	percentage [mass%]	rsd [%]	percentage [mass%]	rsd [%]
024-401-01	99.798	0.54	0.199	0.61	0.00071	9.6	0.0029	9.0
028-401-01	99.799	0.21	0.197	0.28	0.00067	21.5	0.0027	5.0
028-403-01	99.799	1.06	0.198	1.05	0.00059	7.9	0.0028	7.9

Table H.6 Isotopic ratio ^{235}U / ^{238}U

NUC-2002-	isotope ratio ^{235}U / ^{238}U	k [%]	DU of total U [%]	k [%]
024-401-01	0.00199	0.6	100.2	0.2
028-401-01	0.00197	0.7	100.5	0.2
028-403-01	0.00198	0.8	100.4	0.3

Table H.7 Plutonium in [Bq/g]

Code	Sample	Σ Pu-239/Pu-240 [Bq/g]	rsd [%]
NUC-02-024-401	Penetrator	0.0878	5
NUC-02-028-401	Penetrator	0.0175	14
NUC-02-028-403	Penetrator	0.00503	11

Table H.8 Plutonium in [g/g] calculated as Pu-239

Code	Sample	Pu-239 [g/g]	rsd [%]
NUC-02-024-401	Penetrator	38.2E-12	5
NUC-02-028-401	Penetrator	7.6E-12	14
NUC-02-028-403	Penetrator	2.2E-12	11

Table H.9 Neptunium in [Bq/g]

Code	Sample	Np-237 [Bq/g]	rsd [%]
NUC-02-024-401	Penetrator	0.0162	15
NUC-02-028-401	Penetrator	0.0040	62
NUC-02-028-403	Penetrator	<0.004	-

Table H.10 Neptunium in [g/g]

Code	Sample	Np-237 [g/g]	rsd [%]
NUC-02-024-401	Penetrator	6.20E-10	15
NUC-02-028-401	Penetrator	1.52E-10	62
NUC-02-028-403	Penetrator	<1.5E-10	-

Post-Conflict Environmental Assessment

APPENDIX I

Influence of resuspension and deposition processes on the DU air and surface contamination

I.1 GENERAL INFORMATION

In a zero-dimensional model (i.e. there is no dependence on spatial coordinates), the temporal evolution of airborne (mass or activity) concentration is given in the solution of the mass balance equation:

$$dC(t)/dt = [\beta_\uparrow(t) - \beta_\downarrow(t)] \cdot C(t) \tag{I.1}$$

where $\beta_\uparrow(t)$ and $\beta_\downarrow(t)$ are the instantaneous values of resuspension and deposition rates (s^{-1}), respectively.

At times, an additional term is added on the right hand side of this equation describing long-term "memory" resuspension processes (Williams, 1992). Equation (I.1) describes the fraction of contaminant removed from or added to the surface per unit time.

Shortly following the contamination event, the time term can be ignored and, in this case, assuming of resuspension and deposition rates are independent from time, formula (I.1) can be written as:

$$dC(t)/dt = (\beta_\uparrow - \beta_\downarrow) \cdot C(t) \tag{I.2}$$

For subsequent calculations it is convenient to use the interrelation between resuspension flux density $J_\uparrow$ ($g\ m^{-2}\ s^{-1}$) and resuspension rate $\beta_\uparrow$ as:

$$J_\uparrow = \sigma \cdot \beta_\uparrow \tag{I.3}$$

where σ is the surface contamination density, $g\ m^{-2}$.

Equation (I.3) gives a principal opportunity to estimate the value of the resuspension flux density $J_\uparrow$ by using the measurements results for resuspension rate $\beta_\uparrow$ and the surface contamination density σ. The method for estimating the resuspension flux density $J_\uparrow$ is called "eddy-correlation technique". This technique consists of counting all particles crossing a reference area, from both below and above, during a certain time period and determining the net flux density in this manner. It is important that this method not depend on the validity of the gradient transfer approach (ECP1, 1996). It should also be noted that this methodology is extremely difficult and has no wide application.

A simpler and the more frequently used approach is the concept of "resuspension factor". The resuspension factor R is defined by the ratio of airborne contamination concentration C (in $g\ m^{-3}$) at some height above a surface of the ground and surface contamination density σ (in $g\ m^{-2}$) i.e.:

$$R = C / \sigma \tag{I.4}$$

Using the formulas (I.3) and (I.4) it is possible to represent the expression for resuspension rate $\beta_\uparrow$ as:

$$\beta_\uparrow = J_\uparrow \cdot R / C \qquad\qquad (I.5)$$

The deposition flux density $J_\downarrow$ can thus be estimated by using information about the deposition velocity $v_\downarrow$ and airborne contamination concentration C:

$$J_\downarrow = v_\downarrow \cdot C \qquad\qquad (I.6)$$

On the other hand the deposition flux density $J_\downarrow$ is connected with deposition rate $\beta_\downarrow$ by the ratio similar to the formula (I.3):

$$J_\downarrow = \sigma \cdot \beta_\downarrow \qquad\qquad (I.7)$$

Using the given formula, and also formulas (I.6) and (I.4) we obtain:

$$\beta_\downarrow = v_\downarrow \cdot R \qquad\qquad (I.8)$$

After substituting the values for calculation the resuspension and deposition rates using the aforementioned formulas, equation (I.2) becomes:

$$dC(t)/dt = J_\uparrow \cdot R - v_\downarrow \cdot R \cdot C(t) \qquad\qquad (I.9)$$

which has the solution:

$$C(t) = C(0) \cdot Exp(-v_\downarrow \cdot R \cdot t) + J_\uparrow / v_\downarrow \cdot [1 - Exp(-v_\downarrow \cdot R \cdot t)] \qquad\qquad (I.10)$$

It follows from this equation, that at the constant product $v_\downarrow \cdot R$ with increased time t, the concentration of contaminants in air will approach equilibrium conditions equal to the ratio of resuspension flux density $J_\uparrow$ to deposition velocity $v_\downarrow$, i.e. at $t \rightarrow \infty$

$$C = J_\uparrow \cdot / v_\downarrow \qquad\qquad (I.11)$$

Practical use of equation (I.10) is very difficult. However, by using experimental data on resuspension flux density $J_\uparrow$ and deposition velocity $v_\downarrow$ to estimate air contamination, formula (I.11) is sufficient.

Therefore, the most applicable way for a similar calculation is to use formula (I.4) in which the resuspension factor R appears dependent on the period of time after initial soil contamination, as well as from soil surface activity, ground wind speed, particle size and other parameters:

$$C(t) = \sigma(t) \cdot R(t) \qquad\qquad (I.12)$$

Some variable estimates included in formula (I.12), as well as the analysis of certain parameters influencing these variables, are described below.

Soil surface activity

It is appropriate to assume that only soil particles close to the surface can be resuspended. This makes the specific soil activity C_{soil} one of the most important parameters. Various models are used for forecasting vertical migration of radionuclides into the ground, depending on the time after initial contamination. One such model is the generic undisturbed soil model (Brown, 1995). This compartmental soil model is based on the migration in soil for a limited number of elements, particularly Pu, Cs and Sr. The rate of movement of these elements

Post-Conflict Environmental Assessment

into the soil is slow, although there is significant variation between the results of the various observations owing to differences in soil composition and annual rainfall. The soil model consists of four compartments or 'boxes': the 0-1 cm box, 1-5 cm box, 5-15 cm box and 15-30 cm box. There are rate constants to express transfer between and losses from boxes. Resuspension is assumed to occur only from the top 1 cm of soil, i.e. the upper box in the generic soil model (UK, 2002).

The mass of DU at time zero can be calculated in the top box by using the assumptions accepted in the report (UK, 2002). By using the *Reference Case* from the UNEP *DU Desk Assessment Report* (UNEP/UNCHS, 1999) for the initial soil contamination it is assumed that:

- 10 g DU m^{-2} is uniformly distributed in the 0-1 cm box;
- the volume of the top box (with dimensions 1 m x 1 m x 0.01 m) = 0.01 m^3;
- 10 g of DU are deposited on the box; therefore density of DU in the top box = 1 kg m^{-3};
- assume density of soil (generic dry soil) = 1.25 g cm^{-3} = 1.25 x 10^{-3} kg m^{-3};
- concentration of DU in the top box is equal to 0.8 g kg^{-1} (i.e. g of DU in one kg of soil)

Using the Brown model, the concentrations of DU in the topsoil box are presented on Fig. I.1. For comparative purposes, results of similar calculations based on the generalization of experimental data on soil contamination as a result of Chernobyl accident are also shown of the Figure (ECP1). It is shown in the report (ECP1, 1996) that the surface activity concentration follows almost exactly a $t^{0.5}$ dependence (without radioactive decay). It can be seen from this figure that for a period of approximately 7 years (time since DU attacks) the topsoil contamination can be approximately 15-30 % of the original levels of pollution.

Figure I.1   Soil surface activity as a function of time after initial contamination (calculated by Brown and ECP1 models)

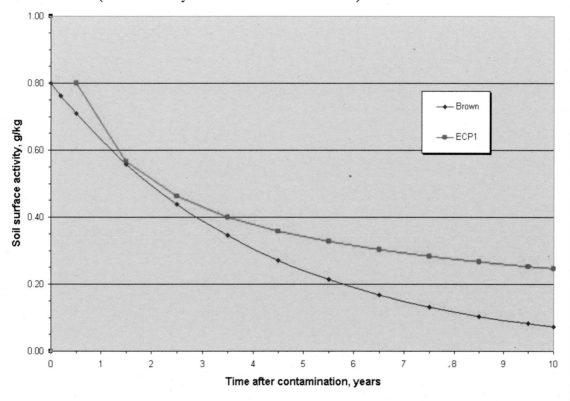

Size particles and deposition velocity

The deposition velocity $v_\downarrow$ for a particle with a diameter of more than 10 μm depends on its weight, the Archimedean buoyant force and aerodynamic resistance restricting the movement of a particle. Falling aerosol particles quickly reach such constant speed (sedimentation velocity) at which aerodynamic resistance of air becomes equal to the effective weight of a particle, i.e. to its weight minus the Archimedean buoyant force:

$$3\pi \cdot \mu_{air} \cdot d \cdot v_{sed} = \pi / 6 \cdot d^3 \cdot (\gamma - \gamma_{air}) \qquad (I.13)$$

where: μ_{air} - viscosity of air, Pa s;
           d - diameter of particle, m;
           v_{sed} - edimentation velocity, m s^{-1};
           γ - specific weight of particle, N m^{-3};
           γ_{air} - specific weight of air, N m^{-3}

Neglecting γ_{air} as contrasted to γ we shall receive:

$$v_{sed} = d^2 \cdot \gamma \, / \, (18 \cdot \mu_{air}) = d^2 \cdot \rho \cdot g \, / \, (18 \cdot \mu_{air}) \qquad (I.14)$$

where: ρ - Density of air, kg m^{-3};

         g - Acceleration of gravity, m s^{-2}.

Equation (I.14) is applicable only for small and constant speeds of particles and their small dimensions when the Reynolds number is in the range of 0 to 1 (Stokes formula). For major Reynolds numbers it is necessary to enter allowances into Equation (I.14) - for example the Klyachko Equation (Idelchik, 1975).

Figure I.2   **Dependence of deposition velocity $v_\downarrow$ from particle size**

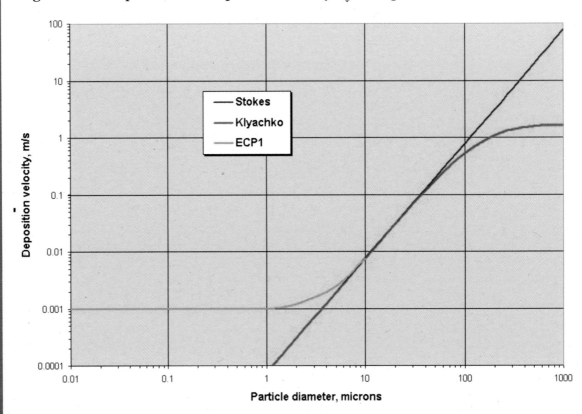

Post-Conflict Environmental Assessment

Thus, for large particles, the deposition velocity $v_\downarrow$ is dominated by particle sedimentation ($v_\downarrow \approx v_{sed}$), whereas for very small particles, the deposition velocity is dominated by Brownian diffusion. For atmospheric particles in the report (ECP1, 1996), it is recommended to use a minimum deposition velocity of 0.001 m s^{-1}. In that case, the reliance of deposition velocity $v_\downarrow$ on particle sizes can look like relationships presented in Fig.I.2.

On the generalization basis of experimental data in the ECP1 report (ECP1, 1996) it follows that a typical airborne cumulative mass size distribution during natural resuspension has the mass median aerodynamic diameter of 4.3 μm, the geometric standard deviation σ_g of 4.0 and the total mass concentration of 57 μg m^{-3}.

Analysing data of air contamination as a result of the Chernobyl accident, the report (ECP1, 1996) asserts that the given total mass concentration correlates favourably with the value of resuspension flux density $J_\uparrow$ at the level of 3.7 10^{-7} g m^{-2} s^{-1}. This corresponds to an average deposition velocity value $v_\downarrow$ of 0.0065 m s^{-1} and to a particle size of about 14 μm.

Wind

Observations show that wind speed statistics follow Weibull distributions. Total effects of non-linear phenomena based on skew probability distributions like the one shown will be largely determined by a few strong events. In view of the very non-linear dependence of resuspension on wind speed, a few strong wind events could dominate resuspension. It is therefore of critical importance to have wind speed statistics for estimating the probability of such events (ECP1, 1996). Importantly, as natural resuspension is closely related to wind erosion, this link provides access to much literature and data on the processes of wind soil erosion.

One of the relationships connecting resuspension flux density $J_\uparrow$ with wind speed at the soil surface u_* is the Gillette relation (Gillette, 1977):

$$J_\uparrow = \psi \cdot u_*^5 \tag{I.15}$$

where the empirical constant is $\psi = 3 \cdot 10^{-6}$ kg s^4 m^{-7}. This reliance is depicted in Fig.I.3.

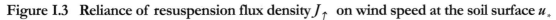

Figure I.3   Reliance of resuspension flux density $J_\uparrow$ on wind speed at the soil surface u_*

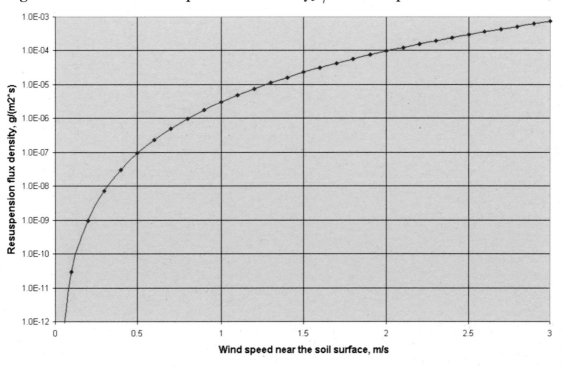

Depleted Uranium in Bosnia and Herzegovina

As this figure indicates, resuspension by wind shear is a highly nonlinear event, therefore considerable fractions of the annual resuspension yield can be produced within short time periods by gusts and dust storms (ECP1, 1996). Data on observable values of deposition flux density $J_{\downarrow}$ at the level of 9.2 - 16 µg m^{-2} s^{-1} are submitted in the ECP1 report. Similar values, ranging between 0.6 - 16 µg m^{-2} s^{-1}, are reported for Karakalpakia (Kuksa, 1994). Wind erosion rates around Lake Aral averaged 2-3 mm per year over the last 30 years are equivalent to 0.10 – 0.15 mg m^{-2} s^{-1} (ECP1, 1996).

It follows that high erosion rates immediately after a primary deposition could effectively resuspend all contamination that would still be at the very top of the soil at that time. In a situation where there is a DU surface contamination density of 10 g m^{-2} and a contamination depth of 1 cm, specific soil activity at the surface 7 years after the initial contamination can be 0.16 g DU in one kg soil (top soil times reduction coefficient of 0.2 is used – see Fig.I.1). In the case for semi-arid and windy conditions, the resuspension flux density $J_{\uparrow}$ of DU at the level of 0.003 – 0.024 µg m^{-2} s^{-1} occurs. Applying formula (I.11) it is obtained that at a deposition velocity $v_{\downarrow}$ at a level of 0.0065 m s^{-1} the concentration of DU in air can be roughly 0.4 – 3.7 µg m^{-3}. The higher value is approximately two times lower than derived by the U.S. Agency for Toxic Substances and Disease Registry's (ATSDR) Minimal Risk Level (MRL) for chronic inhalation exposure of 8 µg m^{-3} (ATSDR, 1999).

Resuspension factor for natural conditions

As previously discussed, the resuspension factor R is defined by the ratio of airborne contamination concentration C and surface contamination density σ. In practice, there are no homogeneously contaminated surfaces and in that case *"the airborne concentration is a sum of the local resuspended contamination and contamination carried from upwind resuspension, minus that carried away by the wind"* (UK, 2002). A large uncertainty exists in the values of resuspension factor R in the short time after initial contamination. In this period of time, the resuspension factor can range from 10^{-9} to 10^{-5} m^{-1} (Linsley, 1978).

PNNL analyzed air concentrations of resuspended DU in the contaminated area of the North Compound after the 1991 Doha fire (OSAGWI, 2000). PNNL estimated air concentrations for each of the periods of the recovery effort assuming resuspension factors. Thus, it was taken into account that the density of the DU oxides was 4.5 g cm^{-3}, the average surface contamination was 0.383 g m^{-2} and a reasonable estimate for wind speed was considered to be 7 m s^{-1}. It was revealed that before any cleanup activity the resuspension factor R by wind erosion was 1 10^{-4} m^{-1}, and it reduced to 1 10^{-5} m^{-1} after completing the cleanup operations (OSAGWI, 2000).

In Hanover 12 – 22 days after primary deposition following the Chernobyl accident, resuspension rates in the range 2 10^{-6} to 2 10^{-5} m^{-1} were found, depending on wind speed (Hollander, 1994).

To assess the time dependence of the resuspension factor, Garland has suggested the following formula (Garland, 1979; 1982):

$$R(t) = 1.2\,10^{-6} \cdot t^{-1} \tag{I.16}$$

where t is the time after initial deposition in days. Another dependence resuspension factor for time, built by integrating data on Chernobyl accident, is presented (ICP1, 1996):

$$R(t) = 2.09\,10^{-4} \cdot t^{-1.67} \tag{I.17}$$

Both of these dependences are shown on Fig.I.4.

According to the ECP1 report (ECP1, 1996), the exponent value -1.67 in formula (I.17) is very reasonable considering the surface activity concentration decay proportional to $t^{-0.5}$ (see Fig.I.1), which would have to be added to the exponent of -1.07 expected from theory (Reeks, 1988). Thus, using the technique from this report is preferable as it also takes into account the time history of the of soil contamination density of the top layer.

Figure I.4 Dependence of resuspension factor R from the time after initial soil contamination

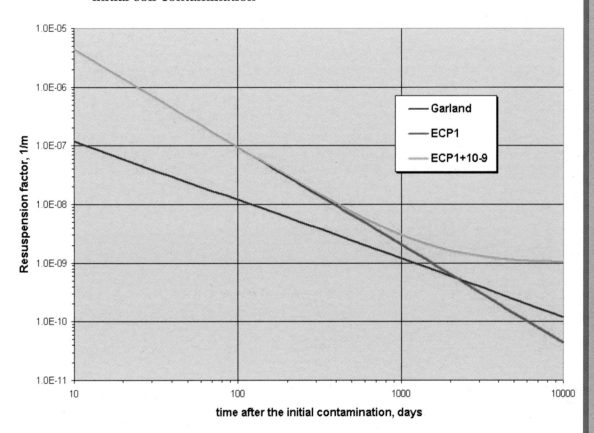

From figure 1.4 it is evident that with increasing time the resuspension factor R is constantly reduced and for t = 10 000 days becomes at a level of 10^{-10} and even less. It does not fully correspond to the measurement data which were conducted on experimental sites through a considerable space of time (Anspaugh, 1975; Linsley, 1978; Müller, 1999). To eliminate this discrepancy (UK, 2002), a time dependence of the resuspension factor R is suggested in the formulas for estimating and increasing the additional long-term resuspension term of be equal to 10^{-9} m^{-1}. In that case the formula (I.17) can be rewritten as:

$$R(t) = 2.09 \; 10^{-4} \cdot t^{-1.67} + 1 \; 10^{-9} \tag{I.18}$$

Allowance for this concept is added on Fig.I.4 in the curve titled "ECP1+10^{-9}". Substituting into equation (I.7) to estimate the deposition rate $\beta_\downarrow$ from equation (I.8) we obtain:

$$J_\downarrow = \sigma \cdot v_\downarrow \cdot R \tag{I.19}$$

By integrating the equation (I.19) with time, assuming constancy with time, surface contamination density σ and deposition velocity $v_\downarrow$, the integral deposition flux density $J_\downarrow$ was estimated as a function of time after initial soil contamination. Results from these calculations are depicted in Fig.I.5. Thus, it was calculated that the deposition velocity $v_\downarrow$ is 0.0065 m s^{-1}, the initial DU surface contamination density σ - 0.8 g kg^{-1} and time dependence of resuspension factor R can be described by equations (I.17) or (I.18).

Depleted Uranium in Bosnia and Herzegovina

Figure I.5 **Integrated DU deposition flux density as a function of time after the initial soil contamination**

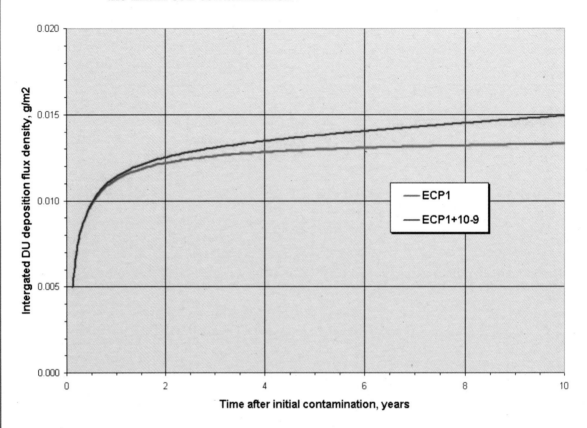

Figure I.5 shows that, for *Reference Case* conditions, the integrated level of surface contamination (UNEP/UNCHS, 1999) as a result of resuspension processes 7 years after contamination will not exceed 13 - 14 mg m^{-2}, i.e. only 1.6 % from a level of initial soil contamination.

It is also possible to remark that in the 1996 ECP1 report, the dependence of the resuspension factor R from the soil humidity obtained during experimental work in areas contaminated after Chernobyl is presented as:

$$\mathbf{R = R_0 \cdot \exp(-\lambda \cdot r_{sh})} \qquad (I.20)$$

where: R_0 - the resuspension factor R for dry soil, m^{-1};
   λ - the constant, which value in the report (ECP1, 1996) is equal0.6, non-dimensional value;
   r_{sh} - the relative soil humidity, %

Assessments by using equation (I.20) show that a change of relative soil humidity from 9 % to 1 % results in the resuspension factor R increase of 120 times.

Resuspension factor for anthropogenic activity

In addition to natural resuspension, the resuspension factor R as a result of anthropogenic activity essentially depends on a period of time following initial soil contamination. In the first days following contamination of military machinery by DU, the resuspension factor R appropriate to vigorous working on a contaminated surface is assumed to be 0.001 m^{-1} (Fish, 1967; Mitchell, 1967).

The report (The Effect, 2001) affirms that for UK conditions as a result of moderate mechanical activity (regular disturbance of the surface by vehicles or pedestrians) a resuspension factor of $10^{-5}\,m^{-1}$ may be more applicable. For a worst case (desert conditions and high mechanical activity), it is recommended to use the resuspension factor R at a level of $1.2\ 10^{-4}\,m^{-1}$. This value was chosen on the basis of the measurements which were made on the Maralinga test site, 0.3 m from a moving vehicle. The resuspension factors in these measurements were reported to range from $5.0\ 10^{-7}\,m^{-1}$ to $1.0 \times 10^{-3}\,m^{-1}$.

In a situation where a long time has elapsed since initial contamination, to assess the value of the resuspension factor R stipulated by anthropogenic activity, equations (I.16) - (I.18) introducing padding multipliers can be used:

- 10 – for population in desert conditions;
- 100 – for professionals (e.g. tractor drivers) in desert conditions and high mechanical activity

To note, these values are in reasonable accord with results of calculations using equation (I.20).

Dust Loading Approach

Another method commonly used in environmental assessments is to consider "dust loading" (Wilkins, 1994; UK, 2002). This approach assumes that contaminant activity concentrations in airborne dust at a particular location is the same as that in the surface layer of soil:

$$C = C_{soil} \cdot S_E \tag{I.21}$$

where: C - the estimated concentration of the contaminant in air, $g\,m^{-3}$;

C_{soil} - the concentration of the contaminant in soil, $g\,kg^{-1}$,
         (i.e. g of contaminant in 1 kg soil);

S_E - the equivalent soil concentration or dust-loading in air, $kg\,m^{-3}$

Still, problems exist in using the dust-loading approach. First, the soil concentration is expressed in terms of $g\,kg^{-1}$. However, as a rule, the results of measurements are generally reported as $g\,m^{-2}$ and knowledge of the depth of contamination is required. A short time after contamination, it is difficult to define what the real depth of the surface soil layer is and how this depth will change with time.

The normal average value of dust load S_E is 50 $\mu g\,m^{-3}$. In real conditions this value can be (Wilkins, 1994):

- in the range of 5–50 $\mu g\,m^{-3}$ in non-urban areas; and
- between 100–800 $\mu g\,m^{-3}$ in large industrial areas

The report (UK, 2001) states that for UK conditions, and soldiers carrying out a range of activities, $S_E = 50\ \mu g\,m^{-3}$ can be used as a reasonably cautious value for dust-loading. For desert conditions and intensive vehicular movement, this report recommends to use dust load $S_E = 30\ mg\,m^{-3}$. This value is based on measurements from the Maralinga and Emu nuclear test sites in Australia, which quoted values of S_E from 0.37 to 65 $mg\,m^{-3}$ for sitting in or near a moving vehicle. Finally, the worst case assumes desert conditions and normal living conditions of a population and recommends to use dust load $S_E = 2\ mg\,m^{-3}$, based on measurements from Maralinga and Emu nuclear test sites for children playing.

Comparison of calculated values of mid-annual DU concentrations in air is estimated using a technique of the resuspension factor R or dust loading approach as given in Fig.I.6. At its construction, initial soil contamination by DU at the level of 10 $g\,m^{-2}$ was used according to a *Reference Case*.

Figure I.6   Comparison of mid-annual DU concentrations in air estimated using a technique of resuspension factor *R* or dust loading approach

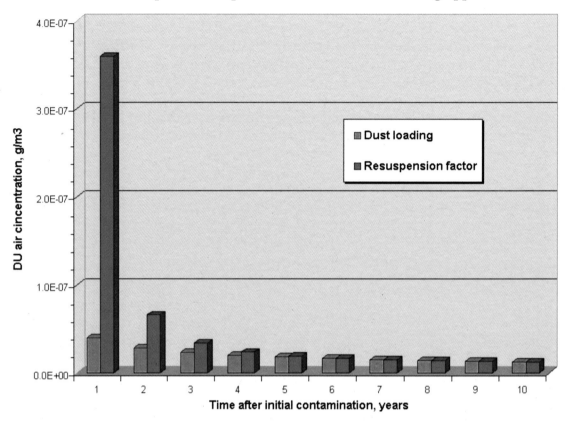

This figure shows that in the first years following initial soil contamination, the technique based on the dust loading approach gives values of DU concentrations in air which are almost 10 times lower than estimated by using the resuspension factor R procedure. However, after a period of 5 years, the results of both techniques practically coincide.

Conclusions

- The most convenient way for the assessment of air contamination by the processes of a secondary dust formation is the use of resuspension factors which are dependent on the period of time after initial soil contamination.

- A decrease of contamination of the top layer of soil (0-1 cm) in time can, in 7 years, be at a level of 15-30 % from the initial contamination.

- Natural resuspension can be characterized by the particle sizes about 14 µm, particles deposition velocity of 0.0065 m s^{-1} and resuspension flux density at the level of 3.7 10^{-7} g m^{-2} s^{-1}. In the case of semi-arid and windy conditions, the resuspension flux density by DU can reach 0.003-0.024 µg m^{-2} s^{-1} 7 years after the initial soil contamination at a level of 10 g DU per 1 m^2.

- Design values of the resuspension factor 7 year after the initial soil contamination can be in the range (0.5 – 1.4) 10^{-9} m^{-1}, depending on the applied estimation model.

- For *Reference Case* conditions the integrated level of surface contamination as a result of resuspension processes 7 years after contamination will not exceed 13 - 14 mg m^{-2}, i.e. only 0.13-0.14 % from a level of initial soil contamination.

- In the first years following initial soil contamination, the technique based on the dust loading approach gives values of DU concentrations in air which are almost 10 times lower than estimated by using the resuspension factor R procedure. However, after a period of 5 years, the results of both techniques practically coincide.

I.2   RESUSPENSION FACTORS AND ANALYSIS

Estimations of resuspension factors were completed using equation (I.12) with air contamination data from Appendix G and soil contamination data from Appendix J. Of the 24 air samples collected, 21 outdoor samples and 3 samples inside buildings (samples NUC-02-024-201, NUC-02-024-202 and NUC-02-028-202) were selected. As formation processes for secondary air pollution outside and inside buildings can be different, and considering the complexities in assessing floor contamination inside buildings (see below), it was decided to conduct separate estimations of the resuspension factors for these cases.

Outdoors resuspension factors

By analyzing the coordinates of air and soil sampling locations, it is possible to observe that, as a rule, these points do not coincide. In this respect, it is necessary to choose which point of soil sample splitting is best compared to an air sampling point. To solve this problem, it was decided to average soil samples, including a weighting factor for each separate measurement, and consider the remoteness of the soil sampling point position from the air sampling position. The change was obtained from measured concentrations of uranium isotopes in a layer of 0-5 cm (except for samples NUC-02-024-011 and NUC-02-024-011, selected in a 0-3 cm layer) to their concentration in the layer of soil of 0-1 cm at the moment of initial fallout. It was assumed that the portion of activity of uranium isotopes in the soil sample stipulated by the presence of DU was completely transferred to a layer of 0-1 cm. For the presence of natural uranium in any recalculations, it was assumed that the concentration of uranium isotopes in a layer of 0-1 cm is proportional to their measured concentration in a layer 0-3 or 0-5 cm. Results of these calculations are presented in the Tab.I.1.

The cumulative distribution of estimated average values of outdoors resuspension factors R (the last column of the Table I.1) are presented on Fig.I.7. The median of this distribution is $8.5 \ 10^{-10}$ m^{-1} with the confidence interval of this value in the range of $(0.28 - 2.5) \ 10^{-9}$ m^{-1}. Of note

Table I.1   Estimated values of outdoors resuspension factors, m^{-1}

Air sample Code	Sampling site	Interval of distances, m	Resuspension factors estimated by ...			
			U-238	U-235	U-234	Average
NUC-02-023-201	Hadzici ; [1]	98 - 602	3.44E-10	6.12E-10	7.53E-10	5.70E-10
NUC-02-023-202	Hadzici ; [1]	36 - 399	9.56E-11	1.89E-10	4.75E-10	2.53E-10
NUC-02-023-203	Hadzici ; [1]	35 - 402	3.90E-11	9.07E-11	2.64E-10	1.31E-10
NUC-02-023-204	Hadzici ; [1]	33 - 399	4.36E-11	1.06E-10	2.02E-10	1.17E-10
NUC-02-024-201	Hadzici ; [1]	26 - 462	8.28E-10	8.83E-10	1.17E-09	1.03E-09
NUC-02-024-202	Hadzici ; [1]	14 - 481	2.45E-09	2.05E-09	2.18E-09	2.10E-09
NUC-02-024-205	Hadzici ; [1]	79 - 662	2.45E-10	3.72E-10	5.25E-10	3.81E-10
NUC-02-025-201	Lukavica ; Barracks	113 - 314	4.02E-09	4.00E-09	3.74E-09	3.92E-09
NUC-02-025-202	Lukavica ; Barracks	21 - 415	6.73E-09	6.73E-09	7.87E-09	7.11E-09
NUC-02-025-203	Lukavica ; Barracks	50 - 341	3.82E-09	3.89E-09	3.93E-09	3.88E-09
NUC-02-025-204	Lukavica ; Barracks	67 - 255	3.36E-09	3.41E-09	3.58E-09	3.45E-09
NUC-02-026-201	Hadzici ; [2]	60 - 1870	4.92E-10	4.93E-10	5.34E-10	5.06E-10
NUC-02-026-202	Hadzici ; [2]	45 - 1704	6.50E-10	6.76E-10	6.81E-10	6.69E-10
NUC-02-027-201	Han Pijesak ; Barracks	111 - 608	1.23E-09	1.22E-09	1.09E-09	1.18E-09
NUC-02-027-202	Han Pijesak ; Barracks	79 - 444	8.60E-10	8.62E-10	6.11E-10	7.78E-10
NUC-02-027-203	Han Pijesak ; Barracks	12 - 399	4.90E-10	4.82E-10	4.72E-10	4.81E-10
NUC-02-027-204	Han Pijesak ; Barracks	76 - 537	7.16E-10	5.00E-10	8.84E-10	7.00E-10
NUC-02-028-201	Han Pijesak ; Barracks	79 - 547	1.78E-09	6.35E-10	5.43E-10	9.85E-10
NUC-02-029-201	Vogosca ; [3]	37 - 3580	6.10E-10	5.49E-10	-	5.79E-10
NUC-02-029-202	Vogosca ; [3]	85 - 3301	4.37E-10	4.03E-10	7.42E-10	5.27E-10
NUC-02-030-201	Foca Bridge (Srbinje)	16 - 203	1.19E-09	1.22E-09	2.09E-09	1.50E-09

[1] Tank repair facility   [2] Barracks near ammunition storage area   [3] Ammunition production site

Figure I.7   Cumulative distribution of results of the estimated outdoor resuspension factor *R*

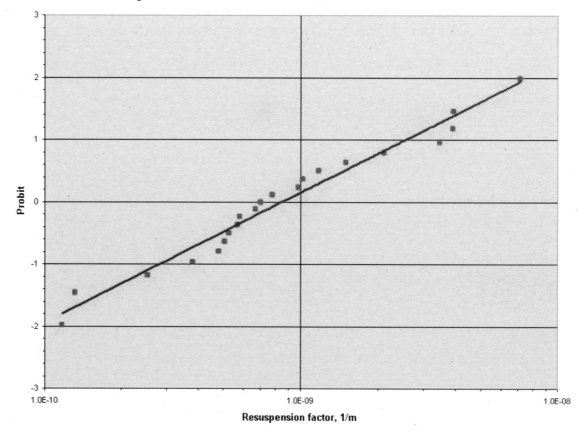

is that this value is in the good agreement with results of assessment of resuspension factors *R* by using the equation (I.18).

Resuspension factors inside the bombed storage barn (Han Pijesak)

The assessment of resuspension factors *R* inside the attacked storage barn (Han Pijesak Artillery Storage and Barracks site) was made using the following data:

- The density of DU contamination on the concrete floor inside the attacked storage barn was 0.7 g m^{-2} (see Appendix J);

- The isotopic composition of uranium on the floor corresponds to the measurement results of the scratch sample (NUC-02-028-302);

- The isotopic composition of uranium in the air inside this barn corresponds to the measurement results from the air filter sample (NUC-020-28-202)

The results of these estimantes are presented in Table I.2

Table I.2   Input data and the results of estimation of resuspension factors *R* inside the storage barn, m^{-1}

Parameter	^{234}U	^{235}U	^{236}U	^{238}U
DU on concrete floor, g m^{-2}	4.78E-06	1.38E-03	2.04E-05	6.90E-01
DU in air inside the barrack, g m^{-3}	2.68E-14	7.26E-12	9.90E-14	3.60E-09
Resuspension factor R, m^{-1}	5.61E-09	5.26E-09	4.86E-09	5.21E-09

An analysis of this table shows that the results using data for different uranium nuclides are very similar. The average value of resuspension factors R inside the attacked storage barn is $5.2 \cdot 10^{-9} \, \mathrm{m}^{-1}$. That value is approximately 7 times higher than the average value for outdoor resuspension factors R (see Table I.1). Differences can perhaps be explained by the current design of this barn as there are major apertures near the floor and wind speed at the floor surface could be much higher than outdoors.

Surface contamination as a result of resuspension and deposition processes

Military machinery has been stored in the barn for some time, but only once the building was repaired following the attack. Therefore, any contamination on the surface would be due to resuspension and deposition. Two smear samples were collected from the surface of a cannon inside this barn (samples code NUC-02-028-303 and NSI-smr-07-03) (results, see Appendix J). A further smear sample (sample code NUC-02-028-304) was taken from a wooden box surface. The input data and results of the estimation ratios of surface to floor DU residues 7 years after initial contamination are presented in Table I.3.

Table I.3   Input data and the results of estimation the ratio of surface to floor DU contamination inside the storage barn

Parameter	^{234}U	^{235}U	^{236}U	^{238}U
DU on concrete floor, g m^{-2}				
	4.78E-06	1.38E-03	2.04E-05	6.90E-01
DU on the smear samples, mg cm^{-2}				
NSI-smr-07-03	3.10E-10	-	-	1.10E-05
NUC-02-028-303	4.00E-11	1.20E-08	1.66E-10	5.90E-06
NUC-02-028-304	1.73E-10	5.40E-08	7.23E-10	2.67E-05
DU on the analyzed surface$^{1)}$, g m^{-2}				
NSI-smr-07-03	1.55E-08	-	-	5.50E-04
NUC-02-028-303	2.00E-09	6.00E-07	8.30E-09	2.95E-04
NUC-02-028-304	8.65E-09	2.70E-06	3.62E-08	1.34E-03
The ratio of surface to floor DU contamination, %				
NSI-smr-07-03	0.324	-	-	0.080
NUC-02-028-303	0.042	0.043	0.041	0.043
NUC-02-028-304	0.181	0.196	0.178	0.193

$^{1)}$ - Taking into account, that the part of taken out activity by using the smear sampling method is near 20 % from the surface contamination density.

This Table shows that the range of results of this contamination ratio is 0.04 – 0.32 %. This value is in the good agreement with results of theoretical assessments that were presented in Fig. I.5.

Conclusions

1. The introduced analysis model for the effects of resuspension and deposition processes on DU air and surface contamination has shown a good correlation with supervising results from the different sites.
2. Estimated on analysis of experimental data, the value of outdoor resuspension factors R is $7.3 \cdot 10^{-10} \, \mathrm{m}^{-1}$ with the confidence interval in the range $(0.23 – 2.3) \cdot 10^{-9} \, \mathrm{m}^{-1}$. This value is in good agreement with assessment results for this factor by mathematical models.
3. The average value of resuspension factors R inside the storage barn is $5.2 \cdot 10^{-9} \, \mathrm{m}^{-1}$. This value is approximately 7 times higher than the average value for outdoor resuspension factors R.
4. The ratio of contamination density of the surfaces – polluted due to the deposition process of resuspended particles – to floor DU contamination density 7 years after initial contamination is in the range 0.04 – 0.32 %. This range is in good agreement with results from theoretical assessments.

Appendix J

DU in Surface Deposits and Special Studies on Surfaces

J.1 DU IN SURFACE DEPOSITS

Background

When penetrators impact on the ground surface, a portion of its DU mass is transformed into aerosols or fine particles and thrown into the surrounding air. The quantity of DU dispersed into the air mainly depends on the hardness of the surface where the impact takes place. The quantity dispersed is greater on hard surface impacts than on softer surfaces. Consequently, aerial dispersion of small DU quantities is expected after impact on soft soil (soil without stones), higher quantities on hard ground surfaces (stony soil, rock, concrete, asphalt), and the highest quantities when the impact occurs on the heavy armour of a tank or APC.

These aerosols and fine particles are normally deposited in measurable quantities on the surrounding ground or on other surfaces within about 100 m from impact. After initial deposit, it is possible that fine DU dust particles are resuspended into the atmosphere together with soil-dust by wind or human activities, leading to secondary air contamination. These particles are then deposited once more on the surrounding ground and other surfaces. If the deposition takes place on surfaces other than soil that are exposed to rain and other meteorological phenomena, the surface deposit will be partly washed off. Surface deposits on soil will penetrate into the topsoil layer with time.

If the deposition of DU aerosols and fine particles takes place on surfaces which are not affected by rain and other meteorological phenomena (e.g. inside a building), surface deposits will accumulate and remain undisturbed over a longer time and can later be collected and analysed by taking smear or scratch samples.

Measurements of surface deposits

During the mission to Bosnia and Herzegovina (BiH), special samples were taken inside a wooden storage barn at the *Han Pijesak Artillery Storage and Barracks* site. Inside this building, shot holes on the concrete floor indicated that the building had been attacked and hit by DU rounds. After the attacks, the DU contaminated building was repaired and used once again to store army material, such as cannons and instruments in wooden boxes. However, the detailed history of the building's management is not known.

One scratch sample was taken from the edge of the concrete floor against the wall; a second one was collected from the horizontal surface of a wooden beam at a height of about 1 m above the floor surface. Two smear samples were taken from smooth, painted horizontal surfaces of army material that had been stored in the barn: one from a cannon, another from a wooden box. The description of the samples and the analyses of results are summarised in Tables J.1 to J.7.

NUC-2002-028-302

DU content of uranium in scratch samples exceeded 99%

The scratch sample from the rough concrete floor surface consisted of sand and dust.

23.8g of the material was collected from a surface of 420 cm². The uranium concentration of the material was 1.89 milligram per gram, representing a surface contamination of 107 μg U/cm², or 1.07 g/m². This uranium concentration is approximately 1 000 times higher than the natural uranium content of soil. The isotope composition shows that the uranium consists to almost 100 % of DU.

The scratch sample from the rough surface on a wooden beam consisted of sand and dust. 2.38 g of the material was collected from a surface of 200 cm². The uranium concentration of the material was 92 μg/g, representing a surface contamination of 1.1 μg U/cm² or 11 mg/m². This uranium concentration is approximately 100 times higher than the natural uranium content of soil. The isotope composition again shows that the uranium consists of almost 100 % depleted uranium.

These two scratch samples mainly represent the primary deposition of debris and dust from the impact of the DU penetrators on the concrete floor inside the building. It is unlikely that this coarse, sandy material was resuspended inside the building at a later time. The measuring results for these samples show that inside a building, the primary surface contamination from impacts of DU penetrators can, as expected, be higher than in the open field. As it is indoors, no influence of weathering effects can occur and the initial superficial contamination will remain preserved at the ground surface, if the floor is not cleaned.

Both smear samples from smooth painted surfaces consisted of fine brown dust. The measured loose surface contamination from the cannon was 5.9 ng U/cm², or 59 μg/m². The measured loose surface contamination from a wooden box was 27 ng U/cm², or 270 μg/m². The isotope composition for both smear samples shows that the uranium consists of almost 100% depleted uranium.

Smear samples from the surface of stored supplies consisted primarily of resuspended particles (secondary deposition)

These two smear samples represent the secondary deposition of resuspended contaminated dust, resulting from the impact of the DU penetrators on the concrete floor inside the building. Because the detailed history of the building management is unknown, it is indeed not possible to discern the length of time elapsed since the dust was deposited on the sampled surfaces. Measurement results from these samples show that – inside a building – the secondary deposition of resuspended dust from contaminated ground surfaces can lead to a DU contamination of objects' surfaces that were brought into the building only after the attack. Indeed, the DU concentration was found to be about 1 000 times less than the primary

Depleted Uranium in Bosnia and Herzegovina

contamination on the ground surface. There is no influence from weathering effects, and the superficial contamination will accumulate and remain preserved on the surface of the objects for a long time.

Table J.1   Special samples from Han Pijesak

Sample Code	Coordinates UTM 34T	Sample description
NUC-02-028-301	CP 35 550 / 84 425	Scratch sample of dust (8x25cm) on beam inside storage barn
NUC-02-028-302	CP 35 550 / 84 425	Scratch sample of dust (6x70cm) on concrete floor inside storage barn
NUC-02-028-303	CP 35 550 / 84 425	Smear sample on horizontal area (10x40cm) of cannon inside storage barn
NUC-02-028-004	CP 35 550 / 84 425	Smear sample (24x40cm) on wooden box inside storage barn

Table J.2   Scratch samples: Isotope concentration of uranium per sample mass

NUC-2002-028-	^{238}U		^{235}U		^{234}U		^{236}U	
	[g/kg]	k [%]	[mg/kg]	k [%]	[µg/kg]	k [%]	[µg/kg]	k [%]
301	0.0917	1.9	0.187	3.6	0.66	23	2.6	17
302	1.89	1.8	3.77	11.0	13.1	35	56	15

Table J.3   Scratch samples: Isotope concentration of uranium per surface unit

NUC-2002-028-	^{238}U		^{235}U		^{234}U		^{236}U	
	[µg/cm2]	k [%]	[ng/cm2]	k [%]	[pg/cm2]	k [%]	[pg/cm2]	k [%]
301	1.09	1.9	2.23	3.6	7.90	23	30.8	17
302	107	1.8	214	11.0	741	35	3158	15

Table J.4   Scratch samples: Percentage DU of total uranium

NUC-2002-028-	Isotopic ratio ^{235}U / ^{238}U	k [%]	Percentage DU of total uranium [%]	k [%]
301	0.00203	1.5	99.4	0.6
302	0.00199	2.0	100.2	0.8

Table J.5   Smear samples: Isotope concentration of uranium per sample

NUC-2002-028-	^{238}U		^{235}U		^{234}U		^{236}U	
	[µg/smear sample]	k [%]	[ng/smear sample]	k [%]	[pg/smear sample]	k [%]	[pg/smear sample]	k [%]
303	2.37	1.5	4.75	2.9	15.9	11	66.3	12
304	25.6	1.5	52.1	8.8	166	16	694	12

Table J.6   Smear samples: Isotope concentration of uranium per surface unit

NUC-2002-028-	^{238}U		^{235}U		^{234}U		^{236}U	
	[µg/cm2]	k [%]	[ng/cm2]	k [%]	[pg/cm2]	k [%]	[pg/cm2]	k [%]
303	0.0059	1.5	0.012	2.9	0.040	11	0.166	12
304	0.0267	1.5	0.054	8.8	0.173	16	0.723	12

Table J.7   Smear samples: Percentage DU of total uranium

NUC-2002-028-	Isotope ratio ^{235}U / ^{238}U	k [%]	Percentage DU of total uranium [%]	k [%]
303	0.00200	0.75	100.0	0.28
304	0.00202	0.99	99.6	0.38

J.2 SPECIAL STUDIES ON SURFACES

Inspector device measurements

Dust in the air and settling over surfaces, both inside and outside, mainly contains radioactive decay products from naturally occurring uranium and thorium in soil. In addition, the dust can include the radionuclides from nuclear weapons tests in the atmosphere, from nuclear accidents (for example – the Chernobyl accident in 1986) and from the airborne release of nuclear installations. Soil-derived radionuclides are present in air in variable amounts, depending on local soil, wind, and moisture conditions. Using assessments, a dust loading of 50 µg m^{-3} was assumed and applied to typical concentrations of natural radionuclides in soil. Some portion of the solid matter in air may not come from the soil, but from organic matter, building dust, smoke, and fly ash from coal burning (UNSCEAR, 2000).

Measurements of radioactive surface contamination using the *Inspector* device were produced on 13 sites during the mission. 175 measurements were made in total. Some information about these measurements is reported in Table J.8.

Table J.8 Surface contamination measurements produced

Site	Number of samples with count rates (cps) in the interval …								Total
	<0.1	0.1-0.2	0.2-0.3	0.3-0.5	0.5-1.0	1-10	10-100	>100	
Sarajevo	2								2
Hadzici [1]	16	6	6	1	1	1	1	2	34
Lukavica; Barracks	11	12							23
Hadzici [2]	4	4	3	1					12
Hadzici; Barracks	1		1						2
Pjelugovici [3]	4	2		1					7
Han Pijesak; Barracks	14	10	4	7	5	8	1	1	50
Pale-Koran: Barracks					1				1
Vogosca [4]	5	6	3	1	1				16
Kalinovik [5]		1	1						2
Kalinovik [6]		1	2	1					4
Foca (Srbinje) Bridge	4	7	4	1					16
Bjelasnica Plateau		3	3						6
Total	61	52	27	13	8	9	2	3	175

[1] Tank repair facility [2] Barracks 1 km from ammunition storage area [3] T55 tank position
[4] Ammunition production site [5] Ammunition destruction site [6] Water reservoir

The cumulative distribution of these results on the total β-activity is shown in Figure J.1. This figure illustrates that the main part of the results stay in the range of 0.04-1.0 cps. The results with count rates less than 0.04 cps are not significant values. On the other hand, the results with count rates over 1.0 cps fall into cases of measurements of a surface contamination or inside the bombed barracks, or near fragments of DU penetrators outdoors.

Following the elimination of these extreme values, the remaining results were segregated into two groups. In one were included the results from sites where DU penetrator fragments were found (*Hadzici Tank Repair Facility*, *Hadzici Ammunition storage* area and *Han Pijesak Artillery Storage and Barracks*). The second group included those sites in which the presence of DU was not revealed. The cumulative distribution of measuring results of beta-surface contamination for these two groups is shown on Figure J.2.

Depleted Uranium in Bosnia and Herzegovina

Figure J.1   Cumulative distribution of measurement results of beta-surface contamination at different sites

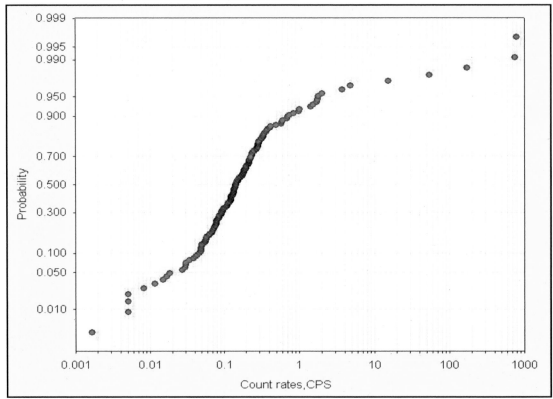

Figure J.2   Cumulative distribution of measuring results of beta-surface contamination in sites with (green ovals) and without (red rectangles) DU

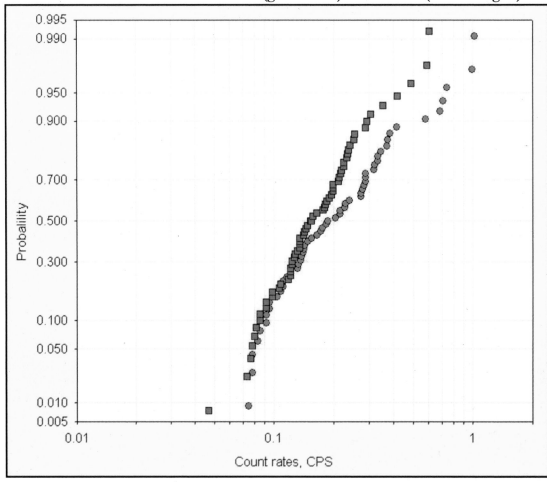

Post-Conflict Environmental Assessment

Table J.9   Beta-activity of concrete floor surface contamination inside wooden storage barn (Han Pijesak)

CODE NSI-Insp-	Duration of measurement	gamma count	gamma+beta count	only beta count	beta count rates, cps	Relative error of beta count rates, %	DU surface conta-mination, mg cm^{-2}
07-34	10 min	391	1313	922	1.54E+00	4.5	0.031
07-35	10 min	425	1273	848	1.41E+00	4.9	0.028
07-36	10 min	328	548	220	3.67E-01	13.5	0.007
07-39	10 min	379	1429	1050	1.75E+00	4.0	0.035
07-41	5 min	220	1333	1113	3.71E+00	3.5	0.074
07-42	1 min	866	11160	10294	1.72E+02	1.1	3.43
07-43	1 min	65	969	904	1.51E+01	3.6	0.30
07-44	5 min	183	785	602	2.01E+00	5.2	0.040
07-45	5 min	193	725	532	1.77E+00	5.7	0.035
07-48	10 min	453	3307	2854	4.76E+00	2.1	0.095

Both of these distributions are close to logarithmically normal distributions. First, for un-contaminated sites, a median contamination density value of 0.16 cps was found and the confidence interval of this result over the range 0.10-0.27 cps. For sites with DU contamination, 0.20 cps and 0.10-0.40 cps, respectively.

For potential follow-up assessments, the greatest interest is present in the measurements of contamination density of the concrete floor inside the attacked storage barn at Han Pijesak as these values will hereinafter be used to estimate the resuspension factor (see *Appendix I*). 10 measurements were conducted inside the building of radioactive floor contamination (Table J.9). To estimate the DU contamination density, the conversion coefficient 0.02 mg cm^{-2} DU was used for count rates of 1 cps by the Inspector device. The cumulative distribution of results from these calculations is shown in Figure J.3.

Figure J.3   Cumulative distribution of estimation results on the DU contamination density of the concrete floor inside the storage barn (Han Pijesak site)

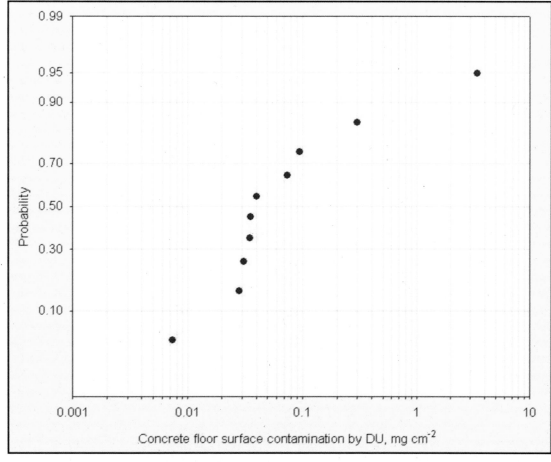

The median value of DU contamination density is 0.069 mg cm^{-2} (0.69 g m^{-2}) with the confidence interval of this value in the range of 0.01 - 0.44 mg cm^{-2} (0.1 - 4.4 g m^{-2}). It should be noted that in this report a *Reference Case* value of 10 g m^{-2} appreciably exceeds the measured values of DU contamination density on the floor in this building.

J.3 SMEAR AND SCRATCH SAMPLES

Two scratch and 34 smear samples were collected from surfaces during the mission. The majority of the smear samples (32) were collected using a scotch tape (IBRAE RAS method). Tape width was 44 mm, length was from 120-190 mm. A low-background alpha-beta radiometer HT-1000 (Canberra Inc.) with four gas-flow detectors was applied for sample activity measurements. The fixed pollution was isolated by sticking on a second layer of scotch tape. A low-background alpha-beta radiometer HT-1000 (Canberra Inc.) with four gas-flow detectors was applied for smear sample total β-activity measurements (see *Appendix C*). The results of these measurements are presented in Table J.10.

Table J.10 Smear samples collected (IBRAE RAS)

Site	Number of samples with density contamination in the interval, mBq cm^{-2}							Total
	<0.5	0.5-1.0	1.0-1.5	1.5-2.0	2.0-5.0	5.0-10	>10	
Sarajevo		1	1					2
Han Pijesak; Barracks	3	1	4	1	4	2	1	16
Vogosca [1]			4	4	1			9
Kalinovik [2]		1						1
Foca (Srbinje) Bridge	2		2					4
Total	5	3	11	5	5	2	1	32

[1] Ammunition production site [2] Water reservoir

Figure J.4 Cumulative distribution of estimation results for the ratio of smear contamination density to surface contamination density

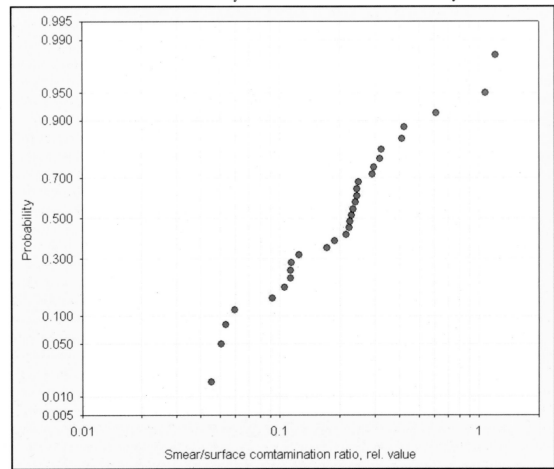

Post-Conflict Environmental Assessment

Data in this table shows that the contamination density of smear samples vary within wide limits. For practical purposes, it is important to estimate the value of the ratio between the measured smear sample contamination densities and the surface contamination density in the location where this smear sample was taken. The results of these calculations are shown on the Figure J.4.

The median value of this ratio is 0.20 with a confidence interval for this value in the range of 0.09-0.46. Thus, the contamination taken on this scotch tape is equal to approximately 20 % from a total density of the surface contamination.

Five scotch smear samples by IBRAE RAS, as well as 2 scratch and 2 smear samples were collected by Spiez and analyzed for DU contamination. The information of these samples is presented in Tables J.11 and J.1.

Table J.11 Smear samples measurement of DU contamination (IBRAE RAS)

CODE NSI-smr-	Sampling site	Coordinates UTM 34T	Type of surface	Selection area, cm2
07-03	Han Pijesak; Barracks	CP 35550 / 84438	metal	106
07-05	Han Pijesak; Barracks	CP 35524 / 84460	metal	119
07-11	Han Pijesak; Barracks	CP 35548 / 84437	concrete	109
07-16	Han Pijesak; Barracks	CP 35974 / 84343	metal	136
10-02	Vogosca [1]	BP 88948 / 64991	metal	119

[1] Ammunition production site

The results of DU contamination density for all 9 scratch and smear samples are given in the Table J.12.

Table J.12 DU surface contamination on the scratch and smear samples collected

CODE	^{234}U		^{235}U		^{235}U		^{238}U		DU [%]
	pg cm^{-2}	k [%]	ng cm^{-2}	k [%]	pg cm^{-2}	k [%]	µg cm^{-2}	k [%]	
NSI-smr-07-03	0.31	39	-	-	-	-	0.011	25	60
NSI-smr-07-05	0.19	37	-	-	-	-	0.0060	26	52
NSI-smr-07-11	34	5.8	11	21	-	-	5.6	2.9	109
NSI-smr-07-16	0.12	58	-	-	-	-	0.0033	47	39
NSI-smr-10-02	0.46	21	-	-	-	-	0.0086	21	< 1
NUC-02-028-301	7.90	23	2.23	3.6	2.6	17	1.09	1.9	99.4
NUC-02-028-302	741	35	214	11.0	56	15	107	1.8	100.2
NUC-02-028-303	0.040	11	0.012	2,9	0.166	12	0.0059	1.5	100.0
NUC-02-028-304	0.173	16	0.054	8.8	0.723	12	0.0267	1.5	99.6

Data in this table shows that the DU density contamination of the concrete floor inside the Han Pijesak storage barn equals 0.107 mg cm^{-2} (sample NUC-02-028-302). This value is in agreement with the assessment results of DU surface contamination density in this building, which was conducted using the *Inspector* device (0.07 mg cm^{-2} with the confidence interval for this value in the range of 0.01-0.44 mg cm^{-2}). Of note, the measured values of ^{238}U contamination density on the cannon surface, estimated by two different types of smear samples (sample codes NSI-smr-07-03 and NUC-02-028-303) and different methods of measurement procedure, are practically equal – 0.011 and 0.006 mg cm^{-2}.

An important observation is the detection of DU in a smear sample taken from a metal surface at a distance of about 400 m from the attacked barrack (sample code NSI-smr-07-16). Assuming that:

- DU contamination of this surface is 5 times higher (by using the above-mentioned ratio between the scotch tape and total density of the surface contamination), i.e. – 0.16 mg m^{-2};

- Deposition velocity of released DU particles at this distance is 0.01 m s^{-1};

- Air dilution factors for a distance of 400 m for weather stability class D is 5 10^{-7} s m^{-3} and 4 10^{-6} s m^{-3} for stability class F

In that case, the DU release in the atmosphere as a result of an attack can range from 4-33 kg for weather stability class F and D respectively. If it is also assumed that about 10% of DU can suspend in air, it can be estimated that the total DU used in the attack at the *Han Pijesak Artillery Storage and Barracks* was 40-330 kg, or 150-1100 penetrators. This assessment is thought to be quite reasonable.

Conclusions

- The use of the *Inspector* device gives the possibility to find places with DU surface contamination densities higher than 0.1 g m^{-2}.

- The median value of DU contamination density of the concrete floor inside the attacked storage barn (Han Pijesak site) was 0.7 g m^{-2}.

- The part of collected contamination on scotch tape is equal to approximately 20 % of the total density of the surface contamination.

- The smear sampling method permits establishing the contamination of surfaces by DU at a level of 3 ng m^{-2}.

- Detection of DU fallout at a distance of about 400 m from the storage barn has allowed to evaluate the total mass of DU used in the attack at a level of 40-330 kg (i.e. 150-1100 penetrators).

Appendix K

Heavy Metals and Other Elements in Selected Water and Soil Samples

K.1 INTRODUCTION

During early negotiation phases for a DU assessment in Bosnia and Herzegovina, the local authorities expressed on a number of occasions their interest in receiving further information and analytical data out of samples that would primarily be analysed for DU content.

UNEP concluded that in the context of a DU field assessment, information on heavy metals other than DU could be of value. Consequently, both water samples and selected soil samples were analysed for their heavy metals and other elements content.

Analyses were performed at Spiez Laboratory in Switzerland under accredited laboratory procedures (testing service) for the determination of main and trace elements, their compounds and selected air pollutants; STS 101. Quadrupole-ICP-MS-technology (ELAN 6000) was used for the determination of the elements. The analysis program "Totalquant-®" of Perkin-Elmer – an element screening analysis - was applied as it allows a rapid, semi-quantitative determination of elements within a precision of ± 10%.

K.2 WATER SAMPLES

All water samples collected by APAT (see Appendix E - *DU in Water*) were analysed using the following sample preparation:

- The original water samples were filtered (0.45 µm filter) following preservation in nitric acid.

- 10 mL of the filtered water sample was post-digested by adding of 0.2 ml nitric acid (30%) according the standard procedure EPA 200.8.

Reference values

For drinking water the WHO Guidelines for drinking water quality (WHO 1998) are relevant.

Results

With the exception of one well water sample, all tap and well water samples respected the WHO guidelines. The well water sample (APAT-BHW01) taken at the Hadzici tank repair facility showed 3.2 µg uranium/L (±10%). This value was also confirmed by HR-ICP-MS technique (Appendix E). The provisional WHO guideline value is set at 2.0 µg uranium/L (WHO 1998). This value has been considered as too low for many countries that use groundwaters as public water. Thus WHO are planning to change this value. A new guideline value of 9 µg/L is suggested (WHO 2002; www.who.int/water_sanitation_health/GDWQ/draftchemicals/list.htm).

No problems concerning heavy metals could be measured in stream and river waters. The values lied beyond the WHO guidelines for drinking water.

Table K.1 Chemicals of health significance in drinking water; Inorganic constituents (WHO, 1998)

Element	Guideline value (mg/litre)	Remarks
Antimony	0.005 (P)[a]	
Arsenic	0.01[b] (P)	For excess skin cancer risk of 6×10^{-4}
Barium	0.7	
Beryllium		NAD[c.]
Boron	0.5 (P)	
Cadmium	0.003	
Chromium	0.05 (P)	
Copper	2 (P)	Based on acute gastrointestinal effects
Cyanide	0.07	
Fluoride	1.5	Climatic conditions, volume of water consumed, and intake from other sources should be considered when setting national standards
Lead	0.01	It is recognized that not all water will meet the guideline value immediately; meanwhile, all other recommended measures to reduce the total exposure to lead should be implemented
Manganese	0.5 (P)	ATO[d]
Mercury (total)	0.001	
Molybdenum	0.07	
Nickel	0.02 (P)	
Nitrate (as NO$_3$-)	50 (acute)	
Nitrite (as NO$_2$-)	3 (acute) 0.2 (P) (chronic)	
Selenium	0.01	
Uranium	0.002 (P)	

[a](P) - Provisional guideline value. This term is used for constituents for which there is some evidence of a potential hazard but where the available information on health effects is limited; or where an uncertainty factor greater than 1000 has been used in the derivation of the tolerable daily intake (TDI). Provisional guideline values are also recommended:

(1) for substances for which the calculated guideline value would be below the practical quantification level, or below the level that can be achieved through practical treatment methods; or (2) where disinfection is likely to result in the guideline value being exceeded.

[b] For substances that are considered to be carcinogenic, the guideline value is the concentration in drinking-water associated with an excess lifetime cancer risk of 10^{-5} (one additional cancer per 100 000 of the population ingesting drinking-water containing the substance at the guideline value for 70 years). Concentrations associated with estimated excess lifetime cancer risks of 10^{-4} and 10^{-6} can be calculated by multiplying and dividing, respectively, the guideline value by 10.

In cases in which the concentration associated with an excess lifetime cancer risk of 10^{-5} is not feasible as a result of inadequate analytical or treatment technology, a provisional guideline value is recommended at a practicable level and the estimated associated excess lifetime cancer risk presented.

It should be emphasized that the guideline values for carcinogenic substances have been computed from hypothetical mathematical models that cannot be verified experimentally and that the values should be interpreted differently from TDI-based values because of the lack of precision of the models. At best, these values must be regarded as rough estimates of cancer risk. However, the models used are conservative and probably err on the side of caution. Moderate short-term exposure to levels exceeding the guideline value for carcinogens does not significantly affect the risk.

[c]NAD - No adequate data to permit recommendation of a health-based guideline value.

[d]ATO - Concentrations of the substance at or below the health-based guideline value may affect the appearance, taste, or odour of the water.

Heavy metals contamination was found in the water sample taken at the Kalinovik ammunition destruction site from the body of water in the karst hole used for blasting of ordnance (APAT-BHW17). Specific results are presented in the tables at the end of this Appendix.

K.3 SELECTED SOIL SAMPLES

Solutions from the HR-ICP-MS DU procedures for soil (see Appendix C) were diluted with nitric acid (2%) for a final concentration of 0.5 g soil per litre and then measured. One analysis was performed from each sample. The analytical procedure was controlled by analysing the Standard Reference Materials ISE 954 ¨Clay soil from Turkey¨ and IAEA-326 ¨Radionuclides in soil". Based on these control measurements, an uncertainty (p=0.95) of ± 10% was estimated for the results.

Table K.2   Dutch standards for soil contamination assessment in total concentration of heavy metals in soils (www.agnet.org/library/image/eb473t6.html)

Elements	Target values	Intervention value
	─ ─ ─ ─ ─ ─ ─ mg/kg soils ─ ─ ─ ─ ─ ─ ─	
As	29	55
Ba	200	625
Cd	0.8	12
Cr	100	380
Co	20	240
Cu	36	190
Hg	0.3	10
Pb	85	530
Mo	10	200
Ni	35	210
Zn	140	720

Notes:
1. Target values are specified to indicate desirable maximum levels of elements in uncontaminated soils.
2. B value: Former B values are to identify whether possible risks are likely (Mocn et al. 1986)
   The former B value is now replaced by the average of the target and intervention values, or (where no target value is listed) by·half the inbtervention values.
3. Intervention value: Intervention values are availavble to identify serious contamination of soils and to indicate when remedial action is necessary.
4. For heavy metals, the target and intervention values are dependent on clay/silt and organic matter content, and the standard soil values must be modified by the formula:
   $$Ib = Is \ [(A + B\% \ clay/silt + C\% \ organic \ matter)] / (A + 25B + 10C)$$
   where Ib = Intervention values for a particular soil
   Is = Intervention values for a standard soils (10% organic matter and 25% clay)
   A, B, and C = compound dependent constants (Table K.7 shows the detail values)

Table K.3   Compound related constants for metals in soils

Elements	A value	B value	C value
As	15	0.4	0.4
Ba	30	5	0
Cd	0.4	0.007	0.021
Cr	50	2	0
Co	2	0.28	0
Cu	15	0.6	0.6
Hg	0.2	0.0034	0.0017
Pb	50	1	1
Mo	1	0	0
Ni	10	1	0
Zn	50	3	1.5

Table K.4   The threshold total concentration of trace elements in contaminated soils proposed by some industrialized countries

Element	Germany	France	U.K.	U.S.A.	Australia	Canada	Netherlands	Japan	Taiwan	Total
	mg/kg dry soils									
As	20	20	10	5.6	20	-	55	15	20	5.6-55
Cd	3	2	3.5	2	-	-	12	1	4	1-12
Cu	100	100	140	45	60	-	190	125	150	45-190
Cr	100	150	600	212	50	120	380	-	200	50-600
Hg	2	1	1	-	-	-	10	-	2	1-10
Ni	50	50	35	31	60	32	210	-		120
Pb	100	100	550	68	-	-	580	-	100	68-580
Zn	300	300	280	50	200	-	720	-	300	50-720

Source: Chen 1998.

Depleted Uranium in Bosnia and Herzegovina

Reference values

Internationally recognized reference values are summarized by Zueng-Sang Chen in SELECTING INDICATORS TO EVALUATE SOIL QUALITY; Department of Agricultural Chemistry National Taiwan University Taipei, 10617, Taiwan ROC, 1999-08-01.

Results

This following results are based on the Dutch target and intervention values (see above).

■ **Vogosca Ammunition Production Site**

In all selected soil samples from this site (NUC-02-030-001 to –005), high concentrations of chromium (280 – 408 mg/kg) and nickel (179 – 330 mg/kg) were recognized. The target values for these metals were exceeded by several factors. Additionally, in most of the samples the intervention values were already reached. A future detailed assessment of the situation concerning the heavy metals for this site could be considered based on these results.

■ **Kalinovik Ammunition Destruction Site**

The soil sample NUC-02-031-002 showed high contamination of zinc (1 900 mg/kg), arsenic (90 mg/kg), cadmium (6 mg/kg) and lead (1 000 mg/kg). The target values for these metals (based on the Dutch target and intervention values for soil) were exceeded by several factors. Moreover, in most of the samples the intervention values were already reached.

The other soil sample (NUC-02-031-003) showed an indication of contamination by heavy metals of the neighbouring environment. The water sample also showed heavy metals contamination.

The overall picture from this analysis suggests a detailed assessment be carried out concerning the heavy metals present at this site, the more so since it is situated in a karstic region and might be the source of streams and rivers supplying drinking water.

■ **Kalinovik region in general**

Results from the other soil samples taken at the Kalinovik water reservoir indicate that naturally high levels of Fe, Mn, Ni, Cu, Pb, etc. already exist. However, too few samples were taken to give more than an indication or come to any definite conclusion. The soil in the area is a thin layer on the limestone, residual in nature, and is formed by in situ weathering. In such soils, the concentration of metals is known to be frequently (much) higher than in the underlying limestone.

■ **Bjelasnica Plateau – Ammunition Destruction Site**

In both samples from this site (NUC-02-035-001 and -002), a high contamination of copper (in the range of 2000 mg/kg), zinc (~460-1650 mg/kg) and lead (~290-600 mg/kg) could be measured. The situation is similar to the one mentioned above for the Kalinovik ammunition destruction site. However, what is alarming in the results for this site – in addition to the lead contamination - is the very high copper concentration in the samples taken.

Specific results are presented in the tables on the following pages.

Table K.5   Water sample codes

Sample (APAT)	Sampling Site	Code	Coordinates	Sample Type
BHW01	Hadzici, Tank repair facility	UA-2003-003-001	34TBP 74215 / 56365	Water form concrete drainage well
BHW02	Hadzici, Tank repair facility	UA-2003-003-002	34TBP 74172 / 56387	Stream water
BHW03	Hadzici, Tank repair facility	UA-2003-003-003	34TBP 74172/ 56370	Well water
BHW04	Hadzici, Tank repair facility	UA-2003-003-004	34TBP 74395 / 56319	Water form concrete drainage well
BHW05	Lucavíca	UA-2003-003-005	34TBP 88560 / 55870	Public tap water
BHW06	Hadzici, Barracks	UA-2003-003-006	34TBP 75321/ 54761	Streem water
BHW07	Hadzici, Barracks	UA-2003-003-007	34TBP 75351/ 54720	Tap water
BHW08	Han Pijesak, Barracks	UA-2003-003-008	34TBP 36022 / 84309	Tap water
BHW09	Han Pijesak, Barracks	UA-2003-003-009	34TBP 35540 / 84380	Stream water
BHW10	Pale, Barracks	UA-2003-003-010	34TCP 05663 / 52318	River water
BHW11	Vogosca	UA-2003-003-011	34TBP 89407 / 65357	River water
BHW12	Vogosca	UA-2003-003-012	34TBP 90083 / 66656	Water reservoir
BHW13	Ustikolina, barracks	UA-2003-003-013	34TCP 20059 / 28289	Spring water collected from tap
BHW14	Ustikolina, barracks	UA-2003-003-014	34TCP 20245 / 27886	Spring water collected from tap
BHW15	Foca Bridge	UA-2003-003-015	34TCP 20390 / 20510	Public water from tap
BHW16	Kalinovik, Water reservoir	UA-2003-003-016	34TBP 93344/ 20528	Spring water
BHW17	Kalinovik, Ammunition destruction site	UA-2003-003-017	34TBP 91610/ 18277	Pond on the bottom of a karst hole used for blasting of ordnance
BHW18	Bjelasnica Plateau	UA-2003-003-018	34TBP 65667/ 46257	Spring water collected from tap
BHW19	Bjelasnica Plateau	UA-2003-003-019	34TBP 66591/ 45775	Stream water

Table K.6   Water sample results

Element	APAT-BHW01 [μg/L]	APAT-BHW02 [μg/L]	APAT-BHW03 [μg/L]	APAT-BHW04 [μg/L]
Li	2.2	9.0	4.8	4.4
Be	<1	<1	<1	<1
Na	6400	2600	1200	2900
Mg	14500	11400	2300	23200
Al	64	2400	183	16
K	9000	3300	4300	2100
Ca	100800	59600	26000	144000
Ti	1.3	2.3	2.6	1.3
V	0.3	1.4	0.5	0.1
Cr	<1	2.8	2.0	<1
Mn	13	94	29	1.3
Fe	240	1100	760	310
Co	0.2	1.7	0.4	0.2
Ni	<0.1	2.2	1.8	<0.1
Cu	1.3	5.2	6.9	3.0
Zn	9.1	42	706	2.5
As	0.4	0.6	3.0	0.1
Se	<1	<1	<1	<1
Sr	110	398	120	724
Mo	0.1	0.1	0.1	0.6
Ag	<0.1	<0.1	<0.1	<0.1
Cd	<0.1	0.1	0.4	0.1
Sb	0.09	0.04	0.59	0.04
Cs	0.03	0.12	0.84	0.01
Ba	56	63	43	30
Ce	0.10	1.52	0.19	0.03
W	<0.01	<0.01	<0.01	<0.01
Hg	<0.1	<0.1	<0.1	<0.1
Tl	<0.01	0.01	0.05	<0.01
Pb	3.8	9.2	9.6	1.2
Th	<0.01	0.04	0.01	0.01
U	3.2	1.2	0.85	1.3

Depleted Uranium in Bosnia and Herzegovina

K

HEAVY METALS

Element	APAT-BHW05 [µg/L]	APAT-BHW06 [µg/L]	APAT-BHW07 [µg/L]	APAT-BHW08 [µg/L]
Li	<1	<1	<1	<1
Be	<1	<1	<1	<1
Na	1000	1200	690	440
Mg	1300	23200	27100	960
Al	89	33	66	9
K	630	680	220	340
Ca	78400	66300	59800	69800
Ti	0.7	0.7	0.5	0.5
V	0.2	0.3	0.2	0.2
Cr	<1	<1	<1	<1
Mn	1.8	2.8	2.0	0.32
Fe	191	169	197	170
Co	0.1	0.1	0.1	0.1
Ni	<0.1	<0.1	<0.1	<0.1
Cu	5.2	0.6	4.4	2.1
Zn	1500	13	400	25
As	0.2	0.4	0.2	0.1
Se	<1	<1	<1	<1
Sr	35	51	56	26
Mo	0.1	<0.1	<0.1	0.1
Ag	<0.1	<0.1	<0.1	<0.1
Cd	0.2	0.1	0.2	0.1
Sb	0.17	0.07	0.12	<0.01
Cs	<0.01	0.02	0.01	<0.01
Ba	11	9	6	3
Ce	0.02	0.04	0.08	0.01
W	<0.01	<0.01	<0.01	0.01
Hg	<0.1	<0.1	<0.1	<0.1
Tl	<0.1	<0.1	<0.1	<0.1
Pb	4.8	1.7	3.3	0.81
Th	<0.01	<0.01	<0.01	<0.01
U	0.08	0.18	0.11	0.06
Element	**APAT-BHW09 [µg/L]**	**APAT-BHW10 [µg/L]**	**APAT-BHW11 [µg/L]**	**APAT-BHW12 [µg/L]**
Li	4.4	1.1	1.8	2.3
Be	<1	<1	<1	<1
Na	2600	3700	1700	2100
Mg	2900	8400	10200	10600
Al	380	314	175	13
K	2700	1500	900	940
Ca	16200	45600	61200	66800
Ti	1.2	1.2	1.1	0.9
V	0.6	0.6	0.4	0.2
Cr	<1	<1	<1	<1
Mn	50	239	5.1	2.1
Fe	288	336	231	285
Co	0.3	0.4	0.2	0.1
Ni	1.5	<0.1	<0.1	<0.1
Cu	1.6	1.4	0.9	1.6
Zn	<5	<5	<5	<5
As	0.31	0.78	0.40	0.23
Se	<1	<1	<1	<1
Sr	51	50	143	201
Mo	<0.1	<0.1	<0.1	<0.1
Ag	<0.1	<0.1	<0.1	<0.1
Cd	<0.1	<0.1	<0.1	<0.1
Sb	0.02	0.02	0.02	0.03
Cs	0.01	0.03	0.01	<0.01
Ba	18	99	35	39
Ce	0.22	0.06	0.08	0.02
W	<0.01	<0.01	<0.01	<0.01
Hg	<0.1	<0.1	<0.1	<0.1
Tl	<0.01	<0.01	<0.01	<0.01
Pb	5.6	1.3	1.3	2.6
Th	0.01	0.02	<0.01	<0.01
U	0.02	0.41	0.14	0.13

Post-Conflict Environmental Assessment

Element	APAT-BHW13 [µg/L]	APAT-BHW14 [µg/L]	APAT-BHW15 [µg/L]	APAT-BHW16 [µg/L]
Li	<1	4.6	<1	4.7
Be	<1	<1	<1	<1
Na	1700	4000	1000	490
Mg	4200	10300	9700	650
Al	8.9	23	156	45
K	280	1800	500	160
Ca	72900	36500	52600	33600
Ti	1.2	1.7	1.4	0.5
V	<0.1	<0.1	0.4	0.2
Cr	<1	<1	<1	<1
Mn	0.36	6.2	4.4	1.1
Fe	160	120	220	90
Co	0.1	0.1	0.2	0.0
Ni	<0.1	<0.1	<0.1	<0.1
Cu	0.6	4.0	11.5	0.2
Zn	<5	5.5	105	<5
As	0.23	0.56	0.12	0.10
Se	<1	<1	<1	<1
Sr	69	67	34	14
Mo	<0.1	0.12	<0.1	<0.1
Ag	<0.1	<0.1	<0.1	<0.1
Cd	<0.1	<0.1	<0.1	<0.1
Sb	0.09	0.01	<0.01	<0.01
Cs	0.07	2.5	0.01	0.01
Ba	43	14	13	2
Ce	0.01	0.02	0.12	0.06
W	<0.01	<0.01	<0.01	<0.01
Hg	<0.1	<0.1	<0.1	<0.1
Tl	<0.01	<0.01	<0.01	<0.01
Pb	0.70	1.2	0.99	3.2
Th	<0.01	<0.01	0.01	<0.01
U	0.23	0.09	0.08	0.04

Element	APAT-BHW17 [µg/L]	APAT-BHW18 [µg/L]	APAT-BHW19 [µg/L]
Li	1.9	2.0	1.2
Be	1.0	<1	<1
Na	230	2200	1300
Mg	960	6000	11200
Al	5700	6.6	52
K	970	310	530
Ca	5700	29000	37300
Ti	1.4	1.0	0.9
V	4.0	0.1	0.2
Cr	3.2	<1	<1
Mn	154	0.17	5.4
Fe	920	60	120
Co	2.0	0.8	0.1
Ni	5.0	<0.1	<0.1
Cu	8.7	0.4	2.8
Zn	18	<5	6
As	0.16	1.7	0.47
Se	<1	<1	<1
Sr	8	693	186
Mo	<0.1	0.2	0.1
Ag	<0.1	<0.1	<0.1
Cd	0.7	<0.1	<0.1
Sb	0.07	0.04	<0.01
Cs	0.09	0.55	0.16
Ba	48	124	93
Ce	10.1	<0.01	0.04
W	<0.01	<0.01	<0.01
Hg	<0.1	<0.1	<0.1
Tl	0.09	<0.01	<0.01
Pb	24	0.25	1.1
Th	0.02	<0.01	<0.01
U	0.18	0.29	0.40

Depleted Uranium in Bosnia and Herzegovina

Table K.7.1　Soil sample codes

Sample	Code	Coordinates UTM 34T
Vogosca Ammunition Production Site		
NUC-02-030-001-01	UA-2003-004-001-01	BP 88 927 / 64 949
NUC-02-030-001-02	UA-2003-004-001-02	BP 88 927 / 64 949
NUC-02-030-002-01	UA-2003-004-002-01	BP 89 334 / 65 067
NUC-02-030-002-02	UA-2003-004-002-02	BP 89 334 / 65 067
NUC-02-030-003-01	UA-2003-004-003-01	BP 89 185 / 65 195
NUC-02-030-003-02	UA-2003-004-003-01	BP 89 185 / 65 195
NUC-02-030-004-01	UA-2003-004-004-01	BP 90 088 / 66 734
NUC-02-030-004-02	UA-2003-004-004-02	BP 90 088 / 66 734
NUC-02-030-005-01	UA-2003-004-005-01	BP 91 215 / 67 689
NUC-02-030-005-02	UA-2003-004-005-02	BP 91 215 / 67 689
Kalinovik Water Reservoir Site		
NUC-02-031-001-01	UA-2003-004-006-01	BP 93 325 / 20 622
NUC-02-031-001-02	UA-2003-004-006-02	BP 93 325 / 20 622
Kalinovik - Ammunition Destruction Site		
NUC-02-031-002-01	UA-2003-004-007-01	BP 91 586 / 18 312
NUC-02-031-002-02	UA-2003-004-007-02	BP 91 586 / 18 312
NUC-02-031-003-01	UA-2003-004-008-01	BP 91 714 / 18 349
NUC-02-031-003-02	UA-2003-004-008-02	BP 91 714 / 18 349
Bjelasnica Plateau - Ammunition Destruction Site		
NUC-02-035-001-02	UA-2003-004-009-01	BP 61 932 / 42 464
NUC-02-035-001-02	UA-2003-004-009-02	BP 61 932 / 42 464
NUC-02-035-002-01	UA-2003-004-010-01	BP 61 877 / 42 288
NUC-02-035-002-02	UA-2003-004-010-02	BP 61 877 / 42 288

Table K.7.2　Results on Vogosca Soil Samples

Element	NUC-02-030-001-01 [mg/kg]	NUC-02-030-002-01 [mg/kg]	NUC-02-030-003-01 [mg/kg]	NUC-02-030-004-01 [mg/kg]	NUC-02-030-005-01 [mg/kg]
V	94	88	91	94	110
Cr	319	292	327	304	408
Mn	1150	1207	910	846	869
Fe	42000	42000	43000	41000	52000
Co	26	23	24	24	29
Ni	212	182	229	206	325
Cu	52	84	68	53	63
Zn	135	207	104	136	206
As	11	14	8.4	7.4	9.1
Sr	105	102	176	86	101
Mo	0.54	0.86	0.54	0.41	0.61
Cd	0.36	0.43	0.19	0.29	0.42
Ba	278	312	229	230	311
Pb	40	54	44	39	68
Th	8.8	8.9	6.9	7.6	8.2
U	1.6	1.7	1.7	1.4	1.6
Element	NUC-02-030-001-02 [mg/kg]	NUC-02-030-002-02 [mg/kg]	NUC-02-030-003-02 [mg/kg]	NUC-02-030-004-02 [mg/kg]	NUC-02-030-005-02 [mg/kg]
V	94	85	97	97	111
Cr	325	280	356	313	406
Mn	1146	1170	980	852	873
Fe	42000	41000	46000	41000	52000
Co	25	23	26	24	29
Ni	205	179	245	207	330
Cu	52	84	72	54	63
Zn	133	201	113	141	204
As	10	13	8.9	7.6	8.9
Sr	105	102	194	90	102
Mo	0.57	0.86	0.77	0.39	0.61
Cd	0.36	0.43	0.24	0.30	0.41
Ba	280	302	245	247	316
Pb	39	53	47	41	69
Th	8.7	8.7	7.4	7.8	8.2
U	1.6	1.6	1.8	1.4	1.6

Post-Conflict Environmental Assessment

Table K.7.3   Results on Kalinovik Soil Samples

Element	NUC-02-031 -001-01 [mg/kg]	NUC-02-031 -001-02 [mg/kg]	NUC-02-031 -002-01 [mg/kg]	NUC-02-031 -002-02 [mg/kg]	NUC-02-031 -003-01 [mg/kg]	NUC-02-031 -003-02 [mg/kg]
V	120	111	282	277	119	121
Cr	84	82	155	140	167	168
Mn	1591	1460	5708	5652	1690	1736
Fe	54000	53000	59000	54000	56000	57000
Co	17	16	23	22	24	25
Ni	58	57	95	86	87	89
Cu	35	34	57	50	109	112
Zn	185	170	1899	1873	185	192
As	26	25	90	88	26	26
Sr	58	54	60	71	60	62
Mo	1.4	1.1	2.3	2.2	1.1	1.1
Cd	3.1	2.9	6.3	6.3	3.4	3.5
Ba	321	293	330	326	323	334
Pb	112	88	987	984	202	212
Th	21.3	20.0	13.4	13.4	20.4	21.1
U	4.3	4.3	3.1	2.9	2.8	2.8

Table K.7.4   Results on Bjelasnica Plateau Soil Samples

Element	NUC-02-035-001-01 [mg/kg]	NUC-02-035-001-02 [mg/kg]	NUC-02-035-002-01 [mg/kg]	NUC-02-035-002-02 [mg/kg]
V	66	70	85	82
Cr	86	91	91	90
Mn	1410	1502	1417	1357
Fe	44000	48000	46000	44000
Co	16.2	17.2	16.0	15.5
Ni	<5	<5	<5	<5
Cu	2027	2087	1768	1917
Zn	1653	1596	477	459
As	20.5	22.1	21.1	21.2
Sr	43.3	46.2	49.4	48.0
Mo	2.4	2.5	1.8	2.2
Cd	20	17.5	4.6	4.6
Ba	247	268	274	266
Pb	603	602	292	286
Th	10.1	10.9	12.9	12.5
U	1.5	1.6	2.2	2.1

K.4   STATISTICAL AND MEASUREMENT UNCERTAINTY

From each sample one analysis was performed. The analytical procedure was controlled by analysing of the Standard Reference Materials ISE 954 ¨Clay soil from Turkey¨ and IAEA-326 ¨Radionuclides in soil¨. Based on these control measurements an uncertainty (p=0.95) of ± 10% was estimated for the results.

Experimental details are available in STS 101 Testing Service "Determination of main and trace elements, their compounds and selected air-pollutants".

Depleted Uranium in Bosnia and Herzegovina

Appendix L
WHO Assessment of the information on cancer in Bosnia and Herzegovina

The assessment presented here of the information on cancer in Bosnia and Herzegovina (BiH) was developed by the WHO as a contribution to the wider UNEP mission to assess depleted uranium (DU) in BiH, which took place on 12-24 October 2002. A health consultant to UNEP, coming from the US Army Center for Health Promotion and Preventive Medicine (USACHPPM), accompanied the WHO in the visits and meetings that were part of the health assessment.

L.1 VISITS

Visits were made to the cities of Sarajevo (in both the Federation of Bosnia and Herzegovina (FBiH) and Republika Srpska (RS)), and Banja Luka.

In Sarajevo (FBiH) the team met with:

- Clinicians and the director of the Clinical Centre, University of Sarajevo, including those persons developing an in-hospital cancer registry;
- A representative of the Institute of Public Health of the FBiH (present at the meeting in the university hospital);
- The group in the Federal Institute of Public Health, who is starting a population based cancer registry for the FBiH;
- The Federal Statistics Agency (which collects information on population, births and deaths by age, sex and cause for the FBiH); and
- WHO liaison office.

In Sarajevo (RS) the team met with:

- Clinicians and director of the Clinical Centre Kasindo.

In Banja Luka the team met with:

- Minister of Health for Republika Srpska (RS);
- Clinicians from oncology and other departments; and
- Persons responsible for the Banja Luka cancer registry.

A visit to the town of Bratunac was planned but transferred to a later date by the organisers, to be undertaken by the UNEP health consultant.

L.2 BACKGROUND

What diseases might be associated to DU, and how strong is the evidence? What health impacts could we expect to find in BiH if it were confirmed that there had been relevant exposure to DU?

Health effects would depend on the route and magnitude of exposure (ingestion, inhalation, contact or in wounds) and the characteristics of the DU (such as particle size and solubility). The potential effects of DU on human health could be due to its chemical form that enters the body, which could lead to both chemical and radiological effects.

In terms of chemical toxicity, uranium can cause kidney damage in experimental animals, and some studies in humans also suggest that long-term exposure may result in pathological damage to kidneys. The types of damage that have been observed are nodular changes to the surface of the kidney, lesions to the tubular epithelium and increased levels of glucose and protein in the urine.

Radiological toxicity comes from DU decay, mainly through emission of alpha particles. These particles do not have the ability to penetrate the skin. However, if ingested or inhaled, they may have an effect on lung or gut epithelium. Exposure to alpha and beta radiation from inhaled insoluble DU particles may, in principle, lead to lung tissue damage and increase the probability of lung cancer. Similarly, absorption into the blood and retention in other organs, in particular the skeleton, is assumed to carry an additional risk of cancer in these organs. In all such cases any additional risk of cancer will depend on the severity of radiation exposure. At low levels of exposure to radiation, the additional risk of cancer is thought to be very low.

- Depleted uranium and uranium are essentially the same, except that the content of ^{235}U is three times lower in DU. Consequently, DU is less radioactive than natural uranium and, thus, a radiation dose from it would be about 60% lower than that from purified natural uranium with the same mass. It is assumed that prior knowledge from scientific (experimental, clinical and epidemiological) studies on uranium can be applied to DU.

- Up to now no adverse health effects of DU have been established in the limited epidemiological studies that have been undertaken. DU may, in principle, cause both nephrotoxic effects and internal exposure to radiation (through inhalation, or wounds contaminated with DU). However, these have not yet been confirmed.

- No consistent or confirmed adverse chemical effects of uranium have been reported for the skeleton or liver. No reproductive or developmental effects have been confirmed in humans.

- In a number of studies on uranium miners, an increased risk of lung cancer was demonstrated, but this has been attributed to exposure from radon decay products. Because DU is only weakly radioactive, very large amounts of dust (in the order of grams) would have to be inhaled for the additional risk of lung cancer to be detectable in an exposed group.

- Risks for other radiation-induced cancers, including leukaemia, are considered to be very much lower than for lung cancer.

- However, evidence is inadequate to completely dismiss an association with lymphatic and bone cancer, even though most studies have shown no effect. Veterans from the 1991 Gulf war who have had DU fragments in their soft tissues since the Gulf war are excreting raised uranium concentration, but neither increased rates of lung and bone cancers nor of leukaemias have been detected among them.

As the current debate on the possible adverse effects of potential DU contamination has focused on cases of leukaemia in the military, it is important to assess the known facts regarding leukaemia and DU. While ionising radiation is known to cause leukaemia, the risk is proportional to the level of radiation exposure. Such exposure from DU is calculated to be low.

Even in war zones under extreme conditions and shortly after the impact of penetrators, the inhalation and ingestion of DU contaminated dust, as determined by the amount of dust that can be inhaled, has been calculated to result in a radiation exposure of less than

10 millisieverts, which represents around half the annual dose limit for radiation workers. Such an exposure is thought to result in only a small proportional increase in the risk of leukaemia, of the order of 2% over the natural incidence of the disease. This increase in the incidence rate is so low that it is fully covered by the annual fluctuation of the background (natural) occurrence of this disease. Furthermore, no increase in leukaemia could be observed in uranium miners, or in workers milling uranium for nuclear reactor fuel elements. Finally, a minimum of ten years is usually needed between exposure to ionising radiation and a clinical manifestation of cancers (i.e. a longer period than the time since the conflict in BiH).

From the existing knowledge of DU and its health impacts, and assuming that a large enough group of the population may have had sufficient exposure to DU, it appears unlikely that any significant increase in cancers and leukaemia would be observed in the elapsed time since the armed conflict.

L.3 MISSION FINDINGS REGARDING DATA ON CANCER IN BiH

This part of the mission and its related report addresses the question of whether there are changes in the frequency of cancers in BiH and, if so, could these changes be attributed to DU or other factors. It examined the existing cancer and population information systems as well as the results they are producing. In addition, it listened to the observations and concerns of clinicians, health experts and others regarding cancers and its possible causes. The findings and conclusions follow.

L.3.1 The information systems on cancers and population in BiH

In order to identify whether a change in the frequency of a disease exists, the number of cases of that disease and the population producing those disease cases over time needs to be established.

During this mission, the available data on the population and their migration patterns was reviewed, as well as on mortality by cause and incidence of cancers, which is needed in order to estimate disease frequencies. It was observed that there are major uncertainties in the information that was provided and necessary to estimate disease frequency in the population.

a. Information on population and on migration.

The population of BiH was last recorded in the 1991 census. The FBiH Statistics Office is calculating estimates of population starting in 1996. Models are based on the following data sources:

- the 1991 census data;
- lists of individuals prepared by the municipalities for the allocation of humanitarian aid (overestimates) available for 1996, 1997 and 1998;
- vital statistics – births, deaths, marriages, from 1996;
- data on refugees (people returning to BiH) prepared by UNHCR; and
- data on persons displaced by the war (mostly those coming into BiH) from 1997.

Very recently, the Organization for Security and Co-operation in Europe (OSCE) prepared a registration list for each municipality for voting in the general elections. They used the 1991 census and invited persons aged 18 and over to confirm that they were still in BiH and where they wanted their vote to be placed. The list is believed to include an element of error (people dead still included, etc.) of perhaps around 10%, but there are no exact estimates of this error. In the future this information should feed into the population size calculations.

Large-scale migration and population movements occurred both during and after the armed conflict and are believed to continue to occur at the present time. There is limited information on this as the International Organization for Migration (IOM) is not working on migration in BiH, but focusing rather on trafficking. Records of migration to different European countries show similar numbers of people returning to BiH and people going from BiH to the same countries. No records for migration in and around BiH are available. It would therefore be difficult to make assumptions on how many people may have been in a potentially contaminated area at a given time.

In conclusion, the information on population and migration remains incomplete and uncertain. This limits the capacity to adequately calculate the frequency of disease adjusted per population. The modelling work being developed by the Statistics Office of the FBiH is encouraging and should be supported. It is providing estimates of the population in FBiH for the last two years. Similar work in the RS should also be encouraged.

b. Information on cause of death and on diseases

Information systems that report on disease occurrence are beginning to be re-established, along with the reconstruction of the health system. Morbidity and mortality data will be collected at the municipal level and forwarded to the regional and central Institute of Public Health (IPH) for analyses and dissemination of results. Still, there are difficulties with the regular transfer of information from hospitals to IPH, and provision of feedback and results to the regions and to the health institutions providing the original data. Reporting of communicable diseases began around Spring 2002, and reports on maternal and child health is being prepared.

Death and birth certificates

Municipalities collect death and birth certificates. The Institute of Statistics of FBiH regularly reporting statistics on cause of death from death certification since 1999. Recently, the death certificates of people dying during the war period were included into the electronic system, but births registered during the war had not yet been included.

In conclusion, both determination of and reporting of deaths and diseases still have many limitations. These can be overcome with targeted efforts to facilitate ongoing and emerging initiatives to set up reporting and information systems.

Information on Cancers

Cancer diagnosis and information flow:

In FBiH, patients with a suspected cancer are referred by their local doctor to one of the regional hospitals and then to the University Clinic in Sarajevo for diagnosis and treatment. Cases referred to the regional hospital in Tuzla are included in the Tuzla cancer registry. Cases arriving at the University Clinic in Sarajevo are included in the intra-hospital cancer registry, i.e. only a portion of the cancer cases are registered in the Federation of Bosnia and Herzegovina.

In the RS, suspected cases of cancer are referred for clinical and pathology diagnosis and treatment to the clinical centres in Banja Luka and Sarajevo (RS). A part of the patients with cancer living in the eastern part of RS go directly to Belgrade for diagnosis and treatment. Suspected cases from the population displaced from Hadzici to Bratunac are referred to Sarajevo (RS). These pathology laboratories have television connection with Belgrade to review diagnosis and compare slides. When necessary, samples of tissue are sent to Belgrade for a second opinion. These centres provide surgical treatments and chemotherapy but do

Depleted Uranium in Bosnia and Herzegovina

not have radiotherapy. Patients needing chemotherapy are referred to Belgrade. The ministry has requested radiotherapy equipment from the IAEA to be installed in Banja Luka. All cancer diagnosis and treatments are paid for by the Health Insurance Fund.

Cancer registries:

In FBiH, one population-based cancer registry and one intra-hospital cancer registry have recently been implemented. An initiative to extend coverage of cancer registration to the whole FBiH was to start in January 2003.

The plan to establish a population-based cancer registry following international standards in FBiH is part of a World Bank funded health system development project. The registry will be based at the Federal Institute of Public Health in Sarajevo, with a stated start date in January 2003 following the appointment of a project leader. An international consultant has made an assessment and recommendations. The links with mortality statistics have been successfully established. However, links with clinicians, oncologists and pathologists have not yet been made.

The intra-hospital cancer registry is for patients which have been seen at the University Clinic in Sarajevo University Hospital, the reference hospital for all FBiH. The oncologists based there would like to use their information to develop a cancer-based registry.

The Canton of Tuzla has had a population-based cancer registry operating for three years, following international standards. This is reported to be working well and has been supported by a Soros Foundation grant.

Issues in implementation of a population-based cancer registry for FBiH:

- **Achieving good coverage.** Coverage is partial. With the exception of the Canton of Tuzla, there is a need to expand coverage for all 10 Cantons. Mechanisms to ensure cancer information is sent to the registry need to be in place, also in view of the continuing population movement. The external consultant has suggested enacting legislation to establish the cancer registry and requiring collaboration of different parties. In addition, the need for establishing good collaboration with clinicians and pathologists should be emphasized. A specific strategy for that should be developed.

- **Ensuring good data linkage.** ID numbers are not yet included in death certificates (all persons in FBiH have a unique ID number and card). Doctors completing the death certificate could be required to enter the persons ID. This would facilitate linkage with cancer registry.

- **Continuing the improvements in population estimates.** The uncertainties with population information will continue as a census is not envisaged (counts of ethnic groups and their location are seen as a sensitive issue). The models being developed should continue to be improved.

- **New cancer registry should follow international standards** and data entry software (IARC).

In the Republika Srpska, the IPH had set up a cancer registry with its own resources a year prior to the UNEP mission. The registry follows IARC methodology. The information entered in the registry comes from all the clinical centres in the RS. Information from death certificates is not yet being included in the registry, but there is a space in the computerized from to include it, and plans to begin doing that. The Cancer Registry (CR) forms a part of the European association of CRs. It relies on two enthusiastic staff members who have not had any external training but are using the IARC cancer registration software. Furthermore, they have an understanding of the issues of cancer registration (e.g. related to coverage, reporting, the need to avoid duplication of entries, use of repeated information as a mechanism to complete missing data, etc).

Issues for the improvement of cancer registration in Republika Srpska:

- **There is a need to include death certification information in the registry.** The death certification office is apparently reluctant to release that information. This issue needs to be addressed.

- **There are difficulties in obtaining the information back from Belgrade** related to patients diagnosed or treated in one of the various hospitals there. The ministry has agreements for exchange of information with only two of those hospitals.

- **Possible ways to improve this information exchange include** a) to make an agreement with the Belgrade cancer registry for the transfer of information of patients who live in RS and are included in the Belgrade Cancer registry; b) to link the payment for the diagnosis and treatment in Belgrade hospitals for patients from the RS health fund to sending information to the Cancer Registry in Banja Luka.

- **A large proportion of the RS health budget is being used to pay for cancer diagnosis and treatment abroad** (largely Belgrade). Possible solutions to address that issue should also ensure that the resulting information is sent to the Banja Luka registry

In conclusion, information on cancers is incomplete, but improving. In particular, the cancer registries aimed at establishing complete ascertainment of cancers and to avoid double counting have been set up in parts of FBiH and in the RS. These efforts to extend coverage of cancer registries are positive and should be supported.

Issues that need to be further addressed include: Linking up with mortality information; exchange of information on diagnosis and treatment across borders; engaging the collaboration and participation of clinicians and pathologists with the cancer registry; continued improvements of population estimates, and to begin regular reporting of cancer information.

Information on numbers of cancers

The WHO was shown counts of the numbers of cancer patients attending three health facilities. These included one each in both FBiH and RS Sarajevo, and in Banja Luka.

The Clinical Centre of the University of Sarajevo had a collection of papers from a meeting held in March 2002, with abstracts in English, showing an increasing number of patients are being diagnosed with cancers in a variety of organs (lung, skin, breast, thyroid), and in the clinics of gastroenterology, paediatric surgery, and neurosurgery. The papers identify the limitations of developing time trends with that type of data, including: the important changes in the population making use of this clinic; loss of records during the period of war (1992-96); the possibility of double counting; and the recent improvement in diagnostic facilities. Authors point out the need for a cancer registry as a means to address those problems. (Ladislav Ozegovic, Dzemal Rezakovic, Jela Vasic-Grujic, 2002)

The Kasindol Clinical Centre in Sarajevo (RS) had prepared a table with yearly counts of cancer diagnosis made at the centre between 1995 and 2001 (the format was table typewritten, in the local language, with ICD code categories provided). All ages were grouped in these counts, which show that more diagnoses have been made in the later years, for all types of cancers (presented in nine broad diagnostic groups). Considering that there is substantial migration and changes in the population receiving medical attention in this centre, it is possible that they may be receiving more people or an older population for diagnosis and treatment. That by itself could explain the larger number of cases diagnosed more recently in this clinic. The staff and individuals met were not familiar with the limitations of the data they had collected.

The Banja Luka clinic had counts of new cancer cases per year (all ages and all types of cancer) diagnosed between 1993–2000. They show a decline in 1994, and a gradual increase back to 1993 numbers by 1999. A similar pattern could be seen for colorectal cancer in men and in women (lower counts between 1996 and 1998). There is an increase in the number of lung cancer cases in females and in breast cancers diagnosed in Banja Luka in that period (Sasa Jungic; Branislava Jakovljevic; Ivanka Rakita et al., no date).

No reliable information on cancer rates and trends exist in either FBiH or RS. Consequently, no conclusions can be made on whether there is any change in frequency of cancers. Claims of increases in many types of cancers were made by physicians based on clinical observations both in FBiH and in RS. These were not substantiated by information on cancer rates, which relate the number of cases to the population these cases come from. Some of these clinicians are fully aware of the limitations of the data they are collecting and are interested in the development of cancer registries to address that discrepancy. Other clinicians are not aware of such limitations.

L.3.2 Concern about suspected increases in the number of cancers and their potential link with DU

There is concern with the clinical reports of increases in cancers, and the suggestion that this would be due to DU. The parliament in RS has established a committee to investigate a link with DU and is requesting action by the government to solve the problem. It asked the Ministry of Health for a clarification on this matter. The Minister of Health would like support from international agencies to proceed scientifically and address these claims with adequate methods and come up with a reliable answer. He argued that there is a need to clarify whether there are changes in cancer frequency, and if so their aetiology; if from chemicals, food, Chernobyl or other radiation, DU, stress, or a combination of those factors.

The Institute of Public Health in FBiH has similar concerns, as stated in their report on the Health Status of the Population and Health Care System in Transition (2001).

The lack of awareness about causes of error in interpretation of clinical findings, and basic epidemiology by some of the clinicians, is contributing to the concern mentioned above as the media reports these both nationally and internationally.

There is a good consensus in the BiH of the need to study the matter adequately, and the initiatives to develop cancer registration are a good demonstration of that.

L.4 RECOMMENDATIONS

1. Support for the authorities is needed in identifying whether there are any changes in cancers, and to help characterize any such changes, including through the further development and extension of coverage of cancer registers. Existing initiatives on cancer registration, cancer diagnosis and treatment and those to improve estimates of population should continue to be developed and improved.

2. Support for the authorities is needed in identifying whether there are significant exposures to DU and other war related environmental risks and, if so, help establish protective measures.

3. Build local capacity in clinical, environmental and cancer epidemiology, and the capacity to interpret health information coming from both clinics and registries.

4. Develop descriptive epidemiological studies to respond to questions of changes in frequency and distribution of cancers in the population.

5. Develop analytical epidemiological studies to investigate the potential contribution of risk factors including environmental risks and DU exposure, as well as other risk factors, to certain types of cancer.

6. The analytical studies mentioned above would require the development of methodologies to estimate exposures to potential risk factors under evaluation that would consider the population moves observed in BiH over the relevant time period for those studies.

7. Facilitate the development of co-operation in the above activities between FBiH and RS researchers and cancer registries, as exchange of information is likely to be necessary to achieve the above goals. Furthermore, studies of rare cancers may require cases from both sides in order to have adequate capacity to respond to the study question.

8. Support for the authorities is needed in the development of a risk communication strategy regarding the measures being taken, and eventual findings

WHO ASSESSMENT

Appendix M
Storage of radioactive waste and depleted uranium residues in Bosnia and Herzegovina

M.1 INTRODUCTION

Since 1997, UNEP and the International Atomic Energy Agency (IAEA) have established a good working relationship and have been involved on a number of projects together, including the two previous UNEP DU assessments. One of the tasks assigned to the UNEP team for this mission was to conduct an investigation of the regulatory and technical infrastructure the country has in place concerning the storage of radioactive waste and, in particular, DU residues. As part of this task, the IAEA representative, accompanied by a UNEP team member, carried out a series of meetings with national authorities and visited the interim low-level radioactive waste storage facility of the Federation of Bosnia and Herzegovina. This Appendix describes the outcome of this investigation.

M.2 GENERAL OVERVIEW OF THE RADIATION PROTECTION INFRASTRUCTURE IN BIH

M.2.1 Organisational infrastructure

At the end of the war, the legal framework in the area of radiation safety was essentially the same as that existing in the former Yugoslavia. The main legal instrument in force was a basic 'Law on Protection against Ionising Radiation' supplemented by a number of regulations. These regulations were produced in 1977 and were inconsistent with most recent international standards, including the IAEA's International Basic Safety Standards (IAEA, 1996).

The division of Bosnia and Herzegovina following the Dayton Peace Agreement into two administratively independent and separate entities, the Federation of Bosnia and Herzegovina (FBiH) and the Republika Srpska (RS), affects regulatory control in the area of health and the environment, including ionising radiation which comes under the remit of the Ministries of Health.

In FBiH, work began in 1997 with the assistance of the IAEA for the preparation of a new legal framework consistent with the new political and administrative situation and in line with the IAEA's International Basic Safety Standards (IAEA, 1996). The new 'Law on Radiation Protection and Radiation Safety', establishing the bases for the new regulatory system, was approved by Parliament in 1999. However, the modification and updating of existing regulations necessary for the practical implementation of the law are still ongoing.

According to the new law, the regulatory powers and responsibilities for radiation and waste safety are attributed to a Federal Administration for Radiation Protection and Radiation Safety (FRPA) of FBiH, an independent department within the Ministry of Health. The FPRA mainly has regulatory responsibilities but also carries out a number of operational tasks, such as personal dosimetry, radioactive waste management, and emergency management. FRPA receives technical support from the Centre for Radiation Protection of the National Institute of Public Health (CRP).

Because of the division of the country into two administratively separate entities (FBiH and RS), the legal framework currently developed in FBiH is not applied in the RS. Similarly the FRPA only has authority in the FBiH.

The regulatory structure in the RS is similar to the one in place in the FBiH, with a Radiation Protection Department operating within the Public Health Institute, which is part of the Ministry of Health. However, the FBiH has received support from the IAEA since the end of the conflict, whereas the RS has only recently benefited from the IAEA's assistance programmes. Consequently, the radiation safety infrastructure in RS is less developed than in FBiH and still inadequate to deal with the requirements of the implementation of a safety regime.

M.2.2 Radioactive sources and radioactive waste safety in BiH

Although there are no nuclear facilities in BiH, a large number of radioactive sources and radiation generators previously existed in the country. These were used in medicine (diagnostic radiography, cancer radiotherapy and nuclear medicine) industry (industrial radiography), research and teaching establishments. Radioactive lightning rods and smoke detectors were also commonly used in the country. The IAEA has estimated that the inventory of radioactive sources and radiation generators was as follows:

- 430 diagnostic X-ray machines used in medical and dental practices;
- more than 20 radioactive sources used in radiotherapy;
- 5 nuclear medicine laboratories;
- 40 X-ray machines used in industry;
- between 120 and 150 radioactive sources used in industry;
- 26 radioactive sources used in defectoscopy (non-destructive testing);
- 535 radioactive lightning rods; and
- about 30,000 radioactive smoke detectors.

During the war, a large number of these sources were destroyed, damaged, lost or removed without proper registration. Afterwards, only a limited number of new sources were acquired, including a new Co-60 source for a teletherapy unit and some Ir-192 sources for industrial use.

One of the priorities of the new Regulatory Body created in FBiH in the aftermath of the war was the identification, recovery and, whenever necessary, safe storage or disposal of these sources. This issue is of high urgency because of the risks associated with the potential exposure to these sources of workers engaged in the reconstruction or repair of damaged buildings and facilities containing these sources, or of the general public who could come in contact with sources or their parts. In many cases, the IAEA found that insufficient attention was given to the protection of people (repair workers, rescue teams, members of the public) who could be inadvertently exposed to radiation and/or contamination by these sources.

Considerable effort was made by the FRPA, with the assistance of the IAEA, to tackle this problem. In January 1997, the IAEA initiated an ad-hoc Project for 'Radiation Sources Search and Rescue in War-Affected Areas', with the participation of the CRP of the FBiH and the Hazardous Waste Management Agency (APO) of Croatia. The situation, however, remains far from being satisfactory. Although comprehensive records of the sources existed before the war, the new national registry of sources is still incomplete, with confusing and inconsistent data still needing to be clarified. The lack of collaboration between the two regulatory bodies in FBiH and RS makes it practically impossible to have a complete picture of the current inventory of sources over the whole BiH.

According to the information provided to the IAEA in 1999, roughly 60% of the sources

Depleted Uranium in Bosnia and Herzegovina

identified in the FBiH were entered into the national inventory kept at the CRP. The validity of this estimate is questionable, as the numbers for some types of sources (lightning rods, smoke detectors) given for the FBiH are the same as the total number of those sources existing in the whole of BiH before the war. Furthermore, other information indicated that a substantial fraction, if not the majority, of those sources were, in fact, in the territory which is now part of the RS.

Due to the current absence of nuclear installations, no significant amount of radioactive waste from regulated practices is generated in BiH. The only radioactive waste produced comes from the disposal of obsolete radioactive sources, particularly the large numbers of lightning rods and smoke detectors. The safe storage of these sources is therefore the main priority of the CRP in the area of radioactive waste.

Shelling during the war had damaged the radioactive storage facility that had previously been used for these purposes for 15 years. An inspection by the IAEA showed that the building was unsafe in view of the gamma radiation levels inside and around the storage facility and of the risk of contamination spreading to the surrounding populated area in the event of an accident. The selection of an adequate waste storage facility to replace the old one was an important part of early IAEA activities in support to the FBiH. The two possible sites originally suggested by the CRP (a former WWII bunker located within an industrial site of the Energoinvest complex and an old, unused railway tunnel 35 km south of Sarajevo) could not be converted due to opposition by the workers at the industrial site and the significant investment involved to convert the railway tunnel into a radioactive storage. In the end, the authorities decided to build a new, interim low-level radioactive waste storage facility in a police complex in the vicinity of the Sarajevo airport, a few kilometres outside the city centre. The interim waste storage facility was completed in 2000 and is now operational.

M.2.3 Control of public exposure to radiation

Control of public exposures, through an environmental monitoring programme, is one of the responsibilities of the new regulatory body (FRPA).

The Institute of Hygiene and Environmental Protection of the Medical Faculty in Sarajevo have carried out some environmental monitoring activities, whereas the Department of Radiology of the Veterinary Faculty appeared to have carried out some control of foodstuffs.

However, this area of work is affected by the same deficiencies (shortage of staff, inadequacy of resources, lack of regulations) that have hindered all activities of the CRP. With the exception of a limited amount of external radiation monitoring carried out at the university, no activities are carried out to ensure the protection of members of the public in areas accessible to them and where radiation and/or contamination risks may exist. This involves not only the possible exposure to sources used in hospitals or in industrial radiography sites, as in any other country, but also the higher risk of exposure to damaged, abandoned or uncontrolled sources as a result of the war disruption.

M.3   FINDINGS OF THE UNEP MISSION

M.3.1 Federation of Bosnia and Herzegovina

On 16 October 2002, the IAEA representative held a meeting with the Director of the Federal Administration for Radiation Protection and Radioactive Security in order to collect information on the overall situation related to radiation safety in the FBiH.

During the meeting, the Director confirmed that work to strengthen the radiation safety infrastructure in order to comply with IAEA's international standards began just after the end of the conflict. He indicated that, since 1997, good collaboration had been established with the IAEA and that the initial shared activities focused on the management of sealed radiation sources in areas affected by the war. He added that substantial progress had been made towards establishing regulations complying with international standards as outlined in the IAEA-TECDOC-1067 (IAEA, 1999) and that the next step would be implementation of regulations for exemption, notification and licensing of radioactive sources. The Director expressed regret for a lack of close collaboration with its counterpart in the RS.

According to the Administration, the most common radioactive sources found in the territory include sources used in hospitals for radiotherapy (Co-60 and brachitherapy sources) and nuclear medicine, lightning rods (containing Eu-152), smoke detectors, as well as sources for industrial radiography (containing Ir-192).

The UNEP mission visited the FBiH's low-level radioactive waste storage facility on 22 October 2002, accompanied by two staff members of the Department of Radiation Protection of the Federal Institute of Public Health. The recently built facility was found to be in very good condition and conforms to the current international safety standards for this type of facility. The staff working at the facility are being trained by the IAEA in areas related to the treatment and conditioning of radioactive waste, as well as radiation protection in general. The staff members appear to have sufficient basic knowledge and expertise to operate the storage facility in a safe and effective way.

The building used as a storage facility is a concrete structure of fairly modest dimensions (approximately 4 m long x 3 m wide and 4 m high). It is, for the time being, more than adequate for the current requirements of storing radioactive materials found in the territory of the FBiH (such as industrial radiography gauges, lightning rods, smoke alarms). An additional fence within the external perimeter fence around the complex encloses the construction. It is under constant police surveillance in order to restrict access. Dose rates measured at the fence are of the order of a few millisieverts per hour ($\mu Sv/h$), rising to about 15 $\mu Sv/h$ in proximity of the building. No particular problems have been experienced by staff members when dealing with the radioactive materials located within the storage facility.

Adjacent to the storage facility, a new building is under construction and will be used as a treatment and conditioning facility for radioactive waste. The construction has not yet been completed due to lack of funds. Authorities of the FBiH are seeking the technical and financial support of the IAEA to proceed with its construction. Once completed, this facility will provide a valuable contribution to the safe disposal of radioactive waste and the authorities of the FBiH should be encouraged to direct their efforts at completing its construction.

M.3.2 Republika Srpska

On 18 October 2002, the IAEA representative met with representatives of the Public Health Institute as part of the UNEP's visit to the Ministry of Health of the Republika Srpska (see Appendix L). The main counterpart at the meeting was the Director of the Radiation Protection Department.

The Director provided information on the general institutional radiation protection structure within the RS and informed UNEP that legislation complying with IAEA's international standards for the protection against ionising radiation was adopted in 2001. Resources, both financial and human, are limited and the work of the Radiation Protection Department is mainly focused on the screening of X-ray machines. The Department needs dosimeters and equipment to carry out environmental monitoring. According to the Public Health Institute, there are approximately 600 sources, including 250 X-ray machines, 5 CT machines, and approximately 50 dental X-ray machines, as well as sources for industrial radiography, lightning rods,

and smoke alarms. The Department carries out the inspection of these machines, but at the moment there is no operating facility for the storage of radioactive waste in the RS. In recent years, a fruitful collaboration has been established with the Vinca Institute of Nuclear Sciences in Belgrade, but legal difficulties prevent the return of some of these radioactive sources to the Vinca Institute.

The preferred option by the authorities of the RS is the construction of a local storage facility for the safe disposal of low-level radioactive waste. A suitable site has been identified in an area under the control of the Army of the RS in the south of the country, but funds are needed to carry out the project. The Radiation Protection Department has benefited in the last couple of years from financial, technical and training support provided by the IAEA. In 2002, the Department submitted four projects to the IAEA with a request for funds, and another proposal for the construction of a radioactive waste storage facility will be submitted in 2003.

M.4   STORAGE OF RESIDUES OF DEPLETED URANIUM IN BiH

Throughout discussions with national authorities on the situation concerning the storage of radioactive waste in BiH, the UNEP Team sought information on the recovery and storage of depleted uranium residues. The authorities indicated that no residues of DU had been recovered or were currently stored in any facility. At the end of the mission, fragments of DU penetrators found during UNEP's investigations of attacked sites were handed over to the authorities of the FBiH for their safe disposal.

M.5   CONCLUSIONS AND RECOMMENDATIONS

1. Commendable efforts have been made in establishing an institutional radiation protection framework in BiH since the end of the conflict. Considering the limited resources available, the achieved results are encouraging. Nonetheless, further effort is necessary in order to improve the radiation safety infrastructure of the country. BiH is currently receiving technical support from the IAEA, through the programme of the Technical Co-operation Department. Continued IAEA support should ensure that the radiation safety infrastructure of the country is strengthened. This programme includes 8 national and 9 regional projects covering different aspects of radiation protection, including control and prevention of illicit trafficking of nuclear and radioactive materials, monitoring of radioactivity in the environment, management of sealed radiation sources in areas affected by war, and technologies for managing radioactive wastes.

2. The existence of two separate legal frameworks and regulatory authorities in the two entities in which Bosnia and Herzegovina was divided after the war (FBiH and RS) results in a duplication of services and activities which is particularly inappropriate in view of the shortage of resources available. The lack of co-operation between the two radiation protection organizations created is also cause for concern and negatively affects the establishment and implementation of an efficient radiation safety regime in BiH. The solution to this issue goes beyond the mandate of the IAEA. However, efforts should be made at the international level to foster a closer collaboration between the organizations responsible for radiation safety in BiH.

3. The low-level radioactive waste storage facility of the FBiH provides an adequate facility for the safe storage of radioactive waste in the territory of the FBiH, including depleted uranium residues. The facility has been recently built and meets the necessary technological requirements for the safe storage of radioactive waste. The storage facility is surrounded by a fence and is located within police property under constant surveillance; access to the area is restricted. All these measures guarantee that good control is exercised

over the facility. The completion of the treatment and conditioning facility for radioactive waste next to the storage facility will improve the capability of the Centre for Radiation Protection to deal with radioactive waste. Unfortunately, no storage facility for low-level radioactive waste is currently operational in the Republika Srpska, although progress has been made to identify a possible location where the facility could be built. The authorities indicated that they will seek the technical and financial support of the IAEA to proceed with the construction of a storage facility. The effort of the authorities of the RS in completing this project should be encouraged and supported by the IAEA.

4. The issue of the storage of DU residues in BiH should be dealt with the wider context of the safe disposal of radioactive waste within the country. Priority should be given to the storage and eventual disposal of obsolete radioactive sources, such as industrial sources, lightning rods and smoke detectors. Efforts should be directed particularly at the recovery and safe storage or disposal of the significant number of radioactive sources remaining, which were lost or damaged during the war. The risks from potential exposure to these sources are significantly higher than those from exposure to DU residues. Nevertheless, the authorities should be alerted to the presence of residues of depleted uranium on the territory of BiH and made aware of the remedial actions proposed by the UNEP mission.

5. While normal environmental monitoring is not a high priority for BiH where there are no significant sources of radioactive discharges from facilities, the problem of monitoring radiation and radioactive contamination in areas affected by the war is a severe one and it necessitates particular attention in view of the risk of 'potential exposures'.

Depleted Uranium in Bosnia and Herzegovina

Appendix N

Military use of DU

N.1 MILITARY SOURCES OF DEPLETED URANIUM

Depleted uranium has multiple uses by military forces. One of its uses, as in the civilian sector, is to serve as counter-ballast in both aircraft and missiles. However, not all counter-ballasts are made of depleted uranium. Because of its high density (19.0 g/cm^3) and resistance to penetration by anti-armour munitions, depleted uranium can also be used in the armour of tanks, although not all tanks have depleted uranium armour.

Depleted uranium is also used in anti-armour munitions and has several properties that make it ideal for this purpose. For example, when a depleted uranium penetrator hits armour, the rod begins to self-sharpen, thereby enhancing its ability to pierce the armour. Since DU is pyrophoric, during this self-sharpening the depleted uranium forms an aerosol, creating fine DU particles that may burn. The amount of depleted uranium which forms as an aerosol will depend upon the munition, the nature of the impact, and the type of target (i.e. whether it is an armoured vehicle or not). Both tanks and aircraft can fire depleted uranium munitions, with tanks firing larger calibre rounds (105 mm and 120 mm) and the aircraft firing smaller calibre rounds (25 mm and 30 mm).

Many of the world's armies possess, or are thought to possess, DU munitions (RAND, 1999). Depleted uranium munitions are conventional weapons and have been used in warfare. As such, these munitions are readily available on the open market to other armies. Munitions containing DU were used in Iraq during the 1991 Gulf War, as well as in Bosnia and Herzegovina (BiH) in 1994-1995. In the 1999 Kosovo conflict, NATO A-10 aircraft also used 30 mm DU munitions at targeted sites, and depleted uranium munitions were fired at sites in southern Serbia and Montenegro. NATO confirmed that over 30 000 rounds of DU had been used in Kosovo, more than 2,500 rounds in Serbia and 300 rounds in Montenegro (UNEP, 2000). In BiH, NATO information states that the numbers of DU rounds fired at any one target range from 120 to 2400, with a total number of confirmed rounds standing at 6 230 although the exact number remains unknown (see Appendix P). According to NATO/KFOR information provided to UNMIK, the mixture comprised 5 DU rounds per 8 fired (KFOR, 2000). Nothing indicates that a different mixture was used in BiH.

The effectiveness of DU in kinetic energy penetrators (the rods of solid metal used as munitions) has been repeatedly demonstrated at various test ranges and in actual military conflicts. Kinetic energy penetrators do not explode but, if they hit an armoured (hard) target, they may form an aerosol of fine particles. Since uranium metal is pyrophoric, the DU particles ignite and burn, forming small particles of uranium oxides due to the extreme temperatures generated on impact (greater than 1000°C). Most of the contamination remains inside any vehicle that has been struck and penetrated, although some of the dust will be dispersed into the air and deposited on the ground of the surrounding environment. Importantly, DU hits on "soft" targets (e.g. non-armoured vehicles) do not generate significant amounts of dust. Most DU dust from hard target impacts remains within roughly 100 metres of the target, 90 % of which is expected within 50 metres of the target (CHPPM, 2000).

Most penetrators that hit non-armoured (soft) targets will pass right through the target and, in most cases, remain intact. A penetrator that hits the ground usually also remains intact and will continue down into the soil. The depth depends on the mass of the penetrator, the flight angle of the round, the speed of the tank or plane, and the type of soil. In clay, penetrators used by the NATO A-10 aircraft have been reported to reach more than two metres in depth. Penetrators hitting hard objects, such as stones, may ricochet and may thus be found on the surface of the ground several metres from the attacked target. As 7 years had elapsed between the conflict and the DU assessment mission, the major interest of the UNEP mission to BiH was to examine the possible risks from DU to ground, water, biota and populations near the impact sites after such a period of time.

The type of DU munition that the NATO A-10 aircraft uses has a conical DU penetrator. Its length is 95 mm and the diameter at the base 16 mm. The weight of the penetrator is approximately 300 grams. The penetrator is fixed in an aluminium 'jacket' (also called 'casing'), with a diameter of 30 mm and a length of 60 mm. The penetrator and jacket fit tightly through the cylindrical bore of the barrel of the A-10's Gatling gun and the jacket assists the round in flying straight. When the penetrator hits a hard object, e.g. the side of a vehicle, the penetrator continues through the metal sheet, but the jacket does not usually penetrate.

The NATO A-10 aircraft is equipped with one Gatling gun. This gun can fire 3 900 rounds per minute. A typical burst of fire occurs for 2 to 3 seconds and involves 120 to 195 rounds. The shots will hit the ground in a straight line and, depending on the angle of the approach, the shots will hit the ground from 1-3 m apart and occupy an area of about 500 m^2. The number of penetrators hitting a target depends upon many factors, including the type and size of the target. On average, not more than 10% of the penetrators hit the target (CHPPM, 2000). It is important to note that not all A-10 attacks are done with DU munitions. These planes also carry bombs and are used for bombing runs independently of any DU attacks.

UNEP has no information that depleted uranium was used in the cruise missiles fired by NATO forces, or that DU tank munitions were fired during the conflict in BiH. The Yugoslavian Authorities say that the FRY forces did not use depleted uranium. In a letter to the journal *Health Physics*, the U.S. Department of Defense Directorate of Deployment Health Support stated that "Tomahawk [cruise] missiles used in combat and Apache [helicopter] 30 mm rounds **do not** contain depleted uranium"(Kilpatrick, 2002). This letter was in response to a previously published article in *Health Physics*, which stated that DU in the warhead of the Tomahawk was "an assumption that was probably not correct" (Durante and Pugliese, 2002); however, the journal editors allowed the assumption to stand as an extreme worst case.

N.2 THE FATE OF DU IN THE ENVIRONMENT

Normally, 10-35% (and a maximum of 70%) of the penetrator becomes an aerosol on impact (with a "hard" target such as a tank or an armoured personnel carrier (APC)), or when the DU dust accumulated inside the hit target catches fire (RAND, 1999). The DU concentrations, rather than the number of DU particles in various particle sizes, will drive the resultant human intakes and internal doses. A DU hit should be confirmed with a radiation detection instrument since other types of kinetic energy penetrators, such as tungsten alloys, may also leave a black dust cover. The use of colour of the dust cover (i.e. light yellow) is an unreliable indicator for the presence of DU and depleted uranium oxides.

After an attack with depleted uranium munitions, DU will be deposited on the ground and other surfaces in the form of DU metal in pieces, fine fragments and dust. If the DU has caught fire, DU will be deposited as dust of uranium oxides. Most of the DU dust around the targets on the U.S. Nellis Air Force Range is reported to have been deposited within a distance of 100 m of the target (Nellis, 1997). These have been used for a long time period as U.S. Air Force training targets.

Most of the penetrators that impact on soft ground (e.g. sand or clay) will probably penetrate intact more than 50 cm into the ground and remain there for a long time. Penetrators that hit armoured vehicles form an aerosol upon impact or ricochet. Bigger fragments and pieces of

DU are initially deposited on the ground surface. Through weathering, the smaller fragments and dust will gradually be transported into the upper soil layer by water, insects and worms. Wind, rainwater or water that flows on the ground may also transport the smaller fragments and DU dust. Depending on soil composition, some of the dust particles will adsorb onto soil particles, mainly on clay and organic matter (iron-oxyhydroxides and/or carbonates), and thus be less mobile.

Due to the fluctuating chemical properties of different soils and rocks, the fate of DU in the environment varies. Penetrators that are buried in clay will remain intact and will not affect the surrounding soil and groundwater. If penetrators are buried in quartz sand, they will weather relatively fast and may migrate to nearby groundwater. Weathering of penetrators buried in residual soils depends on the type of bedrock. If the soil consists of weathered granite or acid volcanic rock, the environment will be acidic and the weathering will be fast. Acid rain will accelerate the weathering, since uranium is acid soluble.

Once located, penetrators and large pieces of DU can be collected. Otherwise, the DU is removed by gradual leaching from rain and melting snow. This weathering process of DU is principally by corrosion into hydrated uranium oxide [U(VI)] that is soluble in water. Other possible uranium compounds have a lower solubility in water. However, various adsorption processes in soil may slow the migration of uranium through soil by several orders of magnitude, essentially making it immobile. Accordingly, it will take many years, perhaps several hundred years, before DU contamination migrates from the site.

Appendix O

Data on Uranium

O.1 PHYSICOCHEMICAL AND RADIOACTIVE CHARACTERISTICS

Natural uranium exists in various physical and chemical forms (Table O.1). Uranium occurs naturally in the +2, +3, +4, +5, and +6 valence states, but it is most commonly found in the hexavalent form. In nature, hexavalent uranium is commonly associated with oxygen as the uranyl ion, UO_2^{2+}. The specific gravity is 19.07g/cm^3 and melting point $1\,132°C$ (Table O.2).

Table O.1 Physical Data on Uranium

Compound	CAS no.	Molecular formula
Uranium	7440-61-1	U
Uranyl chloride	7791-26-6	Cl_2O_2U
Uranyl nitrate	36478-76-9	N_2O_8U
Uranium dioxide	1344-57-6	UO_2
Uranium trioxide	1344-58-7	UO_3
Uranium(V,VI) oxide	1344-59-8	U_3O_8

Table O.2 Physicochemical properties (Lide, 1992–93)

Compound	Melting point (°C)	Boiling point (°C)	Density at 20°C (g/cm³)	Water solubility (g/litre)
U	1132	3818	19.07	Insoluble
Cl_2O_2U	578	(decomposes)	-	3200
N_2O_8U	60.2	118	2.8	Soluble
UO_2	2878	-	10.96	Insoluble
UO_3	(decomposes to U_3O_8)	-	7.30	Insoluble
U_3O_8	1150*	-	8.38	Soluble

*Decomposes at 1300°C to UO_2

Besides the use of uranium as fuel in nuclear power stations, it is also in some uranium compounds used as catalysts and staining pigments. Depleted uranium is also used for shielding against radiation as it is heavy and absorbs gamma radiation (Berlin & Rudell, 1986).

Naturally occurring uranium ([nat]U) is a mixture of three radioisotopes of uranium ([234]U, [235]U, and [238]U), all of which decay mainly by alpha emission (and some weak beta and gamma emissions (Cothern & Lappenbusch, 1983; Lide, 1992–93). Natural uranium consists almost entirely of the [238]U isotope, with the [235]U and [234]U isotopes respectively comprising about 0.72% and 0.0054% by weight of natural uranium (Greenwood & Earnshaw, 1984) – Table O.3.

Depleted Uranium in Bosnia and Herzegovina

Table O.3 Composition of natural uranium by weight

U-238	99.2745 %
U-235	0.7200 %
U-234	0.0054 %
U-235/U-238	0.00725
U-234/U-238	5.54E-5

Table O.4 Uranium-238 series (ICRP, 1983)

Nuclide	Type of decay	Half-life	Average emitted energy per transformation		
			Alpha energy MeV	Beta energy MeV	Gamma energy MeV
Uranium-238 ^{238}U	α	4.468 10^{9}y	4.26	0.010	0.001
↓					
Thorium-234 ^{234}Th	β	24.1 d	-	0.059	0.009
↓					
*Protactinium-234m ^{234m}Pa (99.84%) +	β	1.17 m			
*Protactinium-234 ^{234}Pa (0.16%)	β	6.7 h	-	0.820	0.013
↓					
Uranium-234 ^{234}U	α	2.45 10^{5}y	4.84	0.013	0.002
↓					
Thorium-230 ^{230}Th	α	7.54 10^{4}y	4.74	-	0.002
↓					
Radium-226 ^{226}Ra	α	1600 y	4.86	-	0.007
↓					
Radon-222 ^{222}Rn	α	3.824 d	5.59	-	-
Polonium-218 ^{218}Po	β (0.02%)	3.05 m	6.11	-	-
↓					
*Astatine-218 ^{218}At 0.02%	α	1.6 s	6.82	0.04	-
*Lead-214 ^{214}Pb 99.98 %	β	26.8 m	-	0.291	0.284
↓					
Bismuth-214 ^{214}Bi	α (0.04%)	19.9 m	-	0.648	1.46
↓					
*Polonium-214 ^{214}Po 99.98%	α	1.64 10^{-4} y	7.83	-	-
*Tallium-210 ^{210}Tl 0.02%	β	1.3 m	-	-	-
↓					
Lead-210 ^{210}Pb	β	22.3 y	-	-	0.047
↓					
Bismuth-210 ^{210}Bi	β	5.01 d	-	0.389	-
↓					
Polonium-210 ^{210}Po	α	138.4 d	5.40	-	-
↓					
Lead-206 ^{206}Pb		Stable			

Isotopes existing in depleted uranium (applies to Uranium-238, Thorium-234, Protactinium-234m/234, Uranium-234)

Nuclide		Type of decay	Half-life	Average emitted energy per transformation		
				Alpha energy MeV	Beta energy MeV	Gamma energy MeV
DU*	Uranium-235 ^{235}U	α	7.04 10^8 y	4.47	0.048	0.154
	↓					
	Thorium-231 ^{231}Th	β	25.52 h	-	0.163	0.026
↓						
Protactinium-231 ^{231}Pa		β	3.28 10^4 y	5.04	0.063	0.048
↓						
Actinium-227 ^{227}Ac		α (1.38%) + β (98.6%)	21.77 y	0.069	0.016	- DU*
↓						
* Thorium-227 ^{227}Th (98.6%) +		α	18.72 d	5.95	0.046	0.106
* Francium-223 ^{223}Fr (1.38%)		β	21.8 m	-	0.391	0.059
↓						
Radium-223 ^{223}Ra		α	11.43 d	5.75	0.075	0.133
↓						
Radon-219 ^{219}Rn		α	3.96 s	6.88	-	0.058
↓						
Polonium-215 ^{215}Po		α	1.78 10^{-3} s	7.52	-	-
↓						
Lead-211 ^{211}Pb		β	36.1 m	-	0.454	0.053
↓						
Bismuth-211 ^{211}Bi		α (99.7%) + β (0.28%)	2.14 m	6.68	-	0.047
↓						
* Polonium-211 ^{211}Po (0.28%)		α	0.516 s	0.021	-	-
*Tallium-207 ^{207}Tl (99.7%)		β	4.77 m	-	0.492	-
↓						
Lead-207 ^{207}Pb			Stable			

* Branched decay
* DU Isotopes existing in depleted uranium

^{238}U decays through 14 steps to ^{206}Pb that is stable (Table O.4) and ^{235}U through 11 steps to ^{207}Pb (Table O.5). Among the decay products there are the elements ^{226}Ra, which is a highly radioactive alpha emitter, ^{214}Bi and ^{214}Pb that emit nearly all gamma radiation in the uranium series. In nature, e.g. in an unprocessed uranium ore, uranium almost is almost in radioactive equilibrium with all its decay products from the whole uranium series.

However, in the chemical process when uranium ore is processed to pure uranium, the decay products of ^{234}U and ^{235}U respectively remain in the waste product. Thus, immediately after uranium has been extracted, it only consists of ^{238}U, ^{234}U and ^{235}U (0.72%). After a few months the immediate daughter products of ^{238}U: ^{234}Th and ^{234}Pa and the daughter product of ^{235}U - ^{231}Th, will be in radioactive equilibrium with their parents. That means that pure uranium after a few months emits not only alpha radiation but also beta and some weak gamma radiation. Because ^{234}U has a very long half-life it takes long time for ^{234}U to reach radioactive equilibrium with ^{238}U more than 800 000 years. Similarly because the first daughter of ^{234}U, ^{230}Th, also has a long half-life it is a delay for the decay products of ^{230}Th like ^{226}Ra and is daughters to reach equilibrium with ^{230}Th, etc.

Table O.6 Composition of depleted uranium by weight (defined as U-235 is 0.2 % by weight; the depletion level found to date in DU ammunition)

^{238}U	99.7990 %
^{235}U	0.2000 %
^{234}U	0.0010 %
$^{235}U / \,^{238}U$	0.00200
$^{234}U / \,^{238}U$	1.00E-5

Depleted uranium is uranium that is a residual product obtained from the production of uranium fuel for nuclear reactors. Most reactors need uranium with a higher concentration of ^{235}U than found in natural uranium. The uranium to be used in the reactor, *enriched uranium,* usually has a concentration of ^{235}U that is 3.5% or higher. This is achieved, at the enrichment process, by separation of the heavier ^{238}U isotope from the less heavy isotopes of ^{235}U and ^{234}U. As a result of the enrichment process large quantities of *depleted uranium* are obtained which has a much lower concentration of ^{235}U and ^{234}U than in normal uranium (Table O.6). The definition of DU varies: certain definitions use U-235 less than 0.7 % (the natural level of uranium), others less than 0.35 %, and some less than 0.30 % as depleted uranium.

Table O.7 The relation between the fraction X of DU of the total amount of uranium in a sample and the ratio R = U-235/U-238 in the sample (DU being defined as 0.2% U-235)

X	1-X	R = U-235/U-238 in the sample M	1/R
0	1	0.00720	139
0.1	0.9	0.00673	149
0.2	0.8	0.00620	161
0.3	0.7	0.00567	176
0.4	0.6	0.00515	194
0.5	0.5	0.00462	216
0.6	0.4	0.00410	244
0.7	0.3	0.00357	280
0.8	0.2	0.00305	328
0.9	0.1	0.00253	396
1.0	0	0.00200	499

Depleted uranium is also used for shielding against radiation as it is heavy and absorbs gamma radiation (Berlin & Rudell, 1986).

Based on the DU Assessments in both Kosovo and Serbia and Montenegro, DU used in NATO munitions contains 0.2% ^{235}U (UNEP, 2001; UNEP, 2002).

In a mixture of natural uranium and DU, the ratio $^{235}U / \,^{238}U$ will vary as follows (Table O.7). Assuming an amount M (mg) of uranium of which X is the DU component and 1-X the natural uranium component. The ratio R = $^{235}U / \,^{238}U$ in the amount M (DU defined as ^{235}U = 0.2 %) is estimated by using the formula:

$$R = \frac{0.72 - 0.52X}{99.2745 + 0.5255X}$$

Post-Conflict Environmental Assessment

Table O.8 The specific activity of some radionuclides of interest

Radionuclide	Occurrence Natural = N Artificial = A	Half-life [years]	Specific activity [Bq/mg Radionuclide]
^{238}U	N	4.468E9	12.4
^{236}U	A	2.3415E7	2'400
^{235}U	N	7.038E8	80
^{234}U	N	2.445E5	231'000
^{239}Pu	A (N)*	24065	2'300'000
^{240}Pu	A	6537	8'400'000
^{241}Pu	A	14.4	3'800'000'000
^{242}Pu	A	3.763E5	145'000
^{244}Pu	A	8.26E7	657

* there is a very small natural production of Pu-239 in Uranium through neutron activation (fission and cosmic neutrons)

Table O.9 Specific activity of the common radionuclides in depleted uranium, (0.2% U-235) in terms of activity (Bq) of a radionuclide per mg DU

Isotope	Chemical composition [1]	Specific activity [Bq/mg DU]
U-238	99.7990%	12.38
U-235	0.2000%	0.16
U-234	0.0010%	2.29
Th-234*	Traces (Decay Product)	12.27
Pa-234m	Traces (Decay Product)	12.27
Th-231	Traces (Decay Product)	0.16
	Sum	39.42

*The Th-234 is a parallel way in the decay chain of Pa-234m to U-234, but with only about 0.15 % intensity
[1] Browne et al., 1986.

Specific activity of ^{238}U is 12.4 Bq/mg (Table O.8). In natural uranium, ^{nat}U, in which 99.8% is ^{238}U by weight, ^{238}U and ^{234}U are assumed to be in activity equilibrium. That means that when saying the uranium activity is 12.4 Bq it means that ^{238}U and ^{234}U each has that activity. If all decay products in the ^{238}U series are in equilibrium (down to ^{206}Pb) all have the same activity, i.e. in the example 12.4 Bq/mg ^{nat}U. The activity of ^{235}U in natural uranium (0.7% by weight) is only 0.56 Bq/mg natural uranium.

Depleted uranium is very much less radioactive then the uranium found in nature, which is in radioactive equilibrium with ^{226}Ra and its highly radioactive daughter isotopes. The specific activities of the common radionuclides in depleted uranium are presented in Table O.9.

O.2 DOSE CONVERSION FACTORS FOR URANIUM ISOTOPES AND FOR DU

Committed effective dose per unit intake (Sv/Bq) of various uranium isotopes via ingestion and inhalation for members of the public.

From European Union Council Directive 96/29/EURATOM of 13 May 1996, laying down the basic safety standards for the protection of workers and the general public against the dangers arising from ionising radiation, Official Journal of the European Communities, No L 159, Vol. 39. 26.9.96.

a =   year

$h(g)$ =   the committed effective dose per unit-intake or unit-inhalation (Sv/Bq) for ingested or inhaled uranium by an individual in the given age group.

f_1 =   gut transfer factor (i.e. the fraction of an element directly absorbed from the gut to body fluids) through intake by ingestion or inhalation.

Type F =   denotes fast clearance from lung

Type M =   denotes moderate clearance from lung

Type S =   denotes slow clearance from lung

As seen from the tables of this section, the dose factors for infants and new-born babies (< 1 a) are about a factor of four times higher than for adults (> 17 a) in the case of inhalation, and even greater in the case of ingestion.

Table O.10   Committed effective dose per unit intake <u>via ingestion</u> (Sv/Bq) for members of the public

Uranium-238 (Half-life 4.47 10^9 a)

Half-life	Age ≤ 1a		Age > 1a	1-2 a	2-7 a	7-12 a	12-17 a	> 17 a
	f_1	$h(g)$	f_1	$h(g)$	$h(g)$	$h(g)$	$h(g)$	$h(g)$
4.47 10^9a	0.040	$3.4\ 10^{-7}$	0.020	$1.2\ 10^{-7}$	$8.0\ 10^{-8}$	$6.8\ 10^{-8}$	$6.7\ 10^{-8}$	$4.5\ 10^{-8}$

Uranium-235 (Half-life 7.04 10^8 a)

Half-life	Age ≤ 1a		Age > 1a	1-2 a	2-7 a	7-12 a	12-17 a	> 17 a
	f_1	$h(g)$	f_1	$h(g)$	$h(g)$	$h(g)$	$h(g)$	$h(g)$
7.04 10^8a	0.040	$3.5\ 10^{-7}$	0.020	$1.3\ 10^{-7}$	$8.5\ 10^{-8}$	$7.1\ 10^{-8}$	$7.0\ 10^{-8}$	$4.7\ 10^{-8}$

Uranium-234 (Half-life 2.44 10^5 a)

Half-life	Age ≤ 1a		Age > 1a	1-2 a	2-7 a	7-12 a	12-17 a	> 17 a
	f_1	$h(g)$	f_1	$h(g)$	$h(g)$	$h(g)$	$h(g)$	$h(g)$
2.44 10^5a	0.040	$3.7\ 10^{-7}$	0.020	$1.3\ 10^{-7}$	$8.8\ 10^{-8}$	$7.4\ 10^{-8}$	$7.4\ 10^{-8}$	$4.9\ 10^{-8}$

Table O.11   Committed effective dose per unit intake <u>via inhalation</u> (Sv/Bq) for members of the public

Uranium-238 (Half-life 4.47 10^9 a)

Type	Age ≤ 1a		Age > 1a	1-2 a	2-7 a	7-12 a	12-17 a	> 17 a
	f_1	$h(g)$	f_1	$h(g)$	$h(g)$	$h(g)$	$h(g)$	$h(g)$
F	0.040	$1.9\ 10^{-6}$	0.020	$1.3\ 10^{-6}$	$8.2\ 10^{-7}$	$7.3\ 10^{-7}$	$7.4\ 10^{-7}$	$5.0\ 10^{-7}$
M	0.040	$1.2\ 10^{-5}$	0.020	$9.4\ 10^{-6}$	$5.9\ 10^{-6}$	$4.0\ 10^{-6}$	$3.4\ 10^{-6}$	$2.9\ 10^{-6}$
S	0.020	$2.9\ 10^{-5}$	0.002	$2.5\ 10^{-5}$	$1{,}6\ 10^{-5}$	$1.0\ 10^{-5}$	$8.7\ 10^{-6}$	$8.0\ 10^{-6}$

Uranium-235 (Half-life 7.04 10^8 a)

Type	Age ≤ 1a		Age > 1a	1-2 a	2-7 a	7-12 a	12-17 a	> 17 a
	f_1	h(g)	f_1	h(g)	h(g)	h(g)	h(g)	h(g)
F	0.040	$2.0\ 10^{-6}$	0.020	$1.3\ 10^{-6}$	$8.5\ 10^{-7}$	$7.5\ 10^{-7}$	$7.7\ 10^{-7}$	$5.2\ 10^{-7}$
M	0.040	$1.3\ 10^{-5}$	0.020	$1.0\ 10^{-5}$	$6.3\ 10^{-6}$	$4.3\ 10^{-6}$	$3.7\ 10^{-6}$	$3.1\ 10^{-6}$
S	0.020	$3.0\ 10^{-5}$	0.002	$2.6\ 10^{-5}$	$1.7\ 10^{-5}$	$1.1\ 10^{-5}$	$9.2\ 10^{-6}$	$8.5\ 10^{-6}$

Uranium-234 (Half-life 2.44 10^5 a)

Type	Age ≤ 1a		Age > 1a	1-2 a	2-7 a	7-12 a	12-17 a	> 17 a
	f_1	h(g)	f_1	h(g)	h(g)	h(g)	h(g)	h(g)
F	0.040	$2.1\ 10^{-6}$	0.020	$1.4\ 10^{-6}$	$9.0\ 10^{-7}$	$8.0\ 10^{-7}$	$8.2\ 10^{-7}$	$5.6\ 10^{-7}$
M	0.040	$1.5\ 10^{-5}$	0.020	$1.1\ 10^{-5}$	$7.0\ 10^{-6}$	$4.8\ 10^{-6}$	$4.2\ 10^{-6}$	$3.5\ 10^{-6}$
S	0.020	$3.3\ 10^{-5}$	0.002	$2.9\ 10^{-5}$	$1,9\ 10^{-5}$	$1.2\ 10^{-5}$	$1.0\ 10^{-5}$	$9.4\ 10^{-6}$

Table O.12 — Effective dose coefficients (Sv/Bq) for workers

Uranium-238

Type	Inhalation			Ingestion	
	f_1	$h(g)_{1\mu m}$	$h(g)_{5\mu m}$	f_1	h(g)
F	0.020	$4.9\ 10^{-7}$	$5.8\ 10^{-7}$	0.020	$4.4\ 10^{-8}$
M	0.020	$2.6\ 10^{-6}$	$1.6\ 10^{-6}$	0.002	$7.6\ 10^{-9}$
S	0.002	$7.3\ 10^{-6}$	$5.7\ 10^{-6}$		

Uranium-235

Type	Inhalation			Ingestion	
	f_1	$h(g)_{1\mu m}$	$h(g)_{5\mu m}$	f_1	h(g)
F	0.020	$5.1\ 10^{-7}$	$6.0\ 10^{-7}$	0.020	$4.6\ 10^{-8}$
M	0.020	$2.8\ 10^{-6}$	$1.8\ 10^{-6}$	0.002	$8.3\ 10^{-9}$
S	0.002	$7.7\ 10^{-6}$	$6.1\ 10^{-6}$		

Uranium-234

Type	Inhalation			Ingestion	
	f_1	$h(g)_{1\mu m}$	$h(g)_{5\mu m}$	f_1	h(g)
F	0.020	$5.5\ 10^{-7}$	$6.4\ 10^{-7}$	0.020	$4.9\ 10^{-8}$
M	0.020	$3.1\ 10^{-6}$	$2.1\ 10^{-6}$	0.002	$8.3\ 10^{-9}$
S	0.002	$8.5\ 10^{-6}$	$6.8\ 10^{-6}$		

Table O.13 — Compounds and f_1 values used for the calculation of ingestion dose coefficients

Uranium	0.020	Unspecified compounds
	0.002	Most tetravalent compounds, e.g., UO_2, U_3O_8, UF_4

Table O.14 — Compounds, lung absorption types and f_1 values for the calculation of inhalation dose coefficients

Adsorption type	f_1	Compound
F	0.020	Most hexavalent compounds, e.g., UF_6, UO_2F_2 and $UO_2(NO_3)_2$
M	0.020	Less soluble compounds, e.g., UO_3, UF_4, UCl_4 and most other hexavalent compounds
S	0.002	Highly insoluble compounds, e.g., UO_2 and U_3O_8

However, the volume of air breathed and mass of food and water consumed per unit of time are much smaller for infants and new-born babies than for adults (ICRP Report No. 23 Report of the Task Group on Reference Man 1974). Therefore, with a given concentration (Bq/m^3 or Bq/g) the intakes by adults and infants are not so different. Furthermore, in the case of inhalation of insoluble uranium aerosols, the biological half-life for a substantial part of the initial lung burden is very long, of the order of years. Table O.15 is an example of lung clearance after an intake of 100 Bq ^{234}U as 5 μm S-particles by an adult. Assuming the same clearance rate for children, it is concluded that the major part of the dose is received when the child has grown up. Furthermore, in the case of long-term exposure, childhood accounts for a limited period of time.

Table O.15 Lung clearance and integrated effective dose as a function of time, example ^{234}U.

Time after inhalation of 100 Bq U-234, days	Remaining U-234 activity in the lung, Bq	Received effective dose, Sv
2	8.6	$2.7 \ 10^{-5}$
10	7.8	$1.1 \ 10^{-4}$
100	4.6	$4.0 \ 10^{-4}$
1000	1.9	$6.9 \ 10^{-4}$
10.000	0.12	$9.2 \ 10^{-4}$

On the basis of the circumstances given above, it is assumed that the uptake and resulting doses are those given for adults, type S-absorption (the most conservative), only.

Tables O.16 and Table O.17 show selected committed effective doses per unit intake (Sv/Bq) of various uranium isotopes and of depleted uranium (Sv/mg), respectively.

Table O.16 Committed effective dose per unit of intake (Sv/Bq)

Isotope	Ingestion Sv/Bq	Inhalation Sv/Bq
U-238	$4.5 \ 10^{-8}$	$8.0 \ 10^{-6}$
U-235	$4.7 \ 10^{-8}$	$8.5 \ 10^{-6}$
U-234	$4.9 \ 10^{-8}$	$9.4 \ 10^{-6}$

Table O.17 Committed effective dose per unit of intake of depleted uranium (Sv/mg)

Mode of intake	Sv per mg intake of DU
Ingestion	$6.7 \ 10^{-7}$
Inhalation	$1.2 \ 10^{-4}$ (*)

(*) This value is about 3 times larger than that used in UNSCEAR 2000 and referred to in this Appendix because a more conservative clearance factor is used in this report.

O

O.3 URANIUM NUCLIDES IN THE ENVIRONMENT

Natural uranium exists in various concentrations in all parts of the environment. There are also some artificial contributions of uranium to the environment e.g. by release in waste tailings from mineral exploration, emissions from the nuclear industry, the combustion of coal and other fuels, and the use of phosphate fertilizers that contain uranium.

■ **Soils and rocks**

Natural uranium occurs in higher than average concentration in certain types rocks e.g. some types of granites and some black shales, e.g. alum shale and Chattanooga shale, and various mineral deposits (Roessler et al., 1979; Lide, 1992–93), see Table O.18.

Table O.18	Natural uranium concentrations in common soils and rocks* Higher and lower concentrations occur occasionally (Åkerblom and Mellander, 1997)

Soils	Range, mg/kg	Range, Bq/kg	Reference
World average	3	35	UNSCEAR 2000
World range	0.01-75	1-900	UNSCEAR 2000
Sand	0.5-3	5-35	
Clay	1-8	10-100	
Serbia and Montenegro at the sites visited by the UNEP Mission	1-10	12-120	UNEP 2001
Rocks	**Range, mg/kg**	**Range, Bq/kg**	**Reference**
World average	3	35	Kogan et al. 1971
Basic igneous rocks	0.1-3	1-30	
Granite, normal	2-6	20-500	
Granite, uranium-rich	8-40	100-500	
Limestone	0.2-3	2-30	
Sandstones	0.5-5	1-60	
Chattanooga shale (USA)	20-80	250-1'000	Swanson 1960
Alum shale (Sweden)	50-300	600-3'700	Andersson et al. 1985
Uranium ores of good quality (0.5-30 % uranium)	10'000-300'000	$6.2 \ 10^5-370 \ 10^5$	

Uranium in rocks that are unaffected by weathering or dissolution by groundwater is normally in radioactive equilibrium with all its daughter products down to Pb-206 (see Table O.10). However, this is usually not the case in weathered rocks and in soils where either uranium or radium may have been partly dissolved and leached from the minerals.

35 Bq U/kg soil leads to (with the level of equilibrium of short-lived daughters existing in the ground) an external absorbed dose rate in air of 15 nGy per hour, or 0.02 mSv per year (adjusted for indoor occupancy factor 0.8 and 0.7 Sv/Gy for conversion coefficient from absorbed dose in air to effective dose received by adults).

Depleted Uranium in Bosnia and Herzegovina

■ **Water**

In a survey of 130 sites (approximately 3 700 samples) in Ontario, Canada, conducted between 1990 and 1995, the mean of the average uranium concentrations (range 0.05–4.21 µg/litre; detection limit 0.05 µg/litre)' in treated drinking water was 0.40 µg/litre (OMEE, 1996). Uranium concentrations of up to 700 µg/litre have been found in private supplies in Canada (Moss et al., 1983; Moss, 1985). The mean concentration of uranium in drinking water in New York City, USA, ranged from 0.03 to 0.08 µg/litre (Fisenne & Welford, 1986). A mean uranium concentration of 2.55 µg/litre was reported in drinking water from 978 sites in the USA in the 1980s (US EPA, 1990, 1991).

The daily uranium intake from water in Finland has been estimated to be 2.1 µg (Kahlos & Asikainen, 1980). The daily intake from drinking water in Salt Lake City, USA, is estimated to be 1.5 µg (Singh et al., 1990). On the basis of the results of the survey from Ontario (OMEE, 1996), the daily intake of uranium from drinking water in Canada is estimated to be 0.8 µg. Average value of annual intake by drinking water is 0.04 mg of natural uranium (500 L water per year).

Table O.19   Natural ^{238}U concentrations in water

Water type	Range, µg/l	Range, mBq/l	Reference
Fresh waters	0.1 - 8	1 - 90	
Ground waters	<1 - 12	<1 - 140	UNSCEAR 1993
Finnish values up to	12,100	150,000	UNSCEAR 2000
Yugoslavian values	0.04 - 41	0.5 - 510	UNSCEAR 1993
Yugoslavian values at the sites visited by the UNEP Mission	0.02 - 1.8	0.2 - 22	UNEP 2001
Sea water	1 - 3.3	12 - 40.5	
Reference value for drinking water	0.08	1	UNSCEAR 2000

■ **Air**

In air, the total activity concentration of uranium is about 1 µBq/m^3 and the reported range for the U.S.A. is 0.9 - 5 µBq/m^3 (UNSCEAR, 2000). Mean levels of uranium in ambient air have been reported to be 0.02 ng/m^3 in Tokyo (based on a 1979–1981 survey) (Hirose & Sugimura, 1981) and 0.076 ng/m^3 in New York (based on two samples, each a composite of two weekly air filter collections, from 1985 and 1986) (Fisenne et al., 1987). On the assumption of a daily respiratory volume of 20 m^3 and a mean urban airborne concentration of 0.08 ng/m^3, the daily intake of uranium from air would be about 1.6 ng. Tobacco smoke (from two packages of cigarettes per day) contributes less than 50 ng of inhaled uranium per day (Lucas & Markun, 1970). Inhalation intake of natural uranium is near 0.6 µg per year.

Effective dose caused by inhaled uranium:

• 0.3 µSv per year if all uranium daughters (except radon and its daughters) are in equilibrium;

• 5.8 µSv per year from uranium and its daughters as they are in air (major part caused by ^{210}Pb/ ^{210}Po);

• 0.02 µSv per year from ^{238}U alone and 0.03 µSv per year from ^{234}U alone.

Post-Conflict Environmental Assessment

■ Food

Uranium has been detected in a variety of foodstuffs. The highest concentrations are found in shellfish, and lower levels have been measured in fresh vegetables, cereals, and fish. The average per capita intake of uranium in food has been reported to be 1.3 μg/day (Fisenne et al., 1987) and 2–3 μg/day (Singh et al., 1990) in the USA and 1.5 μg/day in Japan (Nozaki et al., 1970).

In a review of naturally occurring sources of radioactive contamination in food, dietary intakes of ^{238}U were found to range from 12 to 45 mBq/day in several European countries, from 11 to 60 mBq/day in Japan (the higher values were found in uranium mining areas), and from 15 to 17 mBq/day in the USA. The average daily dietary intake was in the order of 20 mBq, or about 4 μg. It was often difficult to determine whether these dietary intakes included intake from drinking water, and it was emphasized that intake from drinking water has sometimes been found to be equal to intake from the diet (Harley, 1988).

In a study by Cheng et al. (1993), the mean uranium concentration in nine different beverages was 0.98 μg/litre (range 0.26–1.65 μg/litre), and the mean concentration of uranium in mineral water was 9.20 μg/litre.

Landa & Councell (1992) performed leaching studies to determine the quantity of uranium leaching from 33 glass items and two ceramic items in which uranium was used as a colouring agent. Uranium-bearing glasses leached a maximum of 30 μg of uranium per litre, whereas the ceramic-glazed items released approximately 300 000 μg of uranium per litre.

Average value of annual intake by food is 0.46 mg of natural uranium.

Effective dose caused by ingestion of ^{nat}U (by food and water) results in ^{nat}U 0.3 μSv per year. Therefore: 33 Bq/kg soil (each of ^{238}U and ^{234}U) leads to a total annual intake by food and water of 6.2 Bq of both ^{238}U and ^{234}U each, which leads to an effective dose of 0.3 μSv per year from both ^{238}U and ^{234}U.

■ Person's body

Average value of body burden is 30 μg of natural uranium (360 mBq each of ^{238}U and ^{234}U, assumed to be in equilibrium).

Effective dose caused by ^{nat}U (in equilibrium, ^{238}U and ^{234}U each contributing about 50 %) in the body is 7.4 μSv per year.

Total effective dose caused by all uranium daughters in the body from ingestion and inhalation is 110 μSv per year (except radon daughters inhaled). The main part is from ^{210}Pb/ ^{210}Po ingested.

■ Urine

The average amount of uranium excreted in urine from natural sources is roughly 0.01 microgram per day. The analysis of exposed persons' uranium concentration in urine can be used as a monitor for internal uranium exposure. Bio-kinetic models exist that can be used to 'back-calculate' past uranium intakes based on actual urine excretion, depending on the intake path and time elapsed (WHO 2001; Royal Society, 2002).

If exposure is to DU and not natural uranium, it is also possible in principle to estimate DU intake by measuring the isotopic composition of excreted uranium. Using high sensitivity

mass spectrometric analyses, like ICP MS or TIMS, can achieve this. However, international experts believe that reliable estimates of uranium isotope ratios in such urine samples using such techniques is still challenging and subject to a number of potential problems. Adequate sensitivity is probably achievable for samples taken up to 10 years or more after acute exposure to DU, but the uncertainties in the assessed intakes are likely to be quite large.

O.4   HEALTH STANDARDS, LIMITS AND LEVELS

O.4.1 Chemical toxicity: health standards

■   **Water**

The WHO derived a guideline for drinking-water quality of 2 µg of uranium per litre. This value is considered to be protective for sub-clinical renal effects reported in epidemiological studies (WHO, 1998).

U.S. EPA 1991 has 30 µg/litre as a limit for uranium in drinking water (EPA, 2000). This is a new standard, the reference being 65 Federal Register (FR) 76708, 7 DEC 2000, National Primary Drinking Water Regulation, Radionuclides, FR USEPA, 2000.

EU Council Directive 98/83/EC on the quality of water intended for human consumption requires the Member States to monitor the concentrations of radionuclides in public drinking water (EU, 1998). If the indicative dose exceeds 0.1 mSv per year, the competent authorities shall investigate to identify the cause and to take justified precautions. For uranium, the reference concentration is 100 µg/l (EU, 2001).

■   **Oral intake**

For oral intake, a Tolerable Daily Intake (TDI) for uranium of 0.6 µg/kg body weight per day has been established by the WHO (WHO, 1998). The U.S. Agency for Toxic Substances and Disease Registry (ATSDR) established an intermediate Minimal Risk Level (MRL) of 2 µg/kg body weight per day (ATSDR, 1999).

■   **Air**

The American Conference of Governmental Industrial Hygienists (ACGIH) adopted the maximum permissible concentration of 0.2 mg/m^3 for soluble and insoluble natural uranium in air. The short-term exposure limit for natural uranium in the air was set at 0.6 mg/m^3 (ACGIH, 1993).

The U.S. National Institute for Occupational Safety and Health (NIOSH) recommends a limit for insoluble uranium of 0.2 mg/m^3 for chronic occupational exposure, and 0.6 mg/m^3 for short-term exposure. When these occupational guidelines are converted for exposure of the general public, they are 0.05 mg/m^3 for chronic exposure and 0.15 mg/m^3 for short-term exposure.

For soluble uranium, the levels are 0.5 mg/m^3 and 10 mg/m^3, respectively (NIOSH, 1994).

The U.S. Agency for Toxic Substances and Disease Registry derived a MRL for chronic inhalation exposure of 8 µg/m^3.

O.4.2 Radioprotection: Recommendations, limits and action levels

■ **Doses**

Background

The world average dose received by man from natural unavoidable radiation is estimated to be 2.4 mSv/year (UNSCEAR 2000). This dose includes exposure to terrestrial radiation from the ground and building material, cosmic radiation, radiation from potassium-40 in the body, ingested radioactive elements in food and water and inhaled radioactive elements in the air (indoor radon and radon progeny is responsible for main part of this dose). Depending on where you live the annual dose may lower or higher. UNSCEAR gives a range of 0.5 to 10 mSv/year. Locally the exposure to individuals can results in much higher doses.

ICRP recommendations (From ICRP 60, 1991 and ICRP 65,1993):

- Trivial dose for the public is below 10 µSv per year
- The dose limit for the public from all man made sources excluding medical and natural sources is defined as 1 mSv per year effective dose.
- The dose constraint for a given source 0.1-0.3 mSv per year effective dose to the public i.e. the practice shall be planned to give doses (far) below that value.
- The dose limit for the public for exposure of the skin is defined as 50 mSv per year.
- The planning dose limit for a given source is 0.1 mSv per year effective dose to the public i.e. the practice shall be planned to give doses (far) below that value.
- Action levels for radon in dwellings are defined as 3-10 mSv per year.
- Action levels for workplaces are defined as 3-10 mSv per year.
- The dose limit for worker is defined as 20 mSv per year effective dose as an average over 5 years.
- The dose limit for workers in a single year is defined as 50 mSv per year effective dose.
- The dose limit for workers for exposure of the skin is defined as 500 mSv per year.
- If expected doses are over 100 mSv, countermeasures to prevent these doses are mostly always justified.
- Actions are probably justified after a nuclear accident or an existing unsatisfactory *de facto* situation if doses 10-100 mSv are prevented.

EU limits

According to Article 9 of the Council Directive 96/29Euratom of 13 May 1996, which lays down basic safety standards for the protection of health of workers and the general public against the dangers arising from ionising radiation (the BSS):

- "the limit on effective dose for exposed workers shall be 100 mSv in a consecutive five-year period, subject to a maximum effective dose of 50 mSv in a single year" (EU, 1996).
- According to Article 10, the dose to a pregnant woman shall be as low as reasonably achievable and not exceeding 1 mSv. These dose limits refer to exposure at work.
- Article 13 referring to dose limits for members of the public sets the maximum effective dose at 1 mSv/year. This limit refers to exposure to artificial sources. Article 2.4 excludes from this limit exposure to natural levels of radiation.

EU Directive on quality of water

EU Council Directive 98/83/EC on the quality of water intended for human consumption requires the Member States to monitor the concentrations of radionuclides in public drinking water (EU, 1998). If the indicative dose exceeds 0.1 mSv per year, the competent authorities shall investigate to identify the cause and to take justified precautions. For uranium, the reference concentration is 100 µg/L (EU, 2001).

O.4.3 Summarising information on uranium (UNSCEAR and WHO reports)

■ **Activity**

- Activity of U-238 is 12.4 Bq/mg. In natural uranium, ^{nat}U, in which 99.8% is U-238 by weight, U-238 and U-234 are assumed to be in activity equilibrium. That means that when saying the uranium activity is 12.4 Bq it means that U-238 and U-234 each has that activity. If all decay products in the U-238 series are in equilibrium (down to lead-206) all have the same activity, i.e. in the example 12.4 Bq/mg ^{nat}U. The activity of U-235 in natural uranium (0.7% by weight) is only 0.56 Bq/mg natural uranium.

■ **Body**

- Body burden 30 µg uranium (^{nat}U; 360 mBq each of U-238 and U-234, assumed to be in equilibrium).
- Effective dose 7.4 µSv per year caused by ^{nat}U (in equilibrium, U-238 and U-234 each contributing about 50 %) in the body.
- Total effective dose 110 µSv per year caused by all uranium daughters in the body from ingestion and inhalation (except radon daughters inhaled). The main part is from Pb/Po-210 ingested.

■ **Air**

- Concentration in air 1 µBq/m^3 each of U-238 and 234 (0.08 ng m^{-3}, ^{nat}U).
- Inhaled 7 mBq per year each of ^{nat}U (~0.6 µg ^{nat}U).
- Effective dose caused by inhaled uranium:

  - 0.3 µSv per year if all uranium daughters (except radon and its daughters)
  - are in equilibrium;
  - 5.8µSv per year from uranium and its daughters as they are in air (major part
  - caused by Pb/Po-210);
  - 0.02 µSv per year from U-238 alone and 0.03 µSv per year from U-234 alone.

- Normal dust load: 50 µg dust particles/m^3.
- Natural uranium in soil: 35 Bq/kg (=3 mg ^{nat}U/kg).
- Uranium in dust as in soil (dust expressed as 3 mg ^{nat}U/kg as the average of soil) , i.e. 1.7 µBq/m^3 air.
- 35 Bq U/kg soil leads to (with the level of equilibrium of short-lived daughters existing in the ground) an external absorbed dose rate in air of 15 nGy per hour, or 0.02 mSv per year (adjusted for indoor occupancy factor 0.8 and 0.7 Sv/Gy for conversion coefficient from absorbed dose in air to effective dose received by adults).

■ **Ingestion**

- Ingested by food are 5.7 Bq/year (0.46 mg ^{nat}U per year).
- The drinking water concentration is 1 Bq/m^3 (0.08 mg ^{nat}U/m^3).
- Intake by water results in 0.5 Bq per year (0.04 mg ^{nat}U per year, 500 L water per year).
- Effective dose caused by ingestion of ^{nat}U (by food and water) results in ^{nat}U 0.3 µSv per year. Therefore: 33 Bq/kg soil (each of U-238 and 234) leads to a total annual intake by food and water of 6.2 Bq of both U-238 and U-234 each, which leads to an effective dose of 0.3 µSv per year from both U-238 and U-234.

Post-Conflict Environmental Assessment

Appendix P
List of NATO Coordinates

NATO UNCLASSIFIED

These coordinates were provided to UNEP in the preparation phase of the field mission and correspond to A10 employment of 30 mm DU munitions during Allied Operations 'Deny Flight – Deliberate Force', 1993-95.

Site #	Date	Target	Rounds	Location
1	5 August '94	76mm AT Self Propelling Gun	860	434432N 182108E
2	22 September '94	T 55 Tank	120	435237N 181702E
3	30 August '95	Warehouse	UNKNOWN	Vicinity Sarajevo
4	30 August '95	Artillery/Bunker	UNKNOWN	Vicinity Sarajevo
5	30 August '95	120mm artillery	UNKNOWN	Vicinity Sarajevo
6	30 August '95	AAA	UNKNOWN	Vicinity Sarajevo
7	30 August '95	Mortar Position	UNKNOWN	Vicinity Sarajevo
8	30 August '95	Mortar Position	UNKNOWN	Vicinity Sarajevo
9	5 September '95	Hadzici Military Repair Facility	800	434932.7N 181122.9E
10	7 September '95	Han Pijesak Army Storage	700	440522.0N 185655.7E 440525.1N 185653.7E 440527.2N 185653.5E 440539.6N 185649.7E 440540.0N 185645.0E
11	7 September '95	Han Pijesak Army Storage	700	440522.0N 185655.7E 440525.1N 185653.7E 440527.2N 185653.5E 440539.6N 185649.7E 440540.0N 185645.0E
12	7 September '95	Han Pijesak Army Storage	500	440539.6N 185649.7E 440540.0N 185645.0E 440540.3N 185642.5E
13	7 September '95	Han Pijesak Army Storage	500	440539.6N 185649.7E 440540.0N 185645.0E 440540.3N 185642.5E
14	9 September '95	Hadzici Military Repair Facility	350	434939.1N 181117.3E
15	9 September '95	Hadzici Military Repair Facility	350	434939.1N 181117.3E
16	11 September '95	Hadzici Ammunition Storage Depot	400	4348N 1812E
17	11 September '95	Hadzici Ammunition Storage Depot	400	4348N 1812E
18	11 September '95	Hadzici Ammunition Storage Depot	550	4348N 1812E
19	11 September '95	Hadzici Ammunition Storage Depot	550	4348N 1812E

* NATO coordinates are also published at the following website:
www.nato.int/du/docu/d010124b.htm

Depleted Uranium in Bosnia and Herzegovina

APPENDIX Q

Units

SI UNITS

SI = Système International d'unités

SI basic units		
Quantity	**Name**	**Symbol**
length	meter (metre)	m
mass	kilogram	kg
time	second	s
amount of substance	mole	mol

SI derived units		
Derived quantity	**Name**	**Symbol**
Activity (ionizing radiations)	becquerel	$Bq = 1/s$
Absorbed dose, specific energy (imparted), kerma	gray	$Gy = J/kg = m^2/s^2$
Absorbed dose rate	gray per second	$Gy/s = m^2/s^3$
Dose equivalent, ambient dose equivalent, directional dose equivalent, personal dose equivalent, organ equivalent dose	sievert	$Sv = J/kg = m^2/s^2$
Dose equivalent rate	sievert per second	$Sv/s = m^2/s^3$
Volume	cubic meter	m^3

SI PREFIXES

exponent (base 10) of decimal numbers: E n = 10^n

	Factor	Prefix	Symbol		Factor	Prefix	Symbol
10^{18}	E 18	exa	E	10^{15}	E 15	peta	P
10^{12}	E 12	tera	T	10^9	E 9	giga	G
10^6	E 6	mega	M	10^3	E 3	kilo	k
10^2	E 2	hecto	h	10^1	E 1	deca	da
10^{-1}	E -1	deci	d	10^{-2}	E -2	centi	c
10^{-3}	E -3	milli	m	10^{-6}	E -6	micro	μ
10^{-9}	E -9	nano	n	10^{-12}	E-12	pico	p
10^{-15}	E-15	femto	f	10^{-18}	E-18	atto	a

EXAMPLES OF UNITS USED IN THIS REPORT

Bq/kg   becquerel per kg; specific activity

mBq/L   milli becquerel per litre; activity concentration

μBq/m³   micro becquerel per cubic meter; activity concentration

cps   counts per second; count rate

d   days

eV   electron volt; 1 eV = 1.602177E-19 joule. Usually expressed in keV (kilo electron volt) in the gamma spectrometry and MeV (mega electron volt) in the alpha spectrometry

g/m²   gram per square meter; e.g. contamination of a surface

g/m³   gram per cubic meter; e.g. contamination of a volume

mSv   milli sievert; effective dose

nSv/h   nano (10^{-9}) sievert per hour; dose equivalent rate

Sv/mg   committed effective dose per unit of intake (in this depleted uranium report)

Sv/Bq   committed effective dose per unit of intake

μR/h   micro roentgen per hour. Unit formerly used for measurements of gamma radiation: 1 μR/h is equal to 0.01 μSv/h.

L   litre

min   minutes

mg/kg   milli gram per kg: equal to ppm – part per million

μg/kg   micro gram per kg: equal to ppb – part per billion

mg/L   milli gram per litre; concentration

μg/cm²   micro gram per square centimetre; e.g. contamination of a surface

mol/L   mol per litre; amount of substance per litre

ppm   parts per million, 1 ppm is equal to 1mg/kg

ppb   parts per billion, 1 ppb is equal to 1μg/kg

y   year

Depleted Uranium in Bosnia and Herzegovina

APPENDIX R

Glossary

A-10

The A-10 Thunderbolt II is the first US Air Force aircraft specially designed for close air support of ground forces. They are simple, effective and survivable twin-engine jet aircraft that can be used against all ground targets, including tanks and other armoured vehicles. Its 30 mm GAU-8/A Gatling gun can fire 3 900 rounds a minute and can defeat an array of ground targets, including tanks. DU is fired using this gun. Some of their other equipment includes an inertial navigation system, electronic countermeasures, target penetration aids, self-protection systems, and AGM-65 Maverick and AIM-9 Sidewinder missiles.

A - 10 Thunderbolt II

Activity

The number of nuclear transformations occurring in a given quantity of material per unit of time. The SI unit of activity is the reciprocal second (s⁻¹) "per second", termed the *becquerel* (Bq).

Activity concentration

Activity (Bq) per unit mass or volume. ISO 921 distinguishes between *specific activity* (see below) as the *activity* per unit mass and the *activity concentration* as the *activity* per unit volume.

Acute biochemical effects

High exposure of radiation doses can cause noticeable/significant consequences such as symptoms of illness or damage to normal body functions.

Absorbed dose (specific energy (imparted); kerma)

The amount of energy deposited in a unit mass of biological tissue. The unit of absorbed dose is the gray (Gy). See also *dose quantities*.

Alpha particle (α)

A positively charged particle ejected spontaneously from the nuclei of some heavy radioactive elements. The charged particle is identical with the helium nucleus, but of nuclear origin. It comprises two neutrons and two protons, and has a mass number of 4 and an electrostatic charge of +2. On capturing two electrons it forms an atom of helium indistinguishable from any other helium atom.

APC

Armoured Personnel Carrier.

Atom

The smallest particle of an element that cannot be divided or broken up by chemical means. It consists of a central core called the nucleus, which contains protons and neutrons and an outer shell of electrons.

Background radiation

The order of radiation from which a member of the public is exposed to natural sources, such as terrestrial radiation from naturally occurring radionuclides in the soil, cosmic radiation originating from outer space, and naturally occurring radionuclides deposited in the human body.

Becquerel
SI derived unit for activity (ionizing radiation); Bq

Beta particle (β)
Charged particle emitted from the nucleus of an atom. A beta particle has a mass and charge equal in magnitude to that of the electron. The charge may be either +1 (positron) or −1 (negatron).

Bio-indicators
Lichens, bark, mosses, mushrooms, etc. Analysis of these samples can indicate the possible presence of DU as evidence of earlier or ongoing air contamination.

Careful measurements
This method was often used to complement the measurements derived from line up service. It consisted of measurements made with the *Inspector* beta/ gamma instrument, involving more careful removal of any covering of dust, grass etc., and measuring over a longer time period, to detect any possible shielded beta radiation from *localised ground contamination* or even *widespread contamination*.

Clean-up
See decontamination

Committed effective dose
Following an intake into the body of a radioactive material there is a period during which the material gives rise to an equivalent dose to one or several organs and an effective dose to the whole body. The committed effective dose is the time integration of the effective dose rate. If the time interval is not specified it is implied that the value is 50 or 70 years, as defined by the regulator or assessor.

Confidence Level
The range (with a specified value of uncertainty, usually expressed in percent) within which the true value of a measured quantity exists.

Contamination
1. Radioactive substances on surfaces, or within solids, liquids or gases (including the human body), where their presence is unintended or undesirable, or the process giving rise to their presence in such places. Also used less formally to refer to a quantity, namely the *activity* present on a surface (or on unit area of a surface).
    The English language term *contamination* refers only to the presence of *activity*, and gives no indication of the magnitude of the hazard involved.

2. The presence of a radioactive substance on a surface in quantities in excess of $0.4\,Bq/cm^2$ for beta and gamma emitters and *low toxicity alpha emitters*, or $0.04\,Bq/cm^2$ for all other alpha emitters. This is a regulatory definition of *contamination*, specific to the Transport Regulations. Levels below $0.4\,Bq/cm^2$ or $0.04\,Bq/cm^2$ would be considered *contamination* according to the scientific definition (**1**).

Contamination point
Small area of localised *depleted uranium (DU)* surface contamination found by field beta measurements, typically at the point of a penetrator impact.

Decay (radioactive)
Transformation of the nucleus of an unstable nuclide by spontaneous emission of charged particles and/or photons.

Depleted Uranium in Bosnia and Herzegovina

Decay chain or series
A sequence of radioactive decays starting with one nucleus, a *radionuclide*. The initial nucleus decays into a secondary nucleus 'or progeny nucleus' that differs from the first by whatever particles were emitted during the decay.

Decay product
A new isotope formed as a result of radioactive decay. A nuclide resulting from the radioactive transformation of a radionuclide, formed either directly or as the result of successive transformations in a radioactive series. A decay product may be either radioactive or stable.

Decontamination
Clean up of a site/area targeted with DU. Removal of radioactive contamination.

Depleted uranium (DU)
Uranium having a percentage of uranium-235 less than the naturally occurring distribution of U-235 found in natural uranium (less than 0.711 weight percent U-235).

Dose per unit intake (Dose coefficient)
The *committed effective dose* resulting from *intake* by a specified means (usually ingestion or inhalation) of unit *activity* of a specified radionuclide in a specified chemical form. For intakes, synonymous with *dose coefficient*. Unit: Sv/Bq.

Dose quantities

- **absorbed dose, D**
  The fundamental dosimetric quantity D, defined as:

  $$D = \frac{d\bar{\varepsilon}}{dm}$$

  where $d\bar{\varepsilon}$ is the mean energy imparted by *ionizing radiation* to matter in a volume element and dm is the mass of matter in the volume element. [1]

    - The energy can be averaged over any defined volume, the average *dose* being equal to the total energy imparted in the volume divided by the mass in the volume.
    - *Absorbed dose* is defined at a point; for the average dose in a tissue or organ, see *organ dose*.
    - Unit: J/kg, termed the *gray (Gy)* (formerly, the *rad* was used).

- **collective effective dose, S**
  The total *effective dose* S to a population

- **committed effective dose, E(τ)**

  $$E(\tau) = \sum_{T} w_T \cdot H_T(\tau)$$

  where $H_T(\tau)$ is the *committed equivalent dose* to tissue T over the integration time τ and w_T is the *tissue weighting factor* for tissue T. When τ is not specified, it will be taken to be 50 years for adults and to age 70 years for *intakes* by children. [1]

- **committed equivalent dose, HT(τ)**

  $$H_T(\tau) = \int_{t_0}^{t_0+\tau} \dot{H}_T(t)\, dt$$

  where t_0 is the time of *intake*, $\dot{H}_T(t)$ is the *equivalent dose rate* at time *t* in organ or tissue T and τ is the time elapsed after an *intake* of radioactive substances. When τ is not specified, it will be taken to be 50 years for adults and to age 70 years for *intakes* by children. [1]

- **effective dose, E**

$$E = \sum_T w_T \cdot H_T$$

where H_T is the *equivalent dose* in tissue T and w_T is the *tissue weighting factor* for tissue T. From the definition of *equivalent dose*, it follows that:

$$E = \sum_T w_T \cdot \sum_R w_R \cdot D_{T,R}$$

where w_R is the *radiation weighting factor* for *radiation* R and $D_{T,R}$ is the average *absorbed dose* in the organ or tissue T. [1]

- The unit of *effective dose* is J/kg, termed the *sievert (Sv)*. The *rem*, equal to 0.01 Sv, is sometimes used as a unit of *equivalent dose* and *effective dose*. This should not be used in Agency documents except when quoting directly from other documents, in which case the value in *sieverts* should be added in parentheses.

- *Effective dose* is a measure of *dose* designed to reflect the amount of *radiation detriment* likely to result from the *dose*.

- Values of *effective dose* from any type(s) of *radiation* and mode(s) of *exposure* can be compared directly.

- **equivalent dose, HT**

$$H_{T,R} = w_R \cdot D_{T,R}$$

where $D_{T,R}$ is the *absorbed dose* delivered by *radiation* type R averaged over a tissue or organ T and w_R is the *radiation weighting factor* for *radiation* type R. When the *radiation* field is composed of different *radiation* types with different values of w_R the *equivalent dose* is:

$$H_T = \sum_R w_R \cdot D_{T,R} \quad [1]$$

- The unit of *equivalent dose* is J/kg, termed the *sievert (Sv)*. The *rem*, equal to 0.01 Sv, is sometimes used as a unit of *equivalent dose* and *effective dose*. This should not be used in Agency documents except when quoting directly from other documents, in which case the value in *sieverts* should be added in parentheses.

- A measure of the *dose* to a tissue or organ designed to reflect the amount of harm caused.

- Values of *equivalent dose* to a specified tissue from any type(s) of radiation can therefore be compared directly.

- **organ dose**

$$D_T = \frac{1}{m_T} \int_{m_T} D \, dm$$

where m_T is the mass of the tissue or organ and D is the *absorbed dose* in the mass element dm.

Dose rate

Absorbed dose per unit time. Although *dose rate* could, in principle, be defined over any unit of time (e.g. an *annual dose* is, technically, a *dose rate*). The term *dose rate* should be used only in the context of short periods of time, e.g. *dose* per second or *dose* per hour.

DU round

Complete *depleted uranium* projectile, including *jacket/casing* and *penetrator*.

Effective dose (Sv)

see *dose quantities*.

Depleted Uranium in Bosnia and Herzegovina

Effective committed dose
see *dose quantities*.

Fragment
Part of a broken *depleted uranium (DU)* penetrator or *jacket/casing*.

Gamma particle (ϒ)
Short-wavelength electromagnetic radiation of nuclear origin. Penetrating radiation.

Gray
SI derived unit of the absorbed dose; Gy

Half-life (radioactive)
Time required for a radioactive substance to lose 50 % of its activity by decay. Each radionuclide has a unique half-life.

HR-ICP-MS
High resolution inductively coupled plasma mass spectrometry. A highly sophisticated analytical method used to analyze the isotopic composition of a sample.

ICP-MS
Inductively coupled plasma mass spectrometry.

Individual survey
Single individuals or groups of two individuals together conducted surveys by sweeping, as line up survey, in predetermined directions and areas. This method was used in very special circumstances when very little was known about the precise areas of a given site within which DU had been used.

Insignificant risk
Low level of *contamination* – of the same order of magnitude as the natural uranium level.

Insignificant radiological risk
When the corresponding dose is below 1 mSv

Insignificant toxicological risk
When the corresponding concentration/intake are below WHO health standards, recommendations or guidelines respectively.

Isotope
A nuclide having the same number of protons in the nuclei, and hence the same atomic number, but differing in the number of neutrons and therefore in the mass number.

Isotopic concentration
Unit mass (e.g. mg) of an isotope (e.g. U-238) per unit mass or volume in which the isotope occurs.

Jacket (Casing)
The non-DU part of a projectile, made of aluminium, that holds the DU penetrator.

Line-up survey / In-line survey
A number of people (most often 4-6) were lined up with 1-2 metres between each person. The group walked slowly forwards, maintaining their alignment with one another, while sweeping the instruments at ground level left and right perpendicular to the walking direction in such a way that approximately all the area was measured. The walking speed was 7 ±2 metres per minute depending on the terrain.

Localized ground contamination
A contamination – detectable mainly by analytical methods – around the source of contamination ranging over an area, usually not more than 200 x 200 meters.

Natural background concentration
The concentration or level of a substance that is derived solely from natural sources (i.e. of geological origin) according to ISO 11074-1(1996).

Nuclide
A species of atom characterised by the constitution of its nucleus. The nuclear constitution is specified by the number of protons (Z), number of neutrons (N), and energy content, or, alternatively, by the atomic number (Z), mass number A=(N+Z), and atomic mass. To be regarded as a distinct nuclide, the atom must be capable of existing for a measurable time.

Penetrator
The armour-piercing DU core of a DU weapon projectile.

Pyrophore / pyrophoric
DU, particularly as powder, is pyrophoric, which means that it can ignite spontaneously with oxygen in the air at temperatures of 600-700 °C. When DU burns, the high temperature oxidizes the uranium metal to a series of complex oxides, predominately triuranium octaoxide (U_3O_8), but also uranium dioxide (UO_2) and uranium trioxide (UO_3).

Qualified at random survey
After a briefing on what to expect, how to conduct the survey and where to search, team members were sent out to search for radioactivity in the environment.

Radiation weighting factor, wR
A number by which the *absorbed dose* in a tissue or organ is multiplied to reflect the *relative* biological effectiveness of the radiation in inducing stochastic effects at low doses, the result being the equivalent dose. Values are selected by ICRP to be representative of the relevant *relative biological effectiveness* and are broadly compatible with the values previously recommended for *quality factors* in the definition of *dose equivalent*.

Radioactivity
The phenomenon whereby atoms undergo spontaneous and random disintegration, usually accompanied by the emission of radiation.

Radionuclide
A radioisotope or radioactive nuclide characterised by the constitution of its nucleus.

Reference case
Definition on how it is assumed that the attack happened, how much DU was used in the attack, size of the contaminated area, human exposure to DU, use of the contaminated area in the future and possible long-term effects of DU.

Reference level
Ground-surface contamination of 10 g DU/m^2.

SFOR
NATO's Stabilization Force in BiH

SI = Système International d'unités

Sievert (Sv)
SI derived unit of any of the quantities expressed as equivalent or effective dose.

Depleted Uranium in Bosnia and Herzegovina

Significant radiological risk
A 'significant' radiological risk is defined in this report as one where any expected radiation dose would be greater than 1 mSv per event, or per year.

Significant risk
When the exposure of DU is higher than applicable health standards.

Significant toxicological risk
When the expected concentration or intake would exceed WHO health standards, recommendations or guidelines.

Soil
The upper layer of the Earth's crust composed of mineral parts, organic substance, water, air and living matter, according to ISO 11074-1 (1996).

Specific activity
1. The *activity* per unit mass of a radionuclide.
2. The *activity* per unit mass or volume of the material in which the radionuclides are essentially uniformly distributed.

The distinction in usage between *specific activity* and *activity concentration* is controversial. Some regard the terms as synonymous, and may favour one or the other (as above). ISO 921 [11] distinguishes between specific activity as the activity per unit mass and activity concentration as the *activity* per unit volume. Another common distinction is that *specific activity* is used (usually as *activity* per unit mass) with reference to a pure sample of a radionuclide or, less strictly, to cases where a radionuclide is intrinsically present in the material (e.g. carbon-14 in organic materials, uranium-235 in *natural uranium*), even if the abundance of the radionuclide is artificially changed.

Specific energy (imparted)
see *absorbed dose*

Surface soil
The top layer (a few centimetres) of the soil. In this assessment, soil samples from the first 5 - 10 centimetres were taken.

Undetectable DU contamination
Low level DU contamination. Not possible to differentiate from natural uranium present in the soil. Below the detection limits of the field and/or laboratory methods used.

Widespread contamination
A contamination of the ground surface may be either *localized* or wide spread over a large area, depending on the properties of the aerosols and the prevailing meteorological conditions. Widespread contamination exists in the case where the contamination can be found over a couple of hundred meters from the source of contamination.

Appendix S
References

1. ACGIH, 1993. Threshold limiting values for chemical substances and physical agents and biological exposure indices. Technical Affairs Office ACGIH. Cincinnati. Ohio. USA.

2. Adamo, P., Violante, P., Violante, A., 1989. Contenuto di radionuclidi nel tallo di Stereocaulon vesuvianum (Pers.). Atti S.IT.E. 7,173-176.

3. Agapov A.M., Novikov G.N. and Pavlovski O.A., 2001. Use of ammunition with depleted uranium in Yugoslavia. Journal "MOST", S-Petersburg, #43, April 2001, p.30-33. (in Russian).

4. Åkerblom G. and Mellander H., 1997. Geology and radon. In Durrani S.A. & Ili´c R. Radon Measurements by Etched Track Detectors. World Scientific, Singapore, 21-49.

5. Andersson A., Dahlman B., Gee D. and Snäll S., 1985. The Scandinavian alum shales. Geological Survey of Sweden. Avhandlingar och uppsatser, Nr 56,. 55 p.

6. Annual Book of American Society for Testing and Materials (ASTM) Standards, 1999a. Standard Practices for Sampling Water from Closed Conduits - Designation: D 3370-95a. Vol. 11.01 - (Water I) - Water and Environmental Technology (ISBN 0-8031-2688-5), 255-265.

7. Annual Book of American Society for Testing and Materials (ASTM) Standards, 1999b. Standard Test Method for Isotopic Uranium in Water by Radiochemistry - Designation: D 3972-97. Vol. 11.01 - (Water II) - Water and Environmental Technology (ISBN 0-8031-2688-3), 368-373.

8. Anspaugh L R, Shinn J H, Phelps P L & Kennedy N C (1975). Resuspension and redistribution of plutonium in soils. Health Physics 29, 571-582.

9. ATSDR, 1999. Toxicological profile for uranium, draft for public comment. Research Triangle Institute for Agency for Toxic Substances and Disease Registry, Atlanta. USA.

10. Barbizzi S., De Zorzi P. Galas C., 2002. Metrologia e conduzione del campionamento ambientale. Tutto_Misure, Anno IV, nr. 57, Inserto, AUGUSTA Edizioni Mortasino.

11. Beckett P.J., Boileau L.J.R., Padovan D., Richardson D.H.S. & Nieboer E., 1982. Lichens and mosses as monitors of industrial activity associated with uranium mining in northern Ontario, Canada - Part 2: Distance dependent uranium and lead accumulation patterns. Environmental Pollution 4B, 91-107.

12. Bellis D., Ma R., Bramall N., McLeod C.W., Chapman N. and Satake K.; 2001, "Airborne uranium contamination - as revealed through elemental and isotopic analysis of tree bark" - Environmental Pollution vol. 144, Issue 3, 383-387.

13. Biazrov L.G., 1994. Radionuclide content in lichen thallus in the forests adjacent to the Chernobyl atomic power plant. The Science of the Total Environment 157, 25-28.

14. Blasch E.B., Stuckenbroeker G., Lusky R., 1970. The use of uranium as a shielding material. Nuclear Engineering and Design, 13, 146-182. North-Holland Publishing Company.

15. Bleise A., Danesi P.R. and Burkart W., 2003. Properties, use and health effects of depleted uranium (DU): a general overview. Journal of Environmental Radioactivity 64, 93-112.

16. Bogatov S.A., Gorshkov V.E., Tkalya E.V. and Al'himovich N.N.,1995. The Method of Reconstruction of Air Activities Following a Nuclear Accident. Radiat. Prot. Dosim. 62(3), pp 139-149 (1995).

17. Boileau L.J.R., Beckett P.J., Lavoie P. & Richardson D.H., 1982. Lichens and mosses as monitors of industrial activity associated with uranium mining in northern Ontario, Canada - Part 1: Field procedures, chemical analysis and interspecies comparison. Environmental Pollution 4B, 69-84.

18. Bou-Rabee, F. 1995. Estimating the Concentration of Uranium in Some Environmental Samples in Kuwait After the1991 Gulf War, Appl. Rad. Isot. 46(4), 217-220.

19. Brezzi, G., 1999-2000. Valutazione dell'indice di biodiversità dei licheni di alcune aree del Lazio. Tesi di Laurea. Dip. Biologia Vegetale, Università "La Sapienza". Roma.

20. Brown J & Simmonds J S (1995). FARMLAND. A dynamic model for the transfer of radionuclides through terrestrial foodchains. NRPB-R273. HMSO: London.

21. Browne E., Firestone R.B., Shirley V., 1986. Table of isotopes. Lawrence Berkeley Laboratory, University of California. John Wiley & Sons Inc., New York.

22. Brummitt R.K. & Powell C.E., (eds.) 1992. Authors of plant names. Royal Botanic Gardens, Kew.

23. Burger M., 2002. UNEP DU Post-Conflict Assessment 2001: Serbia/Montenegro. Report of the Swiss Team. Spiez Laboratory Report with 1 annex. Switzerland.

24. Cantaluppi C. and Degetto S., 2000. Usi Civili e Militari dell'Uranio Impoverito: Problemi Ambientali e Sanitari. Atti del XXXI Congresso Nazionale AIRP, Ancona, Sett. 2000.

25. Cenci R.M., 1999, "L'utilizzo di muschi indigeni e trapantiati per valutare in micro e macro aeree le ricadute al suolo di elementi in tracce: proposte metodologiche" - in Piccini C. and Salvati S. editors, Atti Workshop "Bio-monitoraggio della qualità dell'aria sul territorio nazionale", Roma, 26-27 nov. 1998. ANPA - Serie Atti 2/1999, 241-263.

25a Chen, Z.S. SELECTING INDICATORS TO EVALUATE SOIL QUALITY; Department of Agricultural Chemistry National Taiwan University Taipei, 10617, Taiwan ROC, 1999-08-01.

26. CHPPM. 2000. Health risk assessment consultation No. 26-MF-7555-00D. Depleted uranium -Human exposure assessment and health risk characterization in support of the environmental exposure report "Depleted uranium in the Gulf" of the Office of the Special Assistant to the Secretary of Defense for Gulf War Illnesses. Medical Readiness and Military Deployments (OSAGWI), OSAGWI Levels I, II, and III Scenarios, 15 September 2000.

27. Clauzade G. & Roux C., 1985. Likenoj de Okcidenta Europo. Ilustrita Determinlibro. Bull. Soc. Bot. Centre-Ouest, n. s., nr. spéc. 7.

28. Crançon P. 2001. Migration de l'uranium dans un Podzol . Le Role des Colloides dans la Zone non saturee et la Nappe: Application aux Llandes de Gascogne. Ph. Dr. thesis, University of Grenoble 1, France.

29. Croudache I., Warwick P., Taylor R., Dee S., 1998, "Rapid procedure for plutonium and uranium determination in soils using a borate fusion followed by ion-exchange and extraction chromatography". Analytica Chimica Acta 371 (1998) 217-225.

30. Currie L.A., 1968. Limits for qualitative detection and quantitative determination. Anal. Chem., 40; 586-593.

31. Dobson F.S., 2000. Lichen. An illustrated guide to the British and Irish species. The Richmond publishing Co., 431 pp.

32. DOE, 2000. Exposure Assessment Project at the Paducah Gaseous Diffusion Plant. Dec. 2000. (http:/www.eh.doe.gov/ benefits/docs/200012paducah.pdf)

33. DOF, 2000. Depleted Uranium in the Gulf (II). Environmental Exposure Report. US Department of Defense. December 13, 2000.

34. DURANTE and PUGLIESE, 2002. Durante, M. and Pugliese, M., Estimates of Radiological Risk from Depleted Uranium Weapons, Health Physics 82(1): 14-20, 2002.

35. ECP1, 1996. Contamination on surfaces by resuspended material. European Commission. Experimental collaboration project No 1. Final Report. EUR 16527 EN.

36. Erikson R.L. et al. 1990. A review of the environmental behavior of uranium derived from depleted uranium alloy penetrators. Pacific Northwest Laboratory, Richland, Washington. PNL-7213.

37. EU, 1996. Council Directive 96/29/EURATOM OF 13 May 1996 laying down the basic safety standards for the protection of workers and the general public against the dangers arising from ionizing radiation. Official Journal of the European Communities. L 159.Vol. 39. 26 June 1996.

38. EU, 1998. Council Directive 98/83/EC of 3 November 1998 on the quality of water intended for human consumption. Official Journal of the European Communities. L 330/32. December 1998.

39. EU, 2001. Draft modification to OJ L330/46 of 5.12.98 (version 13/03/01). Annex II, Monitoring.

40. EURACHEM/CITAC Guide 2000. Quantifying uncertainty in analytical measurement. 2nd Edition, 2000.

41. European Commission 2001. Opinion of the Group of Experts Established according to Article 31 of the EURATOM Treaty. Depleted Uranium.

42. Exploranium G.S. Ltd., 1989. Portable Gamma Ray Spectrometer, Model GR-256 with GPS-21 Detector. Manual. Exploranium G.S. Ltd. Bolton, Ontario, Canada. Rfv. #4 - 10/26/89.

43. Feige G.B., Niemann L. & Jahnke S., 1990. Lichen and mosses - silent chronists of the Chernobyl accident. Bibliotheca Lichenologica 38: 63-77.

44. Ferry B.W., Baddeley M.S. & Hawksworth D.L., (Eds.) 1973. Air Pollution and Lichens. University of Toronto Press, Toronto.

45. Food and Fertilizer Technologie Center; 5F.14 Wenchow St., Taipei 10616 Taiwan R.O.C. (www.agnet.org/library/ image/eb473t6.html)

46. Galsomies L., Letrouit-Galinou M.A., Deschamps C., Savanne D., Avnaim M., Duclaux G., 2000, "Atmospheric metal deposition in France: Estimation based on moss analysisi. First results" - IAEA-TECDOC-1152, 108-115.

47. Garland J A, 1979. Resuspension of particulate material from grass and soil. AERE-R 9452: London.

48. Garland J A, 1982. Resuspension of particulate material from grass. Experimental programme.1979-1980. AERE-R 10106: London.

49. Garty J., Galun M. & Kessel M., 1979. Localization of heavy metals and other elements accumulated in the lichen tallus. New Phytologist 82, 159-168.

50. Garty J.; 2001, "Bio-monitoring Atmospheric Heavy Metals with Lichens: Theory and Application" Critical Reviews in Plant Science, 20(4): 309-371.

51. Gillette, 1977. Fine particulate emissions due to wind erosion, Trans. ASAE.

52. Goldstein S. J., Rodriguez J. M. and Lujan N., 1997. Measurement and Application of Uranium Isotopes for Human and Environmental Monitoring. Health Phys. 72(1), 10-18.

Post-Conflict Environmental Assessment

53. Grodzinska K., Szarek-Lukaszewska G.; 2001, "Response of moss to heavy metal deposition in Poland - an overview" - Environmental Pollution 114 (2001) 443-451.

54. Guidelines for drinking-water quality, 2nd ed. Vol. 2 Health criteria and other supporting information, 1996 (pp. 940-949) and Addendum to Vol. 2. 1998 (pp. 281-283) Geneva, World Health Organization.

55. Haas J.R., Bailey E.H. & Purvis O.W., 1998. Bioaccumulation of metals by lichens: Uptake of aqueous uranium by Peltigera membranacea as a function of time and pH. American Mineralogist 83, 1494-1502.

56. Harley N.H., Foulkes E.C., Hilborne L.H., Hudson A., Anthony C.R., 1999. A review of the scientific literature as it pertains to Gulf war illnesses. RAND. Washington, USA. 1999. (http://www.gulflink.osd.mil/library/randrep/du/).

57. Hofmann W., Attarpour N., Lettner H. & Türk, R., 1993. 137Cs concentrations in lichens before and after the Chernobyl accident. Health Physics 64, 70-73.

58. Hollander, 1994. Resuspension factors of Cs137 in Hannover after the Chernobyl accident. J. Aerosol Science, 25.

59. Holm E. and Persson B.R.R., 1978. Global fallout of curium. Nature, 273, 289-290.

60. IAEA, 1979. Gamma-ray surveys in uranium exploration. International Atomic Energy Agency, Technical reports series No. 186. p 90.

61. IAEA, 1996. International Basic Safety Standards for Protection against Ionizing Radiation and for the Safety of Radiation Sources, Safety Series No. 115, Vienna.

62. IAEA, 1999. Organization and implementation of a national regulatory infrastructure governing protection against ionizing radiation and the safety of radiation sources. Interim report for comment. IAEA-TECDOC-1067, Vienna.

63. IAEA, 1999. Report on the inter-comparison run for the determination of trace and minor elements in Lichen material . IAEA 336" IAEA/AL/079. NAHRES-33.

64. IAEA, 2000. - Bio-monitoring of atmospheric pollution (with emphasis on trace elements) - Bio-MAP - June 2000, IAEA-TECDOC-1152.

65. ICRP, 1974. Report of the Task Group on Reference Man, 1974. Commission on Radiation Protection (ICRP), Publication No. 23. Pergamon Press, 1975.

66. ICRP, 1983. Radionuclide transformations. Energy and intensity of emissions. Annals of the ICRP. ICRP publication 38, Vol. 11-13, 1983. Pergamon Press. 1983.

67. ICRP, 1991. Recommendations of the International Commission on Radiological Protection. ICRP publication No. 60. Pergamon Press 1991.

68. ICRP, 1993. Protection against Radon-222 at home and at work. Report of the International Commission on Radiological Protection, ICRP publication No. 65. Pergamon Press 1993.

69. Idelchik, 1975. The manual on hydraulic resistances. Moscow, Mashinostroenie Publ., (in Russian).

70. ISO/TEC Guide 17025. General Requirements for the Competence of Testing and Calibration Laboratories. American Association for Laboratory Accreditation (A2LA). Fredrick, Maryland USA.

71. Jeran Z., Byrne A.R. and Batic F., 1995. Transplanted epiphytic lichens as biomonitors of air-contaminated by natural radionuclides around the •irovski Vhr Uranium mine, Slovenia. Lichenologist, 27(5): 375-385.

72. Jeran Z., Jacimovic R., Batic F., Smodiš B. and Wolterbeek H. Th., 1996. Atmospheric heavy metal pollution in Slovenia derived from results for epiphytic lichens. Fresenius Journal Anal. Chem, 354:681-687.

73. Jia G., Belli M., Rosamilia S., Gaudino S. and Sansone U., 2002b, "A new method for determination of uranium isotopes in water, vegetation and soil by alpha spectrometry" - Proceeding of the International Congress on the Radioecology-Ecotoxicology of Continental and Estuarine Environments", Aix-en-Provence, France, 3-7 September 2001 -Radioprotection - Colloques, Vol. 37, C1-957-962.

74. Jia G., Belli M., Sansone U., Rosamilia S., Ocone R., Gaudino S., 2002a, "Determination of uranium isotopes in environmental samples by alpha-spectrometry", Journal of Radioanalytical and Nuclear Chemistry, Vol. 253, No. 3, 395-406.

75. Jovanovic S., 1995, "An experience in Montenegro with atmospheric pollution by means of lichens", J. trace and Microprobe Tecniques, 13 4 (1995), 463-471.

76. Jungic, Sasa; Jakovljevic, Branislava; Rakita, Ivanka et al. "Maligna oboljenja u Klinickom centru Banjaluka od 1993 do 2000 godine". Report of the Klinicki centar Banjaluka, Klinika za onkologiju. (in local language) No date.

77. Kashirin I.A., A.I. Ermakov, S.V. Malinovskiy et al. (2000). Liquid scintillation determination of low level components in complex mixtures of radionuclides. Applied Radiation and Isotopes, 53.

78. Keller M., Anet B., Burger M., Schmid E., Wicki A., Wirz Ch., Spiez Laboratory in cooperation with Chambers G., European Parliament, Directorate-General for Research, Working Paper, Scientific and Technological Options Assessment Series, STOA 100 EN 05-2001. Depleted Uranium: Environmental and Health Effects in the Gulf War, Bosnia and Kosovo. WEB: www.europarl.eu.int

79. KFOR. 2000. NATO/KFOR unclassified release to UNMIK. Subject: Depleted Uranium (DU). KFOR Headquarters, Film City, Pristina, Kosovo, 17 September 2000.

80. Kilpatrick, M.E., No Depleted Uranium in Cruise Missiles or Apache Helicopter Munitions - Comments on an Article by Durante and Pugliese, Health Physics 82(6): 904-905, 2002.

REFERENCES

81. Kogan R. M., Nazarov I. M. and Fridman Sh. D. 1971. Gamma spectrometry of natural environments and formations. Atomizdat. Moscow, 1969. Israel program for scientific translations. Jerusalem. p 1-337.

82. Kuksa, 1994. Southern Seas (Aral, Caspian, Azov and Black) under anthropogenic stress. St. Petersburg, Gidrometeoizdat. (in Russian).

83. Lewis D.L. 1996. Assessing and Controlling Sample Contamination. Principle of Environmental Sampling - Second Edition - Edited by Lawrence H. Keith.

84. Lewis D.L. 1996. Assessing and Controlling Sample Contamination. Principle of Environmental Sampling - Second Edition - Edited by Lawrence H. Keith.

85. Linsley G S, 1978. Resuspension of the transuranium elements - a review of existing data. NRPB-R75. HMSO: London.

86. Loppi S. & De Dominicis V., 1996. Lichens as long-term biomonitors of air quality in Central Italy. Acta Botanica Neerlandica 45, 563-570.

87. McLean J., Purvis O.W. & Williamson B.J., 1998. Role of lichen melanins in uranium remediation. Nature 391, 649.

88. MCNP, 2000. MCNP - A General Monte Carlo N-Particle Transport Code. Version 4C. Los Alamos National Laboratory. April 10, 2000.

89. Mook W.G., and de Vries J.J., 2001. Environmental Isotopes in the Hydrological Cycle. Principles and applications. Volume 1. IAEA.

90. Müller H, Gering F & Pröhl G (1999). Model Description of the Terrestrial Food Chain and Dose Module FDMT in RODOS PV4.0. RODOS(WG3)-TN(99)17.

91. Musílek L., Cechák T., losinská J., Wolterbeek H.Th.; 2000, "Bio-monitoring air pollution in the Czech Republic by means of tree bark" -IAEA-TECDOC-1152, 189-196.

92. NAHRES-60, 2001. Report on the NAT-9 quality control exercise on uranium isotopes in two soil samples. International Atomic Energy Agency, Department of Nuclear Sciences and Applications, Division of Human Health, Section of Nutritional and Environmental Studies. IAEA Report NAHRES-60.

93. Nash K., Fried S., Friedman A.M. and Sullivan J.C. (1981) Redox behaviour, complexing, and adsorption of hexavalent actinides by humic-acid and selected clays. Environmental Science and Technology, 15, 834-837.

94. Nash T.H. III & Wirth V., (Eds.) 1988. Lichens, Bryophytes and Air Quality. Bibliotheca Lichenologica 30.

95. NATO AEP 49. Sampling and Identification of Radiological Agents, Volume 2: Forensic.

96. NATO, STANAG 4590, AEP-49. Sampling and Identification of Radiological Agents Handbook, SIRA Handbook.

97. NELLIS, 1997. Resumption of use of depleted uranium rounds at Nellis Air Force Range. Target 63-10. U.S. Army Corps of Engineers, Nebraska. Draft June 1997.

98. Nieboer E. & Richardson D.H., 1981. Lichen as monitors of atmospheric deposition. In Atmospheric pollutants in natural waters. Ed. by S.J. Eisenreich, 339-88. Ann Arbor, Michigan, Ann Arbor Science.

99. Nimis P.L. and Barbagli R., 1999, "Linee guida per l'utilizzo di licheni epifiti come bioaccumulatori di metalli in traccia" in Piccini C. and Salvati S. editors, Atti Workshop "Biomonitoraggio della qualità dell'aria sul territorio nazionale", Roma, 26-27 nov. 1998. APAT - Serie Atti 2/1999, 279-289.

100. Nimis P.L. and Purvis O.W.; 2002, "Monitoring Lichen as indicators of pollution". Monitoring with Lichen - Monitoring Lichens, Kluwer Academic Publishers, 7-10.

101. Nimis P.L., 1987. I macrolicheni d'Italia. Chiavi analitiche per la determinazione. Gortania. Atti MuseoFriu/.StoriaNat. 8: 101-220.

102. Nimis P.L., 2000. Checklist of the Lichens of Italy 2.0. University of Trieste, Dept. of Biology, IN2.0/2 (http://dbiodbs.univ.trieste.it/).

103. NIOSH, 1994. Pocket guide to chemical hazards. US Department of Health and Human ervices, Public Health Service, Centers for Disease Control and Prevention, National Institute for Occupational Safety and Health.

104. OSAGWI, 2000. DEPLETED URANIUM - Human Exposure Assessment and Health Risk Characterization In Support of the Environmental Exposure Report "Depleted Uranium in the Gulf" of the Office of the Special Assistant to the Secretary of Defense for Gulf War Illnesses, Medical Readiness and Military Deployments (OSAGWI). 15 September 2000. HEALTH RISK ASSESSMENT CONSULTATION, NO. 26-MF-7555-00D.

105. Pavlovski O.A., 2002. External radiation as a factor of radiation exposure under the DU contaminated areas. Preprint IBRAE RAS No 2002-03, Moscow, 2002 (in Russian).

106. Piervittori R., 1999, "Licheni come bio-indicatori della qualità dell'aria: stato dell'arte in Italia" - in Piccini C. and Salvati S. editors, Atti Workshop "Bio-monitoraggio della qualità dell'aria sul territorio nazionale", Roma, 26-27 nov. 1998. ANPA - Serie Atti 2/1999, 97-122.

107. Purvis O.W., Coppins B.J., Hawksworth D.L., James P.W., Moore D.M., 1992. The lichen flora of Great Britain and Ireland. Natural History Museum Publications and The British Lichen Society, London, 710 pp.

108. Ragnarsdottir K.V. and Charlet L., 2000. Uranium behavior in natural environments. In Environmental Mineralogy: Microbial Interactions, Anthropogenic Influences, Contaminated Land and Waste Management. (J. Cotter-Howells J., Batchelder M.,Campbell L. and Valsami-Jones E., eds.), 333-377. Mineralogical Society of Great Britain and Ireland.

Post-Conflict Environmental Assessment

109. Reeks, M.W., J. Reed and D. Hall (1988). On the resuspension of small particles by a turbulent flow. J. Phys. D: Appl. Phys. 21.

110. RESRAD, 2001. User's Manual for RESRAD Version 6. Environmental Assessment Division Argonne National Laboratory. ANL/EAD-4, July 2001.

111. Ribeiro Guevara S., Arribe M.A., Calvelo S. & Roman Ross G., 1995. Elemental composition of lichens at Naahuel Huapi national park, Patagonia, Argentina. Journal of Radioanalytical Chemistry 198 (2), 437-448.

112. Richardson D.H.S. & Nieboer E., 1980. Surface binding and accumulation of metals in lichens. In Cellular interactions in symbiosis and parasitism. Ed. by C.B. Cook, P. W. Pappas and E.D. Rudolph, 75-94. Columbus, Ohio, Ohio State University Press.

113. Richardson D.H.S. & Nieboer E., 1981. Lichens and pollution monitoring. Enddeavour, 5, 127-133.

114. Richardson D.H.S., Beckett P.J. & Nieboer E., 1980. Nickel in lichens, bryophytes, fungi and algae. In Nickel in the environment. Ed. by J.O. Nriagu, 367-406. New York, John Wiley.

115. Rosamilia S., Gaudino S. and Jia G., 2003. "Uranium Isotopes in water samples collected in Bosnia-Herzegovina" Italian Agency for Environmental Protection and Technical Services (APAT) contribution to UNEP DU Post-Conflict in Bosnia-Herzegovina. Prot. APAT.AMB.LAB.058-2003.

116. Rosamilia S., Gaudino S., Jia G., A. Pati, S. Ruisi, A. Pati, Leone P., Bellaria V., 2003b "Bio-Indicators - APAT Report" Italian Agency for Environmental Protection and Technical Services (APAT) contribution to UNEP DU Post-Conflict in Bosnia-Herzegovina. Prot. APAT.AMB.LAB-151-2003.

117. Rosamilia S., Gaudino S., Jia G., Barbizzi S., Ruisi S., L. Zucconi, F. Fornasier, 2003a. "Methodology and Quality Control - APAT Report" Italian Agency for Environmental Protection and Technical Services (APAT) contribution to UNEP DU Post-Conflict in Bosnia-Herzegovina. Prot. APAT.AMB.LAB-150-2003.

118. S.E. International Inc., 1999. Inspector User Manual. S.E. International, Inc. Summertime, TN 38483, U.S.A.

119. Sansone U., Barbizzi S., Belli M., Gaudino S., Jia G., and Rosamilia S., 2002. Italian National Environmental Protection Agency (ANPA) contribution to the UNEP DU Post-Conflict Assessment in Serbia and Montenegro 2001. Prot. ANPA/AMB-LAB 60-2002.

120. Sansone U., Barbizzi S., Belli M., Gaudino S., Jia G., Rosamilia S., Stellato L., 2001a. Uranio impoverito: l'evidenza delle misure. Tutto_Misure, Anno III, 2/01, 172-176.

121. Sansone U., Barbizzi S., Belli M., Gaudino S., Jia G., Rosamilia S., Stellato L., 2001b. Levels of depleted uranium in the soils of Kosovo. Radiation Protection Dosimetry, Nuclear Technology Publishing. Vol. 97, No. 4, pp. 317-320.

122. Sansone U., Danesi P., Campbell M., Ocone R., Pati A., Stellato L., Rosamilia S., Jia G., Gaudino S., Barbizzi S. and Belli M.; 2001, "Radioecological Survey at Selected Sites hit by Depleted Uranium Ammunitions during the 1999 Kosovo Conflict", The Science of the Total Environment 281 (2001.), 23-35.

123. Saphymo-SRAT, 1969. Scintillation meter S.P.P.2NF User Manual. Saphymo-PHY, 5 Rue de Teatre, 91884, Massy, France.

124. Sloof J.E. & Wolterbeek H.Th., 1991. Patterns in trace elements in lichens. Water, Air and Soil Pollution 57-58, 785-795.

125. Spiez Laboratory, 2000. Depleted Uranium, Hintergrundinformation.

126. Spiez Laboratory; Test Report No. UA-2003-003; Element screening analyses of water samples with ICP-mass spectrometry.

127. Spiez Laboratory; Test Report No. UA-2003-004; Element screening analyses of total digested soil sample solutions with ICP-mass spectrometry.

128. Spiez Laboratory; Test report No. NUC-2002-024; Determination of uranium isotopes in soil samples (Hadzici tank repair facility) from the UNEP DU Field Assessment Mission 2002 in BiH.

129. Spiez Laboratory; Test report No. NUC-2002-025; Determination of uranium isotopes in soil samples (Lukavica barracks) from the UNEP DU Field Assessment Mission 2002 in BiH.

130. Spiez Laboratory; Test report No. NUC-2002-026; Determination of uranium isotopes in soil samples (Dobrosevice; T55 tank position) from the UNEP DU Field Assessment Mission 2002 in BiH.

131. Spiez Laboratory; Test report No. NUC-2002-027; Determination of uranium isotopes in soil samples (Hadzici barracks and ammunition storage area) from the UNEP DU Field Assessment Mission 2002 in BiH.

132. Spiez Laboratory; Test report No. NUC-2002-028/A; Determination of uranium isotopes in soil samples 0-5cm (Han Pijesak barracks) from the UNEP DU Field Assessment Mission 2002 in BiH.

133. Spiez Laboratory; Test report No. NUC-2002-028/B; Determination of uranium isotopes in profile soil samples (Han Pijesak barracks) from the UNEP DU Field Assessment Mission 2002 in BiH.

134. Spiez Laboratory; Test report No. NUC-2002-028/C; Determination of uranium isotopes in special samples (Han Pijesak barracks) from the UNEP DU Field Assessment Mission 2002 in BiH.

135. Spiez Laboratory; Test report No. NUC-2002-028/D; Determination of plutonium and neptunium isotopes in three penetrators from the UNEP DU Field Assessment Mission 2002 in BiH.

136. Spiez Laboratory; Test report No. NUC-2002-028/E; Determination of the uranium isotopic composition of three penetrators from the UNEP DU Field Assessment Mission 2002 in BiH.

137. Spiez Laboratory; Test report No. NUC-2002-028/F; Determination of extracted uranium isotopes in profile soil samples (Han Pijesak barracks) from the UNEP DU Field Assessment Mission 2002 in BiH.

138. Spiez Laboratory; Test report No. NUC-2002-028/G; Determination of extracted uranium isotopes in profile soil samples (Han Pijesak barracks) from the UNEP DU Field Assessment Mission 2002 in BiH.

139. Spiez Laboratory; Test report No. NUC-2002-028/H; Determination of extracted uranium isotopes in profile soil samples (Han Pijesak barracks) from the UNEP DU Field Assessment Mission 2002 in BiH.

140. Spiez Laboratory; Test report No. NUC-2002-028/I; Determination of extracted uranium isotopes in profile soil samples (Han Pijesak barracks) from the UNEP DU Field Assessment Mission 2002 in BiH.

141. Spiez Laboratory; Test report No. NUC-2002-028/K; Determination of extracted uranium isotopes in profile soil samples (Han Pijesak barracks) from the UNEP DU Field Assessment Mission 2002 in BiH.

142. Spiez Laboratory; Test report No. NUC-2002-028/L; Determination of extracted uranium isotopes in profile soil samples (Han Pijesak barracks) from the UNEP DU Field Assessment Mission 2002 in BiH.

143. Spiez Laboratory; Test report No. NUC-2002-028/M; Determination of extracted uranium isotopes in profile soil samples (Han Pijesak barracks) from the UNEP DU Field Assessment Mission 2002 in BiH.

144. Spiez Laboratory; Test report No. NUC-2002-028/N; Determination of uranium isotopes in the extraction residues of profile soil samples (Han Pijesak barracks) from the UNEP DU Field Assessment Mission 2002 in BiH.

145. Spiez Laboratory; Test report No. NUC-2002-028/O; Determination of uranium isotopes in profile soil samples (Han Pijesak barracks) from the UNEP DU Field Assessment Mission 2002 in BiH.

146. Spiez Laboratory; Test report No. NUC-2002-030; Determination of uranium isotopes in soil samples (Vogosca ammunition production site) from the UNEP DU Field Assessment Mission 2002 in BiH.

147. Spiez Laboratory; Test report No. NUC-2002-031; Determination of uranium isotopes in soil samples (Kalinovik water reservoir and ammunition destruction site) from the UNEP DU Field Assessment Mission 2002 in BiH.

148. Spiez Laboratory; Test report No. NUC-2002-032; Determination of uranium isotopes in soil samples (Foca bridge) from the UNEP DU Field Assessment Mission 2002 in BiH.

149. Spiez Laboratory; Test report No. NUC-2002-033; Determination of uranium isotopes in soil samples (Ustikolina barracks) from the UNEP DU Field Assessment Mission 2002 in BiH.

150. Spiez Laboratory; Test report No. NUC-2002-034; Determination of uranium isotopes in soil samples (Pale Koran barracks) from the UNEP DU Field Assessment Mission 2002 in BiH.

151. Spiez Laboratory; Test report No. NUC-2002-035; Determination of uranium isotopes in soil samples (Bjelasnica plateau, ammunition liquidation site) from the UNEP DU Field Assessment Mission 2002 in BiH.

152. Spiez Laboratory; Test report No. NUC-2002-036 A; Determination of uranium isotopes in air filter samples from the UNEP DU Field Assessment Mission 2002 in BiH.

153. Spiez Laboratory; Test report No. NUC-2002-037; Determination of uranium isotopes in IAEA reference material: soil, sea water, lichen and seaweed.

154. Spiez Laboratory; Test report No. NUC-2002-038; Determination of uranium isotopes in water and water filter samples from the UNEP DU Field Assessment Mission 2002 in BiH.

155. Spiez Laboratory; Test report No. NUC-2002-039; Determination of uranium isotopes in water samples from the UNEP DU Field Assessment Mission 2002 in BiH.

156. Stevenson F.J. 1985. Geochemistry of Soil Humic Substances. In: Humic Substances in Soil, Sediments and Water. Eds: Aiken G.R., McKnight D.M., Wershaw R.L. and MacCarthy P., John Wiley and Sons, pp13-52.

157. Suschny O.,1968. The measurement of atmospheric radioactivity. World Meteorological Organization. Technical note No.94. WMO - No.231.TP.124. Geneva. Switzerland.

158. Swanson V.E., 1960. Oil yield and uranium content in black shales. Geological Survey, Professional Papers 356-A. Washington.

159. Symposium: Incidence of malignant tumours in BiH and Herzegovina Population. Sarajevo 21.03.2002. Editor in chief Faruk Konjhodzic, editorial board: Ladislav Ozegovic, Dzemal Rezakovic, Jela Vasic-Grujic.

160. Taylor H.W., Hutchinson E.A., McInnes K.L. and Svoboda J., 1979. Cosmos 954: Search for airborne radioactivity on lichens in the crash area, Northwest Territories, Canada. Science, N.Y., 205, 1383-1385.

161. The Royal Society, March 2002, "The health effects of depleted uranium munitions". Document 6/02. ISBN 0 85403 5753.

162. Trembley M.L., Fahselt D. and Madzia S.; 1997, "Localization of Uranium in Cladina rangiferina and Cladina mitis and Removal by Aqueous Washing" - The Bryologis, 100(3) 368-376.

163. Triulzi C., Nonnis Marzano F. and Vaghi M.; 1996, "Important alpha, beta and gamma-emitting radionuclides in Lichen and moss collected in different world areas". Annali di Chimica 86, 699-704.

164. U.S. AEPI, 1994. Health and environmental consequences of depleted uranium use by the U.S. Army. Technical report, June 1995. Army Environmental Policy Institute. Champaign, Illinois, 1994.

165. U.S. Army Material Command, 2000. Tank-Automotive and Armaments Command (TACOM) and army Material command (AMC) review of transuranics (TRU) in depleted uranium armor. 19 January, 2000. Memorandum. ATTN:AMCSF (Mr. Pittenger), 5001 Eisenhower Avenue, Alexandria, VA 22333-001.

166. U.S. EPA, 2000. National Primary Drinking Water Regulations. Radionucliods Final Rule, Environmental Protection Agency. 40 CFP Parts 9, 141, and 142. December 7, 2000.

167. UK, 2001. The health hazards of depleted uranium munitions. Part I. The Royal Society. 2001.

168. UK, 2001. The health hazards of depleted uranium munitions. Part I. The Royal Society. 2001.

169. UK, 2002. The health hazards of depleted uranium munitions. Part II. The Royal Society. 2002.

170. UNEP and UNCHS, 1999, "The Kosovo Conflict: consequences for the environment and Human settlements". United Nation Environment Programme and United Nations Centre for Human Settlements (Habitat).

171. UNEP, 2000. NATO confirms to the UN use of depleted uranium during the Kosovo Conflict. Press Release, 21 March 2000.

172. UNEP. 2001. "Depleted Uranium in Kosovo, Post-Conflict Environmental Assessment. UNEP Scientific Team Mission to Kosovo" (5th-19th November 2000). United Nations Environment Programme, Geneva, March 2001.

173. UNEP. 2002, "Depleted uranium in Serbia and Montenegro. Post-conflict environmental assessment in FRY", United Nations Environment Programme, Geneva, March 2002.

174. UNEP/UNCHS Balkans Task Force (BTF). 1999. The potentials effects on human health and the environment arising from possible use of depleted uranium during the 1999 Kosovo conflict. A preliminary assessment. Geneva. October 1999. 76.

175. UNSCEAR 2000. Exposures from natural radiation sources. United Nations Scientific Committee on the Effects of Atomic Radiation. Forty-eight session of UNSCEAR, Vienna, 12 to 16 April 1996. Preliminary report. Draft. 1999.

176. UNSCEAR, 1993. United Nations Scientific Committee on the Effects of Atomic Radiation. Report to the General Assembly, with scientific annexes. New York. United Nations 54. ISBN 92-1-142200-0. 1993.

177. UNSCEAR, 2000. Sources and effects of ionizing radiation. United Nations Scientific Committee on the Effects of Atomic Radiation. Report to the General Assembly, with scientific annexes. Vol. 1. United Nations, New York, 2000. ISBN 92-1142238-8.

178. UNSCEAR. 2000. Sources and Effects of Ionizing Radiation - Annex B. Exposures from natural radiation sources. United Nations Scientific Committee on the Effects of Atomic Radiation. Vol. I. Sources.

179. Vukotich P., Andjelich T., Zekich R., Kovachevich M., Vasich V., Ristich N., 2001. Field searching for ground contamination from depleted uranium at Cape Arza - Montenegro. 2001 (unpublished report).

180. Wagner G., 1995. Basic approaches and methods for quality assurance and quality control in sample collection and storage for environmental monitoring. The Science of the Total Environment 176 (1995) 63-71.

181. Waite T.D., Davis J.A., Payne T.E., Waychunas G.A, and Xu N., 1994. Uranium (VI) adsorption to ferrihydrite - application of surface complexation model Geochimica et Cosmochimica Acta, 58, 5465-5478.

182. WHO Geneva, April 2001, "Depleted Uranium: Sources, Exposure, and Health Effects". WHO/SDE/PHE/01.1.

183. WHO, 1998a. Guidelines for drinking water quality. 2nd edition. Addendum to Volume 2: Health criteria and other supporting information. World Health Organisation, Geneva, Switzerland.

184. WHO, 1998b. Derived intervention levels for radionuclides in food. World Health Organization, Geneva, Switzerland.

185. WHO, 2001. Depleted uranium. Sources, Exposure and Health Effects. Department of Protection of the Human Environment. World Health Organization. Geneva, April 2001.

186. WHO, 2002; www.who.int/water_sanitation_health/GDWQ/draftchemicals/list.htm

187. WHO. 1998. Guidelines for drinking water quality. 2nd edition. Addendum to volume 2: Health criteria and other supporting information. Geneva, Switzerland.

188. Wilkins B T, Simmonds J R & Cooper J R (Project Managers) (1994). Assessment of the present and future implications of the radioactive contamination of the Irish Sea coastal region of Cumbria. National Radiological Protection Board. NRPB-R267. HMSO: London

189. Williams, 1992. An exact solution of the Reeks-Hall resuspension equation for particulate flow. J.

190. Wirth, V. (1995). Die Flechten Baden-Württembergs. Ulmer & Co., Stuttgart.

191. WISE, 202. WISE Uranium Project. (http://www.antenna.nl/wise/uranium/index.html)

Depleted Uranium in Bosnia and Herzegovina

Appendix T
List of Contributors

Members of the UNEP Mission

Mr. Pekka Haavisto	Chairman of UNEP DU projects
Mr. Mario Burger	Project Coordinator, UNEP
Mr. Andrew Robinson	Report Writer, UNEP
Mr. Jan Olof Snihs	Scientific Leader, Swedish Radiation Protection Institute (SSI)
Mr. Gustav Åkerblom	Technical Leader, Swedish Radiation Protection Institute (SSI)
Mr. Ernst Schmid	Spiez Laboratory, Switzerland
Mr. Markus Astner	Spiez Laboratory, Switzerland
Ms. Silvia Rosamilia	Italian Environmental Protection Agency and Technical Services (APAT), Italy
Ms. Stefania Gaudino	Italian Environmental Protection Agency and Technical Services (APAT), Italy
Mr. Mark Allen Melanson	U.S. Army Center for Health Promotion and Preventive Medicine (USACHPPM)
Mr. Oleg Pavlovski	Nuclear Safety Institute, Russian Academy of Sciences
Mr. Konstantinos Potiriadis	Greek Atomic Energy Commission
Ms. K. Vala Ragnarsdottir	Environmental Geochemistry, University of Bristol, UK.
Ms. Alison Hendry	Environmental Geochemistry, University of Bristol, UK.
Mr. Tiberio Cabianca	International Atomic Energy Agency (IAEA)
Mr. Carlos Dora	World Health Organization (WHO)
Mr. Matti Valtonen	Security Advisor, UNEP
Ms. Caitlin Brannan	Project Assistant, UNEP

Other contributors

Mr. Michael Williams	Press Officer
Ms. Akiko Harayama	GRID
Ms. Nikki Meith	Technical Support
Mr. Peter Hulm	Technical Support
Mr. Matija Potocnik	Design and Layout

UNEP Post-Conflict Assessment Unit

Mr. Henrik Slotte	Head of Unit
Mr. Pekka Haavisto	Chairman
Mr. Pasi Rinne	Senior Policy Advisor
Mr. Mario Burger	Project Coordinator
Mr. Dennis Bruhn	Project Coordinator

Mr. Aniket Ghai	Project Coordinator
Mr. Richard Wood	Technical Coordinator
Mr. David Jensen	Programme Officer
Mr. Ola Nordbeck	Research Officer
Mr. Mikko Halonen	Expert
Mr. Gabriel Rocha	System Administrator
Ms. Ljerka Komar-Gosovic	Administrative Assistant
Mr. Andrew Robinson	Report Writer
Mr. Alain Wittig	Information Assistant
Mr. Frederic Delpech	Project Assistant

Spiez Laboratory contributors

Mr. Mario Burger

Mr. Stefan Roellin

Mr. Hans Sahli

Ms. Ruth Holzer

Mr. Alfred Jakob

APAT Laboratory contributors

Ms. Maria Belli

Mr. Umberto Sansone

Ms. Guogang Jia

Ms. Alessandra Pati

Ms. Patrizia Leone

Ms. Sabrina Barbizzi

Ms. Vanessa Bellaria

University of Viterbo contributors

Ms. Serena Ruisi

Ms. Laura Zucconi

Ms. Francesca Fornasier

USACHPPM

Mr. David P. Alberth

Mr. John Collins

Mr. Gordon Lodde

Ms. Fran Szrom

SIA RADON contributors

Mr. Alexander Sobolev

Mr. Alexander Ermakov

Depleted Uranium in Bosnia and Herzegovina

E.0.III.D.7